D1447452

JOURNAL FOR THE STUDY OF THE NEW TESTAMENT SUPPLEMENT SERIES
185

Sheffield Academic Press

Luke's Stories of Jesus

Theological Reading of Gospel Narrative and the Legacy of Hans Frei

David Lee

Journal for the Study of the New Testament
Supplement Series 185

This study is dedicated to Janet, Simon and Jonathan Lee
in appreciation of all that they contributed

Published by
Sheffield Academic Press Ltd
Mansion House
19 Kingfield Road
Sheffield S11 9AS
England

Typeset by Sheffield Academic Press
and
Printed on acid-free paper in Great Britain
by Bookcraft Ltd
Midsomer Norton, Bath

British Library Cataloguing in Publication Data

A catalogue record for this book is available
from the British Library

ISBN 1-84127-013-X

CONTENTS

ACKNOWLEDGMENTS

I would like to acknowledge the general encouragement and support given to me initially by the Church Missionary Society and subsequently by the Right Revd Mark Santer, the Bishop of Birmingham, during the preparation of the original thesis 'Jesus in the Lukan Gospel Narrative' presented to the University of Birmingham for a PhD in 1996. I particularly appreciated the stimulus of Professor David Ford, who introduced me to the thought of Hans Frei, and the wisdom of Professor Frances Young, who encouraged the transformation of various interesting explorations into the coherence of a thesis.

I would like to record my thanks to the staff of the libraries in Birmingham who have assisted my search for periodicals and books, and in particular I would like to salute the generous support given to me by Sheila Russell, the librarian at Queens College, Birmingham, both during the research and subsequently as this book took shape.

I am grateful for the encouragement of Professor Porter and the staff of Sheffield Academic Press for their helpfulness in the writing of this book.

Finally I would like to thank my wife Janet, who has patiently supported this part-time work which has required much more than part of the time.

ABBREVIATIONS

Bib	*Biblica*
BibInt	*Biblical Interpretation: A Journal of Contemporary Approaches*
BTB	*Biblical Theology Bulletin*
CBQ	*Catholic Biblical Quarterly*
Conc	*Concilium*
CritInq	*Critical Inquiry*
IBS	*Irish Biblical Studies*
IDB	George Arthur Buttrick (ed.), *The Interpreter's Dictionary of the Bible* (4 vols.; Nashville: Abingdon Press, 1962)
IDBSup	*IDB*, Supplementary Volume
Int	*Interpretation*
JAAR	*Journal of the American Academy of Religion*
JBL	*Journal of Biblical Literature*
JLT	*Journal of Literature and Theology*
JR	*Journal of Religion*
JSNT	*Journal for the Study of the New Testament*
JSNTSup	*Journal for the Study of the New Testament*, Supplement Series
JSOT	*Journal for the Study of the Old Testament*
JSOTSup	*Journal for the Study of the Old Testament*, Supplement Series
JTS	*Journal of Theological Studies*
LSJ	H.G. Liddell, Robert Scott and H. Stuart Jones, *Greek–English Lexicon* (Oxford: Clarendon Press, 9th edn, 1968)
ModTh	*Modern Theology*
NB	*New Blackfriars*
NeoPh	*Neophilologus*
NIV	New International Version
NLH	*New Literary History*
NovT	*Novum Testamentum*
N and Q	*Notes and Queries*
NRSV	New Revised Standard Version
NTS	*New Testament Studies*
Phil & Lit	*Philosophy and Literature*
PTL	*A Journal for Descriptive Poetics and Theology of Literature* [*Poetics Today*]

PToday	*Poetics Today*
REB	Revised English Bible
RelE	*Religious Education*
RelS	*Religious Studies*
RSV	Revised Standard Version
SE	*Studia Evangelica*
SJT	*Scottish Journal of Theology*
Str–B	[Hermann L. Strack and] Paul Billerbeck, *Kommentar zum Neuen Testament aus Talmud und Midrasch* (7 vols.; Munich: Beck, 1922–61)
TDNT	Gerhard Kittel and Gerhard Friedrich (eds.), *Theological Dictionary of the New Testament* (trans. Geoffrey W. Bromily; 10 vols.; Grand Rapids: Eerdmans, 1964–)
TTod	*Theology Today*
TynBul	*Tyndale Bulletin*
UBSGNT	United Bible Societies' *Greek New Testament*
ZNW	*Zeitschrift für die neutestamentliche Wissenschaft*

Part I

THE LEGACY OF HANS FREI FOR NEW TESTAMENT STUDIES

Chapter 1

HANS FREI AND THEOLOGICAL READING OF GOSPEL NARRATIVES

The Context and Promise of the Contribution of Hans Frei

If theological interpretation of the Bible is in short supply, those who
want it must first reconsider its character and the conditions under which
it thrives.

Morgan with Barton 1988: 193

The historical-critical approach to the New Testament Gospels has been
pre-eminent in Western biblical scholarship for many years. This
approach exemplifies the pretensions to both objectivity and a universal
normativity that are typical of 'modern' thought. A recent and increasing unease with these global claims has now generated a more modest
assessment of the usefulness of the historical-critical approach and has
been accompanied by the emergence of a variety of alternative ways of
handling the New Testament Gospels.[1] One group of these approaches
may be characterized as explicitly 'theological'.[2]

One of the illusions that frequently accompanies the historical-critical
approach is the assumption that its use will generate theological readings of the texts whenever these studies are carried out by Christian
believers. It quickly becomes clear that this is not necessarily the case
in practice because the theological respect for the canonical form of the
Gospel narratives is subverted by the disintegration of that canonical
form when the texts are interpreted with historical-critical tools.[3] The

1. The analysis of Morgan with Barton in *Biblical Interpretation* (1988) is one
of a number of surveys which discuss the limitations and their consequences of the
historical-critical approach to the New Testament. Needless to say, some argue for
the revision and rehabilitation of historical criticism (cf. Burnett 1990).
2. Recent proposals in this field are offered by Morgan with Barton 1988;
Wright 1988; Jeanrond 1988, 1991; Jasper 1989; Watson 1994 and Fodor 1995.
3. Hans Frei traces the disintegration of the narrative form of the Gospel texts
in 'modern' scholarship in his *The Eclipse of Biblical Narrative* (1974). 'The his-

Christian faith of those who practise the historical-critical approach is formally disavowed in the interest of 'objectivity', yet masks the true nature of the exercise they conduct. The unknowing collusion of Christian communities reinforces this illusion.

The development of the interest in specifically theological reading is in part a reaction to the definite but limited usefulness of the historical-critical approach. The challenge is to construct a *new* way of reading the texts *which is theological* and which avoids the improper manipulation of the texts in some dogmatic and popular theology. In the past, such misuse of the Scriptures contributed to the emergence of the rational historical-critical approach to the texts, which was itself supposed to be free of ideological influence. The historical-critical approach signalled the release of the reader of the Bible from the improper tyranny of dogmatic theologians. Clearly, a contemporary theological reading cannot entertain that kind of subjection. Instead, the search is on for a critical theological reading practice appropriate for an increasingly postmodern Western Christian reading community.

The discussion of what constitutes a critical theological reading of the New Testament Gospels occupied the North American theologian Hans Frei for the last 20 years of his life. Although Frei's work was a preparation for a larger project in Christology, these hermeneutical questions so absorbed his time and attention that his prolegomena came to be his major contribution to contemporary theology.

Frei's thought is an appropriate place to begin a discussion of a theological reading of the Gospel narratives for a number of reasons. First, his work exerted a significant influence upon his theological colleagues working in this field. Second, Frei is one of the few *theologians* to address these issues at length.[4] Third, and most importantly, Frei's thought moves through two phases which may be broadly characterized as 'modern' and 'postmodern', and the transition between these phases

---

tory of gospel scholarship over the last two hundred and fifty years could well be judged to have been an escape from narrativity' (Kelber 1988a: 130).

4.   'It is one of the plagues of theology in our day that theologians, justly aware of their limitations in biblical exegesis, retreat from biblical commentary in their theologies. As many forms of biblical scholarship in the meantime become more and more non theological (even anti-theological) the theological situation worsens' (Tracy 1990: 62). While Frei did address the issues involved, and did so with great acumen, it is also true that he produced very little biblical commentary. Frei focused principally upon the *methodology* of a theological hermeneutic.

produces a clear analysis of the issues involved, albeit often at the level of a semi-popular discussion with the associated tendency to generalization and minimal qualification.

The inadequacy of the 'modern' approach to the Gospels for a theological reading is demonstrated by Frei's critical reflection upon his own attempt to use such an approach. As a consequence of this failure, and after more than ten years of work, Frei turned to a quite different way of reading the Gospels which he considered better served the theological concerns of the reader. Within the thought of this one man, the Rubicon is crossed between the 'modern' era and the 'postmodern' era. Frei's analysis of these issues continues to influence the North American theological world, even if his particular constructive proposals now seem dated.

What is it that characterizes a theological reading of the New Testament Gospels as distinct from a literary, a philosophical or a historical reading? In what way does the theological commitment of the reading community engage in the reading practice of the community without robbing the practice of its critical power? How may a Gospel text be read as Scripture in a postmodern context? What might such a reading look like? May theologians employ literary-critical schemes within their theological projects? There are probably as many answers to these questions as there are students of the New Testament. The value of Frei's contribution is that he offers an analysis of the fundamental issues involved which is both clear and seminal.[5] The value of Frei's particular proposals which flow from his analyses is more debatable, and I argue that an alternative is preferable. Nevertheless, Frei opens up the discussion in a most useful and instructive way.

This book addresses the question 'How may the legacy of Frei's thought contribute to the practice of a contemporary critical theological reading of a Gospel narrative?' The rest of this chapter introduces a

---

5.   The sympathetic Garrett Green, who edited *Scriptural Authority and Narrative Interpretation* (the volume of essays to honour Frei), comments that 'Frei has done for theologians something akin to what Freud does in another venture. By recovering for us a portion of our own intellectual history, he has discovered the roots of some contemporary quandaries and unleashed new energies for our continuing work' (Green 1987: x). David Tracy, whose thought is thoroughly criticized by Frei, comments that 'the work of Frei, Lindbeck and their many colleagues has much to teach all theologians—even unrepentant correlational theologians like myself' (Tracy 1990: 36).

descriptive overview of Frei's thought and his two principal proposals. The following two chapters offer a critical analysis of Frei's two proposals for a theological reading of the Gospels. A set of criteria is assembled from these critiques, which may be used to identify 'theological reading' and which then informs the construction of an alternative to Frei's proposals. The present discussion does not examine Frei's Christology from the perspective of systematic theology, but concentrates instead upon the hermeneutical issues involved.

This critique will argue that in the first phase of his thought, Frei maps a cogent formal possibility for the theological reading of a Gospel narrative in which he looks to literary theory and criticism for the tools with which to approach the New Testament texts. At the same time, Frei's decision to 'bracket' historical questions associated with the texts is a necessary temporary move in order to create 'methodological space' in which to attend to the literary features of the Gospel text in preparation for a theological reading. However, Frei's formal interest in the Gospel narratives is insufficiently developed in practice and the lack of careful engagement with actual Gospel texts impoverishes his argument, because it removes the opportunity for the complexities of the texts to challenge him and stimulate possible refinements to his proposal.

Frei eventually concludes that these literary-critical approaches fail because they are examples of 'modern' critical studies, and so he turns to the reading community as the replacement primary resource for the determination of the meaning of the readings of the Gospel narratives. This decentring of the literary interest which is typical of Frei's second phase of thought leads to the abandonment of the central importance of the text which was clearly fundamental in Frei's model of theological reading. Frei's turn to the study of the reading practice of the Christian community partially succeeds in the 'postmodern' task of formally including the reader or community within a reading practice, but at the same time it fails to include the respectful attention to the text which was a key aspect of Frei's kind of theological reading. This failure poses the question: 'How may a postmodern theological reading involve a literary-critical appreciation of the Gospels?'

The recent development of a New Testament narrative criticism would seem to offer a way of reading the Gospel texts that pays careful literary attention to the texts, including their narrative features. However, I will argue that the first generation of narrative critics are incapable of being rigorously critical of their own reading practice due to their choice of literary theory. Furthermore, for a variety of reasons, the readings they produce remain literary-critical exercises and never rise to be genuinely theological. Literary-critical reading is a necessary stage in the production of a theological reading but the 'modern' kind of literary critical practice adopted by many of these New Testament narrative critics fails formally to include the ideological stance of the reader or reading community. The work of the sometime narratologist Mieke Bal includes both of these dimensions, and so a revision of her narrative-critical proposal is developed, which is integrated with Frei's theological strategy to produce a new way of reading the texts theologically.

The last and longest part of the book employs this approach to construct a preliminary christological reading of the Gospel of Luke, in which three sets of narrative descriptions of Jesus illuminate the identity of the Lukan Jesus. This theological reading practice is more than a revision of Frei's proposals, but it would not have been possible without the fundamental analyses of Hans Frei.

An Overview of the Thought of Hans Frei (1922–88)

> At stake is a simple question: How shall we speak of Christ's presence? I shall of course not try to prove that he is present, but simply ask what belief in his presence means for Christians.
>
> Frei 1975: 1

Hans Frei was a theologian of considerable influence within North America who still remains little known in Europe, apart perhaps from his magisterial study of eighteenth- and nineteenth-century hermeneutics *The Eclipse of Biblical Narrative* which was published in 1974. Frei thought slowly and published sparingly and it is only in recent years that his more significant articles and lectures have been edited and published by two of his doctoral students, George Hunsinger and William Placher.[6] Throughout his life, Frei addressed the hermeneutical

---

6. During his lifetime, Frei published two books and less than a dozen major articles. The books are *The Eclipse of Biblical Narrative* (1974) and *The Identity of Jesus Christ* (1975). With the kind assistance of Frei's widow, Hunsinger and Placher have edited and published revised forms of several lecture series as *Types of Christian Theology* (1992) and gathered together key papers in *Theology and Narrative* (1993).

challenge of how to read the Gospel narratives of Jesus as an example of narrative Christology.

Most of Frei's work is concerned with formal questions of method rather than the task of producing exegeses of the biblical narratives, and this is both the strength and the limitation of his achievements. Nevertheless, Frei's sustained theological interest in biblical narrative has proved to be influential in late twentieth-century Western theology, particularly in North America.

Hans Frei began university life at North Carolina State University as a student of textile engineering.[7] A lecture by H. Richard Niebuhr provided the catalyst for a change of direction in Frei's studies. Eventually, with Niebuhr's encouragement, Frei began theological studies at Yale Divinity School. Frei completed his BD in 1945 and became the minister of a Baptist church in a small town in New Hampshire. Two things became clear during his pastorate—the calling to an academic life and the attraction of the greater theological freedom within the Episcopalian Church. Frei returned to Yale in 1947 to begin his doctoral studies (supervised by Niebuhr) in the area of nineteenth-century theology and Barth's break with liberalism. In 1950 Frei took a teaching position at Wabash College and three years later moved to the Episcopal Seminary of the Southwest.

In 1956, after nine years, Frei completed his doctorate and joined the faculty of Yale Graduate School of Religion which was to be his academic home for the rest of his life. Frei taught mainly in the Graduate School of Religion, and took some classes in the Divinity School. Beyond Yale, Frei's involvement with the church was modest; for him, the university was his institutional home. Frei's thought gradually became more widely known when he started to publish in the mid 1960s.[8]

Frei, together with colleagues David Kelsey and George Lindbeck, established during the 1970s and 1980s what some in theological circles described as the 'Yale School' whose approaches were in marked con-

---

7.   This sketch is drawn principally from Placher's 'Introduction' to *Theology and Narrative* (Hunsinger and Placher 1993: 3-25), with some further contributions from Ford 1992: 203-14.

8.   'The earliest essays in the collection *Theology and Narrative* were written when Frei was in his mid forties and had already arrived at his mature theological views, though he continued to develop and modify them' (Hunsinger and Placher 1993: 5).

trast to the work of Paul Ricoeur and David Tracy at Chicago. Frei himself was always hesitant about 'schools' and 'disciples'. A better impression of Frei's wider influence is reflected in the range of the contributors to *Scriptural Authority and Narrative Interpretation*—a collection of essays collated by Garrett Green for Frei's 65th birthday.[9] At the time of his unexpected death in 1988, Frei had completed the preliminary studies for his larger project on the recent Western history of Christology.

In 1990, the Karl Barth Society of North America devoted its annual conference to the theme 'Hans Frei and the Future of Theology', 'because the Karl Barth Society wished to honour the memory of a thinker whose modest work has done much to redefine the agenda of Christian Theology in North America and beyond'.[10] The importance of Frei's continuing influence may be gauged by the posthumous publication of lectures and papers, and the wider interest that has stimulated studies such as this one.

Frei argues that the identity of Jesus Christ is constituted by the Gospel story about him. This leads Frei to place great emphasis upon the narrative form of the story and makes him wary of any reading practice that does not respect the narrative aspect of the texts. Frei develops the hermeneutical importance of reading this story in such a way that it describes or introduces the present reality of Jesus for the reader.

During his life, Frei's thought moves through two distinct phases, and within each of these there is continual revision and development.[11] The first phase may be characterized as 'modern' and the second phase as 'postmodern'. For the purpose of this discussion, 'modern' describes 'a rational, objective approach to reality, through the natural and social sciences' (Griffin, Beardslee and Holland 1989: 2). The growing dissatisfaction with this approach has generated a variety of 'postmodern' proposals. The term 'postmodern' is used here in a general and non-

9. Green 1987.

10. The conference papers were subsequently published in *Modern Theology* 8.2 (April 1992: 103-237), together with a preface from which this quotation is drawn.

11. The importance of the second period of Frei's thought can be underappreciated. For example, a recent study of Frei by Demson (Demson 1997) concentrates upon the earlier period as if it is typical of Frei's thought; Demson does not even take account of Frei's own criticism of his earlier work!

technical way to denote 'a diffuse sentiment that humanity can and must go beyond the modern' (Griffin 1989: xii).[12] In biblical studies the historical-critical approach is a prime example of the modern approach, and Frei's analysis eventually led him to a proposal which may be described as 'postmodern'.[13]

In both periods Frei offers a proposal for how his strategic concern might be realized. In the first phase of his thought he employs a literary New Critical approach to the interpretation of the narrative texts which at least ensures that the narrative meaning of the text is respected. In his later phase, Frei turns to the tradition of 'literal' reading of the text within the church as the safeguard for the meaning of the text. This approach, long established within the Christian tradition, involves a social anthropological model of the church which is then used to provide an appropriate hermeneutic for Christian theology.

Frei's First Phase: A 'New Critical' Interest in Realistic Narrative

> [Commentators] lacked the distinctive category and the appropriate interpretative procedure for understanding what...has actually been recognized: the high significance of the literal, narrative shape of the stories for their meaning. And so, one might add, it has by and large remained ever since.
>
> Frei 1974: 10

Frei was interested in how Christian theologians may speak of Jesus Christ today. The first period of his work starts with an interest in the possible ways in which Jesus can be 'present' to the believer. If Jesus is able to be 'present', Frei argues, then it must be as a consequence of the kind of person he is, which leads him on to discuss the identity of Jesus.

This first period in his thought is introduced by the essay 'Theological

---

12. Although 'postmodern' can be characterized as 'emphasis upon indeterminacy, the production of meaning by the reader, and in many cases the refusal to appeal to consensual criteria in order to adjudicate between different readings' (Burnett 1990: 51), Frei does not necessarily embrace any of these characteristics in his later thought. For a useful summary of the historical context see Klemm 1986: 1-24.

13. Placher suggests that Lindbeck's phrase 'post-liberal' could describe Frei's theology (Placher 1989: 117); others have described his work as 'post-critical'. These labels are of limited use—they simply signify that for Frei, the modern critical approach to biblical narrative had to be left behind in order to create a methodological 'space' for the recovery of the narrative features of the biblical texts.

Reflections on the Accounts of Jesus' Death and Resurrection' which was published in *The Christian Scholar* in 1966 and serves as a programmatic statement of Frei's conception of the irreducible narrative identity of Jesus.[14] Frei's proposal is best understood when seen within its wider theological context, which he provides in a lecture given at Harvard in 1967 entitled 'Remarks in Connection with a Theological Proposal'. In this lecture, Frei surveys contemporary Western theology and concludes that it is dominated by 'modern theology' which he considers to be bankrupt, due to its 'apologetic' mode of thinking.[15]

While working on the Harvard lecture Frei refined his initial proposal in an extended article 'The Mystery of the Presence of Christ' which was published in the adult education periodical *Crossroads* (1967a). This article was sufficiently definitive for it later to form the core of Frei's book *The Identity of Jesus Christ*, which was published in 1975.[16]

According to Frei, the main difficulty with the apologetic mode of doing theology is the way in which possibilities of theological meaning are determined by criteria of meaning generated by non-theological contemporary thought. Frei is convinced that a productive alternative is a kind of dogmatic theology, whose formal mode is nearer to Anselm's *fides quaerens intellectum* (faith seeking understanding). Such an alternative 'describes' and 'explicates' what is already given in the theological text, without having to justify each 'given'.[17] In this 'dogmatic'

14. I propose in all the references to Frei's work to use a different convention for referring to them. Instead of using the date of publication, I will use the date of *production* of the piece, because the later date when his essays were published as collections masks the sense of development in his thought. The publication date is clearly indicated alongside the date of production in the Bibliography where the requirement to locate the publication is a prime concern.

15. 'The conviction underlying these pages is that the story of modern Christian theology (beginning with the end of the seventeenth century) is increasingly, indeed, almost exclusively that of anthropological and christological apologetics...that this has now just about run its course, and that whether it has or not, it is time to search for alternatives' (Frei 1967b: 27).

16. The introduction and epilogue of *The Identity of Jesus Christ* were written in 1975; the rest of the book is a virtually unrevised form of the 1967 *Crossroads* article.

17. Frei's christological project is not typical dogmatic theology. Instead it is 'an outline of dogmatic or systematic theology that takes for its presupposition faith in the presence of Christ. In a sense, therefore, there is no argument to be developed' (Frei 1975: 1). Frei's proposal is a more modest enterprise of 'reflection within belief...a kind of descriptive expansion' (Frei 1975: 4-5). Yet, in the first

mode, the emphasis falls upon the exposition of the 'meaning' of the texts themselves, rather than a discussion of how their 'meaning' and 'possible truthfulness' may be assessed at the bar of contemporary reason.

Frei adopts this 'dogmatic' mode of doing theology and introduces his striking combination of two quite different insights which enable him to address the question of the identity of Jesus Christ. Frei combines the philosophical concept of 'person' which anchors a person's identity in the story of their actions, with a literary interest in the texts as stories which most clearly render their characters in the unfolding narrative of their actions. The result is Frei's proposal that the personal identity of Jesus Christ is constituted by the Gospel story of Jesus Christ.

The Philosophical Concept of 'Personal Identity as Constituted in Action'

The first element of Frei's proposal concerning the identity of Jesus Christ relates to the interpretative 'bridge' between the world of the text and the world of the reader. To cross this hermeneutical distance, Frei adopts a contemporary concept of 'identity' to serve as a 'tool of interpretive analysis'.[18] While supervising a research student in the 1960s, Frei read the works of Gilbert Ryle and came across a conceptual tool which he was later to employ in his own christological project.[19] Ryle argues that 'a person's identity is not some possibly unknowable inner

period of his thought the significance of 'belief' is carefully qualified, for Frei hopes that 'the exegetical and accompanying hermeneutical inquiry will show that, no matter whether one is a believing Christian or not, one can make sense of the Gospel story in its own right' (Frei 1975: xvii). In his later writings Frei becomes more clearly Anselmian.

18. 'We meet with the problem of interpretation. Without some perspective of our own the story has no discernibly significant shape for us; but on the other hand we must not imprint either our own life problems or our own ideological analyses on it. The proper approach is to keep the tools of interpretive analysis as minimal and formal as possible, so that the character(s) and the narrative of events may emerge in their own right' (Frei 1966: 47).

19. Frei supervised Robert H. King's doctoral thesis 'The Concept of Personal Agency as a Theological Model', which was completed in 1965. In the preface to *The Eclipse of Biblical Narrative*, Frei wrote 'My debts in the present work are innumerable. Among authors who have been particularly influential on my thought I want to mention Eric Auerbach, Karl Barth and Gilbert Ryle' (Frei 1974: vii).

essence but is constituted by the pattern of the particular person's speech and action' (Hunsinger and Placher 1993: 12). Frei takes up this idea and to the question 'what is a man?', replies that 'a man...is what he *does* uniquely, the way no one else does it. In that kind of passage from free intention into action, ordering the two (intention and act) into one harmony, a free man gains his being' (Frei 1966: 57; Frei's italics). Thus 'a person's identity is constituted (not simply illustrated) by the intention which he carries into action' (Frei 1966: 63).

Frei avoids the tangles which face those interested in the 'inner life' of Jesus by arguing that there is no separable inner life.[20] Next, he needed an account of the actions of the person Jesus that would provide the occasion of Jesus' intention being carried into action. The Gospels are the obvious source, but Frei needed a literary interpretative concept in order to press beyond a close reading of the Gospel stories which would be little more than a paraphrase. Auerbach's concept of 'realistic narrative' provided what Frei requires: 'let's start with the Synoptic Gospels, or at least one of them, because their peculiar nature as narratives, or at least partial narratives, makes some hermeneutical moves possible that we don't have available elsewhere in the New Testament' (Frei 1967b: 32).

The Literary Interest in the Gospels as a 'Realistic Narrative' Type of Story

The second element in Frei's proposal is the literary recognition that the Gospels are sufficiently 'novel-like' narratives to be read literally and not symbolically or historically (Frei 1966: 45). To develop what is involved in texts that are 'novel-like' or 'realistic', Frei drew upon the work of the historian of literary style Auerbach, who in his *Mimesis* described the characteristics of 'realistic narrative' and suggests that biblical narrative is one example of this type with the nineteenth-century novel as another.[21] As a theologian Frei was struck by Auerbach's analysis of biblical narrative, and in particular, his observation that 'the

---

20. Placher notes that 'in the 1960s the "new quest for the historical Jesus" was widely discussed' (Hunsinger and Placher 1993: 11). Frei instances the work of Bornkamm, Fuchs and J.M. Robinson (cf. Frei 1967b: 38-39).

21. 'Eric Auerbach suggests that the realistic tradition has persisted through the ebb and flow of its own fortunes in Western literature. But he also sees three historical high points in its development: the Bible, Dante's *Divine Comedy* and the nineteenth century novel, especially in France' (Frei 1974: 15).

world of the Scripture stories is not satisfied with claiming to be a historically true reality—it insists that it is the only real world' (Auerbach 1953: 15).[22] If this is the case, then the meaning of the text is firmly grounded *in the world of the text* and not elsewhere, and so for the literary character Jesus, Frei can conclude that 'Jesus *is* his story' (Frei 1967b: 42).

The difficulty Frei then faced is the curious fact that in modern Western biblical studies, an appreciation of the 'story form' of the Gospels is largely absent. Frei began a detailed study of eighteenth- and early nineteenth-century interpretation of the history-like stories of the Old and New Testaments and came to the startling conclusion that 'this realistic characteristic though acknowledged by all hands to be there, finally came to be ignored, or—even more fascinating—its presence or distinctiveness came to be denied for lack of a method to isolate it' (Frei 1974: 10). Frei published this study in 1974 as his first book *The Eclipse of Biblical Narrative*. The study is not a general history of hermeneutics, but rather a study of one segment of the history of the theory of biblical interpretation, and a history 'under a thesis'. Frei's study is an extended argument for the recovery of biblical narrative which is to be achieved by the historical exposition of how this narrative aspect came to be eclipsed (1974: chapters 2–16). The argument is preceded by a key sketch of what the recovery of the narrative aspect of the biblical texts might involve (1974: chapter 1). According to Frei, the way forward is to treat biblical narratives as examples of literary 'Realistic Narrative'.

The analysis of *The Eclipse of Biblical Narrative* concludes that biblical commentators 'lacked the *distinctive category* and the appropriate *interpretative procedure* for understanding what...has actually been recognized: the high significance of the literal, narrative shape of the stories for their meaning. And so, one might add, it has by and large remained ever since' (Frei 1974: 10; my italics). In the introduction to the book Frei outlined his proposal to adopt the literary concept of realistic narrative as the missing 'distinctive category' and to adopt AngloAmerican New Critical reading as the missing 'interpretive procedure'.[23]

---

22. 'What the Biblical narrator wrote was 'not primarily oriented towards realism (if he succeeded in being realistic, it was merely a means, not an end); it was oriented toward truth' (Auerbach 1953: 114).

23. Frei did not use the title of 'New Criticism' until his later review of this

Under the influence of Frei's reading of Auerbach, which is itself not uncontested, the concept of 'realistic narrative' is linked to the realistic writing of the English and French nineteenth-century novel. The comparison that Frei made between these two literary genres is understandable but has also provided grounds for considerable criticism.[24]

Frei's difficulties were not yet over for he was writing during the hegemony of the 'modern' historical-critical approach to the Gospels. In order to create the methodological 'space' in which to work with the literary category 'realistic narrative' when reading the Gospels, Frei introduced the important distinction between the 'history-like' qualities of the realistic biblical text and the 'historical claims' of the realistic biblical text. 'History likeness' is first and foremost a *literary* quality of the text which contributes to its narrative meaning and is not to be confused with any historical claim of the text to truthfully represent past events.

Frei argued that the assumption that the literary 'history-like' quality of a biblical text is equivalent to making a 'historical claim' about the past 'is a classic instance of a category error'.[25] The confusion is compounded by historical-critical analyses of narrative history-like texts which disintegrate their narrative form with its 'history-likeness', and so raise doubts about whether their supposed 'historical reliability' is any more than just a literary construct.[26] Frei procedurally bracketed such historical discussions in order to attend to the literary dimension of the Gospel texts.

The Eclipse of Biblical Narrative has become a classic work and is still in print today. As a 'study in eighteenth- and nineteenth-century hermeneutics' which engages with Western literature and theology, the book addresses theologians, literary scholars and biblical scholars.

period of his work, when he wrote that 'the resemblance of [my] view to Anglo-American New Criticism is obvious and has often been pointed out' (Frei 1983: 63).

24. Frei was working in a period when the 'view of narrative literature [was] almost hopelessly novel-centred' (Scholes and Kellogg 1966: 8).

25. 'Modern interpreters were concerned to show...how Scripture was "likely history" rather than "history-like"' (Fodor 1995: 264).

26. The discussion of any historical claim of such texts filled Frei with foreboding for another reason. Frei feared that in so doing, he might slip back into an apologetic mode of thought, and so he avoided the discussion for as long as possible. The question was not addressed until the 1986 lecture 'Conflicts in Interpretation' and only then in a tentative and heavily qualified way.

Fellow theologians were the largest group to engage with Frei's thesis, and their response ranged from the appreciative to the highly critical.[27] Frei's version of literary history and his adoption of realistic narrative drew critical though not fatal fire from some literary scholars.[28] However, a virtual silence reigned amid the guild of biblical scholars.[29] There seemed to be a great gulf between the worlds of dogmatic theologians and biblical scholars, despite Frei's endeavour to bridge it.[30] However it seems to be true that while not many New Testament

27. *The Eclipse of Biblical Narrative* initially received mixed reviews. These ranged from J.K. Riches's 'a book of rare and excellent character' (Riches 1976: 117) to Anthony Yu who lectured at the University of Chicago: 'it is unfortunate that a book...may leave us with the impression that its author is being reactionary without trying to offer a constructive alternative' (Yu 1978: 203). There was a widespread view that Frei's work was only part-done, needing 'a second volume to bring the argument to a satisfactory conclusion' as G.H. Boobyer put it (Boobyer 1975: 580), which was provided the following year in *The Identity of Jesus Christ*. With others, Frederick Borsch commented upon the difficulty of Frei's writing (Borsch 1975: 572; cf. Keck 1975: 367). However, within the twin growing streams of narrative theology and narrative New Testament criticism, Hans Frei is instanced time and again as a seminal influence. This consensus about the importance of 'narrative' among North American theologians attracts the wry amazement of Edward Oakes in his article 'Apologetics and the Pathos of Narrative Theology' (Oakes 1992: 37-58).

28. The critic George Steiner comments that 'even at its best, it is not sufficient to infer a full basis for Frei's case from Auerbach's background presence. The force of demonstration must reside in concrete examples. These are lacking almost throughout the book, and most damagingly when Frei implicates his own view of the missed alternative' (Steiner 1977: 242). Frei acknowledged this lack in the Preface to *The Eclipse of Biblical Narrative*: 'This essay falls into the almost legendary category of analysis of analyses of the Bible in which not a single text is examined, not a single exegesis undertaken' (Frei 1974: vii). The literary critic Stephen Prickett opened up a different critical front when he wrote that 'we have no reason to suppose...that biblical authors subscribed to a similar literary convention to that of the nineteenth century realistic novel, but I think it is not too far-fetched to assume that they did not' (Prickett 1989: 5).

29. In the Festschrift *Scriptural Authority and Narrative Interpretation* (Green 1987), Green assembles details of 23 reviews of *The Eclipse of Biblical Narrative*, only 5 of which are written by recognized biblical scholars. It is also significant that not one of the contributors to the Festschrift is primarily a biblical scholar.

30. This state of affairs is discussed by the hermeneutical theologian Werner Jeanrond among others, who comments that 'the lack of proper integration of biblical and theological studies in most faculties has long been a cause for grave concern' (Jeanrond 1993: 85). 'We are now at a juncture in history when both subdis-

scholars knew his work, it was also the case that Frei was just as unaware of the renewed interest of biblical scholars in the literary qualities of the texts.[31]

Frei's proposal attracted acute criticism because of his strategic separation of the literary feature of 'history-likeness' from the historical claims of the text. In modern historical-critical studies, the 'truthfulness' of the Gospels had been reduced to arguments about 'historical truthfulness'. Frei's strategy raised suspicions that he was not interested in the truth claims of the Gospels, and the fact that he deferred addressing the issue confirmed that suspicion for many.[32]

A weakness of *The Eclipse of Biblical Narrative* is that its constructive proposal is limited to a 16-page introductory outline,[33] and there is not a biblical passage in sight.[34] Frei was sensitive to this omission, and decided to offer a substantive proposal which would work with the biblical text and also provide an introduction to the methodological issues involved. The easiest way was to use material already to hand, and so Frei's second book emerged. Frei published *The Identity of Jesus Christ* in 1975. The essay is an exposition of how a combination of the con-

ciplines of Christian reflection—biblical criticism and Christian theology—may go their separate ways' (Jeanrond 1992: 218).

31. It is illuminating that with his interest in the Gospel narratives, Frei, writing in 1974, shows no evidence of acquaintance with Beardslee's *Literary Criticism of the New Testament* (1970), or the relevant work of New Testament scholars in the Society of Biblical Literature seminars held in North America.

32. One example is the 1983 paper of Gary Comstock, later published in the *Journal of Religion* as 'Truth or Meaning: Ricoeur versus Frei on Biblical Narrative'. Comstock suggests that 'when Frei says that "the meaning of these narratives is autonomous, they refer only to themselves", then at that point Frei avoids the discussion of correspondence to reality and any associated truth claims' (Comstock 1986: 120, quoting Frei).

33. Anthony Yu wrote: 'Frei has told us, often with devastating insight, what should not have happened, but he does not tell us what should have happened' (Yu 1978: 202).

34. Frei was aware of this irony, as his preface makes clear: 'There is no denying the odd result of a book about the Bible in which the Bible itself is never looked at. Nevertheless, I am confident that the essay may have significant implications for the study of the Bible' (Frei 1974: vii). It is clear that Frei considered himself to be 'a Christian theologian rather than a literary or biblical scholar' (Frei 1983: 36), for apart from *The Identity of Jesus Christ* he never again attempted sustained work on the biblical narratives, and concentrated instead on questions of 'theological method'.

cepts of narrative identity and realistic narrative may form a hermeneutical basis for a Christology. The book is actually a very slightly revised
form of his 1967 essay 'The Mystery of the Presence of Christ' with the
addition of two extra chapters.[35]

The Identity of Jesus Christ is a theological proposal which seeks to
engage with the text of the Gospel stories. As theological proposal it
has been hailed as opening up new possibilities for all theology by
theologians ranging from the sympathetic George Lindbeck to the critical David Tracy.[36] In its engagement with the texts, its first achievement
is the introduction of the New Critical way of reading the Gospels as
'realistic narrative' which was more widely interpreted as an argument
for reading the Gospels for their 'plain sense'.[37] The second achievement of the book is the establishment of a necessary link between the
story form of the Gospel narrative and christological reflection.

The Identity of Jesus Christ is illuminating in several ways. First, it
sets out Frei's strategic objective which occupied him in various guises
throughout his life's work. Frei was convinced that the narrative identity of Jesus Christ is a constructive way of engaging in contemporary
theological reflection and the way to achieve this is by the production of
a christological reading of the Gospel narrative. Frei argued that the
integration of a dogmatic theological approach with a literary formalism
akin to Anglo-American New Criticism could produce a christological
reading.[38]

The Identity of Jesus Christ is illuminating in a second way, for it is
the only occasion when Frei provides a substantial exposition of biblical texts. A theologically derived and non-negotiable criterion for Frei's
proposal is that readers should respect the plain reading of the narrative
form of these texts, for he maintains that the narrative text constitutes
the identity of Jesus Christ.

35. The change in the title from 'presence' to 'identity' for what is virtually the
same piece of writing is due to Frei's increasing hesitation about the concept of
'presence' but his continuing interest in the notion of 'identity' (cf. Frei 1975: vii).

36. 'In his constructive christological work on the identity and presence of Jesus
Christ as rendered in and through a "literal" or "plain" reading of the passion narratives of the gospels, Frei's work has proved a breakthrough for all theology' (Tracy
1990: 37).

37. Cf. Tracy 1990; Tanner 1987: 59-78.

38. 'Frei thus upholds a rigorous New Critical formalism...[in] a comprehen-
sive union of theology and literary criticism, Barth and the New Critics' (Poland
1985b: 469).

The Eclipse of Biblical Narrative and *The Identity of Jesus Christ* were the only two books Frei ever wrote, and they provide a fitting summation of this first period of Frei's thought. *The Eclipse of Biblical Narrative* contributed to the recovery of interest in biblical narrative within Christian theology, and to a lesser extent within biblical studies. *The Identity of Jesus Christ* mapped a strategy and demonstrated how we might speak about Jesus Christ today. However, the 'popular' level of writing in *The Identity of Jesus Christ* and its failure to persuade many theologians may explain the fact that the book is not as well known as *The Eclipse of Biblical Narrative*.[39]

Frei's Second Phase: The Turn to the Sensus Literalis *of the Christian Community*

> It is the case that description of the Christian religion, especially in the West, has included a description of its sacred text in which at the very least certain portions regarded as central were to be read not allegorically or spiritually but literally. Another reading may be allowed, but it must not offend the basic literal sense of those crucial sections.
>
> Frei 1982: 102

Hans Frei changed his mind in a fundamental way during the early 1980s. He realized that he could no longer look to the literary-critical concepts which he had employed in order to preserve the literal reading of the Gospel narrative text which his christological project required. So he began a second period of constructive theological work in an endeavour to achieve this literal reading of the Gospel.[40]

---

39. Green (1987) assembled 12 reviews of *The Identity of Jesus Christ*, over against the 23 reviews of *The Eclipse of Biblical Narrative*. Significantly, while *The Eclipse of Biblical Narrative* is now available in paperback, *The Identity of Jesus Christ* is out of print.

40. Both Hunsinger and Placher also suggest that Frei's thought falls into two periods divided by the important watershed of Frei's 1983 lecture 'The Literal Reading of Biblical Narrative in the Christian Tradition'. I agree that this lecture is the significant turning point in Frei's thought, and for the purposes of this discussion, the twofold division is sufficiently useful. In fact, within both the earlier and later periods, there is enough development to merit further subdivision into a total of four periods within his thought:

    (1) The interest in 'presence'—'The Mystery of the Presence of Jesus Christ' (Frei 1967a);

    (2) The interest in 'Narrative Identity'—discussed in the introduction to *The Identity of Jesus Christ* (Frei 1975);

Frei's change of mind was first signalled in the lecture 'Theology and the Interpretation of Narrative: Some Hermeneutical Considerations' which he gave in a joint presentation with Paul Ricoeur in 1982.[41] Frei expounded his revised theological approach which was based upon the practice of reading for the *sensus literalis* of the text within the Christian tradition, and used Kermode's *The Genesis of Secrecy* (1979) as a foil for his own exposition.

The clearer and more powerful statement of the new position was given in 1983 in the lecture 'The Literal Reading of Biblical Narrative in the Christian Tradition: Does It Stretch or Will It Break?'[42] This time Frei adopted Ricoeur's phenomenological hermeneutics as his foil, for Frei recognized it as 'the current defender of the concern to read narrative texts as *narrative* texts' (Frei 1983: 36-37). Frei concludes that 'the defence is a failure, so that...the literal reading will break apart under its ministrations' (Frei 1983: 37).[43] Finally, Frei proposes a way of literal reading 'with a far more modest theory'.

(3)   The interest in the literal sense—discussed in 'Theology and the Interpretation of Narrative' (Frei 1982); and in 'The Literal Reading of Biblical Narrative in the Christian Tradition' (Frei 1983).

(4)   The interest in literal reading—discussed in 'Narrative in Christian and Modern Reading' (Frei 1988b) and in the revision of the lectures which comprise the posthumous *Types of Christian Theology* (Frei 1988c).

41.   Haverford College invites two distinguished scholars in a field to make a joint presentation, during which each would then respond to the other's paper. This would require Frei to engage at length with Ricoeur's hermeneutical theory. He considered it to be a most important contribution. 'In the midst of the mounting crescendo of dissent from thematic readings of narratives, including scripture stories, as normative guides for living and believing as well as reading, hermeneutical theory is the most prominent contemporary champion of the embattled tradition' (Frei 1983: 37).

42.   The lecture was presented at the conference 'The Bible and the Narrative Tradition' held at the University of California in 1983, and published as *The Bible and the Narrative Tradition* (McConnell 1986).

43.   The contrast between the 1982 and 1983 papers is very clear. In 1982, Frei used Kermode's *The Genesis of Secrecy* as a foil for his own argument, and refers to 'the literal sense [as] a paradigm case of what Professor Ricoeur has so wisely called the hermeneutics of restoration in contrast to the hermeneutics of suspicion' (Frei 1982: 111). By 1983, Frei had closely studied Ricoeur's hermeneutical theory, concluded that it fails in what it endeavours, and so uses it as a foil for his 'The Literal Reading of Biblical Narrative in the Christian Tradition' lecture.

The key insight that emerges in the encounter with Ricoeur's general hermeneutical theory is Frei's assessment of the limitations of 'general interpretation theory', and his desire to distance his thought from such global schemes.[44] The illustration of this withdrawal is Frei's abandonment of his own earlier use of realistic narrative and New Critical reading when he eventually realized that they are both examples of a regional application of general theory.[45] Frei turns instead to the traditional way the Christian community reads for the *sensus literalis* of the text, which Frei considered succeeds in preserving the literal sense of the biblical narratives. In this move, Frei drew upon Brevard Childs's discussion of the *sensus literalis*.[46]

Implicit in this decision is the turn away from the literary features of the text as the principal determinants of the meaning of the text, and a turn to the consensus about the meaning of the text which is built up through the history of the reading of the text in the Christian community.[47] Paradoxically, Frei considered that from a theological perspective, this turn away from literary-critical reading provides the way to preserve the literal reading of the text.[48]

44. It is no accident that two of the more penetrating recent studies of Frei's hermeneutical proposals are actually parts of larger discussions of Ricoeur's phenomenological hermeneutics, for the contrast in the thought of Ricoeur and Frei is mutually illuminating. (Vanhoozer 1990: 148-89; Fodor 1995: 258-330).

45. Frei wrote in his earlier work that the 'less high-powered general theory that upholds the literal or realistic reading of the Gospels may be just as perilously perched as its more majestic and pretentious hermeneutical cousin' (Frei 1983: 64).

46. Frei acknowledges his indebtedness to Childs's article 'The *Sensus Literalis* of Scripture: An Ancient and Modern Problem' (Frei 1982: 102 n. 10).

47. Hunsinger correctly observes that 'a cultural-linguistic turn, under the influence of George Lindbeck, has been effected in Frei's thought' (Hunsinger 1992: 128).

48. The interest in hermeneutics and Christology that appears in the earliest of Frei's essays continued throughout his career, but different contexts led to different emphases and further development of his position. At the beginning of his career, the dominant approach to the biblical texts, influenced by Bultmann, had been to analyse individual pericopes. Frei had to make the case for attending to the narrative shape of the Gospel texts as a whole. With the influence of redaction critics, literary approaches to the Bible and Frei's own work, that argument no longer needed to be made by the 1980s. However, Frei was convinced that many theological interpreters 'failed to take the narratives as narratives with sufficient seriousness' (Placher 1993: 15).

This second phase of Frei's thought is characterized by three recurring themes which inform Frei's theological hermeneutic and illuminate the battle which he was fighting.

The Subversion of the Literal Sense by 'General Theory'
Frei had long been cautious about the role that interpretation theory should play. In the earlier work *The Identity of Jesus Christ*, he insisted that 'in the instance of realistic narrative interpretation...the amount of theory is minimal. There should be enough to elucidate what is actually being done in exegesis, and no more' (Frei 1975: xv). His subsequent engagement with hermeneutical theory brought into focus the unseen but far-reaching influence of 'general theory' and led to Frei's withdrawal from interpretative schemes governed by this kind of theory. Frei concluded that whenever general theory is used in an explanatory way, it *always* subverts the particular, literal and hence narrative, sense of the text.

Frei employed the phrase 'general interpretive theory' as a shorthand for any scheme in which the meaning of the text is determined primarily by reference to a general scheme rather than by reference to the specifics of the particular text. Frei concluded that this had happened (albeit unwittingly) in his earlier literary proposal to treat the Gospel narratives as realistic narratives, for 'even though less high powered, general theory it remains: the Gospel narratives "mean" realistically because that is the general literary class to which they belong' (Frei 1983: 64).

Frei concludes that 'it is doubtful that any scheme for reading texts, and narrative texts in particular, and biblical narrative texts more specifically, can serve globally and foundationally, so that the reading of the biblical material would simply be a regional instance of that universal procedure' (Frei 1983: 59). The power of any general theory lies in its authority to explain what meaning or meanings a particular text may or may not bear, with the consequence that interpretation of a specific text is subject to these general criteria of meaning. Frei's alternative may be considered metaphorically as the importance of allowing the text 'space' in which it may 'speak for itself'.

Frei's imaginative response to this dilemma was to re-define the function of general interpretative theory. In order to achieve a case-specific reading, he proposed that interpretative theory be used in a *descriptive* way.[49] Instead of *explaining* (and thus determining) how such a reading occurs, the theoretical categories are now to be used *descriptively* in a case specific reading which 'governs and bends to its own ends whatever general categories it shares—as indeed it has to share—with other kinds of reading' (Frei 1983: 67).

This development in Frei's assessment of general theory took place under the influence of wider concerns within his thought. The first was his work on a theological typology of possible relationships between particular sacred texts and general interpretative theory.[50] The second influence was Frei's increased knowledge of secular literary criticism, and particularly deconstructionist thought,[51] and the third influence was his encounter with the philosophical hermeneutics of Paul Ricoeur. Ricoeur does treat the Gospel texts as narratives, but it seemed to Frei that the 'objective world of descriptive discourse is consigned to a decidedly peripheral and ambiguous status...(and eventually) under its auspices the literal reading of the Gospel narratives vanishes' (Frei 1983: 45-67).

Frei's engagement with these issues is important because he considered that the role of general (or foundational) theory within theological hermeneutics is one of the fundamental issues in contemporary Western theology. The outcome for Frei was the withdrawal of his theological hermeneutics from the domain of global general theories in order to give his respectful attention to the particularities of specific biblical texts.[52]

Frei's respect for the particularities of these narrative texts springs from his theological interest in the texts. How may the Christian speak of Jesus Christ, the unique Son of God? It is clear to Frei that general categories generated from human experience cannot suffice, for no

49. This move 'involves lowering our theoretical sights yet further to the level of mere description rather than explanation, to the specific set of texts and the most specific context, rather than to a general class of texts (eg. realistic narrative) and the most general context (eg. human experience)' (Frei 1983: 67).

50. Frei discusses the range of possible relationships in the 1982 paper given at the Haverford College. The typology was developed and expounded in the papers which constitute his *Types of Christian Theology*.

51. Frei had studied Frank Kermode, Harold Bloom and Derrida among others.

52. Frei later acknowledges that in this move, he emulates Barth, for 'Barth almost always proceeds from the priority of the singular and from the particular to the general' (Frei 1988c: 87).

general category can portray a unique entity.[53] Instead when these categories of thought are used of Jesus (which Frei acknowledges as necessary) their meaning has to be refashioned by the identity of the person of
Jesus.[54] And Frei finds that identity in the Gospel narratives of Jesus.[55]

Frei maintained that a normative reading of the biblical text is possible, even if he gradually recognized that it is very difficult to achieve.[56]
A major task which faces a reader is the recognition of *which* reading of
several is normative. Initially under the influence of New Critical
thought, Frei held that normative interpretations (of the Gospels) may be
possible 'because the meaning of the texts remains the same no matter
what the perspectives of succeeding generations of interpreters' (Frei
1967b: 32). The interpreter recognizes the meaning by attending to the
literary features of the text and employs general literary theory and criticism to help interpret these features. Once Frei turned away from the
use of general theory in an explanatory way, an alternative is required.

Frei turned to the history of the Christian communities' reading for
the *sensus literalis* in order to provide criteria for the recognition of the

53. Frei's discussion in the 1987 Edward Cadbury Lectures of the category 'history' well illustrates the inadequacy of some supposed 'factuality'. 'However one
wishes to bring together the ascriptive subject of the New Testament portraits with
general meaning or explanatory theory or with some specific discipline exem-
plifying theory, relating the Christ of faith to the Jesus of history is not the way...
The category "factuality" is simply inadequate (not wrong) for the interpretation of
this text' (Frei 1988c: 85).

54. Frei is at pains to point out that the Gospel narratives do not describe Jesus
in general terms, but rather *ascribe* to Jesus qualities which are only found in this
combination in this particular person. So it is appropriate, he argues, to describe the
person of Jesus as 'unsubstitutable'.

55. Frei's concern to protect the primacy of the text may be seen as a literary
concern with a theological purpose. Does not this approach recall the pre-critical
conviction that the world of the text is the real world, and that the reader and his
thinking were to be assimilated to it?

56. Frei's conviction about the possibility of the 'correct interpretation' of a text
becomes less and less certain. In the earlier period of his thought, under the
influence of New Critical thought, he considered that his 'exegetical and accompanying hermeneutical inquiry will show that, no matter whether one is a believing
Christian or not, one can make sense of the Gospel story in its own right' (Frei
1975: xvii). In his later period, Frei writes: 'let us assume that the notion of a right
interpretation of the Bible is not in itself meaningless, but is eschatological' (Frei
1988c: 56).

meanings of the biblical texts. This withdrawal from the realm of general theory inevitably attracts the criticism of those who maintain that theological hermeneutics is a regional example of global hermeneutical theory, for they argue that Frei has withdrawn from the wider public debate about hermeneutics.[57] This is true, but the criticism betrays a failure to understand Frei's argument. Frei took this step *after* engaging with global hermeneutical theory when he recognized that 'global theory' is formally incapable of handling the unique features of the person of Jesus Christ. Now Frei develops his second proposal by narrowing his focus to the reading of the Gospels within the Christian tradition.[58]

The Possibilities Offered by the Community's Sensus Literalis
Frei declares in his programmatic 1983 essay that 'as a Christian theologian rather than a literary or biblical scholar, I shall not try to position the Bible in relation to this [narrative tradition in literature]; instead I will comment on what I perceive to be a wide...consensus among Christians in the West on the primacy of the literal reading of the Bible' (Frei 1983: 36).[59] The essay begins with a historical sketch of the primacy of the literal sense in Christian interpretive tradition, and after an analysis and critique of phenomenological hermeneutics, the paper closes by proposing that literal reading is a more modest and

57. Jeanrond criticizes Frei's approach: 'There are those Christian thinkers like Stuhlmacher, Lindbeck and the late Hans Frei who feel that they ought to determine the specifically Christian vision predominantly from inside the church and biblical theology...this group is not willing to be engaged radically in the hermeneutical reflection on its methodological foundations...I do not wish to dwell any longer on...the group's hermeneutical self-limitation. Rather I would like to show what Christian theology may have to gain for its own self-understanding by getting involved in the contemporary conversation upon hermeneutics. Thus, I do advocate a return to the traditional theological occupation with questions of method' (Jeanrond 1991: 163-64). Jeanrond's criticism fails to appreciate the serious attention which Frei paid to general hermeneutics in the preparation of his proposal, and the substantial difficulties which Jeanrond's position entails.

58. Such a reading 'is not only case specific but as such belongs first and foremost into the context of the socio-linguistic community, that is of the specific religion of which it is a part, rather than in a literary ambience' (Frei 1983: 67).

59. Once again, Frei's paper is a 'strictly second-order affair, commenting on theories pertinent to the past as well as the present and future conditions for the literal reading as a religious enterprise' (Frei 1983: 37), and engages in no actual exegesis.

appropriate enterprise. The substantial proposal in the paper is the reading of the narrative text for its *sensus literalis*. Such 'literal reading' looks for the literal or plain sense of the text, and in so doing, Frei expected that it will inevitably respect the literal (and hence narrative) form of the Gospel text.

Frei's review of the history of the reading of Scripture by the Christian community revealed that the *sensus literalis* is not simply the 'literal sense', as a translation might suggest. Instead, it is a flexible concept, whose actual meaning varies in a context dependent way.[60] Frei draws upon this varied history of the reading for the *sensus literalis* in the Christian tradition and concludes that the literal sense is 'the natural, plain, obvious meaning which the community of faith has normally acknowledged as basic, regardless of whatever other constructions might also be properly put upon the text' (Frei 1982: 104).[61] The variety of readings of the same biblical texts down the centuries is now explained as the particular forms of 'the customary use to which the text has been put in the context of the community's belief and life' (Frei 1982: 110).[62]

Frei offers a bipolar model for the *sensus literalis*.[63] In his 1982 paper Frei explains that until the rise of modernity, the *sensus literalis* had encompassed both the textual pole (the literal sense of the text) and the pole of the reading practice of the Christian community (the literal reading) and that usually preference was given to the reading pole. Frei

60. Frei's position approaches George Lindbeck's reconceptualization of Christian doctrine (Lindbeck 1984), in which Lindbeck argues that the primary significance of doctrinal statements is their function within a context dependent discussion, rather than the actual meaning of their content. 'To distinguish doctrines from the concepts in which they are formulated is to state these doctrines in different terms that nevertheless have equivalent consequences' (Lindbeck 1984: 93).

61. Frei adopted this description of the 'plain sense of the text' from Charles Wood (1981) to which Frei was 'deeply and generally indebted' (Frei 1982: 115 n. 13).

62. 'This is the setting in which it is appropriate to reach for that saying of Wittgenstein that has so often and wrongly been given the status of a general principle: "Don't ask for the meaning; ask for the use"' (Frei 1982: 104).

63. Frei actually provides his longest discussion of the three principal meanings of *sensus literalis* in his 1982 paper at the Frei-Ricoeur presentation. These are (1) the fit of the text with the author's intention; (2) the descriptive fit between sense and reference; and (3) the 'use-in-context'. The first meaning is not directly relevant to this discussion, for the pre-moderns tended to consider that the author of scripture was God himself.

argues that the *sensus literalis* in the Christian tradition is usually a discussion of the significance of the biblical text for 'the reader's present'
rather than a debate about the historical 'fit' of the text with the ancient
past.[64]

During the modern period, the interest in the textual pole had been
transformed and reduced to a critical discussion of the historical reliability of the narratives, and the pole of the significance for the reader
simply neglected, largely due to the supposed uninvolved 'objectivity'
of the modern 'Cartesian' reader. Recalling his proposal in *The Eclipse
of Biblical Narrative*, Frei distances himself from the modern historical
debate, and turns to the Christian reading community for assistance.

For the rest of his life, Frei worked upon the consequences of this
sociological turn and his thought is set out most clearly in the posthumous *Types of Christian Theology*.[65] 'You should not ask at all...
what is the meaning of a text—but rather how is the text used and in
what context. That is a better, less abstract question than What is the
meaning of the text?' (Frei 1988c: 16). 'The usefulness of the theories
we employ is discovered in the process of application, of actual exegesis' (Frei 1988c: 86). Therefore 'the literal meaning of the text is precisely that meaning which finds the greatest degree of agreement in the
use of the text in the religious community' (Frei 1988c: 15). These
statements are the logical consequence of Frei's decision to consider the
sensus literalis 'as a communal consensus rather than as a literary
structure' (Hunsinger 1993: 263).[66] This paradigm shift explains why

64. 'Augustine for example understood the plain sense of Scripture to be that
which conduces to faith, hope and the twofold love of God and neighbour' (Frei
1982: 105).

65. Frei proposed that current theological enterprises may be approached by
enquiring how each of them relates general explanatory schemes of *Wissenschaft*
(scientifically grounded knowledge) to the modest self description which the community uses of God and of itself. Frei's position is closest to that in which 'applying
a general scheme to specific reading may well be an *ad hoc* affair, rather than a
matter of systematic or tight correlation between text and reading, but that in order
to use schemes in an ad hoc fashion, we will have to *subordinate* them to the text in
the context of the self description of the Christian community' (Frei 1988c: 85).

66. 'I am persuaded that in the search for an answer to the question of how to
understand the texts as texts, the closest discipline to theology is not history at all.
When I ask what external discipline is potentially most useful to theology, I come
up with an answer that surprises me, and it is a certain kind of social anthropology
that bears some relationship to a kind of literary inquiry' (Frei 1988c: 11).

Frei now discusses the *readings* generated when a text is read, rather than the intrinsic *meaning* of the text as he had done formerly.[67]

What is the role of the Christian tradition for Frei? On the one hand, Frei insisted that 'there is no such thing as a community's assuming dictatorship of interpretation principles' (Frei 1988c: 57). And on the other hand, it is the case that 'by reason of the centrality of the story of Jesus, the Christian interpretive tradition in the West gradually assigned clear primacy to the literal sense in the reading of Scripture' (Frei 1988b: 151). Frei employs the history of the reading of the Scriptures to serve a formal function. First, it commends a reading of the narratives for their literal sense. Second, it 'probably sets reasonable bounds on what can and cannot be done' (Frei 1988c: 57) and so performs a normative function.

While developing this approach, Frei became more sceptical about the possible contribution of literary theory for a theological reading of the biblical narratives, in part because it operates 'usually in a nontheological context...especially secular literary reading' (Frei 1988b: 152-53),[68] and in part because it is an example of 'general theory'. In 1988 Frei wrote that 'the Babel of contemporary literary theory is such that it is too early to tell whether literary inquiry into the New Testament narratives will prove a bane, blessing, or neither to the literal tradition' (Frei 1988b: 154).

The irony of Frei's position is that his change of direction signals a move away from the 'primacy of the literal sense of the text' which had characterized his earlier work. The narrative qualities of the text are in danger of being eclipsed all over again, and this time by the reading consensus of Christian communities.

The Meaning and Truth of Biblical Texts in a Postmodern Context
In contrast to 1973, when he completed *The Eclipse of Biblical Narrative*, Frei could write in 1988 that 'Biblical narrative has re-emerged as

---

67. Frei's thought moves on from the ground-breaking essay 'The Literal Reading of Biblical Narrative in the Christian Tradition'. In the 1988 essay 'Narrative in Christian and Modern Reading' the first section is an illuminating revision of the opening section of the 1983 essay 'The Literal Reading of Biblical Narrative in the Christian Tradition'. For example, 'the primacy of the literal sense' becomes 'the primacy of the literal reading' (Frei 1988b: 150).

68. Frei seems to assume that postmodern theories of reading are almost always secular, but he never argued any necessary link between these two aspects, nor the criteria for the possible theological use of postmodern literary theory.

an engrossing topic while the preoccupation with historical explanation as a necessary even if not sufficient criterion for the "meaning" of the narratives has faded. Biblical texts became thought of once again as texts, rather than sources or clues that mean by referring beyond themselves' (Frei 1988b: 152).[69]

One of Frei's moves during his earlier period had been to bracket out the 'historical claims' of a 'history-like' narrative, in order to create methodological space in which to attend to the literary significance of its 'history-likeness'. Significantly, Frei never completely relinquished an interest in the extra-textual historical referential claim of the narrative, for he still considered that 'Christians do have to speak of the referent of the text. They have to speak historically and ontologically, but in each case, it must be the notion of truth or reference that is re-shaped extravagantly, not the reading of the literal text' (Frei 1986: 354).

Frei's bracketing of these historical questions can only be justified as an interim position; however, the interim seemed to extend indefinitely. Frei's continuing avoidance of this question eventually attracted sustained criticism (e.g. Comstock 1986). Frei's reading in secular postmodern literary theory and criticism in the early 1980s led him to return to this most difficult of questions. The thoroughgoing deconstructionist criticism of the stability of textual meaning and the associated impossibility of establishing criteria of 'true' readings outflanked Frei's hesitations over the complex questions of reference and truth. Although Frei denied that the Gospel narratives made any kind of simple historical claim as was popularly understood by those with quasi pre-critical assumptions about historical correspondence between the text and reality, he was convinced that the narratives did 'mean one thing, and not another' and did make truth claims. So in the 1986 Thompson Memorial Lecture at Princeton Theological Seminary, Frei addresses the relationship between meaning and truth.

In the lecture, Frei plays off the 'modern' and the 'postmodern' approaches to the Gospel narratives, and then offers his own tentative suggestion as a third option. The modern view maintains that the meaning of the text is stable and accessible when the text is read with due reasonable care. Furthermore, the 'history-like' qualities of the Gospel

---

69. Many Western, historically orientated biblical scholars are conceptually ill-equipped to cope with the text as primarily 'text' and not as 'source', with the consequence that 'the narrative "means" what is written, even when the written sense does not correspond to an "actual" state of affairs' (Frei 1988b: 153).

narratives signal a claim to represent historical reality. Conservatives then argue that past historical reality is like the world of the text, and Liberals argue that sometimes historical reality—as critically reconstructed—is not like the text, and so only those parts of the text which accord with the reconstruction are historically reliable and may be considered true. Frei points out that both approaches are mistaken, yet paradoxically both employ 'a shared understanding of the sense of the text'.[70]

A more radical challenge emerges from the postmodern situation with its abandonment of 'the single sense view of the meaning of texts, a single sense redolent upon a real world' (Frei 1986: 349). To Frei it seemed that 'modern secular interpreters of the Bible...want to emphasize the text itself, and they do not wish its interpretation to be governed by a criterion of meaning strongly connected to truth' (Frei 1986: 353).[71] Frei returned to Kermode's *The Genesis of Secrecy* as an example, in which the melancholic Kermode concludes that 'the pleasures of interpretation are...linked to loss and disappointment, so that most of us will find the task too hard...and then, abandoning meaning, we slip back into the old comfortable fictions of transparency, the single sense, the truth' (Kermode 1979: 123; quoted in Frei 1986: 350).

Frei writes: 'I agree with structuralists and post-structuralists that we should treat textuality (what is written) and the referent or truth of a text (what it is written about) as two different things...[but] *I do not say, finally, that they have no bearing on each other*' (Frei 1986: 350; my italics). Yet Frei remained cautious, because in his experience of Christian interpretation, 'the move from text to truth or language to reality, whatever form it takes, is almost always premature' (Frei 1986: 350).

Frei proposes a revised form of the traditional Christian primacy of the literal sense as a way forward.[72] Significantly, Frei does not argue a

70. 'It cannot be said often and emphatically enough that liberals and fundamentalists are siblings under the skin in identifying or rather confusing ascriptive as well as descriptive literalism about Jesus at the level of the understanding the text, with ascriptive and descriptive literalism at the level of knowing historical reality' (Frei 1988c: 84).

71. Frei oversimplifies the argument by conflating the two aspects of (1) the religious approach and (2) the theoretical approach in his sketch, and then describes the modern view as essentially Christian, and the postmodern view as typically secular. In this discussion, only the theoretical analysis is considered.

72. For Frei, the pre-critical way is inadmissible for in the contemporary context, it would seem to require the reader to agree an uncritical correlation between

theoretical case for his proposal, but simply commends it to his reader. When pressed, Frei is agnostic about what can be said in explanation: 'of course Christians want to live and speak the truth or speak truth-fully, but we ought to be careful at what point and in what way' (Frei 1986: 350). The primacy of the literal sense requires 'the condescension of the truth to the depiction in the text, and not vice-versa... [Frei pleads] for the textuality of Scripture, the importance of its linguistic-depictive shape this side of metaphor (or better, with metaphor as a secondary instrument under the governance of the literal sense, rather than the other way round)' (Frei 1986: 355).

As regards Jesus, the primacy of the literal sense means '*literally about Jesus*, in which certain descriptions are literally ascribed...and are not literally descriptive' (Frei 1986: 356; my italics). Frei concludes with a plea for the primacy of the literal sense and its puzzling but firm relationship to a truth towards which we cannot thrust.

> The *modus significandi* will never allow us to say what the *res significata* is... There is a fit due to the mystery of grace between truth and text. But that, of course, is a very delicate and very constant opera-tion to find that fit between textuality and truth. The Reformers saw the place where that fit was realized in the constant reconstitution of the church, where the word is rightly preached and the sacraments are duly administered (Frei 1986: 356).

With this relocation of theological reading within the Christian com-munity Frei removed himself from a thoroughgoing accountability to general philosophical discussion of hermeneutics. This development is seen more clearly in the papers published as the posthumous *Types of Christian Theology*. The challenge which faces this later proposal of Frei is how to relate such a church-orientated practice to a philosophi-cally rigorous general hermeneutical debate. This overview of Frei's thought provides the context for the following analysis and critique of the two major proposals Frei developed.

the narrative and the events described, and so misrepresent what is meant by the 'literal sense' of the text. The 'modern' approach is inadmissible, for it makes the extra-textual referent more important than the text itself, reducing the function of the text to an 'evidential' role, and so dissolving the literal sense. Finally, the typi-cally postmodern position which does take an interest in the literal sense is inadmissible because it procedurally declares the impossibility of truth or reference.

Chapter 2

THE NEW CRITICAL READING OF REALISTIC NARRATIVE

One way and another there has been a Christian belief that Jesus Christ is
a contemporaneous person, here and now, just as he spans the ages…
[who] shares his presence in a very particular way with *you* personally.
Frei 1975: 12; Frei's italics

Frei's first period of thought opens with his Anselmian kind of theological hermeneutics for the reading of biblical narratives. This chapter
expounds its principal features and in a constructive critique draws out
its fundamental assumptions. The discussion treats the hermeneutical
dimension of the important Christological text *The Identity of Jesus
Christ* which exemplifies Frei's proposal 'at work'. I suspect that the
lasting achievement of the book will be its contribution to theological
hermeneutics rather than to contemporary Western Christology; certainly, *The Identity of Jesus Christ* argues cogently for 'the restoration
of the christologically centred narrative sense of scripture to its original
primacy' (Lindbeck 1987: 161).[1]

While Frei's theological reading proposal begins with a literary-critical stage, he considered himself to be a theologian and not a literary
critic nor a historian. For Frei, theological reading is a way of reading
in which the Christian reads the Gospel account in order to speak truthfully *today* of God and Jesus Christ. Frei's interest in literary concerns
is the consequence of his theological convictions, and so this discussion
begins with Frei's theological concerns.

'What is the essence of Christianity today?' With disarming simplic-
ity, Frei's answer during this period amounts to 'Jesus, the Jesus of the

---

1.   So also David Tracy, with whom Frei disagreed. 'Both in his magisterial
work on the eclipse of narrative understanding in modern historical-critical biblical
interpretation and in his constructive christological work on the identity and presence of Jesus Christ as rendered in and through a "literal" or "plain" reading of the
passion narratives of the gospels, Frei's work has proved a breakthrough for all
theology' (Tracy 1990: 37).

Gospel narratives'. In his later period, when the interest in the literary Gospel narratives had been demoted, Frei continued to maintain that 'the central persuasion of Christian theology, not so much to be de-fended as to be set out, is that Jesus Christ is the presence of God in the Church to the world' (Frei 1988c: 8).[2] Therefore, the task for the Chris-tian theologian is to speak of the contemporary person Jesus Christ.[3]

Frei's literary interest in this phase concentrates upon the New Tes-tament stories and in particular 'the Synoptic Gospels, or at least one of them, because their peculiar nature as narratives, or at least partial nar-ratives, makes some hermeneutical moves possible that we don't have available in other parts of the New Testament' (Frei 1967: 32). Frei makes clear in *The Identity of Jesus Christ* that 'the outline to be fol-lowed is largely, though not exclusively that of Luke' (Frei 1975: 92 n. 17).

This chapter argues that Frei is broadly correct in his analysis and in his suggestions for engagement with the fields of literary-critical stud-ies. At the same time, this discussion argues that the particular New Critical proposal which Frei selected is a mistake. The present critique draws out key issues involved in theological reading and also the ways in which theological convictions can inform this activity. Chapter 3 will then consider Frei's reasons for his eventual rejection of this scheme.

The Rationale of Frei's Approach

> It is one of the plagues of theology in our day that theologians, justly aware of their limitations in biblical exegesis, retreat from biblical com-mentary in their theologies. As many forms of biblical scholarship in the meantime become more and more nontheological (even anti-theological) the theological situation worsens.
>
> Tracy 1990: 62

2. In his last public lecture 'H. Richard Niebuhr on History, Church and Nation' (in Hunsinger and Placher 1993: 213-33) Frei enquired 'why, we might ask of H. Richard Niebuhr, be a theologian in our utterly untheological times? I think he would have made short shrift of that question. He would have asserted, I believe, that our responsibility to affirm the glory of the Lord, and his glory alone has not altered one whit, and that this remains our duty in propitious or unpropitious times.'
3. Frei would concur with Jüngel's description of the theological task: 'To account for something (an event, a person) dogmatically means to represent its sig-nificance now in the horizon of our current awareness of truth (with the possibility of critique of the latter)' (Jüngel 1995: 83).

Frei's search for alternative ways to address the Christological task began because he was thoroughly disillusioned with 'modern' theology. Instead of attempting the usual 'modern' apologetic task of demonstrating the reasonableness of Christian thought before a sceptical modern world, Frei offers a modest project with a completely different approach which he described as a 'reflection within belief' in the Anselmian tradition of *fides quaerens intellectum*. Frei took it for granted that in some way or other Jesus is 'present' to the Christian believer and therefore the theological task is to explicate what this entails.[4] 'Reflection about the presence of Christ is for the believer a pleasurable exercise... ordering his thinking about his faith and—in a certain sense—a praise of God by the use of analytical capacities' (Frei 1975: 5).

Frei's interest in the presence of Christ led him to begin with the Gospels, for he was convinced that these texts are normative for the Christian in ways analogous to pre-critical ways of reading the biblical texts which led to the believer's world being accommodated to the world of the text.[5] In practice, however, largely due to the unrecognized influence of modern criticism, Frei did not develop the formal role of the world peculiar to the believer. Instead, he expounded how a Christian might reflect upon his or her belief and do so in a way that is accessible to every kind of reader.

The inner coherence of Frei's proposal may be displayed by tracing the rationale of his project. Frei's thought may be presented as a sequence of steps:[6]

Step 1. Frei begins with the question of the presence of Christ. The

4.   At the beginning of *The Identity of Jesus Christ*, Frei invokes the Matthaean text 'Lo, I am with you always, to the close of the age [Mt. 28.20]' (Frei 1975: 3).

5.   This form of the relationship between text and reader is typical of pre-critical reading of the Bible, which considered that 'the world of the Bible was the one and only real world [which] in principle embraces the experience of any present age and reader. Not only was it possible for him, it was also his duty to fit himself into that world' (Frei 1974: 3). I suggest that one important way of appreciating Frei's theological hermeneutic is to consider it as a 'postmodern retrieval of a pre-critical way of reading the biblical text'.

6.   This description of Frei's thought necessarily draws upon the relatively early *The Identity of Jesus Christ* from 1967, for it is his only substantive proposal. However, the theoretical discussion of this position is found primarily in the introduction to *The Eclipse of Biblical Narrative* (Frei 1974) and the preface to *The Identity of Jesus Christ* (Frei 1975).

ability of Christ to 'be present', that is, his identity is a consequence
who he is.

Step 2. Frei develops a version of Ryle's proposal that a 'person' can
be so defined that *their story constitutes their identity*.

Step 3. Frei proposes that the place to start a discussion of Jesus'
identity is the story of Jesus which is found in the Gospels. This step
begins the long and unfinished detour within Frei's christological project
as he engages with hermeneutical questions.

Step 4. Frei reviews how the Gospel story of Jesus has been read
within the modern period of biblical scholarship, and discovers a consistent failure to appreciate the *story form* of the Gospel. Consequently,
it is now impossible to read the Gospels as *texts*. Instead, most modern
biblical scholars read the Gospel story as a *source* for historical reconstruction, which inevitably decomposes the form of the Gospel story.

Frei attributes the failure to appreciate the story form of the Gospels
to the deficient methodology of the biblical critics, who lacked both a
concept of what the text is, and a *way* to read the text. Frei's response is
to find a suitable concept of the text and an appropriate way to read it.

Step 5. Frei argues that the deficiency in the historical-critical
approach to the text lies in the *historical* demands of the enterprise. Frei
proposes a distinction whose function is to create methodological
'space' in which the Gospel text could be read free from this relentless
historicism. Frei suggests that the 'history-likeness' of the Gospel text
is a *literary* feature whose function is to help create a 'lifelike' and
accessible story-world and that there is no necessary historical claim
associated with this literary feature.

The distinction between a literary or synchronic reading and a historical or diachronic reading of the Gospel text sets in train two separate
interpretative enquiries. Frei addresses the synchronic literary approach,
and brackets (for years!) the historical issues.

Step 6. The distinction between the 'history-like' and the 'historical'
aspects of the Gospel texts informs the selection of a *concept* of text
and the choice of a *way* to read the text. Frei selects the fictional category 'Realistic Narrative' which he draws from the thought of Auerbach, and for a reading practice, Frei draws upon Anglo-American New
Critical reading of the text.

Step 7. Frei produces *The Identity of Jesus Christ*. The book is a
reading of the Gospel of Luke which combines Frei's textual category

and interpretative procedure, together with the concept of narrative identity developed from Ryle.

The Preliminary Decisions in Frei's Theological Hermeneutic

> Christian faith involves a unique affirmation about Jesus Christ, viz., not only that he is the presence of God but also that knowing his identity is identical with having him present.
>
> Frei 1975: vii

Frei's proposal begins with two preliminary decisions discussed below which duly inform and largely determine his selection of elements for the construction of his theological hermeneutic.

Theological Reading of the Gospels as the Narrative Identity of Jesus Christ

In *The Uses of Scripture in Recent Theology*, Frei's colleague David Kelsey produces a 'theological criticism' (Kelsey 1975: 9) of various theologians at work and concludes that theologians take a prior decision before constructing their theologies, when they choose 'how to characterize the *mode* in which God is present among the faithful' (Kelsey 1975: 160).[7] Kelsey suggests three broad ways of doing this in recent Western Christian theology:

1. 'The *ideational* mode', when God is taken to be present 'in and through the teaching and learning of the doctrine asserted by scripture' (Kelsey 1975: 161). As a consequence, the theological task becomes a critical reflection upon the community's belief and its use of the propositional inheritance, primarily in scripture. The central emphasis falls upon believing and on what is to be believed.

2. 'The mode of *concrete actuality*' in which God is taken to be present in and through an agent rendered by Scripture, or in and through a cosmic process. In this approach, the central emphasis falls upon an 'identity description of the person and work of Jesus Christ' (Kelsey 1975: 162).

3. 'The mode of *ideal possibility*' in which God is taken to be present in and through existential events that are occasioned by Scripture's

---

7.   'At the root of a theological position there is an imaginative act in which a theologian tries to catch up in a single metaphorical judgment the full complexity of God's presence in, through and over-against the activities comprising the church's common life' (Kelsey 1975: 163).

kerygmatic statements. In this approach, the central emphasis falls upon the transformation of human subjectivity.

Frei's enterprise is typical of the second group, in which the presence of God in Christ is considered as concrete actuality, and the identity of this Christ is found in the Gospel narrative texts.[8]

Dogmatic and Apologetic Modes of Theology

Frei's approach to doing theology is a sustained withdrawal from the influence of general theoretical schemes of thought.[9]

> The conviction underlying these pages is that the story of modern Christian theology (beginning with the end of the seventeenth century) is increasingly, indeed, almost exclusively that of anthropological and Christological apologetics, that the new hermeneutics by and large serves the same aim, that this development has now just about run its course, and that whether it has or not, it is time to search for alternatives (Frei 1967b: 27).

Frei initially divides the Western theological enterprise into two broad categories which he characterizes as dogmatic theology and apologetic theology. Frei considers that apologetic theology is characteristically cast in the mode of 'explanation'. Explanatory theology endeavours 'to show the credibility or (in our day) the 'meaningfulness' of Christianity to sceptical or confused contemporaries' (Frei 1975: xi). As a consequence, 'the rationale of how one comes to believe comes to control, indeed to be virtually identical with the logic of belief... [exercising] a

---

8.   Kelsey does not examine Frei's theological enterprise, but his comments about the Barthian use of Scripture could just as well apply to Frei's work. 'It is clear that narrative is the authoritative aspect of scripture...as Barth expressly and repeatedly points out, he authorises his theological proposals by appeal to the New Testament narratives just as they stand in the received texts' (Kelsey 1975: 45). Frei acknowledges his indebtedness to 'Barth's biblical exegesis [as] a model of the kind of narrative reading that can be done in the wake of the changes I describe in *The Eclipse of Biblical Narrative*' (Frei 1974: viii).

9.   In the 1967 lecture at Harvard, Frei set out his two fundamental assumptions. First, 'the meaning of a text is found within the text', which opposed the current phenomenological hermeneutics in which meaning and the interpreter's understanding are dialectically related in the hermeneutical circle. According to Frei, meaning is independent of the interpreter who reads the text, so that 'the meaning of the text remains the same no matter what the perspectives of succeeding generations of interpreters might be' (Frei 1967b: 322). Second, the involvement of Global Theory should be minimal because, as Frei later summarized, it 'dictates to, not to say overwhelms exegesis' (Frei 1975: xvi).

tyranny over the way that Christian concepts mean' (Frei 1975: xii).

This apologetic mode of Christian theology employs a form of correlation between Christian concepts and aspects of contemporary experience, in which the meaning of the Christian concept is considered to be a particular expression of a general truth about contemporary existence. Frei recalls Bultmann's observation that 'all theological assertions are anthropological assertions' (Frei 1967b: 28).[10] Theology in the apologetic mode requires theological statements to be primarily accountable to the 'world view' of the theologian and not to the text, and the interpretative theory used is constructed upon this premise. The consequence is that the interpretation produced is primarily accountable to the interpretative theory rather than to the text.[11] Frei doubted whether such apologetic theology is ever useful, but for theological reflection he considered it as simply inappropriate.[12] This observation is typical of Frei, rooted in his 'unrelenting insistence on the freedom of God's sovereignty in revelation' (Fodor 1995: 261), which sprang from his doctoral research upon the theology of Karl Barth.

Frei responds formally and practically to the *impasse*. Formally, he argues for a different mode of theological reflection, in which the biblical text is normative and theological reflection is the explication of the text. Frei characterizes this alternative as in the dogmatic mode, which is a 'reflection within belief…in which I shall simply try to explore a certain notion and what is contained in it' (Frei 1975: 4). This theological exercise is 'an exercise in clarification…adding no new information and providing no new conclusions. We talk about the relation to Christ as if it were already established and simply wanted a kind of descriptive expansion' (Frei 1975: 5). Frei's approach is an example of a non-foundational theology, which in its 'celebration of narrative's importance…

---

10. In such an approach, 'Christology becomes the mere form to which anthropology provides the real content' (Hunsinger 1992: 106). It is possible that there is a ' total diffusion of Jesus into our presence so that he no longer has a presence of his own' (Frei 1975: 34).

11. This paragraph summarizes what Frei demonstrates at length in *The Eclipse of Biblical Narrative*. The historical-critical world view precluded aspects of the text that were not amenable to historical investigation.

12. 'I am convinced that the passionate and systematic preoccupation with the apologetic task of showing how faith is meaningful and/or possible is largely out of place and self-defeating—except as an *ad hoc* and highly various exercise. In this arena an ounce of living is usually worth a pound of talk, and especially of writing' (Frei 1975: xii).

focuses on the conditions for adequate *description* rather than the conditions for adequate *expression*' (Kelsey 1987: 123).[13]

Practically, Frei concedes that some interpretative theory is necessary to avoid interpretation becoming reiteration, and so employs two stratagems to prevent the use of interpretative theory leading to a slide back into the apologetic mode. First, he reduces hermeneutics to the rules of interpretation, which is not dissimilar to *pre-critical* kinds of interpretation.[14] Second, Frei argues for the rules to be subject to and revised by the process of interpretation of the text.[15] These proposals then allow 'just enough theory to describe the rules and principle used in an actual exegesis, and no more' (Frei 1975: xvii).

Theological Hermeneutics without a Formal Interest in History

I am well aware of, but not terribly distressed by, the fact that my refusal to speak speculatively or evidentially about the resurrection of Christ while nevertheless affirming it as an indispensable Christian claim may involve me in some difficult logical tangles.

Frei 1975: xiii

Frei introduces the distinction between the history-like quality of a narrative text and any possible historical claims of the text. The realism of the Gospels has usually been construed in modern New Testament studies as constituting a historical claim to represent past events, and so historical criteria are brought to bear in a critical reading practice. Frei argues that the realism of the Gospels is primarily a *literary* and not *historical* feature.

As a consequence, he argues that there are two separate discussions to be conducted in critical studies of the realism of the Gospel texts. The first discussion attends to the literary quality of 'history-likeness' and what it contributes to the meaning of the text. Frei develops his treatment by the adoption of 'realistic narrative' which is a secular

13. Kelsey contrasts Frei's approach with the foundationalist approach of Ricoeur which is based upon a prior conception of human experience as fundamentally narrative, and thus gospel narratives are a particular expression of a general anthropological condition' (cf. Kelsey 1987: 123-26).

14. 'Hermeneutics I define in the old-fashioned, rather narrow and low-keyed manner as the rules and principles for determining the sense of written texts, or the rules and principles governing exegesis' (Frei 1975: xvi).

15. 'The exegetical practice is indispensable to the theory of exegesis, and ruled use governs the statement of the rules actually used' (Frei 1975: xv).

literary concept that includes the characteristic of 'history-likeness' and whose qualities are illuminated by the discussions of realism in European fiction.[16]

The second discussion treats the relationship of the realistic text to past events—which regrettably never took place in Frei's published works in this period. The principal reason for this omission is not the complexity of the task, nor the more serious fact that historical criticism threatens the narrative integrity of the Gospels—Frei has simply established to his own satisfaction that, for his purposes, the discussion is unnecessary.[17]

Frei argues that a theological reading of a Gospel narrative is interested in the meaning of the text and that meaning is inherent within the narrative structure of the text. The distinction he introduces between 'history-like' and 'historical' serves to create methodological 'space' in which the narrative form of the whole text may be read, *apart* from the 'decomposition' which happens when read with historical criticism. This attention to the literary form of the text is a *literary* critical decision. Frei's adoption of this emphasis upon the literary form of the text is ultimately rooted in a theologically serious respect for the text *appropriate for reading the Gospels as Scripture*. However, as Frei wishes to retain the accessibility of the meaning of the Gospels for every kind of reader, whether a believer or not, he does not use the description 'Scripture'.

Frei's claim that history is not *directly* relevant to a theological reading is weakened because he never argues the claim in detail.[18] Whereas

16. European realism in literature developed from late eighteenth-century philosophy (cf. Wellek 1960) whose 'encompassing motto is succinctly summarised in Balzac's claim...that "All is true"' (Furst 1992: 2). Frei in his earlier writings considered biblical narratives to be a kind of realistic narrative which were akin to the realism of the nineteenth-century novel. 'What is involved in understanding *historical* narrative apart from the question of fact estimate, I would regard as having many features in common with fictional, novelistic narrative' (Frei 1967b: 34; Frei's italics).

17. In this earlier period of Frei's thought, the distinction between 'history' and 'history-like' always led to the relegation of the question of history to some other discussion, which Frei never conducted.

18. 'I shall not attempt to evaluate the historical reliability of the Gospel story of Jesus or argue the unique truth of the story on the grounds of a true factual "kernel" in it. Instead I shall be focussing on its character as a story. As for history, I shall take for granted only what most commentators agree upon: that a man, Jesus

Frei's omission of an interest in historical reconstruction is a *de facto* statement that a theological reading has to do with the contemporary context of the reader and the text, it cannot justify a blanket dismissal of historical interest.[19]

In practice Frei does not fully relinquish historical concerns and his exposition of *The Identity of Jesus Christ* does require a factual resurrection. Yet even then, Frei does not employ historical arguments to establish the resurrection, for Frei considered that would be a complex and probably impossible task.[20] Frei's emphasis upon the world of the text and his relegation of the historical world 'behind' the text fits well with the pre-critical conviction that the world of the Gospel narrative is the real world, and all else is to be subordinated to this world. In so doing, the claims of positivist history are distanced, and a postmodern possibility emerges.[21]

Frei's suggestion that theological reading can continue *apart* from the critique of the historian raises important questions about the function of historical study.[22] How can Frei's theological reading engage with 'modern' readings of the Gospel in which 'truth' is commonly held to be a judgment upon the accuracy of historical correspondence of text and historical event? After discussing Frei's proposal, Goldberg comments that for 'the biblical narratives which portray a historically conditioned reality, the historical facticity of the events narrated in those

---

of Nazareth, who proclaimed the kingdom of God's nearness, did exist and was finally executed' (Frei 1975: 51). Frei adopts this minimalist historical reconstruction because it is all that historical criticism can ever achieve. The resurrection is certainly still a fact, but one beyond the range of historical argument, so that 'there is no historical evidence that counts in favour of the claim that Jesus was resurrected' (Frei 1966: 86).

19. Theologically Frei's position is in keeping with his descriptive mode of doing theology, in which apologetics has no place. For Frei, historical reconstruction is an example of apologetic theology.

20. Hunsinger offers a brief exposition and critique of the relationship between faith and history in the thought of Frei (Hunsinger 1992: 125-26). Frei 'cogently points out that biblical narrative was not abandoned for some more directly available world or reality; instead, the biblical story was exchanged *for another story...* [In effect, modern theology is] a clash between stories' (Goldberg 1991: 160).

21. Thiemann writes: 'The [scriptural] text's authority lies not in its ability to coerce or compel but in its ability to persuade and convince the reader' (1987: 28).

22. These questions include 'what is involved in the historical discussions of the Gospels?', 'what is the function of historical reconstruction within theology?' and also 'what kind of "truth" is at stake?'

stories must affect the truth of any claims which have them as their basis' (1991: 185). Goldberg clearly has historical truth in mind, whereas Frei is committed to an exposition of the *theological truth* of the Gospels which he considers to be conceptually distinct from historical truth.[23] As the modern world usually employs this historical model of truth, Frei deliberately restricts his exposition to the *meaning* of the narratives and not to their 'truth' as popularly understood, in order to avoid the diversion of historical questions.[24] Frei's decision not to attend to the historical question of the texts is in keeping with his respect for Barth's model of biblical exegesis.[25]

23. Comstock argues that Frei considers that 'the meaning of the narratives is autonomous, they refer only to themselves' and are thus not open to 'the rigorous debate about truth conditions' (Comstock 1986: 123). In response, Green correctly argues that Frei allows that texts may refer outside themselves, even though this is not the meaning of the texts (Green 1987: 95 n. 14). The confusion arises from a form of the 'referential fallacy'. Frei considers that the 'narrated world is as such the real world' (quoted in Schner 1992: 160 n. 14) and its claims to be true are not accountable to or adjudicated by any external, secondary world. Thus Comstock's analysis is correct, if truth is conceived as correspondence to an external historical event. However, Frei seems to assume (without a clear exposition of the position) that there are distinctions between 'theological truth and historical truth'. In his article 'Two Types of Narrative Theology', Comstock observes that Frei's postmodern narrativism 'collapses explanation into description' (1987a: 692). The question of truth is 'the most severe fault line that is undermining the foundation of narrative theology' (Oakes 1992: 56).

24. It is this decision which invites so much criticism. Philosophically, Comstock and Oates consider Frei's refusal to discuss historical claims as a failure to be interested in truth. Biblically, Meir Sternberg considers Frei's dismissal of the problem of the relationship between the 'constrained historian and the licensed fiction-maker as well-intentioned, even laudable, but theoretically misguided' (1985: 81-82). The narrative theologian Stanley Hauerwas wrote 'that Frei's suggestion would be disastrous if it is an attempt to make irrelevant whether Jesus in fact did not exist and act in a way very much like the way he is portrayed in the gospel accounts' (quoted in Goldberg 1991: 185). The kind of truth claims the Gospels make proved to be one of the central issues within the wider debates between those of 'Yale' and those of 'Chicago' (cf. Stroup's criticism of the quality of the debate [1991: 425]) Vanhoozer extrapolates and exaggerates, but correctly senses that 'Frei's stratagem of dissociating literal sense from the historical referent threatens to eclipse not the biblical narrative, but the biblical claims to truth' (1990: 175).

25. 'Barth distinguishes historical from realistic reading of the theologically most significant biblical narratives, without falling into the trap of instantly making history the test of *meaning* of the realistic form of the stories' (Frei 1974: viii).

Frei claims to create 'methodological space' in order to respect the text. However, when Frei expounds the Lukan Gospel narrative in *The Identity of Jesus Christ*, he fails to comment upon the places in the text where it is clear that the narrative makes explicitly historical claims (Lk. 1.1-4; 2.1-2; 3.1). If a reader is committed to the kind of respect for the text which Frei enjoins, and the text makes extratextual historical claims, should not these be taken seriously? It seems that Frei's ideological commitment overrides his sensitivities to the literal meaning of the text!

Frei's failure to establish the relationship between the 'history-like' text and its historical claims is a serious tactical mistake. The consequence was a widespread misunderstanding about his project, typically represented by Wood's comment: '[Frei] recommended reading the stories as realistic but historically unreliable narratives' (1976: 81).

There is also a serious internal difficulty that arises due to the failure to engage with the question of history. The problem surfaces when Frei discusses the resurrection event, which is the one point where he acknowledges that history intersects with the world of the text.[26] Although he argues that a historically warranted resurrection cannot serve as a ground for Christian belief, Frei attracts legitimate criticism when he tries to employ a historical resurrection without a return to historical discussion!

Frei's distinction between 'history-like' and 'historical' is an important contribution to the task of theologically reading the Gospels, and a revised form of the distinction is adopted in the argument of this book.[27] However, unlike Frei, the 'historical' dimension is considered important in a subsidiary way *within the proper historical constraints*, because it seems to be a requirement of the text when read with respect.[28]

---

26. Frei's attempt at maintaining the facticity of the resurrection is discussed below. Watson is broadly correct when he writes that 'Frei had no conceptual tools with which to deal with the resurrection' (1994: 25). There is an ambiguity in Frei's reading practice at this point because he *needs* to engage with Jesus' resurrection as a historical event, even if he cannot demonstrate it historically. This ambiguity is betrayed in Frei's prose, for 'it is not clear whether Frei is speaking about the depicted Jesus, the historical Jesus, or both' (Fodor 1995: 281).

27. 'It is difficult to exaggerate the importance of this narrative insight for Christian theology' (Tracy 1990: 35). The literary critic Kermode hesitated about Frei's version of literary history, but appreciated his distinction between 'history' and 'history-likeness' whose confusion 'we still suffer from' (1979: 121).

28. The subsidiary, distinctive and necessary function of historical reconstruc-

Theological Hermeneutics with a Formal Literary Contribution

One lacked the distinctive category and the appropriate interpretive procedure for understanding what one had actually recognized: the high significance of the literal narrative shape of the stories for their meaning.

Frei 1974: 12

If the first surprise is that Frei turned his back on historical-critical work as a guide to the meaning of the Gospels, the second surprise is his turn to the world of literary criticism. Frei considered that the failure to appreciate the narrative quality of the Gospel texts arose because interpreters 'lacked the distinctive *category* and the appropriate *interpretive procedure*' (Frei 1974: 12), and so he proposes to adopt 'realistic narrative' to serve as the distinctive category together with a New Critical reading practice to serve as the appropriate interpretative procedure. Frei then integrates them into an interpretative practice informed by the biblical exegesis of the 'incomparable Karl Barth'.[29]

Frei's proposal is shaped by the research he undertook for *The Eclipse of Biblical Narrative*. To avoid another 'eclipse' of biblical narrative, Frei develops a tight linkage between the literary form of the text and the theologically generated respect which is paid to the text. The only appropriate expression of this respect for the text is an interpretative practice which respects the literary features of the text. And clearly, for the Gospels, these features include the narrative form of the texts.

The Category of 'Realistic Narrative'

Frei adopts the literary category of 'realistic narrative' in which what the biblical stories 'are about and how they make sense are functions of the depiction or the narrative rendering of the events constituting them' (Frei 1974: 13). Frei's version of realistic narrative was stimulated by Auerbach's *Mimesis*, which surveys 'realistic works of serious style and character' (Auerbach 1953: 556). Frei draws upon Auerbach's suggestion that the realistic tradition has three historical high points in its development: the Bible, Dante's *Divine Comedy* and the nineteenth-century novel.[30]

tion for theology is a large and separate discussion, as argued in Jüngel 1995: 83-119.

29. 'Barth's biblical exegesis is a model of the kind of narrative reading that can be done' (Frei 1974: viii).

30. Frei considers that biblical narratives, history writing and the traditional

Auerbach notes that biblical narratives are not written for pleasure, as other works, but with a passionate concern for truth. 'Far from seeking like Homer merely to make us forget our reality for a few hours, the Biblical narrative seeks to overcome our reality: we are to fit our own life into its world... The Bible's claim to truth is not only far more urgent than Homer's, it is tyrannical—it excludes all other claims' (Auerbach 1953: 15).

Frei lists three characteristics of his version of 'realistic narrative' which are drawn from *Mimesis* and also includes a fourth extratextual qualification for the interpreter. First, Frei notes that 'the narrative rendering, in effect a cumulative account of the theme, is indispensable' (Frei 1974: 13), because 'what [narratives] are about and how they make sense are functions of the depiction or narrative rendering of the events constituting them...[so] if one uses the metaphorical expression "location of meaning", one would want to say that the location of meaning in narrative of the realistic sort *is the text*, the narrative structure or sequence itself' (Frei 1974: 280; my italics). 'There is neither need for nor use in looking for meaning in a more profound stratum beneath the structure (a separable "subject matter") or in a separable author's intention or in a combination of behind-the-scene projections' (Frei 1974: 281).

The second characteristic is seen when 'characters or individual persons in their internal depth or subjectivity as well as their capacity as doers and sufferers of actions or events, are firmly and significantly set in the context of the external environment, natural and more particularly social' (Frei 1974: 13). Frei recalls Henry James: 'What is character but the determination of incident? What is incident but the illustration of character?'[31]

The third characteristic of realistic narrative is that in style and content, 'the sublime mingles inextricably with the quality of what is casual, random, ordinary and everyday' (Frei 1974: 14). This feature

novel all display aspects of the category 'realistic narrative'. For example, 'they all literally mean what they say' and so 'the kind of theological proposal consonant with this essay rests on a reading of the Gospel narrative to which I have applied the term "realistic narrative" ' (Frei 1975: xiii-xiv).

31. Poland suggests that this conviction offers one reason for Frei's rejection of the existentialism of Bultmann, which 'tends to view self-identity or self-understanding as separable from public circumstances and social contexts and structures... [and so distorts the subject self]' (Poland 1985a: 127-28).

was identified by Auerbach in 'the story of Christ, with its ruthless mixture of everyday reality and the highest and most sublimest tragedy' (1953: 555).

Frei's qualification for interpreting biblical realistic narrative is the extratextual requirement that the literary meaning is independent of any historical claim for 'in order to recognize the realistic narrative feature as a narrative feature in its own right...one would have had to distinguish sharply between literal sense and historical reference' (Frei 1974: 11). The complications this brings have already been discussed.

Initially the literary category 'realistic narrative' seems a brilliant choice for Frei's project, for it embraces his 'history-like'/'historical' distinction and it fits well the assumptions of the New Critical reading practice which Frei also adopts. In a realistic narrative the function of the history-like features of the text is to construct the 'common public world' to which all readers have easy and non-technical access. 'Believable individuals and their credible destinies are rendered in ordinary language and through concatenations of ordinary events' (Frei 1974: 15).

However, Frei's adoption of realistic narrative attracted severe and ultimately compelling criticism. Critics persuasively argue that first, Frei misunderstood the concept;[32] second, he overplayed the similarity between the Gospels and the novel;[33] and third, he showed no appreciation of the reasons why this kind of realism in literary studies had eventually been discarded by the literary critics who once employed it.[34]

32. Yu observes that Frei has missed the scientific conventions intrinsic to such modern literary realism. An example of a 'scientific convention' is the concern 'to bring about natural events by easy means, and to keep up the curiosity without the help of wonder' (Dr Samuel Johnson, *The Rambler*, No. 4, quoted by Yu 1978: 201-202).

33. The contemporary literary critic Stephen Prickett drily comments of Frei's work that 'we have no reason to suppose...that biblical authors subscribed to a similar literary convention to that of the nineteenth century realistic novel, but I think it is not too far-fetched to assume that they did not' (1989: 5; so also Fodor 1995: 285).

34. There is 'a well documented collapse of nineteenth century realism in literary studies...and the type of realism employed in the Victorian novel has itself come under severe criticism within literary studies... Frei does not seem to be aware of the problematic status of realism' (Prickett 1989: 3-6). One of the reasons for this collapse is suspicion about narrative's covert ideological function. Recent studies of narrative and ideology suggest that 'most of the controversy over the "postmodern" centres on issues connected with narrative... Narrative, simply

58   *Luke's Stories of Jesus*

Reviewing Frei's project, the literary critic Stephen Prickett criticizes those who 'have wanted to see biblical narrative less as history than as an essentially *literary* creation analogous to prose realism' (1989: 20). Literary critics who have inspected Frei's proposal generally agree that fictional realistic narrative has insufficient similarity to the biblical history-like narratives.[35]

Frei's choice of 'realistic narrative' is mistaken, and an alternative is required for the textual category. Nevertheless, Frei's choice illuminates the requirements for whichever textual model is chosen. First, the model will allow the literary aspects to operate as a *literary* feature, untroubled by historical-critical discussions; second, the model will locate the primary meaning of the text within the form of the text itself, so that 'the texts literally mean what they say' (Frei 1975: xiv); and third, this literary category should comprise the realistic kind of narrative writing which renders a world accessible to a general reader.

These criteria are generated by a theological concern to read the Bible in a way analogous to the way it used to be read in the pre-modern church. Frei's proposal formally treats the text in a way reminiscent of Western pre-critical biblical interpretation. Frei's exercise in theological hermeneutics is actually *a narrative argument for a postmodern form of a pre-critical way of reading the biblical text literally.*

An Interpretative Procedure: A New Critical Reading with Hermeneutical Instruments
'Nor can we probe the intentions and themes or even the cultural contexts of the Gospel writers that underlie the story. Our task is rather to observe the story itself: its structure, the shape of its movement and its

because it tells a story, is under suspicion' (Tambling 1991: 93). For a view more sympathetic to Frei's proposal, see Nuttall 1989.

35. At the time when Frei was writing there were other literary alternatives open to the interpreter of biblical narrative. New Testament literary studies were embryonic. David Gunn, in 'Narrative Criticism' (1993: 173) traces the slow emergence of the narrative studies in the Old Testament in the 1960s, and notes that even in the crucial formation period of the 1970s a number of significant contributors worked in relative isolation from each other. It is therefore understandable how little impact was made at that time upon North American thinking by the work on Old Testament narrative. This related realm of literary study even today plays little part in the narrative reading of the New Testament Gospels. Meir Sternberg published articles from the late 1960s onwards, which became the basis for his influential *The Poetics of Biblical Narrative* (Sternberg 1985).

crucial transitions' (Frei 1975: 87). Frei adopts a New Critical reading practice as his 'appropriate interpretive procedure', for he considers that it addresses his theologically generated concerns about many contemporary interpretations of the text.[36]

Frei's interpretative procedure includes characteristics typical of the formalism of New Criticism: (1) the meaning of the text is distinct from its reception; (2) the interest is in Jesus as he is presented in the Gospel story, and there is a minimal interest in the Jesus of history; (3) the dismissal of the contribution of the intention of the author; (4) the primary significance of the structure of the text for its meaning, with a consequent wariness of the 'heresy of paraphrase', in which paraphrase alters the structure, and thus inevitably modifies the meaning; and (5) the immediate accessibility of the world of the text for the interpreter.

One attraction of the New Critical approach for Frei is the recovery of a way of reading which respects the integrity of the text in its final form, which is similar to an attitude to Scripture which had been widespread in the history of the church. Poland persuasively argues that there is a formal congruity between the New Critical approach and the

---

36. 'New Criticism' is an umbrella term to describe common features in the approaches of literary scholars such as T.S. Eliot, Cleanth Brooks, Allen Tate, John Crowe Ransom, Robert Penn Warren, I.A. Richards and William Empson. Inevitably not all of them welcomed the description, e.g. 'I do not know what the New Criticism is... I merely acknowledge the presence of the myth' (Tate 1970: 169). The title 'The New Criticism' was coined by Ransom, writing for *The Kenyon Review*. The New Criticism began in the 1920s and is generally considered to have ended in the 1960s (cf. Lentricchia 1980).

The New Criticism is a reaction to the Romantic celebration of the author as genius which spawned much 'specialized rubbish—put there...by professors of literature which stands between the reader of the poem and the poem' (Rice and Waugh 1989: 25). Instead, the New Criticism claimed to view the verbal object as in itself it really was, free from distractions of biography, social message, even paraphrase. 'A distinguishing feature [was] a hostility to or neglect of the historical method' (Tate 1970: 168) which matched Frei's unease with the historical-critical approach.

The characteristics of New Criticism were developed in studies of poetry and include: (1) the literary work as autonomous and which needs no extratextual assistance; (2) the meaning of the literary work is constituted by the *structure* and substance of the work, and therefore to paraphrase is heresy (Brooks 1968: 158-65); (3) the poem is a verbal icon which creates its own world, and does not refer beyond itself. 'Poetry gives no truth of correspondence... [only] the truth of coherence' (Graff 1970: xi).

Barthian Neo-Orthodoxy which was such a major influence upon Frei's thought.[37]

The difficulty with Frei's adoption of the New Critical approach is that it inevitably includes the problems which eventually led to the demise of New Criticism in literary studies.[38] To begin, there are several practical difficulties which result from the adoption of this approach. The first is illustrated in the claim that the 'common public world' of the Gospels is accessible to the twentieth-century Western reader. The New Critical reading of a poem dismissed interest in the historical context of its generation, but is it appropriate to do this in the reading of an ancient narrative text with historical associations?

The second difficulty lies in the tight identification of meaning with the structure of the narrative, for it leads to unwelcome consequences for Frei. If there is no gap between the representation and what is represented, as Frei maintains, then in the narrative identity of Jesus, 'does Frei mean that the *representation* of Jesus in the Gospel stories *is* ontologically Jesus Christ?' (Poland 1985a: 134; Poland's italics). And if that is the case, the further question arises: 'how many Jesuses are there—four to accommodate four Gospel narratives?'[39]

The principal difficulty with the New Critical programme is that it is typically 'modern', based on the myth of the reader who brings nothing to the act of reading and, in particular, to the identification of the

37. 'For Barth's sovereign Word...Frei seems to substitute the autonomous biblical text' (Poland 1985b: 469). 'These recent alliances between neo-orthodox theology and modern literary criticism appear to be, if not marriages made in heaven, then at least unions of kindred spirits' (Poland 1985b: 459). Fodor argues that there is an ethical dimension which also issues from Frei's adoption of New Criticism (1995: 276-78). However, Fodor seems to confuse the thought of the earlier and later Frei. In later writing, Frei develops a use of texts as part of the sociolinguistic approach, and this certainly includes the life of the reader. However, with the earlier Frei, meaning is independent of reader engagement with the text, and the reader respectfully gazes on the verbal icon, which is an analogue for the believer before the Sovereign God.

38. Poland provides a penetrating critique of Frei's adoption of the New Critical programme (1985a). The observation by Watson about biblical scholars applies equally to Frei: 'Banished from literary studies on grounds of superannuation, "new criticism" takes refuge in the midst of biblical scholarship which naively believes that the predicate "new" is still applicable' (1994: 79).

39. As is argued below, Frei actually works with his own generalized version of the Gospel story rather than the four Gospel narrative texts, and so he never faces this difficulty.

meaning of the text. The context and ideological commitment of the reader have no formal place in the practice of interpretation.[40] So Frei could claim that 'the meaning of the text remains the same no matter what the perspectives of succeeding generations of interpreters may be' (Frei 1967b: 32).

At one level, the consequence is that the cultural differences between the world of the reader and the world of the text are trivialized, and the hermeneutical challenge is avoided.[41] More seriously, the failure formally to include the ideological reader leaves the reading practice open to surreptitious ideological abuse without the resources to recognize and correct it. The disintegration of the New Critical programme may be construed as a part of the complex transition between the 'modern' and 'postmodern' world of literary studies, in which the formal emergence of the ideological reader is key. For Frei, the failure formally to include the reader is one reason for his later abandonment of this approach.[42]

Frei is correct when he argues that the theological concerns of the reader should inform the choice of an appropriate literary reading practice. The task is to find an approach which respects the narrative form of the text *and* includes the reader within the reading practice; such a radical revision of New Critical formalism might produce a kind of 'neo-formalism' (Bal 1991a: 12). And when such a literary scheme is incorporated within a theological reading, the combination should not prejudice the critical freedom of the literary-critical reading.

Theological Hermeneutics and the Non-literary Concept of Narrative Identity

When we can say that (a given person) was most of all himself, we should say that his action in that instance does not merely *illustrate* or

---

40. 'My hope is…that no matter whether one is a believing Christian or not, one can make sense of the Gospel story in its own right' (Frei 1975: xvii). However, Frei concedes that 'talk that is not talk in the course of becoming actually acquainted with the one talked about is in this instance meaningless to the non-believer's mind' (Frei 1975: 6).

41. 'It remains unclear…how seriously Frei confronts the cultural distance between the first and twentieth centuries' (Poland 1985a: 134).

42. 'It is artificial and dubious to claim a purely external relation of text and reading, which in effect sets aside the mutual implication of interpretation and textual meaning' (Frei 1983: 64).

represent his identity. Rather it *constitutes* what he is. A person *is* what
he *does* centrally and most significantly.

Frei 1975: 92; Frei's italics

Once Frei had chosen his literary-critical tools, he was able to produce
a New Critical literary reading of the Gospel texts. However, this is not
enough for a theological reading of the text. Frei now pressed beyond
literary-critical reading to argue that the character Jesus of the Gospel
narratives is *more* than a literary character. Frei maintained that Jesus is
a person who in some way is present to the contemporary believer, and
so Frei now required a way of talking about the notion of 'person' in a
contemporary way which would relate to the narrative texts.

While seeking to use the least amount of theoretical assistance in
reading these texts, Frei recognizes that 'we must approach the Gospels
with some conceptual tool in hand, otherwise we understand nothing at
all' (1966: 58).[43] The conceptual tool that Frei proposes is the notion of
'narrative identity' which he developed from his reading of Gilbert
Ryle. Yet at the same time, Frei recognizes that contemporary readers
'must not imprint either our own life problems or our own ideological
analyses on the story...[and so] the proper approach is to keep the tools
of interpretive analysis as minimal and formal as possible, so that the
character and the narrative of events may emerge in their own right'
(1966: 46).

Frei begins with the concept of 'person' in Ryle's philosophy and
proposes that the identity of a person is the sum of his actions and
nothing more, so that the reader does not need the 'superadded factor'
of a separate invisible 'soul'.[44] Thus, 'a person is not merely illustrated,
he is *constituted* by his particular intentional act at any given point in his
life' (Frei 1975: 44). Frei is careful to restrict his use of Ryle's thought
to examples of 'description', and avoids any metaphysical analysis.[45]

43. 'Without some perspective of our own, the story has no discernibly significant shape for us' (Frei 1966: 46).

44. 'This is a difficult puzzle that the sages of Western culture since the time of
Plato and Aristotle have not been able to solve... [Yet] if we now enter into this
argument, we have in effect gone beyond our own task of purely descriptive talk
and into metaphysics... That is precisely what I am not going to do... We are
saying [that] the theory of the "superadded factor" is not helpful' (Frei 1975: 42).

45. It seems that Frei's adoption of Ryle's understanding of the person flows
from the usefulness of this notion in resolving Frei's dilemma. Ryle's *The Concept
of Mind* was published in 1949, as one example of the 'Physicalist' tradition within

It is 'perfectly proper to describe what a person *is* by what he *does*, and *who* he is by what he is and does' (Frei 1966: 62; his italics). Frei then develops two 'intellectual instruments' as he calls them, which together facilitate the recognition of this 'narrative identity'. The first instrument is the notion of 'intention-action' which operates when a person is engaged in a particular event. The second instrument is the notion of 'self-manifestation' which treats the continuity of identity through time.

Frei introduces this approach to narrative identity as a hermeneutical bridge between the world of the text and the world of the reader. In both worlds, the identity of the person is considered to be a function of their story. The ability to discern some kind of formal relationship between the Gospel narrative and a contemporary understanding of person admirably suits Frei's ultimate objective of speaking of Jesus today.[46] Frei maintains that 'Jesus was most of all himself in the description of the Gospels. This was his identity. He was what he did and underwent: the crucified human saviour' (1966: 57). However, though carefully defined, Frei's two instruments also have limitations which eventually make them unworkable.

Instrument One: The 'Intention-Action' of a Person

The 'intention-action' pattern is the first of the hermeneutical instruments to help the reader recognize the identity of Jesus in the Gospel narrative. The concept assumes an intimate continuity between intention and action in a person so that 'a person is not merely illustrated [but]...is *constituted* by his particular intentional act at any given point in his life' (Frei 1975: 44; Frei's italics). 'The appropriate answer to the question what is he like? is look at what he did on this or that occasion. Here he was characteristically himself' (Frei 1975: 91). The restriction of interest to what a person *does* avoids the complexities of the inner

the field of the philosophy of the mind. The question of whether the mind is physical 'occupies the central place in the modern philosophy of the mind' (Scruton 1994: 547). Ryle's position is that the Cartesian dualism of mind and body is a mistake which rests upon a grammatical illusion, and so there is no requirement for a separate 'ghost in the machine'. Frei's discussion of Ryle's proposal is severely limited, because criticism of Ryle's position is not addressed and though Frei was writing 17 years after *The Concept of Mind*, in this area of philosophy, 'the agenda has changed radically since Ryle's day' (Scruton 1994: 537).

    46. 'It is assumed that both the New Testament writers and we ourselves hold in common some of the same sorts of description of human identity' (Frei 1975: 46).

life of a person, for the person is reduced to only those intentions that issue in action. Conceptually, however, it reduces a person's identity to a sequence of their 'intended' actions.

In the actual reading of a narrative, this reductionism is clear. 'Intention-action' is inextricably involved in *only* the 'activity' of a character, which is prioritized over all other narrative elements which might also contribute to their identity. This instrument procedurally brackets out much of the narrative. For example, in the reading of the Gospel text, there is no place to incorporate the teaching of Jesus unless it bears directly upon his action, nor to hear what the Hebrew Scriptures say of this Messiah figure. In *The Identity of Jesus Christ* the question is posed 'Who was Jesus?', and Frei answers 'Jesus was what he did' (1975: 111). Surely there is more that we can say?

Instrument Two: The Pattern of 'Self-Manifestation' through Time
The second instrument tries to 'point to the continuity of a person's identity throughout the transitions brought about by his acts and life's events' (Frei 1975: 127), and to do this 'without returning to the ghost in the machine position' (Frei 1975: 95). Frei concedes that this is a difficult task given the assumption that the 'person in action' is all that can be said about a person.

Frei argues that the two manifestations of the person are his word and his body. But let the reader be clear, 'they are not merely manifestations of the self; they are also the self manifest' (Frei 1975: 98). Therefore the identity of self-manifestation through time traces what a person says and does as the story unfolds.

The qualifications that Frei repeatedly makes illustrate that this notion of the self is a contrivance based upon the prior decision to consider the person as only 'intention coming into action' with all the attendant restrictions it entails. These limitations are seen most clearly in Frei's exposition in *The Identity of Jesus Christ*.

The Theological Hermeneutic of The Identity of Jesus Christ

Let's start with the Synoptic Gospels, or at least one of them, because their peculiar nature as narratives, or at least partial narratives, makes some hermeneutical moves possible that we don't have available elsewhere in the New Testament.

Frei 1967b: 32

All the streams of Frei's thought in this early period flow into *The Identity of Jesus Christ*, which is his proposal for a christological reading of the Gospel narrative.[47] After all the analysis in *The Eclipse of Biblical Narrative*, Frei now sets out 'to show how exegesis can be done' (Frei 1975: xv). The following discussion examines three major areas of his theological hermeneutic at work, and draws out their significance.

The theological task begins with the question: 'How may we speak of Jesus Christ today?' Frei assumes that 'to have Christ present is to know who he is and be persuaded that he lives...[for] the right order for thinking about the unity of Christ's identity and presence is to begin with his identity' (Frei 1975: 6).[48] *The Identity of Jesus Christ* duly begins with a non-technical discussion of 'presence' and its implications for identity.[49]

The second part opens with a discussion of a descriptive form of 'identity' in general and suggests that identity comprises two aspects: the 'ascriptive' and the 'temporal'. These two facets of identity form a descriptive model of personal identity and are then adopted as two hermeneutical instruments. This twin-faceted identity description finds its natural expression in the *story* form, and so lends itself to the reading of the Gospels, which are 'in large part, and at crucial points a story' (Frei 1975: 47).

The longest part of the book is a discussion of the particular story of Jesus as found in the Gospels, employing the twin hermeneutical instruments Frei has introduced. Frei concludes that the Gospel story displays Jesus' 'identity as that of a singular unsubstitutable person, especially in the sequence from his passion to his resurrection' (1975: 52).

---

47. The *Identity of Jesus Christ* comprises four sections: (1) the Preface and Introduction, which describe Frei's approach to the task; (2) Parts 1–3 discuss the categories of 'presence' and 'identity', and consider unsatisfactory accounts of Christ in contemporary theology and literature; (3) Part 4 introduces four exegetical chapters which form the core of the proposal; (4) Part 5 endeavours to demonstrate how the one in the Gospel story may be present today.

48. 'The governing conviction is...that in Jesus Christ identity and presence are so completely one that they are given us together' (Frei 1975: 4).

49. This first part of *The Identity of Jesus Christ* is the least satisfying and, with hindsight, it would have been better had Frei rewritten it. Frei acknowledges his own dissatisfaction in the Preface, and in the light of the development in his thinking, changed the title of the study from 'The Mystery of the Presence of Jesus Christ' to 'The Identity of Jesus Christ'.

Unfortunately, this exegesis offers only occasional insights amid a seriously distorted and impressionist reading of the Gospel stories. The scale of this failure is masked by the influence of Frei's orthodox theological concerns about Jesus. The following discussion identifies and inspects three major weaknesses in Frei's theological reading practice, and draws out their significance.

The Gospel Story or the Gospel Stories: The Failure to Respect the Narrative Text

Frei argues that 'in the Gospels, which tell us most of what we know about Jesus, his identity is grasped only by means of the story told about him' (1975: 87). The first question is 'which story?' A close reading of *The Identity of Jesus Christ* reveals that Frei fails to distinguish between 'the Gospel story' and 'the Gospel stories' and actually works with an abstracted and idealized 'common story'. Astonishingly, after all the analysis, rhetoric and argument, Frei's analysis simply *fails to engage with the New Testament texts*.

The problem is illustrated in his claim that 'in the *Gospels*, which tell us most of what we know about Jesus, his identity is grasped only by means of the *story* told about him' (Frei 1975: 87; my italics). Frei mentions Gospels in the *plural* and story in the *singular*, and gives no clue to their relationship with each other. In practice, Frei does not work with the Gospel narratives themselves, but with a 'story' which he has composed from the Gospels.[50] While Frei can select convenient elements from all four Gospels, he avoids the methodological difficulties which arise as a consequence of there being four canonical Gospel texts, each of which presents a different story of Jesus.[51]

The failure to address the *variety* of stories about Jesus is replicated in the treatment of the Gospel of Luke. Frei's selective and aggregative

50. *The Identity of Jesus Christ* acknowledges the differences between the Synoptic and Johannine Gospels, and then ignores them. Frei writes that 'our earlier statement that Jesus' helplessness is a theme in the Synoptics must be drastically modified, if not eliminated, when one looks at the fourth Gospel' (Frei 1975: 113). But he neither modifies nor eliminates the statement!

51. 'If Frei does mean to assert that literary form directly compels meaning…then he must also argue that each of the four New Testament Gospels has a different meaning, and renders a different Jesus—a conclusion Frei would certainly not wish to maintain' (Poland 1985a: 136). 'When Frei considers the Christian text in its more restrictive, literary sense—as a written artefact—the narrative integrity of each gospel account seems to be compromised' (Fodor 1995: 275).

approach is incapable of appreciating the variety of christological perceptions within this single Gospel narrative, and so Frei's Christology
is unrepresentative of the Gospel text. In practice, Frei's reading practice is seriously deficient because it is unchallenged by the text which it
seeks to interpret.

The argument of *The Identity of Jesus Christ* actually engages with
Frei's 'idealized story of Jesus' and not with the story of any actual
text, despite Frei's insistence that 'meaning is firmly grounded in the
text and nowhere else' (1967b: 42).[52] The recognition that Frei works
with an abstract, idealized story is confirmed by the way that short passages from any of the Gospels are conveniently mixed together without
any attention to their various literary contexts.

The irony of Frei's reading practice is that having established the
need to attend to the narrative form of the Gospel text, and correctly
argued that this can only happen when the reader engages closely with
the text, Frei fails to do it himself.[53] This study argues that a serious and
critical reading of *one of the Gospel stories* is the only way to develop a
reading practice that demonstrates the 'respect' for the text which Frei
champions.

52. It is difficult to suggest why this is the case. Frei acknowledges that he
works as a Christian theologian and not as a biblical scholar (Frei 1983: 36).
Furthermore it is clear if one works through the corpus of Frei's works that his
interest is primarily in the formal questions, rather than the substantial matters. *The
Identity of Jesus Christ* is the only extended treatment of the form and content of a
Gospel text that Frei ever produced. It is also generally the case that recent Western
theology has seen the emergence of a division between biblical scholars and
dogmatic theologians, with a consequent lack of appreciation of the significance of
the methods each employs for the other discipline (see Jeanrond 1991: 159-61).
Perhaps one clue lies in the *style* of *The Identity of Jesus Christ*. The work is
'popular' and impressionist, and does not engage with any option in detail. Nevertheless there is a strange paradox within the thinking of one who claims that 'by
speaking of the narrative shape of these accounts I suggest that what they are about
and how they make sense are functions of the depiction or narrative rendering of the
events constituting them' (Frei 1974: 13).

53. 'The evangelists surely differ substantially among themselves. Yet Frei is
content to speak of the New Testament story...if he had been true to his own
method he would have taken far more account of the differing forms of narration
within the New Testament' (Wiles 1976: 261-62).

The Practical Limitations of Frei's Concept of the Narrative Identity of Jesus Christ
Frei turns to the Gospel text with his two-part concept of narrative identity, and contrary to his concern that the reading practice 'should leave the story as unencumbered as possible' (Frei 1975: xv), both of these instruments seriously distort the reading of the Gospels.

Instrument One: The 'Intention-Action' of a Person. Frei's difficulties begin immediately for he can only find two places in the Gospel story where Jesus' intention is sufficiently clearly expressed and immediately followed by its outworking in action.[54] These moments are the story of the temptation of Jesus in the wilderness and the story of Jesus in the garden of Gethsemane. Although there are only two examples, Frei is undisconcerted for 'there is just sufficient to indicate the passage of intention into enactment' (1975: 104).

Frei observes that the most important feature of the story of Jesus 'is not...that [Jesus'] love to men was his only or even his predominant behavioural quality. Rather, he was perfectly obedient, and his obedience to God was one with his intention to do what had to be done on men's behalf' (1975: 103).[55] Frei suggests that the emphasis in the Gospel that is placed upon the obedience of Jesus succeeds in keeping the reader engaged with the character of Jesus in the story, rather than constructing the person of Jesus *apart* from the story.[56] In this way, 'the characterizing intention of Jesus that becomes enacted—his obedi-

54. Frei is restricted to these two parts of the story by four criteria that he introduces. There are 'four patterns of meaning embedded in the narrative itself...which display the identity of Jesus in terms of his *intention-action* description' (1975: 126). To recognize Jesus' intention is 'to claim an inside knowledge of him that we do not have' (1975: 106). This lack of 'inside knowledge' is typical of first-century literary characterization, and is not peculiar to the story of Jesus.

55. There are many places in the New Testament where the obedience of the Son is described, and *The Identity of Jesus Christ* instances some of them (Rom. 5.19; Phil. 2.8; Heb. 5.8). However there is no evidence given for the claim that 'obedience' is 'the predominant behavioural quality of Jesus in the story' (Frei 1975: 102).

56. The construction of a person 'apart' from the story would be easier if inherent personal characteristics, such as his faith, were portrayed. But 'to draw it would be to claim an inside knowledge of him that we do not have' (Frei 1975: 106). In this comment, Frei is actually making a virtue out of necessity, probably without recognizing it, for the paucity of 'inside knowledge' is typical of first-century literary characterization, and is not peculiar to the story of Jesus.

ence...is shown in the story with just enough strength to indicate that it characterizes him by making the purpose of God who sent him the very aim of his being' (Frei 1975: 107). However, the evidence for this claim is meagre, and this begins to look like eisegesis.

There are considerable problems with the use of this 'intellectual instrument'. The practical difficulty is that there are only two occasions that possibly portray Jesus' inner intention together with its subsequent enactment, and one of those is not completely suitable.[57] Any interpretative tool which purports to assist in the reading of the Gospel narrative and produces one significant insight is clearly of very limited use.

The second difficulty emerges when treating the resurrection as the literary climax to the story, because Frei's intention-action device falls into illogicality. In the resurrection it is *God* who intends to raise and does raise Jesus; however, for Frei, the resurrection is important as part of the identity description of Jesus. Yet in the resurrection, Jesus does nothing at all. The difficulty forces Frei to enquire 'whether in some way Jesus enacted his own resurrection! At this point the nature of the narrative...imposes a limit on theological comment' (Frei 1975: 125). To a student of the New Testament Gospels, it seems much more likely that it is the nature of Frei's interpretative scheme that imposes the limit.

The third difficulty is that the intention-action device disenfranchises most of the Gospel narrative from contributing to the identity of Jesus. For example, *The Identity of Jesus Christ* suggests that during 'the first two chapters of Luke, the person of Jesus is identified wholly in terms of the identity of the people of Israel. *He is not the individual person Jesus*, not even of Nazareth' (Frei 1975: 128; my italics). Ascription of the identity of the baby Jesus is procedurally excluded because the baby is not a person within Frei's concept of person as enacted intention.

There is a further difficulty of how to incorporate the substance of Jesus' teaching, as well as the activity of teaching. It is clear by now that Frei's interpretation of the narrative structure as a whole is actually *transformed* by this concept of identity. The concept of enacted intention is intensely individualistic, for it claims that Jesus' identity can only be revealed through the medium of his own enacted life. Frei fails

---

57. When *The Identity of Jesus Christ* combines this insight with the 'self-manifestation' literary device, it emerges that only *one* of these examples is significant, namely, Jesus in the garden of Gethsemane for 'as nowhere else, the story points "from the inside" to his obedient intention' (Frei 1975: 109).

in a way reminiscent of his fear about others: 'such intellectual instruments have a habit of taking charge of the materials described' (1975:
45). In short, Frei's formal respect for the Gospel texts is not matched
by his exegetical practice.

Instrument Two: The Pattern of 'Self-Manifestation' through Time.
Frei's second hermeneutical instrument is the pattern of 'self-manifestation description…[which is] the structuring of the Gospel story as a
whole into a single developing series of stages in the identification of its
persisting subject Jesus of Nazareth' (1975: 127).[58] Frei divides the
Gospel story into three stages and pays particular attention to the transition points.

The first stage of Jesus' story includes the birth and infancy stories, in
which Jesus 'is Israel under the representative form of the infant king
figure' (Frei 1975: 8). However, Jesus is 'not the individual person
Jesus, not even of Nazareth… He is a representative, stylized figure in
the form of an individual' (1975: 8). The baptism of Jesus marks the
transition to the second stage, in which the public ministry of Jesus is
displayed. Now '[Jesus'] identity is largely defined in terms of the
kingdom of God' (Frei 1975: 130). In a limited way, Jesus appears as
an individual in his own right, but 'his identity is established by reference to the kingdom of God' (Frei 1975: 132).

The characteristic feature of the third stage is clear—Jesus himself
takes centre stage in his unsubstitutable 'unadorned singularity' (Frei
1975: 134).[59] No longer are scriptural fulfilment, the kingdom of God or
the 'Messianic titles' the clues to the identity of Jesus; in fact the story
of Jesus renders them increasingly ambiguous. This third section is 'the
part of the story [which is] most clearly history-like in the sense that it
describes an individual and a series of events in connection with him'
(Frei 1975: 133). Finally, in the resurrection, Jesus 're-establishes the
link between himself and the kingdom of God and the Messianic titles in

---

58. 'The Gospel accounts, regarded as a story and taken as one self-contained
whole, do provide us with a kind of order-in-sequence, consisting of a series of distinct transitions from stage to stage. Each of these stages is marked off from the
preceding by providing a further insight into the identification of who Jesus is' (Frei
1975: 127).

59. The transition between the second and third stage is located differently at
various points of Frei's exposition. At its earliest it is the moment when Jesus sets
his face to go to Jerusalem, and at its latest when Jesus enters Jerusalem.

a striking way. The unsubstitutable Jesus now makes the stylized titles his own…Here, then, he was most of all himself' (Frei 1975: 136).

The use of this hermeneutical instrument presents two major difficulties. First, as the device of 'self-manifestation' requires, by definition, a clear sequence of actions by the same character, it only works well with the Passion sequence, which is 'most clearly history-like in the sense that it describes an individual and a series of events in connection with him' (Frei 1975: 133).[60] And conversely 'Jesus is not available to us directly or unambiguously—either as a character in a story or historically—in the portion of the Gospel accounts describing his ministry' (Frei 1975: 143).[61] Clearly the narrative is being 'reconstructed' in the light of the requirements of Frei's non-literary and extratextual concept of narrative identity.

The second difficulty is the way in which Frei treats the climax of the resurrection within the narrative structure, for he claims that for Jesus, 'a non resurrection becomes inconceivable' (1975: 145). But does the unfolding narrative of Jesus 'require' a resurrection? The suggestion that there is a *literary* necessity for the resurrection within the narrative is debatable and still debated. Once again, Frei's interpretative scheme is interfering with the narrative reading, and the matter can only be addressed by a more careful reading of the Gospel text.

Finally, the use of this non-literary concept of narrative identity is problematic because it includes an unacknowledged conceptual confusion between literary character and real people. It could be argued that Frei reduces the concept of a real person until it approximates to a literary construction, but even that is only part of the problem. There is a range of features of literary characters which denote the difference between literary character and people in real life, but are useful conventions employed by authors for their literary ends. For example, in the

60.   In the case of Luke, Frei's preferred Gospel, this decision accords more weight to the last 6 chapters and less weight to the preceding 18.

61.   Frei suggests that the quality of the historicity of the accounts improves as the story moves through the three stages. For example, Frei allows virtually no historicity to the infancy narratives, some in parts of the middle stage, and most in the third stage. There is an interesting parallel development in the change in portrayal of the character Jesus, for as the person Jesus becomes more accessible in the story so the historical worth of the account improves. Frei is then left with the logical consequence that as the resurrection makes most plain who Jesus is, it is the event whose historicity can, and must, be established. Yet Frei argues that he cannot and will not discuss historicity.

Gospels the ability of the reader to 'see inside the minds' of the characters is so unremarkable that it does not subvert the illusion of realism. Frei endeavours to minimize the differences between literary characters and real people in order to build his hermeneutical bridge between the literary character Jesus and the real Jesus who is present to the believer, and in so doing overlooks the distinctive contribution of a literary Jesus who is mediated to the reader through the literary Gospel story.

Unsurprisingly this version of narrative identity has not won many followers, for Frei unwittingly demonstrates that he fails to prevent these interpretative instruments from distorting the reading of the text. Theologically Frei is committed to the primacy of the literal reading of the Gospel narrative, but he has not attended sufficiently to the integration of a literary-critical approach within a theological hermeneutic, and the result is that literary sensitivities are swamped by hermeneutical requirements.

The Difficulty of the Anselmian Move beyond the World of the Text

Frei considers the resurrection of Jesus as the *literary* climax of the 'passion-resurrection' sequence. Although the resurrection may be highly problematic historically, in story terms Frei argues that it is the literary resolution of the unfolding narrative, and its believability is dependent upon whether the resurrection provides a *coherent* end to the story. In the story-world, literary readings are not governed by the constraints of our physical world.[62] Frei claims that the literary momentum of the story leaves no other option for the character Jesus: the resurrection is the only conceivable end.

This interpretation of the function of the resurrection is in part a consequence of using the hermeneutical instruments Frei adopts. The climax is the stage in the story where 'Jesus is most of all himself' (Frei 1975: 141-42), and, according to Frei, Jesus is himself most plainly in the most integrated 'history-like' sequence of his activity within the Gospel. What the accounts are saying, in effect, is that 'the being and identity of Jesus in the resurrection are such that his non-resurrection becomes inconceivable' (Frei 1975: 145). This literary assessment is problematic in itself, but even if it could be established, there is a more serious difficulty in Frei's argument.

---

62. 'Even such miraculous accounts are history-like or realistic (but not therefore historical and in that sense factually true)…if the depicted action is indispensable to the rendering of a particular character' (Frei 1974: 14).

Frei acknowledges that the 'history-like' Gospel story becomes most like history in the final sequence of the passion and resurrection, which so 'tends to force the question of factuality' (1975: 146). How are literary necessity and facticity related—if at all? Frei claims that this literary recognition does not *require* that such an event happened, but it presses the question. The continuing significance of the 'story resurrection' is then developed. The literary sequence climaxes with the resurrection of Jesus, in which the literary character Jesus is raised from the dead and displays the ability to be present with the story character disciples wherever they go.

Frei's 'move' from this literary resurrection to a factual resurrection opens up the question as to whether the ability of the literary character Jesus to transcend geography and circumstance could allow Jesus to transcend the boundaries of the literary world, so that Jesus can be with readers wherever they go. Frei addresses 'the possibility of making the transition from a literary description to historical and religious affirmation...although explaining how this transition becomes possible...is impossible' (1975: 147).

The Resurrection: Literary Text and Historical Reality. Frei's hesitations about history preclude him from looking to historical studies for assistance in the discussion of the resurrection event.[63] At the same time, Frei's theological concern cannot settle for a merely literary reading of the Gospel story, because it does not include the question of truth. Frei introduces an Anselmian-like move and argues that 'to grasp this identity, Jesus of Nazareth...is to believe that he has been *in fact* raised from the dead' (1975: 145; Frei's italics).[64]

As the resurrection is unique, Frei argues that there is no evidence that directly demonstrates that it happened, but because the accounts are 'more nearly fact like than not, reliable historical evidence *against* the resurrection would be decisive' (1975: 151; Frei's italics). As Frei's theological hermeneutic is conducted in the dogmatic and not apologetic

---

63. 'The criteria for historical reliability in regard to the Gospel story will—in the absence of external corroborations—always rest on shifting sands' (Frei 1975: 141).

64. Frei immediately defends himself from enquiries about hope for other fictional characters by claiming that 'the argument holds good only in this one and absolutely unique case...[for] [h]e *is* the resurrection and the life. How can he be conceived as not resurrected' (Frei 1975: 146; Frei's italics).

mode, this is not a disguised argument for the factuality of the resurrection, but it does reveal the inability of Frei's approach to integrate these two concerns.[65] This Anselmian-like move is an extension of an implication of faith.[66] 'For believers, the logic of their faith requires them to say that disbelief in the resurrection of Jesus is rationally impossible' (Frei 1975: 151). The historical discussion is left with the limited role of possibly proving the resurrection to be false. For the believer, Jesus is raised, until history shows otherwise.

This exposition of the resurrection hinges upon the cogency of the literary argument that the resurrection is the necessary outcome of the Gospel story, despite the fact it is only one of the range of possible readings of the text.[67] In fact, Frei unwittingly concedes that the Synoptic stories are ambiguous when he has to turn to John's Gospel and looks to the Johannine Jesus for the claim to be the resurrection and the life.

The Presence of Jesus: The Text and Theological Reality. Finally Frei returns to the question which began the exercise: 'how may we speak of the presence of Jesus today?' In regard to a theological kind of reality, Frei recalls his opening argument that once a person knows the identity of Jesus then the discussion of his presence may proceed.

The story of Jesus is the key. The resurrection climax in which God raises Jesus from the dead makes plain 'the complex rather than simple identification of God and Jesus—an identification that can only be narrated' (Frei 1975: 164).[68] To speak of God now cannot be done without speaking of Jesus at the same time, for God's identity is manifested in the action of raising Jesus from the dead. Consequently 'to speak of the

---

65. As the exercise is one of explication, it does not attract the criticisms made of Anselm's ontological argument for the existence of God. In fact, on historical grounds, Frei remains convinced that there is no compelling argument for the resurrection. Faith is the ground for the assurance, until history disproves it.

66. 'Jeffrey Stout has called Frei's work an instance of "Anselmian *ad hoc* apologetics carried out by historiographical means" and goes on to call Frei the leading Anselmian theologian of his generation' (Vanhoozer 1990: 153).

67. Steiner reviews *The Eclipse of Biblical Narrative*, and on this point comments that 'both D.H. Lawrence and Robert Graves have shown that there need be nothing ludicrous about rendering the story of Jesus and concluding it by his literal survival and self-effacement among men' (Steiner 1977: 243).

68. The relationship between God and Jesus is conceived as the identicality of the intention-action patterns in the story.

identity of Jesus, in which he is affirmed by believers to be present, is also to speak of the presence of God' (Frei 1975: 154).

Frei then develops the way that the contemporary presence of God is described as 'Holy Spirit' in Christian tradition. Just as the resurrection story makes clear Jesus' oneness with God, so the Holy Spirit may fittingly represent the presence of Jesus. Frei then explores the ways in which the Spirit who is present within the church, the Word and the sacraments is also within the lives of believers. However, it is not clear that the story of the resurrection is a narrative statement that Jesus is the one who is one with God. Could this be a dogmatic presumption by Frei?

Frei's readings of the Gospel story are preliminary, uncritical, eclectic and conveniently selective. Frei's exposition may be a possibility but it is not a necessary reading, and the suspicion is that dogmatic and hermeneutical concerns are driving the theological reading and improperly closing down reading options. In short, Frei's first theological hermeneutic does not truly respect the text, despite his advocacy of the highest respect for the text.

Chapter 3

READING FOR THE *SENSUS LITERALIS* OF CHRISTIAN SCRIPTURE

> The tradition of the *sensus literalis* is the closest one can come to a consensus reading of the Bible as the sacred text in the Christian church.
>
> Frei 1983: 37

In the early 1980s, Frei changed his mind. He concluded that his New Critical literary approach which treated the Gospels as 'realistic narrative' was a failure because the New Critical approach is both a 'modern' exercise and an example of 'general theory' at work. Frei turned to the practice of reading for the literal sense of the Gospel narratives as the basis for his development of a theological hermeneutic. Instead of the earlier emphasis upon '*the* meaning *in* the text', Frei now concentrated upon 'readings *of* the text'. Significantly, Frei's rejection of his earlier proposal rests upon a theoretical critique, and *does not spring from a failure of the approach to illuminate meaning in the Gospel texts.*

The key to Frei's thought in this later period is his conception of the *sensus literalis*, which is 'a much more supple notion than one might first suspect' (Frei 1983: 37). This *sensus literalis* is *not* a literary feature of the narrative text; it is a description of how the text has been read in the light of particular decisions and interests that have governed the reading of the Bible in the history of the Christian church. In his study of Christian biblical interpretation, Frei made the happy discovery that the *sensus literalis* often describes *a way of reading* the Gospels which respects their ascriptive quality as they narrate the story of Jesus, and which is largely indifferent to questions concerning the Jesus of history. Frei then adopts a sociolinguistic perspective to investigate the significance of the variety of readings produced by different Christian communities as they read the same texts.

This second period of Frei's thought is characterized by his development of the implications of this sociolinguistic approach. While not completely relinquishing a literary interest in the biblical text, this turn to 'reading for the *sensus literalis*' signals a relaxation of his formal interest in the literary-critical component of a theological reading and this leads to the decentring of the text within the reading process.[1] Ironically, Frei's new proposal risks a new eclipse of biblical narrative.

This chapter begins with the two failings that Frei detected in his original proposal and that led to the paradigm shift in his thought. The chapter then examines Frei's use of the *sensus literalis* in his theological hermeneutic and investigates the consequences for a literary interest within such a theological reading, bearing in mind Frei's contention that a theological 'respect for the text' entails a respect for the literary features of the text. As Frei did not produce any exegetical work to demonstrate his new hermeneutic, this discussion is based upon his theoretical writings.[2] The chapter argues that Frei's project would be better served if Frei had retained the central emphasis upon a literary interest in the texts as he developed the significance of reading for the *sensus literalis*.

The 'Modern' Failing within Frei's New Critical Reading

It is similarly artificial and dubious to claim a purely external relation of text and reading, which in effect sets aside the mutual implication of interpretation and textual meaning.

Frei 1983: 64

The first reason for Frei's abandonment of his earlier proposal is the *modern* aspect of the formalism of New Criticism. There are three

---

1.   Frei's displacement of a literary concern is evident when he writes: 'when I ask what external discipline is potentially most useful to theology, I come up with an answer that surprises me, and it is a certain kind of social anthropology that bears some relationship to a kind of literary inquiry also' (Frei 1988c: 11).

2.   The principal sources for this exposition of the later Frei are: (1) 'Theology and the Interpretation of Narrative: Some Hermeneutical Considerations' (1982), which was a lecture given in a joint presentation with Paul Ricoeur at Haverford College; (2) The pivotal paper 'The Literal Reading of Biblical Narrative in the Christian Tradition: Does It Stretch or Will It Break?, read at the conference 'The Bible and the Narrative Tradition' in 1983; (3) the less well-known Alexander Thompson Memorial Lecture 'Conflicts in Interpretation: Resolution, Armistice, or Co-existence?' given at Princeton in 1986; and (4) the papers edited posthumously by Hunsinger and Placher in *Types of Christian Theology* (1988c), in which chapters 2–4 are revisions of the 1983 Shaffer Lectures given at Yale Divinity School, chapters 5–7 are revisions of the 1987 Edward Cadbury Lectures given in Birmingham, and Appendices A and B are revisions of the 1987 Princeton Lectures.

assumptions within the proposal that are typically modern, and these are significant both in their own right and for the theological concerns they can represent.[3] These characteristics of a 'modern' literary criticism include:

1. *The 'self-referential' text.* The concept of 'the self-referential text which is apart from any true world' (Frei 1983: 64) was introduced to locate the meaning of the text within the structure of the text itself, in contradistinction to meaning being subject to extra-textual constraints: 'the text is a normative and pure meaning world of its own which... stands on its own' (Frei 1983: 63).

2. *The unchanging meaning of the text.* Frei maintained that the meaning of the text is a function of the structure of the narrative text, and so meaning remains fixed as long as the narrative structure remains unchanged. 'The constancy of the meaning of the text is the text and not the similarity of its *effect* on the life perspectives of succeeding generations' (Frei 1967: 32; his italics). This characteristic enabled Frei to claim that the stories mean what they say, and not something else.

3. *Meaning independent of the interpreter.* Frei held that 'the meaning remains the same no matter what the perspectives of succeeding generations of interpreters may be' (1967b: 32). As a consequence, Frei sought a 'category of understanding which is "non-perspectival"...detached from the perspectives we bring to our understanding, *including our commitment of faith*' (1967b: 31; my italics).[4]

These three literary characteristics flowed from the New Critical concept of the aesthetic text, upon which the observer can only gaze. Frei acknowledges that the New Critical approach springs from an ideological commitment to an 'aesthetic kind of truth in literature' (1983: 64) which he chose because it expressed his theological respect for the scriptural text.[5]

---

3. Watson correctly observes that 'literary critical judgments...serve as surrogates for theological concerns that never explicitly appear yet constantly make their influence felt' (Watson 1994: 23).

4. Frei held that his earlier 'exegetical and accompanying hermeneutical enquiry will show that no matter whether one is a believing Christian or not, one can make sense of the Gospels' (1975: xvii), for this kind of text allows 'across-the-board access to all reasonable people...[by] the authority of self-evident intelligibility' (1983: 63). This view is akin to the argument in Hirsch 1967.

5. 'In regard to aesthetic or quasi-aesthetic texts, particularly narratives, and the Gospels are such in part, "normative interpretations may be possible"' (Frei 1967b: 32).

The paradigm shift began for Frei when he realized that it is 'artificial and dubious to claim a purely external relation of text and reading, which in effect sets aside the mutual implication of interpretation and textual meaning' (1983: 64).

Once Frei turns away from this modern literary approach he also concedes the notion of a meaning determined solely by the literary text. Frei's alternative is to attend to the history of reception within the reading practice of the community—a typically postmodern step.[6] An initial and major difficulty for Frei's project is that the reading practice of the community does not require a formal 'respect for the text'.

I agree with Frei that the modern literary formalism of the New Criticism is untenable and that an alternative interpretative approach is required which formally includes the reader or reading community in the production of a reading of the Gospel narrative. Unlike Frei, I suggest that to reflect the theological position he advocates, the replacement approach must retain a serious interest in the primacy of the text in the act of reading. I consider that it is not necessary to lose this 'centrality of the text' in the quite proper rejection of a New Critical practice.

The 'General Theory' Failing within Frei's New Critical Reading

> The theoretical task compatible with the literal reading of the Gospel narratives is that of describing how and in what context it functions.
>
> Frei 1983: 68

Frei was a theologian implacably opposed to the semantic tyranny exercised by interpretative forms of general theory.[7] In his pivotal 1983 paper 'The Literal Reading of Biblical Narrative in the Christian Tradition: Does It Stretch or Will It Break?' Frei considers two ways of reading biblical narratives which are examples of general theory at work, and traces the difficulties they produce despite their explicit

6. At the beginning of the second period of Frei's thought he retains a qualified interest in New Critical reading: 'As for the New Criticism, a literal reading of the Gospels is appropriate under its auspices, but only because and to the extent that it is in fact a disguised Christian understanding of them and not a reading under a general theory' (1983: 67). The comment illuminates the fact that Frei is content to use literary-critical assistance only within *and subject to* a larger frame of thought.

7. Frei's dramatic language (e.g. 'tyranny' and 'overwhelm') conveys his perception of the seriousness of the threat exercised by 'general theory'.

interest in the narrative form of the texts. The first example is Frei's own earlier proposal and the second example is the phenomenological hermeneutics of Paul Ricoeur. Frei concludes that both approaches so distort the *sensus literalis* that it breaks apart, and his analysis attributes the failure in both cases to the rule of general theory. Frei's analysis in each of these two cases is sufficiently similar formally to be illustrated by a discussion of the critique of his own proposal.[8]

Frei's analysis of his New Critical approach is important because many of the New Testament narrative critics adopt a form of New Critical reading.[9] The principle difficulty Frei identifies is that general literary criteria of meaning overwhelm the particularities of the Gospel narrative when these interpretative schemes identify the meaning of the narrative by reference to categories and criteria which are *external to the text and its world*.[10] Frei considers that 'it is doubtful that any scheme for reading texts, and narrative texts in particular, and biblical narrative texts even more specifically, can serve globally and foundationally, so that reading of biblical material would simply be a regional instance of the universal procedure' (1983: 59).

At the same time, Frei recognizes that it is impossible to read the texts without the use of some hermeneutical tools, for that would reduce interpretation to reiteration, and faith to '*fideism* simpliciter' (Buckley 1990: 332). Moreover, such tools will necessarily have been developed

8.   Frei's analysis of Ricoeur's hermeneutics produces the same criticism of general theory as the analysis of his own work, and so it is not discussed here. Frei offers a brief analysis of Ricoeur's hermeneutical theory as employed by David Tracy and argues that it is a 'regional' theological expression of a general hermeneutical theory. Frei concludes that Ricoeur's approach constitutes a 'subsumption of theology under a general philosophical *Wissenschaftlehre*, [which] under the governing auspices of the latter...seeks to correlate specifically Christian with general cultural meaning structures' (1988c: 3). Although there is debate about the accuracy of Frei's portrayal of Ricoeur's position (Lowe 1992: 137), this is not material to the present discussion. For more detailed discussions of the relationship between the hermeneutical thought of Frei and Ricoeur cf. chapter 7 'The Literal Gospel' in Vanhoozer 1990: 148-89, and chapter 7 'Ricoeur versus Frei: Extra-linguistic Reference and the Absorbing World of the Bible' in Fodor 1995: 258-330.

9.   In the United States, Poland could write in 1985 that 'the majority of Biblical scholars who have employed literary criticism, at least in the initial phases of this movement, have turned to the writings of the New Critics' (Poland 1985a: 5).

10.   The difficulty Frei wrestles with is the place of 'foundationalism' within Christian discourse, i.e. the 'attempt to interpret the Gospels by means of general theories of meaning and truth' (Vanhoozer 1990: 172).

in analyses of 'general' reading practice. Frei's innovative move is to retain the contribution of 'general theory' but to reverse the semantic dependency in its application. Instead of the categories of the Gospel story finding their semantic roots in general categories of thought, their meaning is primarily determined by the Gospel story of Jesus: the Gospel portrayal of Jesus becomes 'ascriptive' and not 'descriptive'.

'Descriptive' categories draw their meaning from general categories of love, peace, righteousness, and so on. According to Frei, Jesus is more than a man with this mix of general attributes; Jesus is peculiarly himself. Therefore he in his story is the source of the meaning of these attributes when applied to him. These general categories of thought begin life in general theories of interpretation, but in the process of an 'ascriptive' reading they are modified by the story of Jesus, rather than the story of Jesus being explained in terms of these general categories.[11] Frei's proposal does not collapse into tautology because the reader has the *stories* of Jesus which function as the narrative exposition of these qualities.

Frei describes this scheme as an *ad hoc* way of employing general theory categories in a way that privileges the story of Jesus over general hermeneutical theory. This *ad hoc* approach is developed not because of some failure of nerve, but because there are categories of meaning concerning Jesus which any general description is conceptually incapable of managing. Frei writes as a Christian theologian, and his proposal may be considered the hermeneutical consequence of his theological conviction about the uniqueness of the incarnation.

Werner Jeanrond is typical of those theologians who oppose this approach and instead champion the explanatory use of general hermeneutical theory within a theological reading of the Gospels.[12] Jeanrond suggests three camps in Christian theology when grouped in the light of their relationship to general hermeneutical theory. The first group Jeanrond labels as the 'dialogical' camp, in which theologians (e.g. Tracy, Jeanrond) participate in conversation and debate with all kinds of hermeneutical thinkers. The second group is the 'intratextual' camp

11. 'What we have in the *sensus literalis* is a reading about which one needs to say first that it governs and bends to its own ends whatever general categories it shares—as indeed it has to share—with other kinds of reading (eg. meaning, truth as well as their relation). It is a case specific reading which may or may not find reduced analogues elsewhere' (Frei 1983: 67).

12. Jeanrond's theological hermeneutic is clearly expounded in Jeanrond 1991.

who employ general hermeneutical theory in a qualified way when interpreting specific Christian texts (e.g. Stuhlmacher, Lindbeck, and Frei). The third group are the 'fideists' (my title, as Jeanrond doesn't suggest a title) who typically consider that the Scriptures do not need any assistance from general interpretative theory (e.g. Barth).

Jeanrond considers Frei's approach as a failure 'to be willing to engage radically in the hermeneutical reflection on methodological foundations' (Jeanrond 1991: 163). However, the reverse is actually the case, for Frei proposes his intratextual approach *as a consequence of his radical engagement* in the wider hermeneutical debate. Frei senses the hubris of modernity in the global aspirations of general hermeneutical theory, which Jeanrond does nothing to dispel. Formally integrating the unique and the singular has always been the Achilles heel of general theory.[13] For the purpose of the present discussion, in contrast to the totalizing claims of modern hermeneutics, Frei's proposal offers a persuasive low level and modest 'case specific' way forward, in which general theory is fully employed within theological hermeneutics, but in a 'non-dominant' way.

Frei's Alternative: Reading for the Sensus Literalis of the Gospel Narrative

> A theological interpretation of the community's Scripture…gives priority to the *sensus literalis*, including the 'literal sense' of its narrative portions.
>
> Frei 1982: 102

One principal difference between the thought of the early and the later Frei is the way that the meaning of the biblical text is established. Originally, Frei held that the meaning of the realistic narrative Gospel text inheres within the narrative structure and is identified by the use of literary-critical tools generated by literary theory. In Frei's later thought the meaning of a text is established in the way that the reading com-

---

13. The uniqueness of Jesus Christ is the theological reason for caution in regard to the contribution of 'general interpretative theory'. 'If you are going to investigate Jesus historically, the "real" historical Jesus, then by definition he won't be unique, he cannot be the Christ. It is forbidden not only by the outcome of the actual historical investigation but also by the assumptions of historical method, which arranges things into a naturally explicable sequence of similar occurrences' (Frei 1988c: 10).

munity *uses* the biblical text.[14] Frei follows 'the saying of Wittgenstein that has so often and wrongly been given the status of a general principle: Don't ask for the meaning; ask for the use' (1982: 104).

Conceptually Frei moves from the view of meaning as 'the property of a text' to a view of meaning as a 'sociolinguistic construct'. The earlier notion of meaning fixed by the structure of the text and independent of the reader is relinquished, for now text *and reader* play a part in the construction of what becomes the 'reader's meaning'.[15] This change achieves the formal integration of the reader or reading community within the act of interpretation of the biblical narratives, while not relinquishing a place for the 'text'.

This paradigm shift requires a change from an analytical literary approach to a descriptive phenomenological approach with a literary dimension. As the relationship between these two aspects is difficult to construct due to a basic conceptual difference, Frei relates them in an eclectic manner with his fundamental perspective built upon the sociolinguistic model for reading.

This paradigm shift is a significant development in Frei's thought and explains his re-evaluation of the history of biblical interpretation in the Christian community. Instead of a particular interpretation of the Gospels being assessed primarily in the light of the literary meaning of the texts, the interpretation is now assessed primarily in the light of the consensus meaning the community agrees. Frei's study of how the church in the West developed the tradition of 'reading for the *sensus literalis*' now has a hermeneutical significance as well as historical interest. 'The tradition of the *sensus literalis* is the closest one can come to a consensus reading of the Bible as the sacred text in the Christian church' (Frei 1983: 37).

A major attraction of this sociolinguistic approach is the way in which it can account for situations when different reading communities

14. Frei approvingly quotes Lindbeck: 'Meaning is constituted by the uses of a specific language rather than being distinguished from it. The proper way to determine what "God" signifies, for example, is by examining how the word operates in a religion and thereby shapes reality and experience, rather than by first establishing its propositional or experiential meaning' (Frei 1983: 72).

15. As pointed out earlier, in Frei's first phase of thought, he had held that 'normative interpretations may be possible. That is to say, the meaning of the text remains the same no matter what the perspectives of succeeding generations of interpreters may be' (Frei 1967: 32).

read the same text and produce different readings.[16] Instead of the insistence that there is one meaning and interpretations of the text are assessed by how close they approach the single meaning, now Frei acknowledges that a reading community can generate legitimate readings of the text and that these will inevitably differ from readings of the same text produced by other communities in other contexts.[17]

Frei's historical review concludes that in the phrase 'the literal sense', the term '*literal* is not referentially univocal, but embraces several possibilities' (Frei 1988c: 5). Frei agrees with Brevard Childs, that 'the *sensus literalis* varied much more through the ages than we used to think' (Frei 1982: 102).[18] Indeed, Frei concludes that the *sensus literalis* 'changes so much...that I'm not sure that I want to try and give a specific definition. It can't be done' (Frei 1988c: 15). Once Frei adopted his new sociolinguistic paradigm, it is impossible to define *sensus literalis* unless account is taken of the *use* of language. Frei traces three ways in which the Christian community has used the phrase *sensus literalis*.

First, *sensus literalis* is used to describe the 'fit' between the author's intention and what the text actually says, and is based on the premise that the text is *able* to enact the intention of the author. This can be construed as an expression of a 'high view' of the scriptural text.[19]

Second, *sensus literalis* is used of the descriptive fit between the

16. Frei considered that 'while the substantive content of the *sensus literalis* remains contestable, and while it may have varied much more through the ages that we used to think, the notion itself nevertheless constitutes one of the most impressive features of Christian continuity' (Fodor 1995: 285).

17. The immediate consequence is the emergence of a pluralist model of the reading of the texts, which is a welcome move for thinkers such as Tracy and Lindbeck in their management of Christian theological variety.

18. Frei commends the discussion of Childs 1977. There are questions about Frei's version of literary history and his analysis of the use of the *sensus literalis* within the Western church. Childs's article is strongly criticized by Barr 1989: 3-17; cf. Childs's reply in Childs 1990: 3-9; cf. Noble 1993a: 1-23. For the present discussion, even if Frei has partly misread the history of interpretation, the interest lies in the way he uses his version of reading for the *sensus literalis*.

19. 'The primacy of the *sensus literalis* is in effect an assertion of the fitness and congruence of the "letter" to be the channel of the "spirit" ' (Frei 1982: 108). Demson comments that 'by emphasizing the doctrine of creation, Frei extends his point about the language of scripture, in which there is no gap between text and meaning' (1992: 148).

sense and the reference of the text. In premodern reading of narrative texts, the reference was to the 'literal world' of the text, and not to the historical past. In the case of the biblical text, this literal world was considered to be the 'real world'. This way of reading broke down when the modern reader became more interested in the historical or ideational world *outside* the text.[20]

Finally, *sensus literalis* is used to describe 'the sense of the text in its sociolinguistic context—liturgical, pedagogical, polemical and so on' (Frei 1982: 104). 'The *sensus literalis* is that which functions in the context of the Christian life...[For example] Augustine understood the plain sense of Scripture to be that which conduces to faith, hope and the twofold love of God and neighbour' (Frei 1982: 105). Frei discovered that pre-modern Christian readers were usually much more concerned with the significance of the text for themselves in their context rather than any historical 'fit' with the past.

Frei's reading of the history of Christian interpretation of the Bible suggested that which of these three options became the predominant way of reading was largely dependent upon the reader's context. Frei then enquires about which would be most appropriate for today. In a postmodern situation, the author's intention is suspect, despite the rearguard arguments of Hirsch and others. The modern addiction to the referential dimension of the text has problematized the status of the final form of the text and its associated 'literal world'.[21] Frei argues that the potential for the recovery of reading for the *sensus literalis* lies in this third approach and its focus upon the way communities use the texts.

Within the practice of reading for the *sensus literalis* there have always been the two 'poles' of *text* and *reader* in a dialectical relationship. Frei's first proposal had prioritized the text, and now his revised proposal prioritizes the reader or, more precisely, the reading community.[22] Within this sociolinguistic reading, Frei continues his interest in

20. In a blend of the categories drawn from literary theory and insights identified in *The Eclipse of Biblical Narrative*, Frei states that pre-modern reading for the *sensus literalis* occurs when the community which reads the narrative text treats 'the narrated world as the real world, and not a linguistic launching pad to language transcending reality' (1982: 104).

21. The modern literary approach leads to the 'referential fallacy' in which the world of the text collapses as a consequence of the assumption that language refers directly to extratextual realities; cf. further discussion in Petersen 1978a.

22. The change of emphasis toward 'reading' and away from narrative 'sense' is illustrated by changes in Frei's revision of his 1983 paper. In 1983, the paper

the literary text, which is now '*in the service*' of the sociolinguistic study.[23] Frei still insists, but unfortunately does not demonstrate in argument or example, that 'the hermeneutical instruments we have looked at have been shaped toward the text' (1988b: 161).[24]

Frei's historical survey concludes that the principal characteristic of reading for the *sensus literalis* is an *interest in Jesus Christ*. 'Literal sense here applies primarily to the identification of Jesus as the ascriptive subject of the descriptions or stories told about and in relation to him' (1988c: 5). Reading for the *sensus literalis* is primarily a christological reading of the biblical texts which Frei argued is governed by three modest criteria.

First, the Christian reading of Christian Scriptures *ascribes* to Jesus those occurrences, teachings, personal qualities and religious attributes that are associated with him in the stories. The ascriptive mode signals that the person who is described defines what the description means, so that meaning is determined by him in his story.

Second, no Christian reading may deny either the unity of Old and New Testaments or the congruence of that unity with the ascriptive literalism of the Gospel narratives.

Third, any readings not in contradiction to the (above) two rules are permissible, and two of the obvious candidates would be examples of historical-critical and literary reading. In this way, Frei *permits* literary- and historical-critical interpretation as secondary activities alongside his Christological project, whenever they are not in contradiction with the practice of reading for the *sensus literalis*. Frei's proposal is akin to

includes a section entitled 'The Primacy of the Literal *Sense* in Christian *Interpretation*' (Frei 1983: 39). A later but virtually unchanged text entitles the same section 'Narrative and the Primacy of "Literal" *Reading* in the Christian *Tradition*' (Frei 1988b: 150).

23. In *Coming to Terms* (Chatman 1990a), Chatman provides the idea of one discipline in the 'service' of another discipline which is itself the 'lead' discipline and forms the context for the contribution of the first discipline. The suggestion addresses the difficulty of integrating different disciplines which have little or no conceptual common ground.

24. The secondary role of literary-critical reading is made clear in Frei's mature description of his second proposal: 'When I ask what external discipline is potentially most useful to theology, I come up with an answer that surprises me, and it is a certain kind of social anthropology that bears some relationship to a kind of literary inquiry also' (1988c: 11).

the thought of his colleague George Lindbeck, with the interest in a cultural-linguistic and intratextual interpretative theological scheme.[25]

The question remains: does Frei's proposal succeed in fulfilling his own theological requirement of 'respecting the narrative Gospel text'? The Christological kind of reading which Frei considers equivalent to reading for the *sensus literalis* has no *necessary* interest in the literary form of the text. Frei's history of reading also makes clear that reading for the *sensus literalis* as Christological reading frequently does not produce a literal reading. This 'decentring of the text' is the principal failure in Frei's new scheme, and makes clear that a fundamental revision of his proposal will be needed to reintroduce the importance of the literary text within a sociolinguistic reading.

The Flight from the Literal Sensus Literalis

When I ask what external discipline is potentially most useful to theology, I come up with an answer that surprises me, and it is a certain kind of social anthropology that bears some relationship to a kind of literary inquiry also.

Frei 1988c: 11

In Frei's history of 'reading for the *sensus literalis*', a reading for the *literal sensus literalis* is only one option, and, moreover, not the most common. Instead, Frei's analysis suggests that a christological concern is most typical of the *sensus literalis* in the history of biblical interpretation, although this view is disputed.[26] Frei looks to this tradition of reading as a model for reading the texts today. As Frei did not demonstrate what this approach might look like the implications of his proposal have to be deduced from his theoretical writings.[27]

---

25. Although Frei does not adopt Lindbeck's approach, sufficient elements of Frei's work are close enough to the thought of his colleague George Lindbeck to allow David Tracy to discuss Frei in a Festschrift for Lindbeck (Tracy 1990: 35).

26. 'Until the end of the eighteenth century...the literal meaning of the Bible was seen as being only one among many ways of understanding it. Not merely did allegorical, figural and typological modes of reading coexist with the literal one, they were often in practice (if not in theory) accorded higher status' (Prickett 1991: 6). Frei's christological form of the *sensus literalis* is thus only one option in a still disputed field.

27. The lack of exegesis does not restrain Frei as he continues to insist that 'the usefulness of the theories we employ is discovered in the process of application, of actual exegesis' (1988c: 86).

Frei is now able to introduce the concept of 'Scripture' for the biblical texts in this later period of thought, because his scheme now formally includes the Christian community, and it is the community which attributes scriptural status to the text.

In his eclectic mix of literary interests in the service of sociolinguistic reading of Christian Scripture, Frei stresses that 'the community must not assume dictatorship of interpretation principles' (Frei 1988c: 57). Yet two features of Frei's exposition raise doubts about whether this dictatorship has been avoided.

First, Frei omits a discussion of the contribution of the literary aspects of the texts in the task of reading the Gospels. This omission is strange because it is clear that in one aspect of his thought, Frei remains committed to the discussion of the meaning of texts in much the same conceptual way as he had treated the subject in his earlier proposal.[28]

Second, Frei attaches fundamental importance to the function of the Christian community in the task of adjudicating upon possible readings. The role that was fulfilled by the literary-critical analysis of the biblical text has now been taken over by the community. 'The plain sense of the text is a consensus reading, interpretation having distilled into conventional opinion, when a certain approach to texts has come to be a community's unselfconscious habit' (Tanner 1987: 63). When a difficulty arises, Frei turns to the 'community of interpretation… [where] right exegesis, like right moral sentiment and action, is what sane, judicious, and fair-minded judges declare it to be' (1988c: 57). In this community, whatever an individual reader suggests, 'if this finally stretches the imagination to the breaking point, as the Antiochene theologians said of Origen, then that assessment probably sets reasonable bounds to what can and cannot be done' (Frei 1988c: 57).[29]

With the sociolinguistic approach to the reading of the Gospels as the fundamental paradigm, the consensus of the community is the logical and proper criterion for the determination of 'good reading practice'. Respect for the literary features of the text need not play a central role in reading practice, although the community may choose to read the

28. Frei's interest in the literal meaning of the text is well expressed in his lecture 'Conflicts in Interpretation' (1986), and is also clear in the papers which make up his *Types of Christian Theology* (1988c).

29. In contrast to the approach of George Lindbeck, Frei proposes that the meaning of the texts may still be generated in traditional literary terms, and then assessed by the community of interpretation.

text in that way. Frei's study recognizes that in the past some Christian communities were interested in literal readings, and many were not. From a phenomenological perspective there is no necessity for the consensus of the reading community to be linked to a particular approach, whether literal or not.

'Respect for the text' is a literary expression of a particular theological decision about the status of the biblical text as Scripture. Metaphorically, one practical implication of a high view of Scripture is the ability of Scripture to criticize the readings of it. In Frei's revised proposal, it is not clear how the text is able to criticize the reading of the text once the interest in the literal reading of the text is made optional.[30]

In Frei's phenomenological approach, it is not the case that all readings are equally acceptable. Every community develops its critical tradition, and 'the theoretical task compatible with a literal reading of the Gospel narratives is that of describing how and in what context it functions...[so that particular readings are] warranted by their agreement with a religious community's rules for reading its sacred text' (Frei 1983: 68). As the literary interest is always 'in the service' of the sociolinguistic approach, it has lost any independent normative function.[31] Instead, the interpretative guidance offered by a particular Christian community becomes the warrant for particular readings.[32]

I wish to argue that the Christian community of interpretation is necessary within a theological reading practice, for the community can provide the ideology and experience which relate to the world of the text. Furthermore, the community can comment upon (though I argue, not determine) particular readings. However, as suggested above, it seems that the relationship between literary interest and sociolinguistic reading requires restructuring so that reading for the *sensus literalis* includes a central concern for the literary text.[33]

---

30. Tanner notes this difficulty, but is more optimistic about the way in which the text may criticize its readers (Tanner 1987: 59-65).

31. In his earlier period of thought, Frei considered that 'meaning' could be identified by following the conventions of 'realistic narrative' when interpreting the Gospel narratives, and the meaning identified would be independent of the reader and the reader's context. Reading and misreading would be recognized by the use of New Critical categories of meaning.

32. 'If the believing community's rules determine what counts as a literal reading of the Gospels who is to determine which communities are the believing ones? Why not Alexandria rather than Antioch?' (Vanhoozer 1990: 174).

33. The need to develop contemporary understandings of the *sensus literalis* is

The Sensus Literalis *and Questions of Truth*

For the Christian interpretive tradition, truth [of the Scriptures] is what is
written, not something separable and translinguistic that is written about.

Frei 1982: 108

Frei's thought in this later period encompasses two kinds of 'truth'
which may be described as referential truth and theological truth.
Referential truth claims arise when the Gospel narratives refer extra-
textually to either factual events which lie metaphorically 'behind' the
text, or to the reader's experience of reading the text, which lies 'in
front of the text'. Frei describes these extra-textual realms as historical
and ontological respectively. Both employ a correspondence model of
truth, in which a correspondence is established between the text and the
extra-textual reality, and truthfulness is a measure of the accuracy of the
correspondence.

Unlike referential truth claims, theological truth claims are concerned
with the world of the text, and the characters who inhabit that world.
The theological enquiry whether the story of Jesus is true invites a
reversal of the inner dynamic of the correspondence model of truth. If
the usual correspondence model is employed, the reader's enquiry
could investigate whether the Jesus of the Gospel stories corresponds to
the Jesus who is alive today and known to the Christian community.
Such an exercise is impossible in any rigorous way because the experience of the presence of Jesus within the Christian community is various
and partial, although the changed lives of believers certainly support the
claims that he is present.

Frei offers a different approach, based upon the ability of the biblical
text to 'absorb the world'.[34] Theological truth is experienced when the

---

signalled by Childs: 'In the light of the present confusion in the discipline of
biblical interpretation, I would suggest that one of the burning issues of theology
lies in a search to recover a new understanding of the *sensus literalis* of Scripture'
(Childs 1977: 92), and also by Scalise: 'A new definition, that perhaps is principally
the revival of an ancient one, dating as far back as early Rabbinic exegesis is
urgently needed' (Scalise 1989: 64). Rowan Williams offers a preliminary suggestion of a diachronic, analogical and eschatological reading for the *sensus literalis*
(1991: 121-34).

34. The phrase 'absorb the world' captures Frei's understanding of the pre-

reader encounters the person Jesus in the world of the text, and when, in the light of this encounter, the reader's extra-textual experiences of Jesus are accommodated to the Jesus of the Gospel stories. The ability to distinguish whether this happens is a function of the consensus derived from the community's experience of the presence of Christ.[35] In practice, this happens 'midst the cacophonous debate within the community as to what is the consensus which may assist the reader' (1988c: 57).[36] This 'normative reality' is found in and mediated through the world of the text, and not in our reconstructions of history or our sense of being. So what is the role of historical discussion of the Gospel texts?

The Limited Usefulness of Historical 'Truth Claims'
In his earlier period of thought Frei *relegated* history rather than completely dismissing it, principally because he did not consider history useful for his theological enterprise. Frei's later proposal considers historical reconstruction more difficult and even less useful: 'If I have a

modern biblical reading practice, and comes from Lindbeck: 'Intratextual theology redescribes reality within the scriptural framework rather than translating scripture into extrascriptural categories. It is the text, so to speak, which absorbs the world, rather than the world the text' (Lindbeck 1984: 118).

35. A criticism of two realms of 'truth' is offered by David Fergusson in a discussion of Lindbeck's thought which helpfully illuminates key aspects of Frei's proposal. Fergusson describes Lindbeck's intrasystematic kind of truth which works with 'coherence with context', in contrast to the extratextual ontological kind of truth which works with the model of 'correspondence'. Fergusson correctly argues that the use of language about God in a particular reading of a text may fit the consensus of the community, but that very consensus is unable to determine whether it is a true statement about God. 'If a statement is ontologically true, it is not because it is being properly used; it is true because of the way things are independently of my asserting them to be so' (Fergusson 1990: 197). But this criticism hinges on the premise that God is an identifiable extratextual entity. For Frei, God is not an extratextual entity who may be identified independently of the text. In the revision of his thought, Frei backs away from his earlier identification of Jesus with the story of Jesus. Nevertheless, the extratextual Jesus is encountered through the world of the text, as 'the text is witness to the Word of God' (Frei 1985b: 209). Both Fergusson's ontological truth and Lindbeck's intrasystematic truth are inadequate, and so Frei in effect argues that in this one case alone, 'access to the reality of Jesus is textually mediated' (Watson 1994: 223).

36. For further discussion of Frei's treatment of 'meaning and truth in the Gospel narratives cf. Hunsinger 1992: 124-26.

continuing theme, it is that I agree with structuralists and post-structuralists that we should treat textuality (what is written) and the referent
or truth of a text (what is written about) as two different things' (1986:
352).[37] Yet Frei also acknowledged that 'Christians want to live and
speak truth or speak truthfully, but we ought to be careful at what point,
and in what way' (1986: 353).[38]

Historical reconstruction is of limited usefulness because it deals with
a concept of 'factuality' which is established upon the basis of general
criteria. And 'factuality' overstates the case, for all historical factuality
is a 'constructed reality'—just as the world of the Gospel text is a constructed reality.[39] So when the theologian comes to speak of the relation
of Jesus to God, Frei asks 'are you seriously proposing that the relation
is best specified under the interpretive category "fact"? Surely not,
unless you are ready to say that "God" is a historical fact'…the concept
of "fact" is simply inadequate (not wrong) for the interpretation of this
[Gospel] text' (1988c: 85).[40] For the modern reader who is wedded to a
particular concept of 'fact' Frei concedes that 'of course I believe in the
historical reality of Christ's death and resurrection, if those are the

37. The reason for the separation between meaning and truth is that 'the textuality of the text goes down the drain when "what it is about" is identified as the
meaning of the text, to which all the rest, its semantic sense and its semiotic structure is subservient' (Frei 1986: 352).

38. It would be interesting to discover whether Comstock's article 'Truth or
Meaning: Ricoeur versus Frei on Biblical Narrative' (first draft 1983, published
1986) contributed to Frei's 1986 lecture 'Conflicts in Interpretation'.

39. The interest in historical factuality is actually more complicated. A 'fact'
may be commonly understood as 'a datum of experience' (*The Concise Oxford
English Dictionary* [1964: 432]), which is in contrast to the 'constructed' reality of
the narrative. Goldberg agrees with Frei when he 'cogently points out that biblical
narrative was not abandoned for some more directly available world or reality;
instead, the biblical story was exchanged *for another story* thought to depict reality
in some truer and more meaningful way' (Goldberg 1991: 160; Frei's italics).

40. 'From the Enlightenment on, the very concept of "fact", historical or
physical, was adapted in the vocabulary of Christian students of the Bible. It
became constitutive part of their own common or group thinking' (Frei 1986: 347).
In a response to a paper by the evangelical Carl Henry, Frei expanded upon the
sense in which he considers that the Gospel narratives 'refer to the real world' (Frei
1985b: 208). 'When speaking of the storied Jesus we have to use historical
referencing, but in a different way from normal. Is Jesus Christ a "fact" like other
historical facts?…I can talk about "Jesus" that way, but can I talk about the eternal
Word made flesh in him in that way. I don't think so' (Frei 1985b: 211).

categories which we employ. But they were not always the categories employed by the church' (1985b: 211).[41]

For a historical reconstruction to have a bearing on a theological reading of the text, it is necessary to establish the link between the Jesus of historical reconstruction and the Jesus of the Gospel narratives. These two constructed realms are governed by quite different criteria, and so Frei concludes that there can be no simple 'correlation between heterogeneous equals' (1988c: 4). Eschatologically 'there can be no ultimate conflict between them, but in finite existence and thought we cannot know how they fit together in principle' (1988c: 85).[42]

Just as earlier in *The Identity of Jesus Christ*, Frei fails to acknowledge and thus respect moments of 'historical extravagance' in the Gospel narratives. The 'history-likeness' of the narratives certainly contributes to their realism, which helps draws the reader into the story-world.[43] This world is sufficiently similar to the reader's world to make the transition possible, and sufficiently different to offer the possibilities of defamiliarization and reader re-orientation. But the narrative moments that display an extravagance of historical reference, far beyond that which is needed for the 'realistic' quality of 'history likeness', still await the reader's attention.

What the *substance* of these passages of 'historical extravagance' contributes is a separate discussion which will depend upon the complex relationship between text and historical reconstruction. However, the *function* of these passages is significant. It seems that the passages

41. Frei would not demur at the claim by Goldberg that 'for the biblical narratives which portray a historically conditioned reality, the historical facticity of the events narrated in those stories must affect the truth of any claims which have them as their basis' (Goldberg 1991: 185). Frei would press him on what kind of 'truth' he describes, and then cautiously say that in his experience 'the move from text to truth or language to reality whatever form it takes is almost always premature' (1986: 353).

42. Frei comments: 'I find myself sympathetic to the position adumbrated by Nils Dahl that faith is *relatively* uninterested in the historical Jesus does not mean that it is *absolutely* uninterested' (quoted in Frei 1982: 93 n. 18). For the view that the historical Jesus is fundamentally significant for the theological concept of the Incarnation see Jüngel 1995: 83-119.

43. 'The narrator does what Jesus himself does in his parables: to force us to enter the world of the narrative. This is what the evangelists do, by and large... We read the narratives] not as a set of secrets to be deciphered but as accounts of lives to which we listen and respond' (Josipovici 1988: 230, 233).

endeavour to relate the world of the narrative to a specific extra-textual historical time and place. Whether the Lukan narrator is historically accurate or not, there is no equally satisfactory alternative literary explanation for the *function* of the extravagance of this type of material.[44] In Frei's theoretical discussion of his sociolinguistic scheme he fails to address this aspect of the Gospel text.

'Christians do have to speak of the referent of the text. They have to speak historically and ontologically, but in each case it must be the notion of truth or reference that is reshaped extravagantly, not the reading of the literal text' (Frei 1986: 353). Frei is correct to affirm that the history-like qualities of the Gospel narratives do not make the historical claims typical of modern historiography, but he is mistaken when he proposes that historical claims are completely detached from the world of the text.[45] Despite an awareness of contemporary discussions about the philosophy of history, Frei's reluctance to address historical truth claims stems from his commitment to keep separate historical and theological reading, because on theological grounds he is convinced that the Word of God encountered in the world of the text needs no historical assistance.[46]

I consider that Frei is broadly correct to argue that the Gospel narratives can be read theologically without the need for a close correspondence between the texts and reconstructions of the historical events which gave birth to them. However, more work needs to be done to

44. The difficulties over the historical and Lukan dating of the census under Quirinius (Lk. 2.2) are important issues to investigate. However, what is more significant for this discussion is to identify the function of this historical material, for it is not seriously prejudiced if there is a degree of inaccuracy.

45. From a different perspective, light may be shed by the rhetoric of the Pauline literature. 'If Christ has not been raised, your faith is futile and you are still in your sins...if for this life only we have hoped in Christ, we are of all people most to be pitied' (1 Cor. 15.17-19). This argument is grounded on the facticity of the resurrection as Frei would put it, and to this end Paul instances the witnesses, 'most of whom are alive, though some have died' (1 Cor. 15.6). What would Frei allow that these witnesses could say?

46. A further reason that caused Frei to hesitate is the nature of the historical enterprise: 'I am uneasy about the way contemporary historians investigate all history, not just the way they investigate the Bible. I no longer know how it is to be done, and I find that there are many historians who no longer know how to do history' (1985b: 211)

elucidate the relationship between possible historical claims of the texts and a theological reading of the Gospels.[47]

The Distinctive Characteristics of Theological Truth Claims
Frei locates the encounter with theological reality *within the world of the narrative text* and not in some extra-textual realm. 'Although the picture is confusing and confused, I take it that until modern times this "fit" between signifier and signified was largely at an intralinguistic or semiotic rather epistemological level' (1982: 103).

In the particular case of a Christian reading of Scripture, 'the linguistic account, that is the narrative itself, renders reality narratively...[so that the] narrated world is as such the real world and not a linguistic launching pad to language-transcending reality, whether ideal essence or self-contained empirical occurrence' (Frei 1982: 103-104).[48] In the one case of the story of Jesus of the Gospel narratives, 'the text did not refer to, *it was the linguistic presence of God*...For the Christian interpretive tradition, truth [of the Scriptures] is what is written, not something separable and translinguistic that is written "about" ' (Frei 1982: 108; my italics).[49] As Frei's thought develops it is clear that for him this linguistic presence of God does not exhaust the possibilities of God's presence, but it is one location through which his presence can encounter the reader.

47. In an unpublished paper, 'The Making and the Discovering of History', I argue that the work of Louis Mink is preferable to the work of Hayden White in the analysis of 'realistic narrative' historical writing, for at the time of his death, Mink was developing a 'critical realism' which could be developed into a 'configured realism' model appropriate for the Gospel narratives.

48. A theological reading of the Gospel narrative assumes that the story is 'the kind of story that does not refer beyond itself for its meaning, as allegory does, [but is] the kind of story in which the "signified" (the identity of the protagonist) is enacted by the signifier (the narrative sequence itself)' (Frei 1982: 112).

49. Frei is able to argue that this pre-modern trust in the biblical text is still possible because of his theological conviction that 'language is, for Christians, a created good and not in principle fallen...and therefore it is not absent from the truth or meaning—that supposed essence which is unlike language, and for which language merely furnishes the transportation' (1982: 109). Fodor suggests that for Frei 'Scripture is uniquely the Word of God and thus pre-conditions for its understanding cannot be determined apart from the Word itself... Frei studiously avoids any appeal to reference...because he believes that any theory of meaning as reference is entirely superfluous to a proper understanding of biblical narrative' (Fodor 1995: 287).

This explains Frei's 'reticence about the transition...from text to truth or from language to reality, whatever form it takes' (Frei 1986: 353). Any move from text to *truth as popularly conceived* is a move out of the world of the text to some extra-textual reality, and thus a move away from the locus of theological truth.[50] Even fundamentalist readers of the Gospels who claim to respect the literal text are led away from the world of the text in their search for extratextual correspondence because they suppose it will confirm the theological reliability of the text.[51]

For Frei, the world of the text is where 'the question of reference is solved descriptively in the case of *this* narrative (whatever may be true of others)' (1982: 103). In this way Frei argues for a postmodern re-covery of the pre-modern conviction that the biblical world is the real world and the reader is required to accommodate their own world to this world.[52]

Frei contrasts the worlds of the textual and the extra-textual but is unable to offer any formal relationship between them.[53] He acknowl-

---

50. From the perspective of a modern historical-critical approach, Comstock is correct to see in Frei an insufficient interest in the referential 'truth' of biblical narratives. Frei is sceptical about how much historical truth can be demonstrated, but his aversion to such an exercise arises from his prior assumption that a different conceptual scheme is required to discuss 'in what way the Gospels are *theologically* true, for the Gospel story renders reality in such a way that it obviates the trans-linguistic reference question as a separate question' (Frei 1988c: 104).

51. 'It cannot be said often and emphatically enough that liberals and funda-mentalists are siblings under the skin in identifying or rather confusing ascriptive as well as descriptive literalism about Jesus at the level of understanding the text, with ascriptive and descriptive literalism at the level of knowing historical reality' (Frei 1988c: 84). James Barr agrees with Frei: 'What then is the sort of truth that is important for the fundamentalist? The answer seems to be: correspondence to external reality' (Barr 1977: 49).

52. At the end of his 1988 discussion of this *ad hoc* approach to the Scriptures, Frei returns to Barth and his reading of the Gospels: '[Barth] reversed the flow of interpretation, claiming that the texts about Jesus were our means of access to incorporating ourselves, or being incorporated, in the world of discourse he shared with us, rather than his specific identity as Redeemer having to be fitted to the criteria of the world of our general experience' (1988c: 87).

53. Watson recognizes Frei's distinction between the world of the text and the world of extra-textual reality and also Frei's 'extreme wariness about letting text and reality touch one another...in order to preserve the integrity of the story in its self-containment and isolation' (Watson 1994: 26). However, Watson does not

edges that popular notions of 'truth' are associated with concepts of referentiality, and so he usually reserves the term 'truth' for that kind of epistemology. In a theological reading 'the question of "truth" addresses the level of *sense* and not of reference' (Frei 1988b: 156; my italics). Of course theological reality is more than the world of the text, but how one refers to it is not yet clear.[54]

The development of the concept of the 'world of the text' raises the interesting question of the potential it might offer for a theological hermeneutics. This world of the text is generated in a theological reading when the reader 'reads for the literal sense' and does not subject the reading to the explanations of general literary theory.[55] Reading for the literal sense involves 'lowering our theoretical sights yet further to the level of mere description rather than explanation, to the specific texts

attend sufficiently to the writings from the later period of Frei's thought, where the consequences of Frei's sociolinguistic turn become clearer and illuminate his earlier work. At the time of his death Frei had not fully developed the implications of the sociolinguistic turn in his analysis, which is based on the premise that *all* reality is linguistically constructed. Therefore Frei's distinction between the world of the text and the extra-textual world is a distinction between different constructed realities (cf. Goldberg 1991: 160). Both Watson and Comstock speak naïvely of 'reality' as if it is an unproblematic notion, and can be easily contrasted with the imaginary world that the reader constructs when reading the text. Watson's claim that for Frei 'the world must not be allowed to contaminate the text' (1994: 26) is simply inadequate. Watson also misses the more profound question about which is the 'more true' of the two constructed worlds. If it is the world of the scriptural text as Frei claims, then a better description of his position would be that 'the world of extra-textual reality must not be allowed to contaminate the world of the text, but must be interpreted so that it is accommodated to the world of the text'.

54. '*How* one refers…extra-textually is a logically different matter. Perhaps we may want to do so analogically rather than literally, or perhaps we may want to say that the truth is something else yet, rather than a matter of corresponding, either identically or analogically with "reality" ' (Frei 1988c: 84).

55. Although literary meaning may contribute in an *ad hoc* way to a theological reading, Frei disagrees with Tracy's correlative approach, in which 'literary-critical methods…develop, challenge, correct theological understandings of the text by explaining the sense of the text in its structure, its form and its creative productivity' (Tracy 1981: 263). The working relationship between literary and theological reading is more modestly sketched by Ryken when he writes that 'the focus on form and technique is what literary criticism is qualified to contribute to New Testament studies. Such a literary approach is not all that needs to be done with the New Testament. But it is a first step in understanding what the New Testament says' (Ryken 1984: 12).

and the most specific context' (Frei 1983: 67). Frei does not need to explain 'why' or 'how' this is the way to read the texts; it is sufficient to demonstrate that historically, the community usually reads the Scriptures in this way.

Although Frei retains a literary interest in the text within his overarching sociolinguistic interest in the reading of the text, it is a convenient but not necessary interest in the literary text. Frei's revision has lost the *formal* 'respect for the text' which he established at the beginning of his work. To recover this respect for the text it is necessary formally to reintroduce a literary-critical dimension to the community's reading practice. I suggest that theological readers will need to develop postmodern *literary-critical* insights suitable for service within their theological reading enterprise.

Chapter 4

THE CRITERIA OF A THEOLOGICAL
LITERARY-CRITICAL READING

This is no game that we are playing. In a harsh and unforgiving world it
is a recall to fundamental issues which are the business of great literature
and belief... Theology needs to understand the nature of literature and to
learn carefully the procedures of textual interpretation.

Jasper 1989: ix-x

Frei's second proposal touches upon issues that are important to the
development of a postmodern theological reading practice. The earlier
proposal made clear that a theological respect for the text entails a
respect for the text in its 'final form'. In addition, the reading of this text
is a literary exercise which attends to the literary features of the text and
their significance for its meaning. In the case of the Gospel stories, Frei
expected the interpreter to attend respectfully to the narrative form of
these stories becuase they are a principal literary feature. Thus a theological respect for the Gospel narratives required a 'formalist' type of
literary criticism. The accessibility of the world of these Gospel texts
happily enabled Frei to use only a modest amount of literary criticism
in his interpretations.

Frei's revised proposal sprang from the recognition of an illusion
within the modern type of formalist literary criticism, in which it pre-
tends to an objectivity which it cannot deliver and a global significance
which is spurious. The adoption of a sociolinguistic approach to reading
allows Frei to attend to the particularities of reading. The history of the
reading for the *sensus literalis* in the Christian church traces a range
of readings which are variations upon the reading of the one text.
Frei developed an interest in how the biblical texts are *used* which led
him to a functional model for 'Scripture', in which the authoritative
status of the texts entails a way of reading them, but does not prescribe
what those readings might look like. Frei's conceptual focus moves
from 'interpretation' to 'reading'; now the reader/reading community is

formally involved in both the generation of and adjudication upon particular readings. I think that Frei's turn to a sociolinguistic approach is fundamentally correct, *except* in the way that Frei discounts an interest in the literary features of a text in favour of the concerns of the community within this new reading practice.

Frei contends that the Gospel stories of Jesus are 'ascriptive' rather than 'descriptive'. This development provides readers with a breathing space (Frei 1986: 353) in which their reading practice is not dominated by the categories and constraints of general theory. However, in his theologically motivated flight from general theory, Frei mistakenly abandons the centrality of the literary text as the appropriate expression of a theologically motivated respect for the text. Frei came to this position when he recognized that literary theory is a type of general theory, which for him vitiates its associated literary criticism as far as a theological reading is concerned.

This wariness about literary theory also distorts Frei's own reading of the history of the *sensus literalis* in the church, and leads to his decision to develop only one aspect of the way that reading for the *sensus literalis* was conducted in the history of Christian biblical interpretation.[1] The consequence is that Frei's reading of the history prioritizes the consensus of the community of interpretation over other ways the scriptural text has been read.

This study commends an alternative reading practice, which takes account of Frei's analyses and the concerns they embody. I propose that Frei's relation between the literary and communal elements is reversed, so that the primary datum in the construction of a good reading is the literary text and not the community consensus. This reading practice is conducted by a theological reader as a member of a community of interpretation in a way that expresses a theological respect for the text through the prioritizing of the text over the reader. This decision respects the theological concerns of the earlier Frei while acknowledging that it is only one of many theological options. Such a respect for the text entails a literary-critical approach to the Gospel narrative that attends to both its literary form and content.

This way of reading does not require a detailed historical-critical analysis of the text to establish the possible meanings of the text. At the

---

1.   Frei retains an interest in the way the reader uses the text, and dispenses with the aspects which relate text and author's intention and text and reference, as discussed earlier in Chapter 3 and in Frei 1982: 102-106.

same time, the historical setting of the text informs the world of the text which the reader constructs in the process of reading; thus historical studies are very important.

The recognition of the 'ascriptive' character of the Gospel narratives is developed further as an appropriate way of including categories generated in literary theory 'in the service' of a theological reading. In this new scheme, every reading produced is peculiar to the particular reader or reading community and so is properly described as the 'reader's meaning'. This reader's meaning then awaits the adjudication of those communities of interpretation which share with the reader a similar theological respect for the text.

This chapter treats key aspects of this new theological reading proposal and identifies the criteria that are employed in the selection of a suitable literary-critical approach. In the next part two literary-critical possibilities are considered and one is adopted. This theoretical discussion prepares for and is refined by a preliminary christological reading of the Gospel of Luke.

The Theological Reader and a Theological Reading

A theological reading is the product of an encounter between a theological reader and a text. The focus of a Christian theological reading is God as he is known in Christ, and the context of the reading is the contemporary experience of the Christian reader within the community of Christian believers. The theological task is to read the Gospel in a way which produces 'true talk about God' (Jüngel 1995: 2).[2] The distinctives that mark 'reading in the theological mode' are provided by the ideology and interests of the reader, together with the thematic interests of the text. The thematic content of the text alone is not sufficient to ensure that a reading is 'theological', for the Gospels may be read in a number of different ways, irrespective of their thematic treatment of God and Jesus.[3]

2.   'The Bible must be read in the theological mode...as a source of true knowledge about the objects described in the Bible—about God, about the creation of the world, about his redemption of mankind, about sin and salvation, about the possibility of a future life' (Barr 1973: 13).
3.   It may be argued that the Gospel texts treat the thematic material in a way that assumes a particular type of reader (Theophilus?) who already has some experience of Christ. If this can be demonstrated, then a theological reading may be the most appropriate reading practice for such readers.

In Frei's earlier version of theological interpretation, he insisted that the reader is a Christian believer, but this feature had no *formal* role in the practice of a theological reading.[4] Such an approach may be attractive to 'modern' readers who suspect that whenever faith is included in the reading process, it can distort the readings produced.[5] Instead, a reading informed by literary criticism or historical criticism alone was mistakenly considered to be more 'objective'. However, Frei recognizes that every reading practice is ideologically directed, including the 'modern' approach. Consequently a responsible reading overtly acknowledges the ideological contribution of the reader. One of Frei's *formal* contributions to the discussion of theological interpretation is the recognition that Gospel interpretation is no longer a function of the text alone.

Frei proposes that a further way in which this ideological contribution may be integrated into a reading practice is to allow the reader's meaning of the Gospel narratives to be subject to the consensus of the reading community. Certainly, the theological interest in the Jesus of the Gospels and experience of Christ within this community are well suited to this role, because there is a congruence in subject matter. The production of readings then involves text, reader and reading community. In this way too the reader is *formally* involved in the interpretation of the Gospels.

Frei surveys the range of 'theological positions' open to the Christian reader and provides an outline of the position which he finds theologically congenial and which informs the work in the second period of his thought. I adopt a theological position which is similar to that of Frei and which informs my proposal for a theological reading practice. Aspects of this theological position are discussed below.

An important challenge for the postmodern theological reader is posed by the centuries of dogmatic theological reading of the Gospels which has been shown to distort to varying extent the meaning/meanings of the Gospel narratives.[6] How may the ideological concerns of the

4.   Frei's earlier model of text interpretation engages in 'a search for categories of understanding *detached* from the perspectives we bring to our understanding, including our commitments of faith' (Frei 1967: 31; my italics).

5.   In the field of biblical studies the historical-critical approach demonstrates a 'commitment to secularity...[for] it is held that anything stemming too directly from "faith" would prove a hindrance' (Watson 1994: 12).

6.   It is argued in Chapter 2 that Frei's exposition in *The Identity of Jesus*

Christian reader inform the *formal* reading practice, while not preclud-
ing the necessary critical dimension to the reading of the Gospel narrative?[7] My argument is that the possibility of a critical reading of the
Gospel narratives is a consequence of the theological position chosen
by the reader.

Finally, with Frei the present proposal abandons typically modern
reading practices, and looks to a postmodern literary approach which is
in keeping with the theological position adopted. The adjective 'postmodern' is used in a modest way to describe simply an alternative
approach which has developed through an appreciation of the usefulness
and the weaknesses of the modern approach.

A Theological Respect for the Gospel Text

An important element within the theology of the reader is the status and
role accorded to the biblical texts. The present proposal follows Frei
(and Kelsey) and considers that the status of the Gospel texts as Scripture is primarily a *functional* concept which describes how these texts
are *used*. What the texts might mean for a particular reader is deferred
until the texts are read.[8] This 'functional' model of Scripture provides
the overarching paradigm within which other aspects of the notion
'Scripture' may be integrated.[9]

Christ also fails to avoid a dogmatic distortion of the reading which is produced.
The description 'distortion' does not necessarily imply a 'modern' view of the text
with a stable, single meaning which is then distorted in the process of interpretation; 'distortion' can also describe a reading practice in which the ideological concerns of the reader have so overwhelmed the reading that there is little consensus
that it is a good reading.

   7.   The crucial importance of a critical dimension to a theological reading
practice is its ability to assist the reader to 'resist theological pressures' (Watson
1996: 125).

   8.   The present discussion is an example of a modest 'reflection within belief'
(Frei 1975: 4) which investigates the implications of a particular theological
position. Thus a consideration of the grounds for the particular theological position
is a separate discussion which is not conducted here. This decision is simply a
'division of labour', and is accompanied by the insistence that such a discussion is
conducted elsewhere.

   9.   Buckley correctly argues for a nuanced and eclectic model for Scripture
which is attentive to the disagreements within single model approaches such as the
'functional' model, or 'contextualists' as he relabels the approaches, considering
that 'what functionalists share in common is an insistence that texts not only have

Within the Christian tradition there is a wide spectrum of views of how theologians may read the texts as Scripture. Frei develops a theological typology to map the principal options for the theological reading of the Gospels as Scripture (1988c). The scheme is built upon the assumption that every theological reading practice comprises the interrelation of a particular theological description and a general literary-critical approach. Frei identifies five options in this spectrum of possibilities, and locates his own approach within them.

The present discussion begins from Frei's position: 'Christian theology is a nonsystematic combination of normed Christian self-description and method founded on general theory...[in which] the practical discipline of Christian self-description governs and limits the applicability of general criteria of meaning in theology, rather than vice versa' (1988c: 4). This pattern of relationship prioritizes Christian self-description (i.e. the Gospel text) so that general schemes of thought are expected to accommodate to the Gospel text in the reading practice. There are three consequences which flow from this choice:

'Respect for the Text' Requires the Reader to Work with the Canonical Text in its Final Form
A theological reading of a scriptural text expresses its respect for the text as Scripture by attending to the text in its canonical form. The decision about which texts belong within the canon and may be used as Scripture is handled by a Christian church and the selection is offered to those within its community who wish to develop their theological reading.

The actual form of the selected texts is under a steady yet modest process of revision which is carried out by textual critics in the field of modern biblical studies. Textual critics offer a range of reconstructed versions of the text which are thought to represent stages in the history of the production of the canonical text. The textual-critical version that serves for the twentieth-century church as the canonical form of the text is the reconstruction of a text which reproduces the words of the original authors or editors, and is usually described as the text in its 'final form'.[10] The description 'final form of the text' is not quite accurate for

subject matters but also contexts' (Buckley 1990: 331).

10. 'Believers need to be convinced that the copy of the scriptures they possess is reliable and reproduces the words of the original authors' (Elliott 1990: 17). For

it describes the best form of the text that textual scholars have reconstructed *so far*.

The phrase 'the final form of the text' is useful, however, because it signals a concern with the text *as a whole and in its entirety*. The theological attention to the text in its final form signals a move from a diachronic interest in origins and redaction history to a synchronic interest in the text as a single artefact. This key paradigm shift within biblical studies is implicit within discussions about the final form of the texts. 'At the heart of the current debate and controversy within biblical studies is the issue of the final form of the biblical texts' (Watson 1994: 15).

One practical consequence of this theological respect for the text is the commitment to engage with the whole of a *particular* Gospel text. In Frei's single extended example of theological hermeneutics, he concentrated upon the Gospel of Luke, though not exclusively so. In order to draw the contrast between Frei's approach and this new approach, this exposition also works with the Gospel of Luke. I argued that Frei championed the importance of close engagement with the text *in theory* but failed to carry it out in practice. In this proposal, the theological respect for the text is expressed in *an extended and close engagement with the Lukan text*; for anything less subverts the 'respect for the text in its final form'.

The attention to the text in its final form includes attention to the *form* of the text. As the Gospels are largely narrative texts, the reader attends to their narrative form. In this sense, a theological respect for the text leads to a *formalist* interest in the texts, and this will inform the selection of a suitable literary-critical approach. The proper abandonment of modern literary-critical practices means that the New Critical and other kinds of modern formalism are no longer options. However, literary theorists are working with neo-formalist possibilities suitable for a postmodern reading practice and their works contribute to the present discussion.

The decision to await the reading of a text before commenting upon the reading produced also applies to the formal analysis of the narrative. The preliminary recognition that a text displays a predominantly narrative form does not lead to any assumptions about whether or not a text is a unified narrative. The unity of a text is not implied by this new

the purposes of this discussion, Elliott's statement of the position is sufficient as it is typical of mainstream Western textual criticism.

formalist interest; a decision about the unity of a narrative can only be established by the reading of the text.

The kind of theological respect for the text commended here involves the recognition that at the beginning of reading the text, the reader does not know and is unwise to presume how the reading of the text will turn out and what kind of reading will be produced—these discussions can only begin as a detailed reading of the text is under way.

'Respect for the Text' Prioritizes the 'Plain' Sense of the Text

Under the influence of Brevard Childs's paper, Frei's version of reading for the *sensus literalis* of the Gospel narrative adopts christological rather than literary criteria claiming that the *sensus literalis* 'applies primarily to the identification of Jesus as the ascriptive subject of the descriptions or stories told about and in relation to him' (Frei 1988c: 5).

The proposal offered here substitutes the *plain* sense of the text for the literal sense in Frei's proposal.[11] The 'plain sense' does not prescribe whether a biblical text is to be taken literally or not; rather it is sufficiently indeterminate to create the methodological space for the biblical text to determine in what way it is to be read. It is only *after* having read the text in this respectful way that the reader may begin to distinguish which parts of the text require a literal or a christological reading.

The christological interest that Frei describes may be brought to the text by the reader *as an enquiry*, but in a respectful reading it is premature to assume that which only the reading of the Gospel text can make clear. The hesitation about the kind of theological reading which prescribes how the text is to read *before* a sustained and respectful engagement with the Gospel arises from a concern that the critical freedom of the reading practice is at risk.

'Respect for the Text' Prioritizes the Particularities of the Text over the Generalities of Interpretation Theory

Respect for the text entails a respect for the particularities of the text. Such a concern for the particular is one expression of the theological respect for the texts as Scripture.[12] Frei argued that for this to happen,

---

11. This substitution is commonly performed in discussions of Frei's work (cf. Tanner 1987; Tracy 1990).

12. Frei approvingly recalls that 'Barth almost always proceeds from the priority of the singular and from the particular to the general' (1988c: 87).

the influence of general theory has to be formally circumscribed. Frei does this by a redefinition of the function of the categories and explanations employed within general schemes of thought: no longer are they used descriptively, but rather ascriptively.

The present proposal adopts Frei's suggestion and treats the stories of Jesus in the Gospel narratives as ascriptive discourse, which means that the descriptions of Jesus are defined by the story of Jesus in the narrative.

A Theologically Informed Selection of a Literary Criticism

A major implication of the argument of *The Eclipse of Biblical Narrative* is that theological respect for the text entails a respect for the literary features of the text, and that this is best achieved by a careful use of a suitable literary-critical approach. The present proposal adopts this position despite Frei's relinquishment of it and with Watson considers that 'literary approaches to the Gospels offer insights and perspectives of considerable theological promise' (Watson 1996: 125).[13]

The literary-critical reading is a key element within a theological reading practice but it is not identical to a theological reading.[14] The principal difference lies not in the literary-critical tools employed but in the ideological position of the reader, and the reading expectations which flow from it. For example, a literary reading of the Gospels may appreciate their qualities as 'imaginative literature' whereas a theological reading of the same Gospels is interested in what is true in what they portray about God and Jesus.[15]

---

13. Watson identifies three initial *formal* contributions: (1) the literary paradigm is at one with an ecclesial-theological approach in holding that the heart of the matter is to be found in the texts as they stand; (2) the literary paradigm seeks the closest possible integration of the parts of the text into the whole in which they are embedded; (3) the literary paradigm is theologically valuable in its recovery of the reality and integrity of the final form of the text, and in its rehabilitation of the category of narrative (Watson 1996: 127-31).

14. 'As for New Criticism, a literal reading of the Gospels is appropriate under its auspices, but only because and to the extent that it is in fact a disguised Christian understanding of them and not a reading under a general theory' (Frei 1983: 67).

15. The recent proliferation of literary studies of the Bible is significant because they arise within an increasingly *secular* context. *The Literary Guide to the Bible* (Alter and Kermode 1987) is representative of one stream within the literary study of the Bible. 'The general reader can now be offered a new view of the Bible as a

Can literary-critical tools be employed appropriately in the reading of Christian Scripture? In the light of the fact that literary criticism was developed to read the classics of literature, one route to an answer is to establish what constitutes literature, and enquire whether biblical texts qualify. The almost insurmountable difficulties in this approach include the continuing debate about what may be described as literature.[16] A pragmatic approach recognizes that 'language...is the medium both subjects hold in common' (Wright 1988: 13) and that both Scripture and literature in the general sense are examples of discourse texts which seem to share conventions for the organization and arrangement of their material. There seems to be sufficient similarity to warrant the use of literary-critical tools with both kinds of text.[17] As these two classes of texts are not identical, whatever literary-critical tools are selected will need to be used in a context-specific way. In Frei's adoption of a literary-critical scheme he demonstrated how a suitable literary scheme

work of great literary force and authority...the Bible, once thought of as a source of secular literature yet somehow apart from it now bids fair to become part of the literary canon' (Alter and Kermode 1987: 2-3; cf. Bal's criticism of the unrepresentative editorial policy of *The Literary Guide to the Bible* [Bal 1985] and Schwartz 1990: 1-15). Wright contends that 'the saving qualities of a finely tuned response to literature [are] quite seriously being offered as a replacement religion, filling the vacuum created by the decline of orthodox Christianity' (Wright 1988: 5).

16. The difficulty facing the reader is that 'literature seems altogether to defy definition' (Wright 1988: 3). One alternative approach is to 'think of literature less as some inherent qualities or set of qualities displayed by certain kinds of writing... than as a number of ways in which people relate themselves to writing' (Eagleton 1983: 9). Wright also claims that 'literature, like theology, is more easily defined in functional rather than ontological terms, in terms of the effects for which readers and critics value certain texts' (Wright 1988: 3). As readers value the Bible, then it may be considered as 'literature before it is anything else, and so to read it "as literature" really means to *read* it again' (Alter 1992: 210; his italics). This minimalist position leaves unexamined the reasons why people value the biblical texts. Is it not the case that 'the Bible has had a literary influence upon English literature not because it has been considered as literature, but because it has been considered as a report of the Word of God'? (Eliot 1935: 390). It is possible that 'those who talk of reading the Bible "as literature" sometimes mean, I think, reading it without attending to the main thing it is about' (Lewis 1958: 10). The notion of 'the Bible as literature' is inadequate, and so it can 'set theological teeth on edge' (Wright 1988: 41).

17. Alter and Kermode are correct when they write that 'the Bible, considered as a book, achieves its effects by means no different from those generally employed by written language' (1987: 2).

can represent theological convictions.[18]

The key to a context-specific way of using literary-critical tools in a theological reading is to ensure that the assumptions that undergird the use of these literary tools are congruent with the theological concerns of the reader. These theological criteria are used in the inspection and eventual selection of a particular literary criticism. In Frei's initial proposal the criteria of a suitable literary-critical approach included a commitment to work with the final form of the text, an approach that prioritizes the text over the reader, an approach that avoids the complex distraction of questions of history, and an approach that is sensitive to the narrative and realistic qualities of the text.

On the two occasions that Frei employs these theological criteria to inform his literary-critical decisions, I argue that he was insufficiently rigorous and selected approaches which were at best only partially satisfactory.[19] Nevertheless, Frei succeeds in demonstrating in general, if not specifically, that the formal task of theologians who read the Gospels is to identify the literary-critical approaches that are *consonant with their ideological stance as theological readers*.

The description 'literary-critical' suggests a proper *critical* freedom as one characteristic of the reading practice. This critical freedom will open up both reader and text to inspection and interrogation. The task for the postmodern reader is to work out how the ever-present ideological commitment of the reader may allow a genuinely critical reading of the text, and also how a respect for the text does not improperly curtail the critical scrutiny of the text for coherence and incoherence. The functional understanding of the Gospel narratives as Scripture which has been adopted here does not preclude a thorough and rigorous critical engagement with the text and the textual world. On the contrary, I

18. The recognition of the central role of literary criticism for a theological reading is a significant achievement which is only partly appreciated by Watson: 'It is one of the peculiarities of *The Eclipse of Biblical Narrative* that, although Frei's motivation is clearly theological, the theological dimension is held in abeyance and literary-critical judgments determine the analysis' (Watson 1994: 23). Frei can do this because he thought that the literary-critical judgments were the expression of his theological concern.

19. Frei's first mistake was when he chose a New Critical reading of the Gospels treated as realistic narrative, which employed an inappropriate category and an obsolete reading practice. The second mistake was when Frei relinquished the central role of the literary-critical component in a theological reading, and subsumed it within a sociolinguistic study of how the Christian community uses the Bible.

suggest that a proper respect for the text requires such seriousness of endeavour.

A Theologically Informed Literary Criticism of the Gospel Text

Once the theological reader has selected an appropriate literary-critical approach, the next step is to identify how to employ such an approach. There are two particular difficulties which seem to mitigate against a truly critical reading of the Gospels and both issue from the theologically derived commitment to prioritize the text over the reader in the reading practice. In the light of this commitment, the first question is 'How may a reader criticize a biblical text in a way that is both respectful and critical?' The second question is 'How may the reader manage their own ideological commitment within the reading practice to ensure that the text is prioritized?'

An Interrogative Use of Literary Criticism

Does a critical reading of a text require that the reader and the text are of equal status in the process of reading?[20] This proposal suggests that a respectful and critical reading may be achieved while retaining the priority of the text over the reader by developing one suggestion of Frei.

To defend the reading of the biblical text against the tyranny of general theory, Frei argued that categories within general literary theory may be employed in a *descriptive* and not *explanatory* way, and that in the particular case of the story of Jesus, the *descriptive* way is further transformed into an *ascriptive* reading.

Accordingly, this proposal adopts Frei's way of employing general categories and takes the suggestion a step further by casting them into the *interrogative mood*. This change of mood represents a formal acknowledgment that the reader *does not yet know what the reading of the text will elucidate*. In the act of reading, the reader enquires of the text whether particular categories are appropriate for the reading of the

---

20. At one stage in her evolution of thought, Mieke Bal bases her critical reading of the biblical texts upon the premise that the reader and text meet 'as two equals speaking to each other, listening to each other, in an attempt to learn something from the encounter: to change' (Bal 1990: 16). This view does not express the theologically rooted priority of the text commended here. In this case, as Thiselton comments, 'the relation between the biblical material and the present situation *cannot be regarded as fully symmetrical*' (Thiselton 1992: 606; Thiselton's italics).

text, and tries them out as the reading proceeds. In this process, the encounter with the text can confirm or dismiss the usefulness of the categories.

The Provisionality of the Reader's Ideology
Every reader is ideologically committed even before beginning to read the text. When readers start to read, their ideology plays a fundamental role in the constructive act of reading. How may this prior commitment be acknowledged and yet still allow the methodological space for a critical reading?

There are three ways through which the improper influence of the reader's ideology may be reduced. The first suggestion is that the reader's ideological stance needs to be *explicit*. The recognition of the ideological commitment of the reader is necessary in order that the reader may manage these commitments. Whereas modern reading cultivated the illusion of a 'studied neutrality', a postmodern style of reading considers it important for the reader to explicitly acknowledge their ideological position formally within the production of their 'reading'.

The second suggestion recommends that all readers' ideological commitment should be treated as *provisional* and thus revisable in the process of reading. The 'theological' ideology which treats Scripture as authoritative in a functional way does not require that readers' meanings should conform to pre-existing readings, and this releases the reading practice from an improper accountability to orthodoxy. These scriptural texts have *functioned* authoritatively for Christian communities in the past, and now they do so for the Christian reader of today. *What* these texts may come to mean for the contemporary reader is not yet clear, and cannot become clear until they are read.

The provisionality of the theological convictions of the readers as they take up the Scriptures also signals a caution about the practice of employing particular theological concepts as fundamental heuristic devices.[21] Whereas theological convictions can inform and shape the questions which the reader brings to the act of reading the text, it is also important that within the activity of reading these convictions are open to revision.

---

21. A recent interesting example of such an approach is Francis Watson's *Text, Church and World* in which he endeavours to construct a 'trinitarian hermeneutic and a corresponding exegetical practice' (Watson 1994: 265).

The third suggestion is that the reading practice is *public*, so that both the community of interpretation and others may comment upon the reading produced. In this way the degree of overt and covert ideological influence within the reading will be more easily identified. Unlike the later Frei, I do not suggest that the individual reading practice is *accountable* to the community of interpretation, for that would usurp the central place of the literary-critical aspect of the reading. Nevertheless, the critical contribution of the Christian community is a necessary component in the theological reader refining his or her own reading of Scripture.

A Theological Concern for the Historical Claims of the Gospel Narrative

Frei successfully reclaims a theological interest in the text by the stratagem of distinguishing historical and theological reading, and then deferring historical reading. This move raises two questions: first, may a Gospel text be read independently of the historical claims it seems to make, and second, if theological and historical reading are related in some way, what is the function of these historical claims within a theological reading of a Gospel text?

A semiotic model for a narrative text provides the conceptual framework with which to address the first question. The narrative text refers to the narrative world generated in the process of reading the text. The construction of this world by the reader involves an encounter with the text, and nothing more. *All* texts refer in this way, whatever else they might or might not do. Therefore the reading of fictional or historical narratives involves the same first steps in the reading process.

The realistic or history-like features of a text facilitate the reader's construction of this narrative world in the reader's imagination. There is no *formal* aspect of a reading process which can distinguish between fictional and historical narratives.[22] Thus the Gospel narratives may be read independently of their possible historical claims. What the postmodern reader requires is assistance to *read well* the narrative texts, and this can be provided by literary- and narrative-critical studies.

---

22. The fact that historical and fictional narratives may be read in the same way allows the employment of literary-critical tools in the reading of biblical texts, even though these tools were developed primarily in the world of narrative studies of fictional literature.

However, this general description of reading needs to be qualified. The distinction between fictional and historical reading is clear within a community of interpretation, and is shown in the way the community uses the texts it reads. Thus in a theological reading of a text, Frei claims it appropriate to employ literary-critical tools in the reading of the narratives without a discussion of the historical claims of the same narratives. Yet as a theological reader, Frei is interested in the characters who inhabit the imaginary narrative world generated by the reader because they are more than just imaginary literary constructs.

The story of Jesus is a narrative declaration of who the character Jesus is within the narrative world of the text, and Frei considers that the narrative world is the location where Jesus meets with the reader. This Jesus who encounters the reader is not the Jesus of history, but the contemporary Jesus who is the Jesus of the Gospel stories. In a way that Frei cannot explain, the imaginative (not imaginary) encounter with the literary character Jesus becomes an encounter with the contemporary Jesus through the presence of the Holy Spirit in the process of reading the Gospel narratives as witnesses to him. The fact that this happens is due to the grace of God.

None of this depends directly upon a consideration of the detailed historical claims of the Gospel narratives. The meaning that the reader generates in the encounter with the Gospel text depends principally upon the literary reading of the final form of the text. The narrative text refers to its own textual world, and not to some extra-textual reference. However, it is clear, as pointed out earlier, that the Lukan text includes examples of historical extravagance, and a theological reader who respects the Gospels as Scripture is committed to attend to whatever is *required by the texts*. In this case, the texts seem to make explicit historical claims, and so respectful fidelity to the narrative texts cannot avoid the issue.[23] These historical claims come as no surprise to the Christian reader, because they are already convinced that Jesus is more than a literary character, and so they expect a relationship between the world of the text and the world of history.[24]

---

23. Goldberg correctly argues that 'no justifiable narrative theology can avoid the fact that a story must at least be *true to itself*. For the biblical narratives which portray a historically conditioned reality, the historical facticity of the events narrated in those stories must affect the truth of any claims which have them as their basis' (Goldberg 1991: 185; Goldberg's italics).

24. Frei expects a relationship between the world of the text and the world of

The world of the past is just as much a construction as the world of the text.[25] These two constructed imagined realities are distinct but they are also related because the Gospel text explicitly relates them. The question of *how* they are related is a complex matter requiring a discussion in its own right. For the present discussion, the question to be addressed is what is the *function* of historical reconstruction for a theological reading? The function of historical reconstruction may be identified from the two ways in which the Gospel narratives employ history.

The first way in which history figures within the narrative is in the assumption of a shared knowledge of general aspects of the first-century world of the Middle East. Although particular features are explained for the reader, many aspects are not. Extratextual historical knowledge contributes to the construction of the narrative world by the reader, and a reading of the text is impoverished to the extent that the reader is unaware of the general 'historical background'.[26]

The second kind of historical interest concerns the particular story of Jesus. The preface of the Gospel of Luke suggests that the narrative is a response to the difficulty of the identification of a reliable interpretation of the life of Jesus amid the various versions available The Lukan version of Jesus' story is the means by which persuasion is achieved, and it is sufficient simply to anchor this story in a wider history as the narrative begins. While it is necessary to demonstrate that Jesus lived, died and rose again in the past, the Gospel narrative attends more to the inter-

history, but he was unable to use the Gospel text to inform his treatment of history because his ideological position had no 'conceptual reserves' for the discussion (cf. Watson 1994: 25).

25. Frei is clear that in the historical-critical approach 'the elements that have been originally woven into one single narrative have now been transposed into another framework. Their meaning, detached from their narrative setting, is now their reference to some other story, some other world, some other context of interpretation' (Frei 1974: 230). 'Frei cogently points out that biblical narrative was not abandoned for some more directly available world or reality; instead the biblical story was exchanged *for another story* thought to depict reality in some truer and more meaningful way' (Goldberg 1991: 160; Goldberg's italics).

26. As Rowan Williams points out, 'the telling of this story is quite overtly a "conversation" with realities that the surface of the narrative does not explicate or display... These are quite simple and contingent points at which it calls for location in its world, since its own frame of reference has the incompleteness characteristic of all genuinely historical discourse' (1991: 127).

pretation of who Jesus is. Consequently it is quite possible to read the Gospel to establish what kind of person is the Lukan Jesus, and in a separate discussion, the reader may investigate the evidence for historical reconstruction.

The Role of the Theological Community in a Theological Reading

The theological 'community of interpretation' plays three subsidiary roles within the kind of theological reading proposed here. The first contribution is the provision of a shared world of experiences of Christ which form the context for a Christian theological reading. The second contribution is the production of the canon, through which particular ecclesiastically acceptable narrative texts are identified and commended for reading. The third contribution is to provide a fellowship of readers whose mutual interaction assists in the criticism and refinement of the reading practice. This last role of the Christian community is the reverse of what Frei commends, for he considers that readers' meanings are subject to the generous but none the less authoritative judgment of the church (Frei 1988c: 57).

Frei maintained that 'there is no such thing as a community's assuming dictatorship of interpretation principles' (1988c: 57) but without further clarification, this caveat fails to prevent the dictatorship, as happened in Frei's later work. In any case, the search for the consensus of the Christian community of interpretation is very difficult due to the wide variety of communities reading Scripture.

When the primacy of the text in the act of reading is restored, Frei's insights may be revised in two ways appropriate for such a respect for the text. First, the relationship between literary and sociolinguistic reading is reversed in order to reinstate the centrality of the literary-critical reading of the text. The sociolinguistic reading becomes one of the resources which is employed in the service of an overarching literary-critical approach to the text.[27]

The second revision follows from the first. Once the centrality of the literary-critical approach is reinstated, it is clear that the community whose assessment of a particular reading will be relevant will be the community that operates with a similar respect for the text. If a particu-

---

27. Tracy, who is appreciative of Frei's work, correctly notes the Reformed roots of Frei's theology, and contrasts it with his own more Catholic approach with its interest in 'how the Scripture is the church's book' (Tracy 1990: 37).

lar Christian community elects a different practice of theological reading, it is likely to produce a range of different readings, and these are less likely to contribute usefully to the assessment of the theological reading under scrutiny.

Formally, a community may avoid the assumption of dictatorship of the interpretation principles if it submits its readings to those interpretative principles that seem to be appropriate to the text, and is willing to revise its consensus readings when necessary. The Christian community forms the context for a theological reading because the experience of the community is congruent (in some way) with the world of the text. Of course those who are not members of the community may read the Gospels with theological questions, and receive illumination of themselves, their experience and their concerns. But any such individual reading is always preliminary and provisional, and requires the *assistance* of the community, which may enquire about the reading, offer possible corrections or extend the reading beyond the horizon of the individual reader.

The Legacy of Hans Frei for a Theological Reading of the Gospels

This discussion of the theological reading of a New Testament Gospel has produced a list of criteria which inform the selection and use of an appropriate literary criticism. The discussion has identified five literary criteria which appropriately express the concerns of the particular theological perspective adopted in this proposal. A theological reading practice which 'respects the text' will display the following criteria:

(1) A respect for the whole of the text in its 'final form';
(2) A literary-critical reading which is distinct from historical-critical interpretation;
(3) A genuine critical freedom in respect of both reader and text;
(4) The inclusion of a formal role for the ideology of the theological reader which prioritizes text over reader;
(5) The inclusion of a formal role for a community of interpretation which also prioritizes text over reader.

The next step in the construction of a theological reading practice is to consider which might be an appropriate literary-critical scheme for the task of theological reading. The next part of the enquiry discusses two possibilities, and commends one for service in theological reading.

Part II

LITERARY-CRITICAL OPTIONS FOR A THEOLOGICAL READING

Chapter 5

THE LITERARY-CRITICAL POTENTIAL OF NEW TESTAMENT
NARRATIVE CRITICISM

> The history of gospel scholarship over the last two hundred and fifty
> years could well be judged to have been an escape from narrativity.
>
> Kelber 1988a: 130

The discussion in Part I concludes with theologically generated literary
criteria that will inform the selection of a literary-critical scheme to
operate within a theological reading practice. New Testament narrative
criticism seems to be a promising candidate for this task, for on first
inspection it seems to meet the criteria identified earlier. These criteria
include working with the final form of the text, prioritizing the text over
the reader, avoiding the complex distraction of questions of history and
being sensitive to the narrative and realistic qualities of the text.

New Testament narrative criticism has opened fresh vistas within the
world of the interpretation of the New Testament. After years of concentration upon the historical significance of the Gospels, New Testament narrative criticism signals a recovery of a literary interest in the
narrative aspects of the Gospels and even the epistles; readers and critics are being recalled to the whole text in its present form.[1] The Gospels
have long been appreciated as narratives, as Frei argues (1974: 1-15),
but the critical tools to proceed beyond this observation were lacking
in modern biblical study. Since the 1980s this deficiency has been

---

1.   'Vying with the venerable historical critical methods for a say on the biblical texts are a host of younger methods, or rather, groups of methods, that are
putting new questions to the texts...Several clusters of criticism are evident...A
profound crossdisciplinary restlessness has been catalytic in the emergence of
several of these clusters—the social and literary clusters in particular' (Moore
1989a: xiii). Moore's *Literary Criticism and the Gospels* (1989a) presents an enter-
taining, illuminating though partisan sketch of this period.

addressed with energy, some critical rigour and no little excitement.[2]

New Testament narrative criticism is peculiar to New Testament studies for although derived from secular literary criticism, there is no equivalent secular critical practice. This new criticism has been created by biblical scholars interested in the significance of the literary aspects of New Testament literature.[3] An overview of the emergence of this new criticism is followed by a theoretical analysis of the approach. The chapter concludes by enquiring whether New Testament narrative criticism can operate within the five literary criteria appropriate to the proposed kind of theological reading and concludes that it can not.

The Emergence of New Testament Narrative Criticism

New Testament narrative criticism emerged on the public stage in the United States in the early 1980s, after ten years of gestation.[4] The para-

---

2. Werner Kelber recalls that 'for many of us the change to the narrative logic of the gospels was an exhilarating experience... It would appear that literary criticism was merely doing the obvious: taking narrative and its logic seriously, and paying attention to its indigenous operations' (Kelber 1988a: 131).

3. Curiously, these scholars show little awareness of very similar work on the Hebrew Bible which predates their efforts (cf. Gunn 1993: 171-78).

4. The emergence of a synchronic literary interest in the New Testament began with the publication of Beardslee's *Literary Criticism of the New Testament* in 1970. Beardslee engages with secular criticism, including Aristotle's *Rhetoric* and *Poetics* and Northrop Frye's *Anatomy of Criticism*.

Whereas in 1960 Mowinkel wrote the entry 'Literature' for the *Interpreter's Dictionary of the Bible*, and concentrated upon the biblical literary genres (Mowinkel 1960: 139-43), Robertson provided a new article 'The Bible as Literature' for the 1976 supplement, and wrote of 'a point of view taken by a relatively small but increasing number of Biblical scholars...united in considering the Bible primarily and fundamentally as a literary document (as opposed to...historical or theological)' (Robertson 1976: 547-51).

Robertson, like Crossan (1982), Rhoads (1982) and Kelber (1988a), considers that this 'new' literary criticism heralds a 'paradigm shift' in New Testament studies. Moore likens this period of fundamental change to 'the last time biblical scholars reeled under the heady influence of a variety of imported critical methods... [which was] when historical criticism of the Bible took its first shambling steps...in a world utterly transformed by modernity' (Moore 1989a: xiii). Brueggemann suggests that this 'enormous change in how we read and interpret the Bible' reflects the loss of confidence in modernity, and the consequent change in 'operative modes of authority...the reader is [no longer] in a posture of control, criticism or explanation' (Brueggemann 1989: 323).

digm shift it represents is the move from a historical-critical approach
to the Gospels to a literary-critical perspective upon these texts. Within
narrative criticism the Gospel text is no longer treated as an artefact to
be employed in historical reconstructions of the life of Jesus or the early
Christian communities. Instead, the best available text of a Gospel is
read and studied as a literary whole.

The lack of literary-critical tools for this study was remedied when
New Testament scholars journeyed to the far country of secular literary
theory and criticism and borrowed from a wealth of different approaches. New Critical approaches were tried, then superseded, by structuralist
criticism and narratology in turn. Virtually all the first generation of
New Testament narrative critics adopted the descriptive narratology of
Chatman's *Story and Discourse* (1978). New Testament scholars became students again as this inter-disciplinary approach spread.

The Book that Broke the News: Mark as Story
The publication of *Mark as Story* in 1982 is generally considered to
have introduced narrative criticism to the wider public.[5] The title *Mark
as Story* is slightly misleading, for the study is actually more of an
'introduction to the narrative of a Gospel' as the subtitle makes clear.[6]
Significantly the book is written jointly by David Rhoads, a New
Testament scholar and Donald Michie, a lecturer in English literature.

Mark as Story introduces the fundamental paradigm shift to a literary
approach to the Gospels. 'The purpose of the book is to recover the

---

In North America, narrative criticism emerged in three phases. The first period is
the 1970s, which was a period of gestation in study groups and papers read at conferences; the second period is the 1980s which is the period of fruition when books
began to appear by Rhoads and Michie (1982); Talbert (1982), Culpepper (1983),
McKnight (1985), Tannehill (1986a), Kingsbury (1986), Aune (1987); these comprise the 'first generation' of narrative critics, whose approach is summed up in
Powell's *What Is Narrative Criticism?* (Powell 1990a). The third phase is the 1990s
which is characterized by many more works and more critical reflection (cf.
Bibliographies).

5.   This discussion of *Mark as Story* also draws on the 1980 paper of David
Rhoads, 'Narrative Criticism and the Gospel of Mark', belatedly published after the
book in 1982. *Mark as Story* is written at a popular level, with just five pages of
theoretical explanation. Consequently the longer discussion in Rhoads' 1980 paper
is particularly important.

6.   *Mark as Story* is the first 'descriptive poetics of a gospel' (Moore 1989a: 41).

experience of the Gospel of Mark as a unified narrative' (Rhoads and Michie 1982: 2). Consequently, 'literary criticism, or more precisely that branch of literary criticism which looks at the formal features of narrative, is one...fresh approach with new questions for Gospel studies' (Rhoads 1982: 411).

Although *Mark as Story* is a short popular work with little theoretical discussion, three methodological choices were made which typify this literary approach and which have been followed by most subsequent New Testament narrative critics. More than 15 years later it turns out that these choices were more significant than the detail of the biblical exposition.

The Emphasis on the Unity of the Final Text. Secular studies of narrative texts drew upon the formalist insight that textual unity is most clearly seen in continuity of literary functions. The extent to which the 'episodic' Gospel of Mark may have a unified and coherent structure is still debated. Formalist literary criticism, however, looks for *formal* criteria to establish unity rather than themes or content of the narrative. Rhoads and Michie drew upon Petersen's study of the continuity of the *point of view* of the Markan narrator through the story (Petersen 1978b) and conclude that 'a literary study of its formal features suggest that the author has succeeded in creating a unified narrative' (Rhoads and Michie 1982: 3).[7]

The Narrative as a Literary Creation with an Autonomous Integrity. Once the unity of the story is acknowledged, Rhoads and Michie claim that the reader is able 'to participate in the world of the story... When viewed as a literary achievement, the statements in Mark's narrative, rather than being a representation of historical events, refer to people, places and events *in the story*' (1982: 3-4).[8] As the reader reads, so she

---

7.   Rhoads describes this first paradigm shift as from 'fragmentation to wholeness'. It was a conscious attempt to work with the whole narrative, and to place emphasis upon the 'unity of the narrative' (Rhoads 1982: 412). Significantly, although Frank Kermode's *The Genesis of Secrecy* is acknowledged in footnotes (Rhoads 1982: 426 n. 2; Rhoads and Michie 1982: 144 n. 5) there is no discussion of Kermode's treatment of aspects of the narrative that subvert the impression of unity. It seems that for Rhoads and Michie, the unity of the narrative is a non-negotiable ideological requirement.

8.   In his 1980 paper, Rhoads described this as 'a shift in perspective from history to fiction', in which fiction is not so much antithetical to history, but

or he enters this story-world.[9] This interest in the story-world of the text is accompanied by a procedural dismissal of historical referentially, because 'recognizing the conceptual autonomy of the narrative world is absolutely essential' (Rhoads 1982: 413).

Narrative Categories are derived from Chatman's Story and Discourse.[10] Chatman's *Story and Discourse* is seminal for most first generation New Testament narrative critics.[11] Typically, Rhoads and Michie drew on Chatman's distinction between *story* as the 'what of a narrative' (e.g. characters, events and settings) and *discourse* as the 'how' of a narrative (e.g. arrangement of events into a plot, type of narrator, point of view, style and rhetorical devices). Chatman's narratology offers more than a just a range of literary categories with which to analyse the narrative text. The New Testament critic Moore considers that 'what the story-discourse model offered narrative criticism was the possibility of systematically accounting for a gospel's narrative in a way that would do justice both to the complexity of the narrative as an instrument of communication and to its unity as an integrated system' (1989a: 45).

Mark as Story was the first in a wave of publications in the fields of literary-critical and narrative-critical interpretations of the New Testa-

signifies that 'in the end the narrative world of the story is a literary creation of the author, and has an autonomous integrity' (Rhoads 1982: 413). Rhoads and Michie agreed with Petersen that an interest in features outside the world of the narrative world is an example of the 'referential fallacy' which fragments the narrative. This is what Frei had argued earlier.

9.   There is a continuing confusion in what Rhoads and Michie mean by 'the reader'. Usually they incorrectly apply it to the contemporary reader, and only introduce the more precise category of the 'implied reader' in their last chapter.

10.   No reasons are given for the choice of *Story and Discourse*. It may be simply that Chatman's work was the only one to hand. Mieke Bal had also published a structuralist introduction to narratology, drawing more upon the Formalist dichotomy of *fabula* and *sjuzhet*, but this was only available in Dutch until 1985.

11.   Chatman was Professor of Rhetoric at Berkeley when he first made his name in the area of stylistics, which drew on Russian formalism, French structuralism, Hjelmslevian linguistics, and the American Schools, including New Criticism. This was the context for Chatman's first venture into narrative theory in which he applied Roland Barthes's 1966 techniques to James Joyce's 'Eveline'. Chatman wrote *Story as Discourse* as a study of how structures are meaning-bearing in their own right. For a discussion of this book see Appendix A: 'The Limitations of Chatman's Narratology'.

ment. The combination of the popular level, the brevity of the work and the novelty of the proposal engendered a mixed response from other scholars. The book that did more to persuade others in the biblical guild was Culpepper's literary analysis and commentary on John's Gospel entitled *The Anatomy of the Fourth Gospel: A Study in Literary Design* (1983).[12]

In 1990 Powell wrote *What Is Narrative Criticism?*, which was published in the Fortress 'Guides to Biblical Scholarship' series, and has become the standard popular introduction to first generation New Testament narrative criticism.[13] Powell had worked in the field of the biblical and literary criticism for some years and drew together a wide reading in the area.[14] The principal limitation of the book arises from its introductory nature, which inevitably places more emphasis upon description than upon theoretical analysis. Nevertheless, when suitably supplemented, it may serve as a useful case study for the following discussion of the elements of New Testament narrative criticism.[15]

New Testament narrative critics look to Frei's *The Eclipse of Biblical Narrative* as an important argument for a literary interest in the Gospels. In contrast to the modern historical-critical approach, and its associated source criticism (commonly and erroneously known as literary criticism in biblical studies), 'literary criticism is concerned with the Bible's literary qualities themselves; it is an example of "aesthetic criticism"' (Powell 1990a: 1).[16] Beardslee (1970), Perrin (1976) and Petersen

---

12. Morgan with Barton are severe in their criticism of *Mark as Story*, but display qualified appreciation of Culpepper's work (Morgan with Barton 1988: 231).

13. The manuscript of *What Is Narrative Criticism?* was read and commented upon by David Rhoads, the pioneer of New Testament narrative criticism and also by Jack Kingsbury, who has written prolifically in the field (cf. Powell 1990a: xi).

14. Powell surveyed the scene (Powell 1991a) and wrote various articles, including three preliminary narrative-critical treatments of the Synoptic Gospels for the journal *Interpretation* (1992, 1993, 1994).

15. The uncritical treatment of theoretical issues, and sometimes their neglect, has contributed to weaknesses within the practice of New Testament narrative criticism, and has made it more difficult to win a wider acceptance for the discipline, not least in Europe. Regretfully, Powell's introductory book shows theoretical inconsistencies. The most *judicious*, and so persuasive, introduction I have found is the brief 1992 essay of Elizabeth Malbon: 'Narrative Criticism: How Does the Story Mean?' (Malbon 1992a).

16. 'The texts are analysed, classified and understood with a view to the enjoyment and instruction readers derive from literature, rather than knowledge of the past... Aesthetic concerns have been far from absent in the [last] two centuries...but

(1978a) had all called for a more literary approach to the Gospels, but there was uncertainty as to how to proceed. The dilemma was whether Scripture could be considered to be literature, if literature is a kind of 'self-consciously imaginary writing' (Wellek and Warren 1963: 20-28). Auerbach's *Mimesis* supplied the breakthrough by arguing that biblical narrative is literature, and influential literature at that. Consequently 'biblical narrative can be studied according to the canons of general literary criticism' (Powell 1990a: 4).

This new and developing literary interest in the Gospels produced a tide of articles, created new journals, gave birth to many books and many more dissertations. And as with most new movements, it encountered resistance and misunderstanding, particularly in its early years within Britain.[17] During the 1990s it is clear that New Testament narrative criticism is now becoming more self-critical.[18] However, the question whether New Testament narrative criticism can establish itself as one of the tools properly available to the New Testament critic is still undecided.[19]

they have remained undeveloped, marginal and exceptional' (Morgan with Barton 1988: 221).

17. A representative British response is seen in the pages of the *Journal for the Study of the New Testament*. Kingsbury published 'The Figure of Jesus in Matthew's Story: A Literary-Critical Probe' in which he argues that the literary feature of the narrator's rhetorical device of 'ideological (evaluative) point of view gives the reader assistance in the identification of Matthew's Christology as preeminently a Son of God christology' (1984: 3). David Hill criticizes Kingsbury's article as unconvincing and ultimately circular, for the literary-critical argument merely arrives at the conclusion with which Kingsbury began, and is therefore 'undeniably subjective' (Hill 1984: 37-52). Kingsbury sets out his answers to the reading and misreading Hill offers of Kingsbury's article, and concludes: 'what strikes me most is that it appears that we have reached an impasse as far as the way in which we approach and interpret Matthew' (Kingsbury 1985: 80). The lack of sympathy for the literary-critical approach is also clear in Morgan with Barton's *Biblical Interpretation*. When they discuss *Mark as Story* there is 'a sense of unease in reading Rhoads and Michie. It is as though the wrong questions are being asked, or at any rate, not the usual questions' (Morgan with Barton 1988: 231) (cf. Moule's misguided and scathing review of the literary-critical elements in Parsons's *The Departure of Jesus in Luke–Acts* [Moule 1989: 187]).

18. The contrast is seen in a comparison of David Rhoads's 1980 paper with Elizabeth Malbon's 1992 article.

19. It is also significant that some narrative critics have become disillusioned

The Elements of New Testament Narrative Criticism

Powell is typical of the first generation narrative critics who adopted the New Critical concept of the 'autonomous text' with its distinction between the extratextual realities (e.g. the real 'historical' author) and the intratextual categories of literary studies (e.g. the literary narrator).[20] Powell argues that the insights of each approach 'will not necessarily be contradictory and so potential exists for the two models to be used in ways that are distinctive but complementary' (Powell 1990a: 10). 'The new literary criticism that has invaded biblical studies in recent years...[draws] upon text-centered (objective) and reader-centered (pragmatic) approaches' (Powell 1990a: 12).

The theoretical basis for New Testament narrative criticism is found in the eclectic work of Chatman, who employs two important conceptual models: (1) the 'narrative communication model' in which the text is modelled as an act of communication between the narrator and narratee;[21] and (2) the dualist distinction between the category of rhetorical devices used by the author which Chatman labels *discourse*,[22] and the study of the narrative elements which are the constituents of what Chatman calls the *story*.

1. *The 'narrative communication' model of the text.* The fundamental step in narratology is to conceive the narrative text as a process of communication.[23] From this conceptual model flows the range of categories and analytical processes which the literary critic traces. The narrator and the narratee conduct this communication within the medium

and 'moved on' for a variety of reasons. Stephen Moore is such an example (1994: 113-17).

20. Four major differences between the newer literary approach and the older historical criticism are: (1) literary criticism focuses on the finished form of the text; (2) literary criticism emphasizes the unity of the text as a whole; (3) literary criticism views the text as an end in itself; and (4) literary criticism is based on a communication model of speech-act theory.

21. The communication model is basic to Chatman's analysis and was employed in combination with the story/discourse model by all first generation New Testament narrative critics. Contra Moore, who argues that Rhoads and Michie did not employ the communication model (Moore 1989a: 46).

22. Powell follows Rhoads and Michie in replacing the label 'discourse' with 'rhetoric', a move which Moore considers 'apt' (Moore 1989a: 44).

23. This idea is usually attributed to Roman Jakobson, and is found as one aspect of the theme of his paper: 'Closing Statement: Linguistics and Poetics' (1958).

of the narrative text, and their ideological positions may be constructed
by the reader through attending to the implications of what is said. The
narrator's ideological position is known as the 'implied author' and is
extrapolated from what the narrator says, while the implied reader is the
reader 'presupposed by the narrative itself' (Powell 1990a: 19) and
deduced from the knowledge, responses and conclusions which the
narrative seems to expect of the narratee.[24] Metaphorically, the communication within the narrative is between the narrator and narratee, with
the reader looking on and overhearing what is going on.[25]

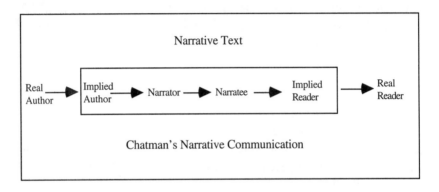

2. *The story/discourse distinction.* Chatman offers his version of the
distinction between *what* is communicated and *how* it is communicated.
The reader is faced with the text which is the combination of the story
(the what) and the way that the story is told (the how or the rhetoric).
Chatman's story/discourse division is a theoretical distinction to illuminate the two aspects which combine to produce the 'story-as-discourse'.
Once there is a discourse, the real author chooses a medium to express
this combination, and in the New Testament the medium is a text.

---

24. 'One of the most pressing issues in literary criticism concerns the question
Who is the Reader?' (Powell 1990a: 19). 'The "implied reader" is an imaginary
reader with the ideal responses implied or suggested by the narrative' (Rhoads and
Michie 1982: 137). Powell concludes that 'the goal of narrative criticism is to read
the text as the Implied Reader' (1990a: 20).
25. Chatman, following Wayne Booth, mistakenly attributes a role in the narrative communication to the 'implied' author and reader. This is a category confusion
and to be avoided (cf. Rimmon-Kenan 1983: 88). The implied author and the
implied reader are ideological positions which the reader infers from the different
voices at work in the text; however, it is voices that communicate, not ideologies!

(a) *The rhetoric.*[26] Powell begins his exposition with discourse which he renames as 'rhetoric' to make clear the the aspects of the text under scrutiny.[27] Although Powell retains the 'implied author', his discussion concentrates upon the narrator in action and the rhetorical devices which he uses. These include devices such as the 'point of view' from which the story is told, the choice of first- or third-person narrator, the degree of omniscience displayed, and the reliability and the profile (or visibility) of the narrator.[28] Powell's brief treatment does not discuss the difference between the implied author and the narrator.[29]

(b) *Story.* Powell follows Chatman in classifying the story elements into three groups: events, characters and settings. Events are 'happenings that occur within the story whose particular contribution is made clear by the way they are presented by the implied author' (Powell 1990a: 35).[30] The story-world is an inference from the narrative world

26. Powell treats the rhetoric dimension in one chapter, misleadingly titled 'Story and Discourse', for he actually treats 'discourse'.

27. There is no consensus among New Testament narrative critics whether it is better to begin the exposition with the rhetoric (so Rhoads and Michie [1982]; Culpepper [1983] and Powell [1990a]), or with the more accessible story elements (as Kingsbury [1986] and Malbon [1992a]). The story elements seem preferable for the beginner.

28. Three other important literary devices employed include symbolism (for which Powell employs the four categories of symbolism suggested by Philip Wheelwright (Powell 1990a: 29), irony and narrative patterning ('often difficult to define, but they include recurrent structural devices and design features that are used to organize and present the story' [Powell 1990a: 32]). Malbon contributed much more work on narrative patterning as seen in her articles listed in the Bibliography.

29. Elizabeth Malbon writes that 'most narrative critics have observed little or no difference between the implied author and the narrator' (Malbon 1992a: 28). To make her point Malbon uses the rather inelegant composite title *implied author/ narrator* in her article.

30. Retaining the classification 'Events' reveals an inconsistency in Powell's thought, and opens possibilities of misunderstanding for the unreconstructed historical critic. The Aristotelian notion of 'plot' has been virtually discarded by structuralist narrative critics, e.g. Rimmon-Kenan: 'I am rather wary of a term which has become too vague in ordinary critical usage' (1983: 135 n. 12). Generally New Testament narrative critics have been eclectic and not thorough-going structuralists, and so have retained the category, and employed it to contextualize 'events' within a narrative. 'Narrative criticism is a story-preoccupied gospel criticism...[which] means, most of all, being preoccupied with *plot* and *character*' (Moore 1989a: 14). Rhoads and Michie (briefly) and Culpepper both have chapters devoted to 'plot'. For them, the significance of an event within a narrative is

generated by the story-as-discourse, and is not identical with what the narrative text displays. The story-world is constructed by the reader and metaphorically represents the events *prior* to their being 'processed' into the 'story-as-discourse'. For example, narrative critics drew upon Genette's distinction between story time and discourse time and the interest generated by the comparison of the two times (Genette 1980). The narrator exercises the freedom to refashion the 'order', 'duration' and 'frequency' of the story events when they are woven into the discourse.

The notion of 'plot' is introduced in Powell's discussion of 'causation' although other critics treat 'plot' as an aspect of the rhetoric of the gospel discourse. Each of the four gospels has a different type of plot, in which causation may be explicitly stated or simply implied (Powell 1990a: 41).[31] The 'plotting of this world is to be seen in the ways its components have been selected and arranged in a sequence of narrated incidents' (Petersen 1978a: 49-50).

Characters are the agents or actors in a story who carry out the activities that comprise the plot. 'We think of them as people, though of course in some literature they may be animals [or] robots' (Powell 1990a: 51). Powell's introduction to the concept of character displays a common failing among New Testament narrative critics, who overlook what is distinctive about *literary character* in contrast to the people we know. Powell also fails to develop the fundamental importance of the *function* of a character within the plot.[32] Chatman's dissatisfaction with structuralist conceptions of character as merely agent had led him to

deduced *primarily* from its place within a plotted sequence, and not by a study of its particular contribution; thus 'plot' is the more fundamental category, within which events are located and then discussed. Culpepper's makes this clear: 'The events are...secondary to the story world or message which gives them meaning' (Culpepper 1983: 85). Matera, in 'The Plot of Matthew's Gospel', similarly concludes that 'Plot is an organizing principle which gives logic and meaning to disparate events' (Matera 1987: 240). Although Powell does consider 'plot' to be a fundamental category (and closes his discussion with a brief treatment of the plot of Matthew's Gospel) his exposition would have been more consistent if he had introduced plot, and then events as a subset of plot.

31. 'Each of the evangelists tells essentially the same story, but the plots and emphases of the gospels differ greatly' (Culpepper 1983: 85).

32. Structuralist thought, following the insight of Vladimir Propp, considers that 'fundamentally, we may classify (characters) in terms of the function they fulfil' (Prince 1987: 72).

develop character as a 'paradigm of traits' (Chatman 1978: 126-38)[33] and this development has been taken up by New Testament narrative critics.

Characters are sketched or 'characterized' for the narratee through statement (telling) and action (showing), together with an often unobserved third *temporal* dimension which is the cumulative interplay within these two aspects through the story. The Dutch narratologist Bal commented that in secular literary theory 'no one has yet succeeded in constructing a complete and coherent theory of character' (1985: 80) and this may partly explain the unsatisfactory quality of Powell's treatment. There is a lack of appreciation of the theoretical issues[34] and little discussion of literary character in secular literary theory, with the consequence that Powell offers an unsatisfactory *ad hoc* eclectic concept of character.[35] Furthermore, Powell does not acknowledge that character

33. The irony is that Chatman's discussion of character is heavily indebted to the rise of the European novel, and that quite different conventions inform the literature of the New Testament period. Malbon reflects that 'narrative critics are generally aware of the differences in characterization between nineteenth and twentieth century psychological novels, for example, and the Gospels. The secular literary theory on which biblical narrative critics so often lean is not particularly supportive at this point. Ways of analysing characterization in the Gospels are still being developed' (Malbon 1992a: 30).

34. One interpretation of North American New Testament narrative criticism suggests that there is a fairly covert theoretical struggle going on. In general terms, Chatman's *Story and Discourse* set out the alternatives and then tried to produce a synthesis (Chatman 1978: 9-12). David Lodge noted that 'in the last couple of decades...the Anglo-American tradition of formalist criticism, essentially underpowered but critically productive, has encountered the more systematic, abstract, theoretically rigorous and "scientific" tradition of European structuralist criticism. The result has been a minor "knowledge explosion" in the field of narrative theory and poetics of fiction' (Lodge 1980: 5) Theoretical rigour is well exemplified by Roland Barthes and Mieke Bal, and the descriptive-formalist approach is typically represented by Wayne Booth. The struggle within the smaller field of New Testament narrative criticism mirrors this. Powell, and others who have adopted Chatman's model, have without theoretical justification moved away from his structuralist concerns and given more weight to the North American 'descriptive' contributions. The result is that they are left with few theoretical critical resources.

35. For example, Powell continues to employ Forster's 1927 distinction between 'flat' and 'round' characters, which is a crude and now obsolete categorization. 'The test of a round character is whether it is capable of surprising in a convincing way' (Forster 1927: 81). The surprise that Forster describes is the effect of a 'rounded character', in which the inner complexity 'shows on the surface'

and characterization in first-century Middle Eastern texts is quite different from that of modern Western literary criticism.[36] Since the publication of *What Is Narrative Criticism?* narrative critics have moved
beyond this naïve treatment of characterization.[37]

Settings provide 'a context for the actions of the characters…[they]
are the adverbs of literary structure: they designate when, where and
how the action occurs' (Powell 1990a: 69). As Bal notes, 'when the
location has not been indicated, readers will, in most cases, supply one'
(Bal 1985: 43). Powell maps three kinds of setting: spatial, temporal
and social. Spatial settings provide the physical environment which
includes the importance of *contrast* (e.g. inside and outside, country/
city; land/sea) and *boundaries* as mediating between opposed locations
(e.g. the seashore). The literary potential of the last two aspects lies
largely undeveloped in the New Testament Gospels.

Temporal Settings are classified as chronological and typological.
Chronological describes time as locative (the point in time when an
action occurred) or durative (the length of time for which it occurred),
whereas typological time is the 'kind' of time (e.g. Nicodemus met
Jesus *at night*). However, as Powell acknowledges, 'references to
temporal settings in our Gospels are typically as brief as descriptions of
the spatial environment…[so] narrative critics cannot assume that all
temporal references and settings possess meaning beyond their literal
function in the story' (1990a: 73).

(1927: 55). But can New Testament characters be usefully categorized in this way
(cf. Bal 1985: 81)?

36. This difference is acknowledged in some recent narrative criticism. Mary
Ann Tolbert writing on Mark observed that 'our modern textual practices often
appear to be a poor "fit" for ancient or culturally distant texts… By exploring how
ancient Greek and Roman writers fashioned characters and how they viewed the
relationship of character to the plot and to the audience, it may be possible to
understand in an entirely new light the nature and purpose of the Markan characters' (1993: 347-48).

37. Elizabeth Malbon rather optimistically claimed in 1992 that 'New Testament narrative critics are generally aware of the differences in characterization
between nineteenth- and twentieth-century psychological novels and the gospels'
(1992a: 30) This has yet to be borne out in the work published in the field!
However, Malbon has contributed usefully to the discussion of developing ways of
analysing characterization in the Gospels (cf. particularly her 'The Jewish Leaders
in the Gospel of Mark: A Literary Study of Markan Characterization' [1989]).

Social settings are important for the real reader, in order to understand the general cultural contexts assumed to be operative in the work. The social settings may be classified as either general or particular. In his introduction, Powell only discusses general social settings.[38] However, the usefulness of this category is limited by 'the paucity of sensory data' in the Gospel narratives (Powell 1990a: 71).[39]

Formal Difficulties within New Testament Narrative Criticism

Once New Testament narrative criticism was launched, three related objections were levelled against it which concern the genre of the Gospels. The first queried whether secular and sacred literature may be treated alike; the second objection doubted that critical tools developed in the world of fiction may be used on non-fictional Gospels; and the third objection queried whether modern literary criticism may be used on the ancient Gospel texts.

Secular Tools for Sacred Literature?
The first attempt to argue for secular literary-critical tools to be used on sacred literature collapsed because of the complex debate about the nature of literature. The second attempt argues that the use of secular narratology is available to the New Testament critic because although narratology has been developed by considering fictional studies which are narratives, it is the *narrative* aspect of the texts which is the focus of the study, and not the fictional status of those narratives.[40] Narratology

---

38. Powell's reluctance to discuss the particular seems to arise from his reluctance to allow any historical referential aspect to the Gospel text. Following Rhoads, Powell writes 'using knowledge of the history and culture of the first century as an aid in understanding a particular Gospel's story world is quite a different matter from using story elements to reconstruct historical events' (Powell 1990a: 74).

39. Powell notes Funk's observation that typically 'the brevity of description is remarkable even for the literature of the time (cf. the writings of Josephus)' (Funk 1988: 141). Powell goes on to suggest that by contrast, when description of a spatial setting is given, it 'calls special attention to such information when it is provided' (1990a: 72). However, Powell does not explore the significance of the 'typical' paucity, which clearly requires further attention.

40. Alter and Kermode argue that 'the Bible, considered as a book, achieves its effects by means no different from those generally employed by written language...indeed literary analysis must come first, for unless we have a sound under-

is the study of the narrative form—wherever it may be found.[41] 'To the extent that the genres of the novel and gospel share narrative forms... both are amenable to narrative analysis' (Powell 1990a: 94).[42]

Non-Fictional Gospels and Literary Criticism Developed in Fictional Studies
Even if 'narrative features' are shared by fictional and non-fictional writings, are not literary-critical tools generated for fictional studies properly restricted to fictional texts alone? The objection that fictional tools are inappropriate for interpreting non-fictional Gospel narratives rests upon a popular understanding of the fiction/history distinction.[43] Fiction is associated with the imaginary or the untrue, and history with the 'true'.[44] When narrative critics employ the term 'fiction' they consider that in *every* kind of narrative 'the narrative world...is a literary creation of the author' (Rhoads 1982: 413). The focus is upon the 'manufactured' or poetic nature of every narrative.

The fiction/history dichotomy is better thought of as a distinction between two aspects of every text: the poetic and the referential. These

standing of what the text is doing and saying, it will not be of much value in other respects' (Alter and Kermode 1987: 2).

41. Chatman introduces *Story and Discourse* thus: 'there are few books in English on the subject of narrative in general... Beyond the analysis of generic differences there lies the determination of what narrative is *in itself*' (1980: 9); cf. Genette, who in his work on Proust discovered that 'by seeking the specific I find the universal... This is the paradox of every poetics...that there are no objects but particular ones, and no science except the general' (Genette 1980: 23). Hence Prince's definition of Narratology as 'the (structuralist inspired) theory of narrative. Narratology studies the nature, form and functioning of narrative (regardless of medium of representation)' (1987: 64).

42. Culpepper argues that it is possible to use secular tools on scared texts. The secular literary critic Frank Kermode commends this in his foreword to Culpepper's book, for 'strongly upholding the position long since enunciated but still widely ignored or disputed, that there can be no sharp distinction between sacred and profane hermeneutics' (Culpepper 1983: vi).

43. Rhoads's characterization of his major shift in perspective as 'from history to fiction' seemed to confirm grounds for suspicion, despite his careful qualification of the term 'fiction'. This part of the discussion was later reworked to try to avoid using the word 'fiction' in *Mark as Story*.

44. 'Fiction is a term often used inclusively for any literary narrative, whether in prose or in verse, which is feigned or invented, and does not purport to be historical truth' (Abrams 1988: 62).

are sufficiently different to be conceptually distinct, and so are not opposed to each other, and consequently do not threaten to subvert each other.[45] Thus narrative-critical tools, which were generated by work on the poetic or literary aspects of fictional narrative literature, may be used on all and any narrative texts. In summary, what this approach encourages is not the reading of the Gospels as if they were kinds of nineteenth-century novel, but rather the reading of the Gospels as examples of the narrative form.

Modern Literary-Critical Tools for Old Narrative Texts?
Finally, there is the charge that narrative critics have 'turned the ancient gospel narrators into our literary contemporaries, creating the illusion of identity' (Kelber 1988b: 12). In point of fact, every text when it is finished leaves behind its author and can be read by people in different times and places. The text is ever contemporary to the reader, simply due to its presence in material representation before the reader. Consequently there will always be a dimension of the treatment of the text which signals that it is a contemporary artefact.

The difficulty that underlies this hesitation is the recognition that some narrative criticism treats the text as *only a contemporary text*. Does not a particular narrative text, which displays synchronic narrative structures, also display the literary conventions of the act of its production? To read an ancient text requires—at some point in the process— an awareness of the historical context and literary conventions of the time in which it was written. Early narrative-critical work dismissed every extratextual kind of reality, and so operated as if the text were only a contemporary text. By 1992, Malbon could write, possibly more hopefully than accurately, 'narrative critics are eager to know as much as possible about the cultural contexts—especially of ancient works' (Malbon 1992a: 28).[46]

45. 'Literary criticism...deals with the poetic function of a text, whereas histori-cal criticism deals with the referential function. This means that literary critics are able to appreciate the story of a narrative apart from consideration of the extent to which it reflects reality' (Powell 1990a: 8).
46. The interest in the wider context of texts was signalled in 1982 by Rhoads and Michie, *but rarely employed:* 'None of these considerations means that our general knowledge of the first century is not helpful in the interpretation of the story; indeed it is often crucial' (Rhoads and Michie 1982: 4) Malbon demonstrated her interest in first-century characterization in her study of the Jewish leaders in Mark (1989).

New Testament Narrative Criticism and Theological Reading

The discussion in Chapter 4 produced five principal characteristics of a literary-critical practice which if met would qualify the practice for inclusion in the kind of theological reading being sought. Four of these are now considered in turn; narrative criticism does not formally involve the community of interpretation, and so the fifth criterion cannot be met.

Criterion One: A Respect for the Literary Text as a Whole

A substantial achievement of New Testament narrative criticism is its contribution to the reintroduction of a literary interest within New Testament studies. This has enabled the critical focus to bear upon the entire text in its present form. Structuralist literary criticism of the New Testament has also endeavoured to focus upon the text itself, but tends to slide inexorably toward discussion of the deep structures of narrative.[47]

Narrative criticism displays a respect for the *literariness* of the literary text, and provides literary categories and conventions to assist the reader when reading the text. What is then needed is a critical procedure for interpreting narratives, which could address the question 'How does the text mean?' (Malbon 1992a: 23).

This respect for the literary text is also displayed in the way that narrative criticism attends to the 'plain sense' of the text, and employs literary-critical tools which respect the biblical texts as kinds of realistic narrative.

Criterion Two: Literary Reading that Is Distinct from a Historical-Critical Interpretation

In his 1980 paper, Rhoads portrayed the change in methodological paradigm as a 'shift from history to fiction' (Rhoads 1982: 412).[48] New

47. Structuralist interpretations of New Testament narratives were an earlier attempt to establish a literary approach to the Gospels. Although a form of literary criticism, in practice, structuralist readings did not work with 'the surface structure of the text' (Patte 1990: viii). Despite the efforts of McKnight, and the indefatigable Patte (with his various popular introductions to structuralism), the structural analysis of texts has not been widely taken up, a fact acknowledged by Patte himself. Although it is a sophisticated and technically demanding approach, I suggest the primary reason for its limited usefulness is that structuralist interpretation is primarily interested in the text as an example of structuralist system and not in the particularity of the literary text itself.

48. Rhoads followed Petersen in accusing critics of committing the 'referential

Testament narrative criticism is more accurately described by Powell as dealing 'with the poetic function of a text, whereas historical criticism deals with the referential function' (Powell 1990a: 8).[49] Malbon distinguishes between the 'internal' or literary meaning and the 'external' or referential meaning.[50]

The argument being advanced is that to appreciate the way a narrative 'means' requires isolation from discussions about the way it refers beyond itself.[51] As a temporary, procedural strategy within an interpretative exercise, that is acceptable. Just as Frei did, many New Testament narrative critics endlessly defer the question of history. A further difficulty arises when the literary insights achieved are introduced to the wider interpretative historical discussion of the text; New Testament narrative criticism struggles to be formally useful at this point.[52]

The relationship between literary text and the historical context of its production has moved back into the forefront of the discussion, so that now there is a growing interest in how the literary conventions and

fallacy' when they displayed an interest in a direct relationship between the text and the Jesus of history. Petersen, following Jakobson, argued that the 'referential function in a narrative is to be located in the world created by the narrative' (Petersen 1978a: 40).

49. In the treatment of the Jewish leaders in the Gospel of Matthew, Powell goes beyond this distinction to claim that the poetic and the referential are not only distinct (e.g. 'the religious leaders...are constructs of the implied author designed to fulfil a particular role in the story') but that sometimes poetic and referential functions are antithetical: 'the religious leaders in Matthew's narrative do not "stand for" any real people in the world outside the story' (Powell 1990a: 66). The strong impression is given that this comment arises from Powell's sense of embarrassment about the text, and is not generated by the text.

50. Malbon proposes that narrative criticism illuminates '*how* does the text mean? This question is literary; it represents a search for the internal meaning rather than external (referential) meaning' (Malbon 1992a: 24).

51. This echoes Frei's proposal in which he had distinguished between 'historical' and 'history-like', in order to create the methodological space to investigate the significance of the history-likeness.

52. The suspicion that New Testament narrative criticism is inevitably ahistorical is compounded by reflection upon its theoretical roots in the world of fictional studies and indirectly in the world of structuralism. The structuralist Barthes claims that 'what takes place in a narrative is from the referential (real) point of view literally nothing. What happens is language itself, the adventure of language which is being constantly celebrated' (1974: 63).

general cultural context of the production of a text influence the production of the narrative text which lies before the reader of any era.

Seemingly unbeknown to most New Testament narrative critics, the relationship between literary narratives and the historical events with which they are associated has been discussed for many years in the field of the philosophy of history. Yet, even if this had been appreciated, the methodological bracketing of history precludes such a discussion.

Criterion Three: The Critical Freedom within the Interpretative Practice

The critical freedom associated with a chosen literary criticism has two related aspects. First, critical freedom may be appreciated as the *freedom from covert reader ideology* in the reading of the Gospel narratives. A 'critical' approach engages with the text in such a way as to allow the process of reading the text to revise the reading which is being generated. There is an 'openness' in the process which awaits the experience of reading before a position is constructed. Critical freedom accords authority to the empirical reading practice.

The second aspect of critical freedom is the freedom to interrogate the whole text, and to attend to those features which seem initially to risk the subversion of the reading produced. This kind of critical freedom expresses its respect for the text in the careful attention given to all the features of the text. Although the consequences await those future readings to become clear, at the least the critical reader has exercised the *freedom to attend to every feature of the narrative*.

The conclusion of this study is that New Testament narrative criticism fails in these aspects of critical freedom. The first failure is illustrated by the 'ideology of the unified narrative', and the second failure is illustrated by the inability to engage with those uncongenial aspects of the text which threaten to subvert the reading.

The Ideology of the Gospels as 'Coherent and Unified Narratives'. Narrative unity 'is not...proved from an analysis of the material. Rather, it is something that can be assumed' (Powell 1990a: 92). At this point the supposedly empirical text-centred critical approach appears to be taken over by an *a priori* ideological concern.

The issue is not *whether* the text forms a sufficiently unified narrative, but what are the grounds for the statement. In the studies of Old Testament narrative criticism where the debate about the narrative unity of texts is more mature, Alter properly insists on *empirical* grounds for any claims for text unity.[53] Moore notes that in Genette's *Narrative Discourse* which is based upon a close study of Proust's *A la recherche du temps perdu*, there was 'room' for the text to 'resist' the poetician.[54] In contrast, the first generation of New Testament narrative critics seem strangely un-disconcerted by the actual Gospel narrative text. Whatever the text includes, it always displays a self-consistent unity![55] These critics have made the unity of the text a part of their ideology, with the result that they are unable to recognize or address those features of the text which threaten the unity of the text.

This mistake is being recognized, if not corrected. Malbon acknowledges narrative criticism's 'holistic passion...its totalizing effect— creating a self-consistent unity of the text' and then acknowledges that 'it is good for narrative criticism to be reminded of what it also knows—and often proclaims—of the tensions, gaps and mysteries of the text itself' (Malbon 1992a: 35).

The Inability to Engage with Deconstructive Aspects of the Text. A critical practice that acknowledges difficulties in the text and then ignores them is clearly suspect.[56] The work of Rhoads and Michie includes

53. '[Some] see the text as an amalgam of conflicting voices. I would concede that this is sometimes so, but I am also repeatedly impressed by the evidence in many instances of a strongly synthesizing imagination which has succeeded in making one disparate voice' (Alter 1992: 7).

54. Genette 'cannot deny in Proust the will for coherence and the striving for design...[yet] just as undeniable in his work is the resistance of its matter and the part played by what is uncontrolled—perhaps what is uncontrollable' (Genette 1980: 266-67).

55. The tortuous gymnastics entailed by the a priori assumption that the Gospel text is a unified narrative may be seen in the treatment of the shorter ending of Mark. Textual critics continue to debate whether this could be the original form of the ending, 'with an increasingly strong inclination to the view that Mk 16.8 is the *intended* ending' (Kümmel 1975: 98-101; my italics). However, Rhoads does not acknowledge this uncertainty, and instead construes this shorter ending as displaying 'the subtlety and ambiguity of that marvellously exasperating ending'. Rhoads implies that the shorter ending 'works' within his construction of the narrative unity, and gives the impression that nothing found in the text can unsettle him!

56. In contrast to the seeming transparency of the reading of Rhoads and Powell, the secular literary critic Kermode concludes his reading of Mark in *The Genesis of Secrecy* with the observation that 'world and book are hopelessly plural; endlessly disappointing...our sole hope and pleasure is in the perception of a

precisely this kind of bad critical practice and invites the response that 'the view of the gospel text which the narrative critics have urged is ultimately a comforting one... In appropriating narrative theory, narrative critics regularly defuse it' (Moore 1989a: 53-54).[57] Moore's comment describes the repeated inability of narrative critics to incorporate in their reading practice the deconstructive as well as the constructive features of the text. The principal reason for this difficulty lies in the fault lines within the narratological model of Seymour Chatman which has been adopted to inform their critical practice.

Chatman's *Story and Discourse* is an eclectic 'amalgam of Anglo-American narrative study...and Russian and French literary semiotics' (Chatman 1980b: 258). The difficulty with eclectic constructions is the lack of a theoretical coherence. Scholes, in a highly critical review of *Story and Discourse*, concludes that Chatman has 'studiously ignored most recent continental criticism...[so that the book] is still, after all, merely formalism' (Scholes 1980: 191).[58] The narrative theory of Chatman produces an essentially uncritical practice, which shapes the New Testament narrative criticism which draws upon his thought. This analysis is developed in the Appendix, 'Limitations of Chatman's Narratology'.

In the area of improper ideological influence and also in its critical inability to address uncongenial aspects of the texts, it becomes clear that first-generation narrative criticism of the Gospels fails as a critical exercise.

Criterion Four: The Role of the Theological Reader
A typical first-generation New Testament narrative-critical practice fails formally to incorporate the theological interests of the reader into its reading practice, and so creates confusion about the status of the

momentary radiance, before the door of disappointment is finally shut on us' (1979: 145). Rhoads noted Kermode's alternative reading, but despite intentions to address it, he neither addressed it, nor the issues raised by such a different reading.

57. The Old Testament narrative critic David Gunn concurs: 'Narrative criticism of the Gospels and Acts has tended to be relatively conservative in its methodology...[and] reluctant to take a literary approach that unravels unity' (1993: 172).

58. Scholes' thoroughgoing criticism is cogent in its analysis, and reflects the breadth of study that contributed to the one-time standard work *The Nature of Narrative*, which he jointly authored with Kellogg in 1966. See discussion in Appendix A.

reading it produces. There are two related difficulties: first, there is the lack of clarity about whether New Testament narrative criticism produces a theological reading of the Gospels or a literary reading of the Gospels. Secondly, under the influence of New Critical thought, there is simply no formal place for extratextual realities, which would include the ideological interests of the reader.

Confusion between a Literary Approach and a Theological Reading. This confusion seems to arise from a tension between literary-critical approaches and institutional expectations. I agree with Kelber when he argues that New Testament narrative criticism is a 'strictly literary reading of biblical narrative' (1988a: 131). In its development, the critical tools employed comprise categories, theoretical models and the critical processes imported directly from the realm of secular literary theory and criticism.

Interestingly, narrative criticism of Gospel texts has begun to attract the interest of secular literary scholars such as Kermode and Bal, because it seems to be an exercise within their professional jurisdiction.[59] Significantly, both of them are quite clear about the nature of the exercise, and they distinguish clearly between literary and religious approaches to the texts.[60] From a literary point of view, the Bible 'has reoccupied literary culture, [and] professional Biblical criticism has been profoundly affected by it' (Alter and Kermode 1987: 3). Within a literary approach, the Bible is not approached as a religious handbook, but simply 'as a set of literary texts' (Bal 1989a: 373).

At the same time, there has been institutional pressure upon many New Testament narrative critics to operate as if they are doing *more* than literary criticism.[61] This difference is illuminated by the concept of

59. As an exercise in literary criticism, biblical and New Testament narrative criticism may correctly be criticized for not having been *literary* enough.

60. Alter and Kermode 1987: 2, and Bal, in her scathing review of Kort's *Story, Text and Scripture* (Bal 1989a: 464).

61. The world of Western New Testament studies had already achieved an academic place within the *Wissenschaft*, in which the rational study of the documents had contributed to the shaping of a discipline. However, the location of New Testament studies within the Departments of Theology tends to mask the fact that most New Testament study is practically a form of literary history, i.e. literature studied from a historical perspective, whereas institutionally it is part of a theological exercise. When scholars began developing narrative criticism, the new discipline natu-

'the text' which is held by the narrative critic. Most hold, even if unacknowledged, a 'quasi-theological view of the text' which inevitably influences the range of literary options open to the critical reader.

The 'quasi-theological' view of the text is a label for a collection of assumptions which have gradually emerged from a theological working with the text.[62] For example, because the text is considered to be Scripture in the theological tradition, the view that 'meaning is single, fixed and located within the text' is most congenial to the Christian tradition. This *preference* has shaped biblical studies, and consequently narrative studies as well. 'The leading question...is that of the location of meaning. New Criticism's claim that meaning is located in the text and only needs close reading to be 'extracted' has remained the implicit presupposition of much biblical scholarship' (Bal 1989b: 374).[63]

The tension between a literary reading and a theological reading leads some narrative critics to conduct a literary-critical reading, and then employ it for a theological end without recognizing the inappropriateness of the ideological basis of the literary criticism which has been used.[64] New Testament narrative criticism is a literary-critical exercise which is informed principally by the ideological concerns of the secular criticism upon which it is based.

Some New Testament narrative critics recognize the need for an inter-disciplinary exercise, but not enough attention has been given to how this new approach of 'field criticism' (Crossan 1982: 200) actually

rally found its home within the world of New Testament scholarship, and was subject to its pressures.

62. Most of the first New Testament narrative critics had received theological training.

63. Moore considers present New Testament narrative criticism to be wedded to the New Critical view of the text: 'American biblical criticism has only recently become preoccupied with the formal coherence of the text, an emphasis in its zenith in American literary criticism in the 1940's and 1950s' (Moore 1989a: 54). Bal goes further to suggest that in biblical narrative criticism, even 'structuralism, which seemed like a reaction to New Criticism, now looks much more like its offshoot...the power of the text is still absolute for many a scholar' (Bal 1989b: 374). Furthermore, Moore observes that there is usually a time lag between an era in secular literary criticism and the subsequent borrowing from it by biblical literary criticism, and this is principally due to the constraint of having to engage with traditional biblical scholarship.

64. Malbon writes optimistically that 'narrative criticism...can help us align ourselves with the implied reader [and then] our own roles as real readers—and re-readers...will surely be enriched' (Malbon 1992a: 47).

works. This book is one such exploration, in which a literary reading is considered as a proper preliminary to a theological reading of the Gospel narratives.

In recent biblical studies there are three primary perspectives from which to approach the text: (1) the literary; (2) the historical; and (3) the theological.[65] Traditional historical-critical study of the New Testament lies within the purview of (2), while New Testament narrative criticism lies within (1) as a form of literary-critical study.[66] This leaves unresolved the question of what constitutes a 'theological reading' of the Gospel texts.

The Formal Role of the Reader. The narrative-critical approach described above omits the real reader in its theoretical model and concentrates upon the communication within an intratextual process. Narrative criticism has never completely abandoned its New Critical formalist heritage, and continues to treat the text as a self-contained aesthetic object.[67] This dismissal of the extratextual real reader (and real author) is claimed by these critics to be a necessary enabling condition for the literary appreciation of the story.

These 'narrative critics generally speak of an *implied reader* who is presupposed by the narrative itself...and the goal of narrative criticism is to read the text as the implied reader' (Powell 1990a: 19-20).[68] Yet this suggestion rests upon a category confusion, for the 'implied reader is a literary device encoded in the text in the very rhetoric through

---

65. These approaches are not dissimilar to Sternberg's suggestion that 'Biblical narrative [is] a complex, because multi-functional, discourse. Functionally speaking, it is regulated by a set of three principles: ideological, historiographical and aesthetic' (Sternberg 1985: 41).

66. The literary-critical nature of New Testament narrative criticism is illustrated in enterprises such as *Literary Guide to the Bible* (Alter and Kermode 1987), edited by *literary* critics, who chose contributors from the areas of biblical studies as well as literary criticism. Secular literary critics are clearer about the literary nature of the enterprise than some New Testament scholars.

67. Kelber characterized the New Critical approach as 'an objective scholar analysing an autonomous text' (1988a: 132). 'Anglo-American New Critics and French Structuralists treated the text as a more or less autonomous object' (Rimmon-Kenan 1983: 117).

68. Powell acknowledges that 'the goal of reading the text as the implied reader may be somewhat unattainable, but it remains a worthy goal nevertheless' (1990a: 21).

which the real reader is required to make sense of the content' (Rim-mon-Kenan 1983: 119). Thus the 'implied reader' cannot substitute for the extratextual reality of the real reader.

In practice, narrative critics increasingly use extratextual factors to inform and enable their reconstruction of the narrative meaning, as Malbon makes clear (1992a: 28). Tannehill's early interest in narrative criticism was accompanied by an interest in the response of real read-ers.[69] Nevertheless, in theoretical terms the real reader is still absent.[70] New Testament narrative critics have in practice recognized the impor-tance of the real reader and offered (simplistic) approximations of the real reader to the implied reader, but the reader or the reader's ideology play no formal part in the reading of the Gospels.

In short, New Testament narrative criticism fails to include the real reader in the hermeneutical activity of reading, and this omission is repeated in respect of the role of the community of interpretation—there is no formal place for either.

The Unsuitability of Narrative Criticism for a Theological Reading

One way of tracing the achievements of a critical procedure is to con-sider the growth of its influence, and the explanations proposed for this growth. There has been an increasing interest in the literary-critical ap-proach to the Bible, particularly in the United States.[71] More speci-fically, in the world of professional New Testament scholarship there seems to have been an increasing interest in narrative criticism, as

---

69. In a study of the disciples in Mark, Tannehill wrote that 'the composition of Mark strongly suggests that the author, by the way in which he tells the disciple's story, intended to awaken his readers to their failures as disciples' (1977: 392). Thus Tannehill integrated narrative and reader-response criticism. Moore considers that the article 'inaugurated the appropriation of reader-response criticism for New Testament exegesis' (Moore 1989a: 73). Powell concludes: 'of all the types of liter-ary criticism...narrative criticism and the dialectical modes...of reader-response are the most similar and they may eventually become indistinguishable' (1990a: 21).

70. The practical employment of extratextual aspects such as cultural contexts is a pragmatic move by narrative critics, for 'both the referential and the formalist [text] models have succeeded in blocking serious reflection upon our role as readers' (Kelber 1988a: 132).

71. 'The effectiveness of this new [literary] approach—or approaches, for the work has proceeded along many different paths—has now been amply demon-strated' (Alter and Kermode 1987: 2).

suggested by the number of articles written, books published and research undertaken. The basic reason for this seems to be that the narrative-critical approach has proved sufficiently seminal as a critical practice to attract the sustained attention of scholars.

Nevertheless, the conclusion to this investigation is that New Testament narrative criticism does not meet enough of the criteria developed in Chapter 4 to be an appropriate type of literary criticism for the kind of theological reading envisaged. Fundamentally, New Testament narrative criticism is both 'uncritical' and also a 'modern' way of reading the texts which disenfranchises the ideology of the reader and the reading community. For the purposes of the present study, it is necessary to consider a further option.

Chapter 6

THE LITERARY POTENTIAL OF THE
CRITICAL NARRATOLOGY OF MIEKE BAL

> Narratology is at an impasse. It has ceased to be perceived as fruitful,
> insofar as it has not succeeded in establishing itself as a *tool*, that is,
> putting itself in the service of critical practice.
>
> Bal 1990: 27

The secular literary theorist and critic Mieke Bal has produced readings
of biblical narrative texts which are thoroughly 'critical', in a way that
has been impossible within New Testament narrative criticism. Furthermore, Bal's approach also explicitly integrates her own ideological
concerns as reader within her critical narrative practice. These twin
achievements commend Bal's work for consideration as a suitable
literary-critical approach for the present theological enterprise.

Some biblical scholars might question whether this is possible after
studying Bal's typically iconoclastic readings of Hebrew biblical texts.
In fact, Bal's theoretical clarity and rigour allow readers to retrace the
paths she took in the production of her readings, and in so doing, readers are then equipped to map alternative paths and produce their own
readings.[1] As Bal's critical practice formally includes within it the
possibility of its own revision, a reader with different ideological concerns may properly develop a revision of her approach.

Bal fiercely opposed readings of texts in which power is appropriated
by the 'dominant' and represses the 'alternative' and the 'other'. Bal's
strategy is to produce rigorous readings of texts which are utterly different to those produced by the 'powerful', and in so doing to subvert
the claims of more traditional readers to declare 'what the text means'.
Bal worked for ten years with the Hebrew Scriptures, during which

---

1. In order to assist students and readers, Bal wrote her *Narratology: Introduction to the Theory of Narrative* for the sake of 'understanding, of the possibility
of exchange of opinions and of emancipation from intimidation' (1985: ix).

time her particular ideological interest increasingly focused on texts which 'have some form or other of misogyny' (Bal 1987: 2).

As well as the 'content' of the texts, Bal's iconoclasm also subjects reading practice to the same ideological criticism. For example, in the literary-critical sphere, the presumption of the 'unity of the text' becomes an ideological claim of the powerful who use it to 'order' the disparate elements of events into a story, and the truthfulness of their reading is supposedly demonstrated by this imposed coherence. Bal observes that to achieve this, all literary features that threaten this fabricated unity are suppressed through being ignored or written out of the reading.

This chapter introduces the writings that Bal produced during those ten years. The theoretical analysis that follows goes on to identify the elements of her critical narratology, to explore whether such an approach may be appropriate within the proposed theological reading and to conclude that a revised form of her critical narratology would be both useful and fitting.

Mieke Bal: An Introduction to her Writings on Critical Narratology

The Dutch literary critic Mieke Bal began her academic life at the National University of Utrecht, and went on to serve as Professor of Comparative Literature and Susan B. Anthony Professor of Women's Studies at the University of Rochester in the United States. During the late 1970s and 1980s, Bal developed what is, as she is quick to point out, '*a* theory of narrative' (Bal 1991a: 73). By the end of the 1980s, Bal's interest had moved on to the hermeneutics of visual perception and she left the field of narratology. Nevertheless, her contribution from that period still offers both stimulus and possibilities for development.

Bal scrutinized various kinds of reading, including those that camouflage uncongenial aspects of the texts. Bal's strategy for clarifying what is going on is to focus on the 'subjects' in the narrative and the way they communicate within the narrative world: 'I enter the analysis with the key question of narrative theory: the question of the subject' (1990: 18). Bal's work upon the concept of the 'subject' produced a key methodological breakthrough during her engagement with Genette's notion of 'focalization' or 'point of view'. Bal developed a more sophisticated appreciation of the 'point of view' of the different 'subjects' within a narrative. Bal published her proposal as *De theorie van vertellen en verhalen* in 1980, which was belatedly published in English in 1985 as *Narratology: Introduction to the Theory of Narrative*. In this work Bal introduces a 'three-layer' model of the communication within a narrative text to accommodate her three kinds of 'subject'.

When Bal published *Femmes imaginaires: L'Ancien Testament au risque d'une narratologie critique* in 1986, she reworked her 1980 model of a narrative text and replaced the insufficiently precise concept of 'narrative agent' as the 'subject' with a more abstract and powerful semiotic concept of 'subject'. This revision is so important that Bal insisted that the original form of her narratology needs to be read in conjunction with this development of her thought (1991a: 74).[2]

In the early 1980s Bal recalls that she began a 'long and serious and pleasurable excursion into the field of Biblical Studies...[which] allowed me to test my theoretical persuasions about narrative against a body of literature foreign to that theory' (1991b: 11). Bal's formidable theoretical work is developed through the process of working with specific texts, for she maintained that theory cannot be simply 'applied' to texts. 'At most, theories can be brought into dialogue with texts...A fruitful encounter between critical theory and the Bible will end...in an interdisciplinary venture' (1990: 16).

Bal was interested in the role of the ideology of the reader, and the risk that it could preclude a genuinely critical reading. In her article 'The Bible as Literature: A Critical Escape' (Bal 1986b) Bal examines works by Alter, Sternberg, and Trible, and criticizes the way that theological ideology improperly interferes with a literary reading and yet manages to escape the proper mutual criticism which is grounded in critical literary theory.

Most of Bal's attention is devoted to Old Testament stories and the female characters which inhabit them. This work led to a trilogy of monographs on biblical narrative. In 1987 she published *Lethal Love: Feminist Literary Readings of Biblical Love Stories*, in which, as she later recalled, she approached 'the texts, a collection of love stories about wicked/or tricky women from the perspective of a critical narrative theory' (Bal 1988b: 2). Bal reveals the dominant ways in which they have been read, 'all of which have some form of misogyny in common' (Bal 1987: 2).[3] Bal's study is a 'case for *difference* which

2.   The relevant excerpt is published in English as 'Narrative Subjectivity' in *On Story-Telling* (Bal 1991a).

3.   'The enterprise was one of confrontation...between ancient texts, the modern rewriting of them, and extant narrative theory' (Bal 1988b: 2).

becomes an argument for the relative arbitrariness of all readings' (Bal 1988b: 2).

Bal's second monograph, *Murder and Difference: Gender, Genre and Scholarship on Sisera's Death* (Bal 1988a), 'confronts the two versions of the murder of Sisera...with various disciplines that constitute the field of scholarship, with the semiotic interest in whether these disciplines "close off or open up meaning?"' (Bal 1988a: 3).

In 1988 Bal published her third study on biblical narrative, *Death and Dissymmetry: The Politics of Coherence in the Book of Judges* (1988b) in which she criticizes 'the politics of coherence' as an ideology for the 'oppression of the other'. As the antidote to the ideological imperialism of (usually male) readers, Bal attends increasingly to the 'gaps and ambiguities' of the texts as the more important tests of attentive reading.[4] Bal's focus changes in this third work in the trilogy: unlike the previous two books, the primary audience is all who have a serious interest in the history of gender relations.

Bal is a rigorous and combative thinker who is highly critical of the unacknowledged ideological commitments of biblical scholars.[5] As a secular critic, Bal operates outside any religious ideological commitment and this gives her a degree of critical freedom not usually found in the guild of biblical scholars. Her formidable grounding in technical literary-critical theory enables Bal to offer penetrating critiques of the work of biblical scholars who enter the field of literary study of biblical texts.[6] The article 'Literature and its Insistent Other' (Bal 1989a) is a

---

4.   'Disturbing because of its violence, fascinating because of its focus on women's lives, useful because of its textual character of both historical and literary narrative, the book of Judges provides more resources for a feminist hermeneutics than I had ever hoped to find...I want to explain why the political coherence is a tool—or should I say a weapon?—in the politics of the critics: a politics of coherence' (Bal 1988b: 2-5).

5.   The Old Testament critic David Gunn, sympathetic to Bal's work, writes: 'A powerful influence since the mid-eighties has been Dutch narratologist Mieke Bal working with what was then for her an unfamiliar language (Hebrew) and text (The Bible)...Schooled in critical theory and wielding interpretive tools borrowed widely from, for example semiotics, psychoanalysis and anthropology, she has challenged biblical critics to take a broader, "interdisciplinary" view of their work' (1993: 177).

6.   Bal could be fiercely critical of both novice and master. Her review of Wesley Kort's *Story, Text and Scripture* concludes that 'the book is wrong in very basic ways' (Bal 1989a: 462), for it caricatures and colonizes literary theory, in

typically trenchant critique of the ideological agenda of Alter and Kermode in their *The Literary Guide to the Bible*; Bal accuses them of simply omitting radical and critical approaches which are uncongenial to the editors.[7] In 1989 Bal edited a collection of essays, entitled *Anti-Covenant: Counter-Reading Women's Lives in the Hebrew Bible*, which addresses the 'issue of readership as an ideological agency' (Bal [ed.] 1989: 7).

As Bal entered the 1990s her interests changed. In her article 'Murder and Difference: Uncanny Sites in an Uncanny World' (1991b), which is a response to Detweiler's appreciative paper on her work, Bal explains that she now treats 'importance of detail' as a tool to resist ideology and reiterates her 'single combat against the politics of coherence' (1991b: 11-19).

In 1991 Bal published *On Story-Telling: Essays in Narratology*, which is an illuminating collection of her essays on narratology from the previous ten years or so. The collection includes a personal critical reflection upon 'the intellectual development of their author from emphasis on the pursuit of theoretical rigour informed by French structuralism to emphasis on social, especially feminist critique, informed by American post-structuralism' (1991a: 4).[8] These essays constitute her

defence of a theological ideology under threat. Her antipathy to Sternberg's *The Poetics of Biblical Narrative* arises because 'his biblical ideology is counterproductive for critique. Left with a circular methodology he can only paraphrase' (Bal 1991a: 66).

7.   Bal reviews and severely criticizes *The Literary Guide to the Bible* for its unargued assumption of both canonical unity and the literary unity of individual biblical books; it is 'nearer to good old New Criticism'. *The Literary Guide to the Bible* excludes just about 'everything that today's literary debates are engaged with'. She concludes that 'this book should not be mistaken for what it is not. It is religious rather than literary; it provides no explicit discussion of what a literary approach can be; it does not demonstrate how a literary reading of the Bible can be useful' (1989b: 382). Bal contributes the essay 'Dealing/With/Women: Daughters in the Book of Judges' to Schwartz's *The Book and the Text* (1990), which styles itself as 'the complementary strain [to *The Literary Guide to the Bible*] whose essays are deliberately engaged in a dialogue between currents in contemporary theory—structuralism, deconstruction, semiotics, hermeneutics, feminism, psychoanalytic interpretation and political thought—and the Bible' (Schwartz 1990: 1). In her essay, Bal demonstrates how the reader, by 'naming' anonymous characters, may move beyond paraphrase of the narrative.

8.   As this collection is so convenient, references will be made to it, rather than the original date and occasion of the publication of individual essays and reviews.

farewell to narratology, as she moved on to interests in the relationship between image and perception heralded in *Reading Rembrandt* (Bal 1991c; cf. Schwartz 1990: viii).

The Critical Narratology of Mieke Bal

This introduction to Bal's narratology sketches her revised critical narratology which takes account of the change of the 'subject' from narrative agent to a 'semiotic subject'. In other respects, her revised position is the same as the exposition she offered in *Narratology*, where 'readers are offered an instrument with which they can describe narrative texts' (Bal 1985: 3).[9] Bal's thought continued to develop and she eventually moved beyond her revised narratology to a position similar to some versions of reader-response criticism.[10] For the purpose of this discussion, the version of her literary theory selected for consideration is that which is most likely to work within the theologically generated literary criteria. Consequently this study treats her critical narratology from her 'formalist' days of the 1980s. It will be argued that her narratology displays great potential and, suitably revised, it will be employed within a theological reading practice.[11]

9.   There are three important sources in English for her narratology and its subsequent refinement. The introduction to the theory is found in the article 'The Narrating and the Focalizing: A Theory of Agents in Narrative' which was republished as 'Narration and Focalization' in *On Story-Telling* (1991a: 75-108). The most systematic exposition of her theory is the 1985 study *Narratology*. Bal subsequently refined the theory in the light of her studies in semiotics. The detailed work is outside the scope of the present discussion, but there is one major change which bears directly on her narrative theory. Bal replaces the concept of 'narrative agent' with a range of 'semiotic subjects'. This development is expounded in a section of her *Femmes imaginaires* (Bal 1986), which is published in English as the essay 'Narrative Subjectivity' (in Bal 1991a: 146-70). The employment of this device is illustrated in the essays entitled *Lethal Love* (1987). Bal considers this revision very important and 'would be reluctant to publish the earlier model today without this essay ['Narrative Subjectivity'] as a companion piece' (1991a: 74).

10.   In 1991 Bal wrote of 'strategies of persuasion that are not objectively inscribed in the text, but are only vital and effective when activated by the response that brings them, so to speak, to life. Authors are also readers, and readers, writing their own (version of the) text are also authors. Working on the Bible has made me more sharply aware of precisely that. Readers of the Bible are constantly engaged in writing it. In this sense, *there is no historical text*' (1991a: 16; Bal's italics).

11.   The narrative-critical tools that are developed from a revised form of Bal's

The Model of the Narrative Text
Bal's critical narratology begins with a conceptual model of a simple, single, narrative text, in which she proposes a 'three-layer distinction—text, story, fabula...as the point of departure for the theory of narrative texts' (1985: 6).[12]

1. *Fabula: The First Layer.* The fabula comprises the elements which are related to each other in ways which are 'experienced by the reader as natural and in accordance with the world' (Bal 1985: 12). The elements include objects (actors, places and things) and processes (development, succession, change, and so on). Metaphorically, the fabula portrays the natural unfolding of events *before* they are incorporated into a story form. If these original events are not directly accessible, then they are reconstructed in the imagination by the reader through inference from the story.

2. *Story: The Second Layer.* The story describes a perspective upon the fabula, in which the elements of the fabula are woven together into an ordered formal structure under the ideological influence of the perspective of the storyteller. If there were an 'original order' to the events prior to the fabrication of the story, then the story may be considered as a 'reordered' account of those events. The order within the story allows the ideological position of the story producer or 'focalizor' to be inferred. Bal introduces her version of 'focalization' as a composite description of *what* is seen and *who* views what is seen. Bal's narrative agent is the location of the focalizor or functionary which views the fabula and reorders it into a story.

When the focalizor is imagined to be a narrative agent, conceptual confusion ensued as readers searched in vain for a narrative agent which functioned in this way. This search was particularly difficult for those whose principle model of narrative agent was a 'person'. Bal eventually adopted the semiotic subject model of the text, which was a great improvement because it avoided the unwitting personalization of the activity. The 'semiotic subject' refined the model of the narrative

critical narratology are introduced and explained in Chapter 7 of this book.
    12. The three-aspect model is also found in other narrative theories, though with a slightly different nomenclature. Genette employs *histoire, récit, narration* (1980: 26-32) and Rimmon-Kenan, *story, text* and *narration* (1983: 3).

text and clarified the contribution of the focalizing semiotic subject without any risk of overlap with other semiotic subjects.[13]

3. *Text: The Third Layer.* 'A narrative text is a text in which a narrative agent tells a story' (Bal 1985: 119). The narrative agent is the narrator, who is neither the external author nor the ideological construct of the 'implied author'; the narrator is 'the agent who utters the linguistic signs which constitute the text' (1985: 120). The narrator sees the story vision which has been constructed by the focalizor, and turns it into a narrative text. Bal is concerned to keep these two narrative agents separate, in order to clarify the different processes which are going on within the text.[14]

These three layers of fabula, story and text provide three locations for different activities within the communication process in the text. Bal's particular contribution is her refinement of the activity of focalization within the middle 'story' layer, which increases the range of analytical categories with which to 'model' the contribution of particular voices because it separates the variety of points of view embodied in the activity of narration. Genette had introduced the concept of 'focalization' in his *Narrative Discourse* when he raised the rather cryptic question whether the 'one who speaks' is 'the one who sees', with the implicit answer 'not necessarily'. Bal recognized the importance of the distinction and also the imprecision in Genette's proposal and so she critically refines it.

Metaphorically, communication moves up and down between the layers in Bal's three layered model of an ideal, simple, single text.[15]

---

13. Bronzwaer criticizes Bal's concept of focalization for the tendency of the focalizor to act like a distinct personal subject rather than a 'position': 'In Bal's theory, focalization does not only refer to the actual process of seeing or observing...but also to such processes as thinking, deliberating, judging, and in particular remembering' (1981: 193-200). Berendsen gives cautious appreciation of Bal's discussion of focalization (Berendsen 1984). The difficulty over the 'focalizor' is eventually resolved when Bal introduces the 'semiotic subject' as the subject of communication in the narrative text.

14. 'The significance of this distinction (between "narrator" and "focalizor") cannot be overestimated; credit for it belongs to Genette. Genette separated the two agents, yet without seeing that they are positioned in narrative hierarchy. While he is not the first to have differentiated the two agents (Henry James, among others did that), he is the first to have separated them in theory' (Bal 1991a: 87).

15. Bal's three-layer model for an ideal single text illuminates the practical

The original events in the fabula occur in the 'bottom layer' and are worked into a story vision by the focalizor in the middle layer. This reworking is the moment when ideology informs and shapes the story vision. Metaphorically, the focalizor does not speak, but silently selects and arranges the fabula elements. The narrator in the 'top layer' sees the story vision and transforms it into a discourse or text. The narrator's modest contribution to the meaning possibilities of the text is the exercise of choice in discourse or text-related issues such as the selection of vocabulary and style, and the distribution of names.

Bal's move to a conceptual scheme of semiotic subjects provides the precision she sought.[16] With semiotic subjects, particular contributions may be attributed much more precisely and the contrast between them is clearer. In contrast, when narrative agents speak, their discourse could include material from a different viewpoint than their own, but this material was difficult to identify and manage. The introduction of the semiotic subject scheme neatly distinguishes different aspects within a single narrative discourse.[17] *A semiotic subject is clearly not equivalent to a narrative agent, but a narrative agent can be treated as equivalent to the sum of the semiotic subjects involved.*[18]

These 'semiotic subjects' engage in signification. For every discrete semiotic contribution to the generation of meaning, a separate semiotic subject is postulated. It is useful to imagine this 'subject' to be a point from which contributions to meaning may be made, so that the semiotic subject is 'a *position*, i.e. a place where different systems intersect' (Bal

---

analysis of actual texts which are usually multi-layered, and often include layers embedded within layers.

16. 'Bal's most far-reaching and usable proposal (again a development of Genette) is for an analysis of texts according to their rendering of *narrative subjectivity*. At the simplest level, she asks of the text "who speaks? ...who sees?...who acts?" How, that is, does the text distribute amongst the narrator and the characters the functions of direct speech, narrative action and focalization?' (Castelli, Moore and Schwarz [ed.] 1995: 92; their italics).

17. Bal's approach to the 'subject' within a narrative is 'directed against two opposed views: the monologic one of classical structuralism, based on one speaker = one subject identification; and the dialogic Bakhtinian view of narrative as an unordered multitude of voices' (Bal 1991a: 1).

18. 'A concept of the *semiotic* subject will be presented as a possible mediator between textual narrative subjects, and the "real" subjects that deal with them, use them and are influenced by them' (Bal 1987: 5).

1991a: 156).[19] Logically each contribution in the realm of focalization or narration will require its own semiotic subject.

Bal's 'semiotic' move does not entail the adoption of a full semiotic analysis with its semiotic squares; instead, Bal offers a modest and focused study of the narrative subject and its communication. Bal suggests that the reader constructs meaning by attending to three separate semiotic aspects, each of which functions in its respective realm or 'layer':

1. Subject as speaker is operative when the subject speaks as a 'voice' within the realm of the discourse text.
2. Subject as focalizor is operative when a 'story vision' is generated within the realm entitled 'story'. This semiotic subject does not have a 'voice'.
3. Subject as actor is that which communicates through the medium of action, within the realm of the fabula.

The consequence of recasting the narrative text model as a web of discrete semiotic subjects is that the realism which is associated with the concept of narrative agent is now replaced by the concept of the narrative world as a semiotic web *in the guise of a realistic story*. Once the more precise semiotic contributions are 'read', they may be approximated to the previous mode of analysis in which the subject is conceived as a narrative agent. Bal successfully uses the appearance of realism as the occasion for an analysis based on the way semiotic subjects communicate in contrast to the way that real people communicate. Consequently her readings of realistic texts disclose some quite unrealistic aspects which can enhance the quality of her critical reading.[20]

---

19. Bal writes of her own work that it is 'the only narratology to my knowledge which offers an alternative to the humanistic, holistic view of the "subject as author", and which does not shun semiotic responsibility' (1991a: 73). It is argued in the previous chapter that Bal's ideological leanings may be distinguished from her general narrative theory, which then permits her model and its rigorous analysis to be used in a way which is both 'humanistic' and attends to the semiotic analysis. This is seen, for example, in the proposal to consider the activity of the narrative agent as incorporating one or more of the semiotic subjects.

20. 'Avoiding the realistic fallacy that challenges any textual aspect that does not fit a preconceived image of "reality"—a logic of realistic representation, mostly derived from nineteenth century Western "realism"—I will try to think the relation between text and reality differently. Rather than seeing the text as a transparent,

Bal is also happy to employ semiotics to inform her revision of 'truth'. Generally, Bal considers that 'truth is a way of colonizing the text, of occupying it and posing as its owner. No method whatsoever can provide the true meaning of a text, because semiotics is not dealing in truth. "Truth" in interpretation is, as in other semiotic practices, a matter of carrying conviction' (1991a: 12).

A Limitation of Bal's Model of 'Communication within the Narrative'
Bal's revised model for the narrative text provides the elements which may be present in a text and models the relationships between them. These various elements are involved in the act of communication that occurs within the text. Bal uses her three-layered model of the text to suggest that communication takes place between one layer and the adjacent layer above it in a *hierarchical* fashion, with the 'audience' of a particular semiotic subject's communication inhabiting the conceptual layer above that which the subject inhabits.

This aspect of Bal's model of communication in the text is problematic, for it confuses theoretical coherence at each of the different levels. In a coherent model, the audience for communication comprises those elements *which inhabit the same world* as the semiotic subject. The practical consequence of Bal's decision to locate the audience in a separate layer is that there is no audience for the communication in the top text layer! As the text model has a boundary beyond which are found extratextual real agents, Bal's hierarchical communication requires that for the narrator in the text layer, the audience is the extratextual audience—the real reader. Bal's proposal thus introduces a confusion of categories, for it requires an internal literary construct (the narrator) to address an external real person!

The difficulty within Bal's scheme is perfectly illustrated by her recognition that there is a narrative agent called the narratee, but she is unable to include the 'narratee' within the intratextual communication because the narrator is busy communicating with the real reader instead. Bal's scheme ends up with a redundant 'narratee! This confusion is removed if the narrative communication is modelled as having its own audience present or implied *within the layer in which the narrative subject functions*.

immaterial medium, a window through which we can glimpse reality, I see it as a figuration of the reality that brought it forth and to which it responded' (Bal 1988b: 3).

Reading the Narrative Text: The Ideological Reader
Bal's reading practice is shaped by her particular ideological concerns. One strength of Bal's scheme is its methodological clarity, for it is clear both where and how her ideology informs her reading practice. Although her interests develop through this period, she characterizes her ideology as broadly 'stemming from a...feminist philosophy and... close to radical scepticism' (1991a: 18).[21] This scepticism leads Bal to an interest in the features of the text which reveal its incoherence and facilitate its deconstruction, and so she deliberately sets out to 'read for the gaps'.[22]

Bal's approach demonstrates that 'interpretation is never objective, never reliable, never free from biases and subjectivity' (Bal 1987: 238). For Bal a *good* reading is one in which the *method* is clear and the reading is a rigorous working within the constraints of the method, even if the method fails and needs revision.[23]

Reading the Narrative Text: The Reader as Conversationalist
'Do I then claim that interpretation is text based after all? Not at all, not *based*. The text is not an object upon which we can operate; it is another subject that speaks to us' (Bal 1988b: 240). The process of reading a narrative text is likened to a conversation between the text and the reader; in the case of actual complex texts with their various voices, a conversation between the reader and the voices which she or he selects.

This approach represents an extension of the narrative communication within the text, for it now involves the extratextual real reader. This

21. 'The force of my interpretations, for example, lies in a very strong motivation which is the desire to understand the relations between gender, violence, and politics in the texts that stand at the roots of out civilization. The meaning of my interpretations, the results, are strongly affected by that force' (Bal 1987: 238).

22. Bal recognizes and attacks the 'tendency toward naturalization, that is the tendency to solve problems and interpret the text in a unifying, reassuringly "natural" way. It is quite possible that the convention of unity, so powerful in our history of criticism is seductive because of its potential to keep the disturbing uncertainty of the subject buried' (Bal 1987: 21).

23. 'The procedure of my analysis has been based on a method. Such methods do not protect us from the influence of our own private motivations. But they do allow us to formulate the findings in a discourse that is or can be made intersubjec-tive...Using the method of narrative theory as a starting point from which my initial questions could be rationally derived, I have made it possible for readers to follow the steps I took, to ask the same questions and to formulate answers that albeit different, are rationally related to the same discourse' (Bal 1988b: 239).

conversational model is one of the reasons for Bal's continued use of the concept of narrative agent when she discusses texts with other readers. The technical semiotic analysis illuminates more precisely the substance and nuances of what these narrative agents are communicating, but is subsumed in her public discussion of the text. Nevertheless, whatever it seems like to other readers, Bal's presentation is not a return to a simple realistic reading of the narratives.

Reading the Narrative Text: The Complexities of Actual Texts
Bal's model for a text provides a set of concepts that illuminate the communication which takes place in the narrative text. This introduction to these concepts is based upon the analysis of a simple, ideal narrative text. The principle feature of an *actual* narrative text is the vast range and number of semiotic subjects engaged in communication within the text.

In realistic narrative texts, this semiotic activity is encountered by the reader in the guise of narrative agents or actors interacting with one another, and with the narrator endeavouring to wrestle some kind of 'order' out of the action. Each narrative agent may make their own narrative statement or 'text' as Bal calls it. Consequently an actual narrative comprises many texts or discourses. There will be the primary narrative text produced by the narrator, and embedded within it are these agents' discourses or texts.

If what an agent says is presented in the form of reported speech, then it forms part of the discourse of the narrating agent which produces the reporting. If agents speak their own discourse, then the discourse or text which is produced is a mini-narrative text in its own right, and may be analysed accordingly. Bal employs the extratextual concept of 'levels' to assist in conceptual clarity when handling different discourses embedded within the one compound text, and these levels are not to be confused with the three layers *within* each discourse.

The first level of narrative text is the primary text produced by the narrator. The discourse of a narrative agent may be embedded within the primary text at a second level, which is metaphorically at a level 'below' the primary text.[24] When an agent speaks in their own dis-

---

24. The simple narrative text is modelled in three layers. When narrative texts are combined, Bal uses the concept of levels. When a character speaks its own discourse, that text is embedded in the primary narrator discourse at a level one step down.

course, the narrator has temporarily handed over the responsibility for the narration of the story and will reclaim it when the agent's discourse is complete. The interaction between these different discourse texts is the principal occasion for the ideological struggle within the narrative which produces the interest for the reader.

Bal states that a narrative agent may communicate through three different semiotic activities. When the agent is a character in the story, all three activities are 'in play', for characters may communicate through their narrating, their focalizing and their acting. In the case of the narrator who is not normally actively involved in the story-world, there can be no 'acting' semiotic contribution, which reduces the narrator's repertoire to two semiotic subjects. This is the case even when a character in a story subsequently becomes the narrator of the story, because when they are narrating, they are not active in the story world.

Reading the Narrative Text: The Limitation of a Critical Narratology
Bal's respect for the text is expressed in her recognition that when reading a text, the experience may demonstrate the limitation of the model of critical narratology, and require a revision or extension of the model. In the encounter between text and reading, 'the heuristics...were double edged: on the one hand, the confrontation exposed limit-cases, the places where the text seemed to obey the "rules"...on the other, transgressions, where the very disobedience produced special effects' (Bal 1991a: 12).

Bal studies at length the cases where her theory doesn't work, for 'precisely where the theory fails...the text reveals its repressed problematic...I think that theory in these cases has a...provisional status' (1991a: 13). The increasing attention which Bal gives to what she describes as 'negative heuristics' is an expression of her ideological iconoclasticism. What is significant for the present discussion is that this demonstrates the *provisionality* of her critical theory in the midst of reading practice.

Critical Narratology and the Requirements
of the Theological Reading

The five criteria established in Chapter 4 are now employed in the assessment of the suitability of Bal's critical narratology for a theological reading. The readings of biblical material which Bal produced are relentlessly iconoclastic and so it may seem unlikely that her approach may be employed within the kind of theological reading under consideration. The irony is that due to her thoroughness as a theoretician, it is clear that her readings are a consequence of the ideological concerns she brings to the reading practice and not a consequence of the approach itself.

Criterion One: A Respect for the Literary Text as a Whole
Bal's critical theory includes the potential to operate within the perspective of a 'respect for the text' in three different aspects of a critical reading.

Attention to the Whole Text. Bal respects the text when she treats the text as a whole. When working with the book of Judges, she writes 'although I do accept the heterogeneous origin of the book, I will deal with text as a whole, composed out of many sources, yet at one time— the time of final redaction—conceived of as one text' (Bal 1988b: 4). This decision does not prejudice her enquiry or suspicions about the possible coherence or unity within the text.

Prioritize the Text over Literary-Critical Theory. The second way Bal respects the text is in the juxtaposition of critical theory and the text within the reading practice. She describes her work in the early 1980s as nearer to a kind of 'neo-formalism' (Bal 1991a: 12) rather than a more philosophical approach.[25] For Bal, 'neo-formalism' expresses her endeavour to *take the text seriously*.[26] This commitment is expressed in the relationship between literary-critical theory and the text: 'for a formalist theory, the literary text is more interesting, more worthwhile than

---

25. Bal's neo-formalism owes nothing to the New Critical formalism, beyond its respect for the text in its narrative form. By way of contrast, Bal's neo-formalism includes the reader within its theoretical model. Bal's writings 'are formalist in this sense. They propose theoretical ideas and concepts which try to formulate a framework for interpretation of narratives which bridges the gap between the text in its structural complexity and its effect upon its readers' (Bal 1991a: 11). Bal later moves away from this version of narratology.

26. Bal contrasts her neo-formalism with the more philosophical approaches, which are demonstrably not subservient to the text. This concern is akin to Frei's concern about the unwarranted claims of 'general theory'.

itself' (Bal 1991a: 12).[27] This 'balance' between text and critical theory changed in her subsequent work.

Attention to All the Literary Features of the Text. The third way that Bal's proposal demonstrates a respect for the text is by attending to the widest range of literary features, which both 'construct' and 'deconstruct' the possible unity and coherence of a text. As time went by, Bal's interest diminished in those aspects of texts which 'construct' coherence, and she became overly attentive to the gaps and ambiguities of the text as an expression of her changed ideological position.

Criterion Two: Literary Reading that Is Distinct from Historical-Critical Interpretation

Bal begins her *Narratology* with a discussion of the question: which texts 'qualify' as narratives? Bal's response is to produce three 'narrative characteristics' which are generated by her narrative theory.[28] What is striking is that these are all *literary* features and that they are present in every kind of narrative, whether fictional or historical. Consequently Bal's narrative theory can inform a reading of any kind of narrative text. It was Bal's interest in the historical dimension of narrative literature that led her to forsake the French novel and to turn her critical attention to biblical narrative.

Although Bal employs her approach upon biblical texts that display some claim to a historical basis, her interest is increasingly the 'history of reception of the texts'.[29] As her thought moved on, she held that 'it

27. Bal did not continue to hold this position. Later she envisages theory and text 'as two equals speaking to each other, listening to each other, in an attempt to learn something from the encounter' (Bal 1990: 16) and acknowledges that she changed her mind. She then held that 'the theoretical text is...a co-text against which the literary text is rubbed or bumped; a collision very close to a collusion, an encounter leading to mixture. Such has been my own attitude in some of my later works' (Bal 1991a: 11).

28. Bal suggests three groups of basic criteria of narrative texts: (1) Two types of spokesman—a narrator and actors; (2) Three layers of Fabula, Story and Text are Discernible; and (3) The content of a narrative is a sequence of connected events caused or experienced by actors (Bal 1985: 8).

29. A historical interest is also practically unattainable. Bal's study of biblical criticism as she worked on biblical texts 'quickly revealed the problems of any historical statement about the context and social structure in which the texts were produced, let alone which historical factors generated them' (1991a: 16).

has never been my goal to account for *historical* meanings of the biblical narratives...because this is usually understood as the author's intention and the original audience understanding...[and] I have given up the
question of the author (intention) long ago, and turned to the reader
instead' (1991a: 15).

Nevertheless, for the purpose of this discussion, Bal successfully
demonstrates that biblical texts may be read as literary narratives
irrespective of the discussion of any historical claims associated with
the text.

Criterion Three: A Genuine Critical Freedom within the Interpretative Practice

Bal's critical narratology displays the potential for genuine critical
enquiry. Bal's close attention to the text had led critics to charge her
with formalism and to rebuke her for assumptions of 'truth disengaged
from ideology, to an objectivity which hides its subject. These are
serious charges. I deny them all' (Bal 1991a: 9). Every act of reading is
ideologically informed and the task of the critical reader is to identify
and acknowledge this aspect and ensure that such an ideological
position is open to criticism in the reading the text. Bal is quite clear
that her ideological position is open to revision in this way: 'critical
literary theory...criticises itself...it must be an open, dialogic theory'
(1990: 17).

There are two kinds of ideological influence that are suspect: that
which is covert and unacknowledged, and that which is not open to criticism and change. Unlike the New Testament narrative critics with their
ideological pre-conceptions about the unity of the Gospel narratives,
Bal argues that there can be no presumption of coherence or unity in the
text, and any such estimate must await the reading of the text.[30]

Criterion Four: The Role of the Theological Reader

Bal is dismissive of many theological readings of biblical narratives but
tireless in her emphasis that every reading is ideologically informed.

---

    30. Bal's own ideological position changes, partly as a consequence of reading
biblical narrative texts, and partly as her interest moves away from critical narratology toward reader-response analyses. By 1991 she contrasts her approach to that of
Trible's *God and the Rhetoric of Sexuality*, and claims for herself that 'the text is
already a reading, that no unambiguous reading is possible, and that the text is not
unified' (Bal 1991a: 17).

This raises the possibility that it is not theological reading per se that presents the problem for her, but the quality of the theological reading. Formally, a theological perspective is just one example of an ideological perspective that can inform a reading practice.

One recurrent reason for Bal's criticism of theological readings stems from their failure to be open to the critical process.[31] Bal commends reading practices in which the ideological component is open to criticism and possible revision as a consequence of reading the text. However some theological readings carefully insulate the theological commitments of the reader from the critical reading practice.[32]

When a reader claims that they have produced a 'truthful' reading, this generates a second set of difficulties for Bal. Ideology that is uncriticizable is bad enough, but ideology that also claims to be 'true' is even more problematic. Bal's practical reservation is that 'truth' can exercise tyrannical power over the critical freedom of the interpretative practice, but ideologically she also entertains a postmodern suspicion of the notion of truth. The practice of some Christian readers is to employ 'truth' improperly and so invite criticism, but I argue that this is not a necessary consequence of choosing to read theologically.[33] A theological reading can be genuinely critical (and so permissible) as long as it is explicit in its stance *and open to criticism and revision* through the reading of the texts.

Criterion Five: The Role of the Community of Interpretation
Bal is interested in the reception of the texts within the wider reading community and the readings which are produced in this process. The variety in these readings form part of the critical discussion, and may serve to inform and criticize a particular reading. As there is no 'definitive' reading within Bal's approach, the wider critical community assists in the determination of what constitutes a good or bad reading.

31. Some theological readings invite criticism on the grounds that they are simply bad literary-critical practice.

32. Bal's critique of Trible's *Text's of Terror: Literary-Feminist Readings of Biblical Narratives* is that 'although Trible is critical toward the characters who abuse women...Yahweh is somehow redeemed from the critique. Hence theology is saved from ideology' (Bal 1991a: 62).

33. 'The positivistic belief in models as purveyors of truth is an authoritarian ideology that, by concealing the subject, supports claims to proprietary rights over texts and meanings' (Bal 1991a: 5)

If my readers have not been able to hear the voice of the text resound in my interpretation, I have simply missed my goal, and will not be believed. Hence there is a third party in the dialogue, the witness who checks what happens and who will refuse to go along when the interpreter overwrites the text (Bal 1988b: 240).

The Potential of Bal's Critical Narratology for a Theological Reading

Bal's critical narratology opens up the process of the critical reading of narrative texts for other readers. The inner coherence of her scheme is accessible to readers who do not share Bal's ideological position. This fidelity to 'method' is one of the bulwarks against *bad* reading (Bal 1988b: 228-30). A further attraction of her critical theory is that it is 'itself open to criticism and revision'. Taken together, these two facts open up possibilities that her critical narratology can form the starting point for those who have quite different ideological commitments to Bal's radical feminism.

Consequently it is proposed that despite the ideological differences, and with some revision, the critical narratology offered by Bal respects and works sufficiently well within the five criteria of a theological reading practice to allow a revised version of this narrative theory to serve within a theological reading. The next chapter develops such a suitable theological reading practice based upon a revised form of Bal's critical narratology.

Chapter 7

A THEOLOGICAL NARRATIVE-CRITICAL READING PRACTICE

> The theory I will use, which is my own version of narratology, will be
> brought to the text as a subtext, one that speaks with or through the bibli-
> cal text, one that opens the text up, asks it questions.
>
> Bal 1990: 16

The Theological Task

'Who is the Lukan Jesus?' Frei developed a theological reading practice
to answer this question in his book *The Identity of Jesus Christ*. I start
with the same question and offer an alternative critical theological
reading of Jesus in the Lukan narrative. By working with the same text,
the contrast between these two approaches is clearly appreciated.

Chapter 6 demonstrated that Bal's critical narratology has the potential required for a theological reading. The first step in this chapter is to
revise her narratology in order that it functions within the constraints of
the theological position adopted. Once the revision is complete, this
chapter will develop a reading practice in which these theoretical categories inform the literary-critical tools used in the reading of the text.

Communication within the world of the narrative text is primarily
considered to be a 'conversation' between different narrative agents.
This conversation embraces all the communication options open to each
narrative agent, and these contributions are recognized with the help of
a 'multi-semiotic subject' type of narrative-critical analysis, in which
the reader reads for the three semiotic subjects associated with each
narrative agent. The 'narrator' and the 'characters' constitute the two
principal kinds of narrative agent with their respective critical reading
practices. This chapter introduces the reading practices for each kind of
narrative agent.

A Preliminary Decision: A Theological Ideology for a Critical Narratology

There is sufficient flexibility within Bal's critical narratology to allow for a thorough revision. The revision begins by 'reworking' her three-layer model of the narrative text by a modest redirection of the communication within each layer of the narrative. The next task is to provide a new theological ideology to guide the implementation of the critical reading practice. Bal's feminist secular sceptical ideology is replaced with the theological ideology discussed in Chapter 4 in which the biblical text is treated as 'Scripture' within the Christian community. The heuristic critical tools which are developed then open up the ideological struggle in the world of the text.[1]

The ideological 'respect for Scripture' adopted here is more 'functional' than 'substantive' and is critical of any inappropriate theological interference in the reading practice. A functional view of the scriptural text deems the text to be authoritative but does not presume to determine what the meanings of this authoritative text might be for the readers. The possible meanings of texts can only be described *after having read the text*.[2]

There is also one important practical difference in contrast to Bal's approach to the texts. Bal increasingly 'read for the gaps' as the only way to open up the ideological struggle within the world of the text. This deconstructionist tendency does not set out to be 'even-handed'. The practical expression of the ideological respect for the text commended in this discussion requires attention to *all the literary features of the texts* and not just those which are conducive to either unity or deconstruction.

The Revision of Bal's Three-Layer Model of a Simple Narrative Text

A narrative text may be considered as a collection of intratextual acts of communication. External to the text, a real life author produces the

---

1.   Bal commends approaches to the narrative texts which 'loosen up the text and our fixed assumptions about it...[and] make room for other meanings to be brought in, not as another truth but as responsible responses that address the position of the text in a social context' (Bal 1989b: 375).

2.   The 'respect for the text as Scripture' is introduced in Chapter 4 of this book.

narrative and a real reader works through the text in the process of reading. Within the narrative text, elements of the narrative structure contribute to the meanings of the narrative which the critical reader constructs. This 'ideal' model of a *simple* narrative text forms the basis for the complex narrative texts found in practice.

A Hierarchical Model of Communication within a Simple Narrative Text
A narrative text involves the four figures of the real author, the narrator, the narratee and the real reader (Fig. 1) The author and reader are external to the text, and play a separate role in the following analysis. The author is virtually inaccessible, and metaphorically, once the text is published, the text is 'orphaned'. The reader has access to just the text itself.

Real Author   Narrator———▶Narratee   Real Reader

Figure 1. *A Preliminary Description of Communication in a Narrative Text*

The narrator and narratee are intratextual narrative agents. The reader plays a key and constitutive role in the construction of these two literary intratextual agents and in 'modelling' the communication process which takes place within the 'world of the text'. The categories of 'implied author' and 'implied reader' found in some narrative theories are not required in this analysis.[3]

The development of the three-layer text model of the communication within a simple narrative text provides a powerful analytical resource for the critical reader. The model is offered as one of the ways in which a narrative text may be understood; its value will be displayed by the increased ability it gives to the reader to enter into the world of the text in a fresh, responsible, interesting and possibly persuasive way.

The three layers of activity are known as the chronicle, the story and the discourse and are named according to what is 'produced' within that layer. The narrative agents that are active within each layer are also

---

3.   Chatman includes the implied author and implied reader in his narratology (Chatman 1978: 151). Conceptually, these two entities are not narrative agents, but are ideological positions constructed retrospectively by the reader. Rimmon-Kenan correctly argues that these entities 'cannot literally be a participant in the narrative communication situation' (Rimmon-Kenan 1983: 88).

shown in the diagram. To make clear that these agents are not 'persons', in this introduction they are referred to in the third person. This model is shown in Fig. 2.

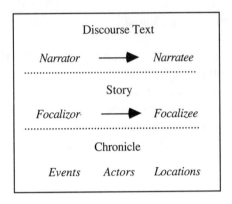

Figure 2. *The Model of a Simple Narrative Text*

The lowest layer is labelled the 'Chronicle' (instead of Bal's fabula) and comprises the different elements of a narrative, and the relationships between them. The next layer is labelled the 'Story' wherein the elements of the chronicle are taken up and processed into a story in the first stage of the processing within a narrative. This activity is performed by the 'focalizor' and is done in the light of the ideological position of the focalizor. The focalizor views the chronicle elements and weaves them into a story. To represent this 'cross-layer communication' the lines of distinction are dotted in the diagram.

The second stage of processing takes place when the story is transformed into a discourse text. The narrator performs this activity and in so doing makes its own contribution. Thus the discourse is twice processed, and disentangling these two contributions is one of the keys to reading well. The real reader encounters the discourse text and reconstructs the 'earlier' stages of the production of the narrative.

The integration of different aspects of the narrative is achieved by relating the various activities *hierarchically*. This means that the intratextual communication moves through these successive layers sequentially, starting at the chronicle layer. Within each layer there is an 'intra-layer' communication, in which a 'product' is *produced for the 'audience' within that layer*. This product may also be 'viewed' (though not influenced) by narrative agents in an adjacent and 'higher' layer. For example, in the story layer, the focalizor views the chronicle of events and processes them into the product which is described as story. In effect, this textual model offers a division of labour between narrative agents of tasks which are popularly thought to be performed by a single agent.

The kind of theological respect for the Gospel texts that is chosen here entails a respect for the literary form of these texts; this inevitably becomes an interest in narrative because the texts display features which suggest a narrative form. Consequently this reading practice may be classified as an example of contemporary neo-formalist literary criticism.[4]

Narrative Agent and Semiotic Subject: The Best of Both Worlds
Bal's three-layer text model includes a narrative subject operating within each layer. In her first version of the scheme, Bal chose 'narrative agents' to function as the narrative subjects, and they display a close resemblance to real life people. In her revision, she replaces narrative agents with semiotic subjects which provide greater clarity and precision *but are not directly comparable to 'people'*. Both schemes provide useful insights for the reader and are employed in the present reading practice.

This approximation of 'narrative subject' to real people allows readers to construct a believable and humane world as they read, and so this approximation is developed as the basic paradigm within which other approaches make their contribution. The analytical potential of this basic scheme is limited and so it is called a 'descriptive scheme'.

In Bal's later 'multi-semiotic subject' scheme, the narrative subject is not an entity but a semiotic position. This semiotic scheme can contribute to the descriptive scheme when all three basic possibilities of

---

4.   'Formalist literary criticism' in both its New Critical and structuralist instances rests upon the assumption of a 'modern' neutral reader producing 'objective' studies, which 'hide the subject'. The kind of neo-formalism which encompasses the approach offered here is well described by Bal: 'formalism proposes theoretical ideas and concepts which try to formulate a framework for interpretations of narratives which bridge the gap between text in its structural complexity and its effect upon its readers...such a theory aims at an encounter with the literary text...as a heuristic tool that helps to illuminate the literary text, which it appears to subject to itself, but to which in fact is subjected. For formalist theory, *the literary text is more interesting, more worthwhile than itself*' (Bal 1991a: 11-12; my italics).

semiotic communication are combined together to approximate to a narrative agent.

Both the descriptive and the semiotic schemes are versions of the activity of narrative subjects in the text and both employ the three-layer model to map the locations of these activities. As two similar but conceptually distinct schemes are used together a clear nomenclature is adopted. The convention is that narrative subjects within the 'descriptive scheme' are narrative agents and are labelled with a *noun* (e.g. narrative agent, narrator, character, focalizor, Jesus, and so on). The activity of these agents is also described using a noun (e.g. focalization, narration). The three kinds of narrative agent are 'actor' (which in the processing becomes a 'character'), 'focalizor' and 'narrator'. Whereas the narrator and characters may appear in a 'people-like way' in the narrative, the focalizor is a purely imaginary and temporary fiction introduced for the convenience of managing one aspect of narration. As Bal discovered, the mixing of agents can lead to conceptual confusion.

In the 'multi-semiotic subject' scheme the narrative subject is denoted with a *present participle*, qualified with the word 'subject' (e.g. narrating subject, focalizing subject). Furthermore, the semiotic activity in the text is described using the present participle alone (e.g. narrating, focalizing, acting). In this scheme all three semiotic subjects exist as points or locations of activity and may be constructed by an analysis of the communication within the text.

The two conceptually distinct schemes may be related by considering an *equivalence of function* between the narrative agent engaged in communication and the semiotic subjects engaged in communication. This equivalence provides the basis for the integration of insights generated under the multi-semiotic subject scheme into a reading which is governed by the descriptive scheme.

In practice an active narrative agent is considered to be the 'location' of the activity of the three associated semiotic subjects. The interaction between these three semiotic contributions when attributed to a single narrative agent is full of interest, because they do not always 'fit together' as might be expected.

The Three-Layer Text Model of an Ideal Simple Narrative Text
The chronicle aspect of a simple narrative text. The chronicle aspect of the narrative text treats the elements of the narrative from the

perspective of an interest in their relations with one another.[5] The elements comprise the *events*, the *actors* involved in events and the *locations* where the events take place.[6] The focus upon the structure of relations leaves the task of the 'development' of these elements to the next layer or stage. An example of this is when the focalizor develops the story aspect of the narrative text. The chronicle is 'a series of logically and chronologically related events that are caused or experienced by actors' (Bal 1985: 5).

The chronicle aspect treats the primary relationships between the elements *before*, metaphorically, the focalizor processes them into a story form. This structure of relations is reconstructed from the narrative text by the critical reader, and so is not 'objective' because different readers do this in their own particular ways. The task of reading well seeks a consensus among critical readers.

Most readers assume a homology between the elements within the chronicle and the reader's experience of the real world. Thus actors are assumed to behave similarly to real people, and argument and logic is assumed to work in the same way in both worlds. Time is assumed to pass in the chronicle world in the same way as in the real world.[7] The value of the hypothetical construction of the chronicle is that it provides the datum against which the reworked material in the story form may be contrasted.

In practice, the ability of a reader to construct the chronicle dimension is limited by the indicators within the text. As a preliminary move,

---

5.   The term 'chronicle' is chosen rather than Bal's 'fabula' because it describes these two important elements: (1) the temporal ordering and (2) the pre-story stage in the process of narration. There is the further attraction for students of the Gospels that whereas the term 'fabula' drawn from Russian formalism evokes but is not literarily equivalent to the fable or imaginative world of Propp's folk stories, so 'chronicle' evokes but is not equivalent to those writings which are 'the predecessors of modern histories' (Abrams 1988: 26).

6.   These concepts have been introduced briefly in the consideration of both New Testament narrative criticism (Chapter 5) and in the discussion of Bal's critical narratology (Chapter 6). The present discussion develops these ideas further as part of the preparation for the construction of a theological reading practice later in this chapter.

7.   'Most [chronicles] can be said to be constructed according to the demands of human "logic of events" provided that this concept is not too narrowly understood. "Logic of events" may be defined as a course of events that is experienced by the reader as natural and in accordance with the world' (Bal 1985: 12).

the reader may identify the two kinds of 'narrative element' which form the structural web of relationships: (1) the dynamic components which comprise the events, and (2) the static components which are the actors and the locations.[8]

Events are dynamic in that change is associated with them and so a temporal dimension is sought alongside any possible logical or causal relationships. In a critical reading practice, the reader's first task is to identify which are the key events in the narrative. Some readers follow Barthes and distinguish between events which are necessary for the thrust of the narrative (labelled 'kernels'), and those events whose removal does not fundamentally change that thrust (labelled 'satellites').[9] However, this distinction is of limited use when reading the Gospel texts due to the way their narratives are structured.

The temporal ordering of events in the chronicle of a realistic narrative such as the Gospels may be considered as a chronological sequence, with time imagined as linear and directional. For other texts, it need not be so, and it is acknowledged that to assume time is linear in Gospel studies invites the charge of ideological intervention: 'linearity in narrative is as crucial a facet of meaning-production as it is illusory as a fact' (Bal 1991a: 2).[10] The debate whether a linear view of time is *only* an ideological construct continues. For this discussion I consider that the reading practice is not prejudiced by a provisional acceptance of the view.

The narrative subject active within the chronicle aspect of the text is the actor, and the range of activity open to it is limited to initiating or

8.   Logically it is possible for both an agent and a location to develop and thus change as narrative time passes, and so the distinction between dynamic and static components is merely provisional, until the specifics of the text require its revision.

9.   The distinctions between kernels and satellites was introduced by Barthes. The distinction between events produces a 'logic of hierarchy' (Chatman 1978: 52).

10.   The linearity of time is not unproblematic, for it can be argued that 'the enlightenment ideology of progress is projected in a sense upon the linearity of the structure of narrative, and the notion of the non-coincidence of the fabula [equivalent to chronicle in my revision—D. Lee] and the story, criticisable as it is in many ways, is valuable if only because it drives home the arbitrariness of that ideology' (Bal 1991a: 2). Tambling argues that 'Our understanding of time as linear is itself a representation with strong ideological associations…there is no original real-life time against which we can check narrative time' (1991: 88). It is doubtful whether the linearity and directionality of time originates as Enlightenment ideology; it is more likely to be an aspect of an attenuated Christian theological legacy.

participating in events. This activity produces a sequence of events called the chronicle, which is 'viewed' by the focalizor and which forms the 'raw material' for the focalizor's activity of processing the chronicle into a story using a variety of literary options.

In semiotic subject terms, each narrative agent can be the location of up to three semiotically significant activities. At the chronicle layer, actors only communicate by 'acting'. The category 'actors' includes all the elements within the narrative world which participate in the action, both personal and impersonal.[11]

Locations are the narrative spaces where the events take place. Initially, 'locations' denotes the spatial location of an action in a way analogous to the set used by players in the theatre. The primary contribution at this stage is found in the structural contrast between locations, as in foreground and background, inside and outside, and 'a special role may be played by the boundary between opposed locations' (Bal 1985: 45). The concept of 'locations' is developed in this proposal to include the spatial places together with temporal and social locations.[12]

The story aspect of a simple narrative text. The ability to distinguish and discuss the 'story' aspect of the narrative text required for Bal the invention of the fictitious focalizor as an imaginary necessity. The task of the focalizor is to represent the activity through which the chronicle is transformed into a story. 'If one regards the [chronicle] primarily as the product of *imagination*, the story could be regarded as the result of *ordering*' (Bal 1985: 49). Within the allocation of the functions in this model, the focalizor is restricted to the ability to 'show' the story by the production of a 'story-vision'; the focalizor does not 'speak' with a voice, but instead informs the narrator, who then may speak.

The focalizor metaphorically 'sees' the events of the chronicle and

11. In the chronicle, the actor is appreciated for its function within the web of relationships in which it finds itself. Structuralist narratology tends to reduce characters to functionaries or agents within the structure of the narrative, and fails to develop the substantial dimension to the category of actor. (For further discussion of the distinction between 'actor' and 'character' cf. Chatman 1978: 108-16.) Chatman argues that structuralist studies of character are inadequate and introduces his own proposal for character (1978: 107-38; cf. Mosher 1980: 175). In my proposal the 'fleshing out' of the actor into a character is carried out in the focalization layer of the text model, in a process of 'characterization'.

12. 'The setting of a narrative...is the general locale, historical time and social circumstances in which the action occurs' (Abrams 1988: 172).

composes a story from them, through the selection and ordering of actors and events, and all this informed by particular ideological interests of the focalizor's point of view. The critical reader traces this 'ordering' and infers what ideological position is likely to have informed this particular way of processing the chronicle material. Bal considered that the 'silent' focalizor is very influential as it exercises 'the most important, most penetrating and most subtle means of manipulation' (Bal 1985: 116).[13]

The significance of the focalizor is the fact that *the focalizor is not the narrator*. When the narrator narrates the perception of the focalizor's story vision, the narrator actually speaks the focalizor's vision in the narrator's language, and thus there are two distinct perspectives at work within the narrated text.

In this analysis, the focalizor is considered to have a repertoire of literary devices reserved for it as it produces the story-vision, which include:

(1)   The selection, ordering and pacing of events. These may be identified by contrasting the story treatment of the events with the hypothetically reconstructed chronicle of the same events (a contrast first developed in Russian literary formalism and later 'mapped' by Genette[14]). This is more problematic than expected, due to the ideological implications of the assumed linearity of time.[15]

13. Bal demands that 'analyses of newspaper reports which aim at revealing the hidden ideology embedded in such reports should involve focalization in their investigation, and not restrict themselves to content analysis' (1985: 116).

14. Narrative discourse as a text-type may be characterized by a doubly temporal logic or 'chrono-logic' (Chatman 1990a: 9) comprising movement through time both in the chronicle dimension and the story dimension. The analysis of the relationships between these two 'kinds' of times in Genette's *Narrative Discourse* has been widely adopted, and is followed here. Genette drew attention to the relative differences of order, duration and frequency in the story form when contrasted to the imagined regular unfolding of time as events occur in the chronicle. Story time is easily accessible in the length of time given to different scenes and discourses within the discourse text, while chronicle time is reconstructed from the narrative on the basis of a homology with our everyday experience of time.

15. Barbara Herrnstein Smith correctly identifies the basic assumption that 'temporal disparities or anachronies will appear especially noteworthy only to the extent that one expects them to be otherwise; only, in other words, if one expects these two time orders to be conformant, equivalent, synchronic or otherwise *corre-*

(2)   The development of the actors into characters. These 'agents-in-relation' of the chronicle are now 'filled out' through the process of literary characterization which can happen directly, indirectly and cumulatively. In the present analysis the focalizor is considered to be responsible for the decision whether to let characters speak their own discourse, or merely have it reported. This convention respects the major ideological significance of these decisions, and in the proposed distribution of responsibilities, the focalizor is the ideological contributor. The importance of the ideological dimension—as distinct from the contribution of the narrator—explains the invention of the fictitious focalizor, for this narrative subject isolates and manages the ideological dimension within the narrator's discourse.

The decision about 'who might speak their own discourse' is conventionally attributed to the narrator. As will be seen in the next section, the 'multi-semiotic' model of a text brings more analytical precision into play, and is able to distinguish two activities going on which approximate to the activity of the narrator. This analysis leads to the very useful but curious practical distinction between the narrator's focalizing and the narrator's narrating. This semiotic revision makes workable the insight which gave birth to the fictitious focalizor.

The discourse aspect of a simple narrative text. The narrator is the narrative agent responsible solely for the production of the discourse text. In the present scheme, the narrator has a modest influence upon the final form of the narrative because the big decisions about the ordering material and who may speak their own discourse are attributed to the focalizor. The narrator produces the discourse, which in the present

---

spondent...Such an expectation of conformity is encouraged and supported by a conception of discourse ['story' in my model—D. Lee] as consisting of sets of discrete signs which, in some way *correspond to* (depict, encode, denote, refer to and so forth) sets of discrete and specific ideas, objects or events. It is precisely such a conception...that dominates contemporary narrative theory, and it is the dualism at the heart of the model of language that provides the scaffolding for the two-levelled model of narrative' (Smith 1981: 221). For Smith, temporal linearity is an ideological import into the process of interpretation. She offers instead a model of language as 'verbal response to various sets of conditions'. In reply, Chatman points out that the distinction between the discourse text level and the narrative events is inherent within the nature of narrative (1980b: 263).

study of the Gospels is produced as a discourse text. The word 'voice' is attributed to this agent, although in fact the narrator is a linguistic functionary and not a person.

The narrator is allocated the following functions:

(1)	the selection of the actual language and style used to 'recount' the story;

(2)	the insertion of 'commentary' within the narrative. This literary device often draws attention to the presence of a narrator at work;

(3)	the management of description within the narrative, including the decisions about the employment of names and titles of characters.

In recent narratology, studies of the act of narration are often theoretically underpowered and amount to an empirical list of stratagems open to the narrator.[16] The inclusion of a semiotic subject analysis within the present scheme significantly increases the potential usefulness of the study of narration. In a semiotic subject analysis, the narrator is a narrative subject whose activities include the two semiotic activities of 'focalizing' and 'narrating'. The narrator does not act within the story-world, and so in a semiotic analysis the narrator model has no 'acting' semiotic subject in operation.

The narrating subject is the only narrative agent with a 'voice', and logically—as with the voice of a person—the narrating subject can only speak in the first person.[17] The common yet mistaken impression of 'third-party narration' occurs when the presence of the narrator is not recognized. 'As soon as there is language, there is a speaker who utters it' (Bal 1985: 121) and so every report 'in the third person' is actually produced by a voice in the first person. However, the narrating subject may be 'invisible', which helps create the illusions of 'third party'

16.	There is limited value in schemes that classify the various types of narrator, a limitation which applies to all global typological schemes.

17.	The traditional distinction between first- and third-person narration is a mistaken analysis of a literary feature within the narrative text. In the example 'Jesus spoke to the crowds', the character Jesus does not produce the text; instead there is an unacknowledged narrator, who can be recognized when a phrase such as 'I tell you' is temporarily prefixed to the sentence. 'From a grammatical point of view, (the narrator) is *always* a "first person" In fact, the term "third-person narrator" is absurd' (Bal 1985: 122).

narration and of immediacy as the story unfolds.[18]

The recognition that subjects can only speak in the first person has a further important consequence. When the narrator requires a character to speak, there are two options available. The narrator may either report the speech, or allow the character to speak in its own words. When the latter happens, the narrator has temporarily handed over the task of narration to the character.[19] In effect, the character becomes a narrator for a time, and a 'mini-narrative' is embedded within the primary narrative.

In a text model based upon a communication model, the significance of the communication hinges upon who said it *and to whom it was said*. Consequently it is important to identify the particular audiences addressed by the various narrative communications. When reading a character, this is an obvious requirement because characters communicate specific things in the light of the audience they address. It is a little different in the case of the narrator for there is only ever one audience and that is the invisible narratee.

Simple and Complex Narrative Texts
The 'ideal' simple text model used so far helpfully introduces different aspects of the analysis. In practice, texts are neither ideal nor simple. Two aspects of narrative texts which are frequently found in actual texts are briefly introduced here.

Mixed texts. The narratologist Seymour Chatman suggests that there are three fundamental types of material incorporated into a narrative texts: description, argument and narrative.[20] In practice, each group includes

18. Chatman initially proposed the idea of 'non-narrated stories' to explain the invisible narrator (Chatman 1978: 166-72); he later and correctly abandoned the idea as 'a contradiction in terms' (Chatman 1990: 115).

19. This simple distinction was developed by Bal into a powerful critical tool. 'The narrator does not narrate continually. Whenever direct speech occurs in the text, it is as if the narrator temporarily transfers this function to one of the [characters]. When describing the text (level) it is thus important to ascertain *who* is doing the narration' (1985: 8). When an actor speaks a separate discourse, the actor functions temporarily as a narrator. This convention establishes a hierarchy of levels within a complex narrative text. For Bal this concept achieves the variety of subjects which structuralist narratology fails to include, and avoids the unordered and unrelated 'carnival' of subjects of Bakhtinian analysis.

20. Some argue for a fourth category 'exposition', but Chatman successfully

material in which a particular type of narrative material predominates, for all texts are actually 'mixed texts'.

If construed as a 'descriptive' classification, these three types of material do not advance analysis very far. If, instead, the *function* of these parts of the text is the distinguishing criterion, what may be described as description or argument may have a different and more insightful role in the narrative.

Embedded texts. When a character in the narrative speaks in their own voice, they produce a 'mini-narrative' which is embedded within the main narrative. These embedded discourses function at different levels within the primary discourse, and so introduce the aspect of narrative 'levels'.

The primary level is the narrator's discourse, within which there are embedded character discourses, which may constitute complete narratives in themselves. If a character's discourse includes another character speaking in the first person, then there is a second embedded discourse within the first embedded discourse text.

As each 'first person' voice produces a discourse in the form of a narrative text, the analytical approach to the simple narrative text developed above may be applied to the embedded text as if it is a free-standing discourse text in its own right. The distinction and relationship between the primary narrative and the embedded narrative is an important area of investigation for it throws light upon otherwise confusing texts.

The Critical Practice of Reading for the Semiotic Subjects

The 'descriptive' analysis of characters speaking and interrelating within the world of the text is greatly improved by the precision and analytical power of the 'multi-semiotic subject' approach, and so the multi-semiotic approach is used as the first stage in a critical reading practice of a narrative text. There are three kinds of semiotic subject, and for each of which there is a particular reading strategy. When the reader has completed reading for these aspects of the narrative, they are integrated into the second stage of reading for the narrative agents of narrator and character using a descriptive scheme.

argues that exposition is not a fundamental category, but rather a composite of argument and description (1990a: 6).

1. *Reading for the 'Acting' Semiotic Subject*

As the name suggests, the contribution of this semiotic subject is made through the activity it engages upon or finds itself caught up in. Within a narrative, there is no possibility for the representation of a character's action 'firsthand' in the way that it is possible to embed a character discourse. The activity of all characters is mediated through the narration. The reader trusts the narrator to describe and report this activity reliably—at least until the point at which this reliability is called into question.

For a character, all three semiotic subjects can come into play. As the narrator when narrating cannot also be involved in action, the narrator cannot communicate through the first semiotic activity of 'acting'.

2. *Reading for the 'Focalizing' Semiotic Subject*

Focalizing encompasses two related aspects. The focalizing subject assumes an *ideological position* or viewpoint, and from there, constructs a *vision* of the story. In a critical reading of the narrative, the identification of the focalizing position is deduced from the vision of the story which is present in the narrative. Occasionally, the focalizing position is identified by a declaration that it is situated in a character. For example, the narrator makes clear the focalizing position is within the crowd when he relates that '[Jesus] was praised by everyone' (Lk. 4.15). One of the most powerful contributions focalizing brings is the ability to distinguish between the character location and the ideological location, so that what is said is not assumed to be said from the point of view of the character who speaks the discourse.

The first stage in reading for the focalizing subject is to establish the vision of events constructed by the focalizing subject, and after that enquire about the ideological significance of the story vision. The vision of events is conveyed through a repertoire of literary devices which 'process' the narrative elements into the 'vision' of the story. This construction of the vision develops the events into a sequence, the agents into characters, and the locations into significant places.

Some discussions of focalizing in narrative texts seem to be a mixture of the empirical and the intuitive rather than inductive. For the sake of clarity, the following literary features are employed to characterize the vision of the story:

The order of the presentation of the narrative elements. The order of the presentation may become significant when the order is unexpected

by the reader. In the Gospel narratives which include a degree of interest in chronology, a different order from the reader's chronological
expectation opens up new possibilities of meaning.

The temporal treatment of the events. 'Narrative time' is the time taken
to recount the scene. One of its significances is based on the premise
that the time allocated to a narrative unit is a key to its importance. In
literary criticism, narrative time may be measured by the number of
words used in the narrative unit. Such a word count has no absolute
value; its usefulness lies in the *comparative* temporal relationship it
reveals.[21]

It is useful to contrast the time an event takes in the narrative with the
time taken by that event in the chronicle, where events are assumed to
take place in a way and at a speed which is the same as experienced by
the reader in the everyday world (unless the text signals to the reader
that this is not the case). The focalizing subject has the ability to vary
the pace of the story events, with the implication of an associated
significance. The slower the speed, the more attention is asked of the
reader, which suggests increased importance. The distribution of temporal exposure in the narrative furnishes a clue to the ideology of the
focalizing subject.

The presentation of character discourse. Although conventionally
subsumed under the narrator's tasks, the decision whether to report or
embed a character's discourse influences whether and to what extent
importance is attributed by the focalizing subject to the discourse, and
indirectly to the character concerned. Although clearly the substance of
a character's discourse includes the contribution of that character, in
this scheme it is the focalizing subject which decides whether a character is allowed to speak.[22]

---

21. For further discussion of 'Word Counts' see the discussion in section 3 of
Appendix B, 'Preliminary Studies for a Theological Reading Practice'.
22. An embedded discourse is a mini-narrative, which employs the literary
stratagems of narrative discourse to construct its meanings. When it is embedded,
the mini-narrative also makes a semantic contribution to the primary discourse in
which it is embedded. When the narrator temporarily 'hands over the stage' to the
character discourse, it signals that a different narrator is in action. It does not mean
that the primary narrator ceases to manage the contribution of the character through
its embedded discourse.

In this thesis it is considered that a character discourse which is embedded signals an increased importance for the focalizing subject in contrast to the presentation of the discourse as reported speech. Generally it is the case that readers pay more attention to an embedded discourse than to a report.

The contribution of the 'Report and Embed' literary pattern. The 'report and embed' pattern is a special case of the possibilities of presentation of character discourse. The pattern is used sparingly and tellingly in the Gospel narratives. In this scheme a dialogue between two characters occurs and the focalizing subject places emphasis upon the contribution of one character by embedding their discourse and merely reports the contribution of the other character.[23] As the embedded discourse attracts greater attention, this literary pattern further emphasizes this importance by the contrast between the two discourses in the dialogue.

The orchestration of different discourses. Focalizing contributes to the characterization of a character through the orchestration of the voices which comment upon the character. The key to the evaluation of such occurrences is the reliability and authority which is attributed to the particular voices, for there is a hierarchy in any complex narrative text, and once the reader has established which are the 'reliable' voices, they are accorded particular attention.

---

23. Rimmon-Kenan correctly argues that all representation of speech is a form of narration or diegesis, even when the use of a separate embedded discourse creates the illusion of mimesis. She instances McHale's proposal of seven types of representation within this diegetic spectrum (Rimmon-Kenan 1983: 106-116). Nevertheless, the pattern of 'report and embed' makes a particular contribution which is dependent upon the distinction between the two types of discourse and their mutual relation. I have been unable to trace work on this feature in the Gospel narratives. As a preliminary and descriptive comment, I suggest that the embedded discourse attracts particular attention, and thus signals an emphasis of the focalizing subjects. In the Gospel narrative there are three types of representation: (1) summary of the speech act (e.g. 'He began to teach in their synagogues' [4.15]); (2) summary of the act and the content of the speech (e.g. 'the crowds wanted to prevent him from leaving them. But he said...' [4.43]); and (3) the separate embedded character discourse.

The significance of the locations. The narrative context of discourses includes the contribution of the location, which includes geographical, social and temporal dimensions. As a story unfolds the associations of particular locations are established in the narrative world and contribute to the possible meanings for the reader.

3. *Reading for the 'Narrating' Semiotic Subject*

The narrating subject is responsible for the production of the narrative text, which includes the responsibility for the choices about what appears in the final text. Although the focalizing has produced the presentation of the story, there are still some decisions left to the subject which produces the final discourse.

Language and style. The study of the language and style of the discourses makes a particular contribution to the communication by the narrating subject. These contributions are established by the reader in the process of reading the text.

The name and the titles. In contemporary narratology the function of the *name* of a character is just beginning to attract the attention of narrative theorists. In part, this lacuna could be due to structuralist emphases upon general structure and function rather than developing discussions of characterization.

The significance of the presence or absence of names in the Gospel narratives makes various contributions for the reader. In the reading of biblical texts, 'more often than not Biblical names have a meaning [and] if they don't have one, they are assigned one in the text's afterlife. Far from being sheerly deictic, like names in Western culture, they have a specific meaning that integrates the character into its life, and that can also imprison it there' (Bal 1987: 73). There is the converse 'problem of anonymity...[because] no names, [means] no power' (Bal 1991a: 19). Such preliminary assessments require further discussion in the light of the cultural and literary conventions of the historical contexts in which the texts were produced.

The contribution of narrative commentary. Narrative commentary is the moment in a narrative text when the action pauses while the usually invisible narrating subject communicates in its own right to the semiotic 'narratee'. Narrative commentary is inserted to offer extra information or evaluation upon a story as it unfolds. Narrative commentary also indirectly illuminates what kind of audience the narrating subject has in view.

Strategy for Reading for the Narrator and for Narrative Characters

The contribution of the narrator is identified by the reader first attending to the two distinct semiotic activities which comprise the production of a narrative—the focalizing of the story and the narrating of that story as discourse text. The activity of these two semiotic subjects then combines to produce the functionally 'equivalent' act of narration in the descriptive model of the text. Reading for the narrator involves beginning by reading for the focalizing activity, which is followed by reading for the narrating activity.

The reader's construction of a character is a more complex affair. A character is the aggregate of the narrative descriptions of the character, and these can be supplied by any narrative agent. Within the world of the text, there may be many narrative agents who through their own discourse or their activity wish to offer their perception of a particular character. Both the narrator and other story characters can contribute to the characterization of the character. All these perceptions are taken up in the process of the reader reading for the character. The result is that the reader's construction of character is a complex, cumulative and aggregative affair which lasts as long as the whole of the narrative.

Furthermore, a story character may make their own contribution to their characterization, either by contributing a character discourse, or perhaps more usually by performing some activity which has implications for the significance of the character. This exercise in 'self-characterization' is clearly seen in the way that Jesus conducts himself in the Gospel stories.

There are three extra aspects to the reader's process of building a character. First, the contribution of a particular story character is usually made to a particular audience within the world of the text, and this qualifies what the character communicates. *Character discourses are audience-specific*, and the critical reader takes this into account when studying such contributions.

The second issue is that the reader needs to form a judgment about the reliability of what is offered as characterization within the story. Although the New Testament Gospels do not major on the unreliability of characters, it is still important to decide how much weight to give to what is discovered in the narrative, for what is said by various characters is not equally reliable.

The third area that requires the reader's attention is the significance of the distinction between the narration and focalization which takes place within a character discourse. Within a single discourse there can be several focalizations, and these are the most influential single feature in a narrative-critical analysis. As readers distinguish which focalizations are operative, so the ideological implications come into view. Chapter 11 displays a quite surprising reading of the demons, in which the identification of the focalizations at work both explains some curious narrative features and makes a significant contribution to the characterization of Jesus.

The Mutual Criticism of Readers' Ideology and the Text

Bal's fiercest criticism is reserved for theological readers who fail to allow a genuine critical freedom within their reading practice. The issue is sufficiently important to be one of the five core criteria developed in Chapter 4, and Bal's narrative theory is chosen in part because it procedurally incorporates the potential for a 'genuine critical freedom in respect of the reader and the text'. How is this achieved in practice?

This study takes up Frei's suggestion of the modest and minimal use of theory and reworks it. As explained in Chapter 4, a 'theologically informed literary criticism' can formally include genuine critical freedom when the reading act is recast as an interrogative exercise. The reader thereby acknowledges both the provisionality of their present understanding and also an openness to persuasion during the reading task before them.

In this way the reader and text are open to a mutual critical engagement. In the kind of theological reading commended here, which asserts a primacy of text over reader, this openness to change on the part of the reader is particularly appropriate. The readings produced through this interrogative approach should be characterized by explicit ideological commitments, a provisional status and a welcome for public inspection and debate.

Part III
STORIES OF JESUS IN THE GOSPEL OF LUKE

Chapter 8

PREPARATIONS FOR A PRELIMINARY
THEOLOGICAL NARRATIVE-CRITICAL READING

'Who is the Lukan Jesus?' This question is now brought to the Gospel text by a theological reader in an interrogative narrative-critical reading. The narrative-critical approach developed in the last chapter is used to analyse some of the narrative agents active in the narrative, whose contributions are constructed by reading each agent with categories drawn from the multi-semiotic subject model of the text. The Lukan Jesus identified by the reader is the composite figure produced by the interaction of the contributions of these various agents.

In this preliminary and ground-breaking study, the Lukan Jesus is constructed through the contributions of three narrative agents: the narrator, Jesus and the demons. This reading of the Gospel of Luke attends to some but not all aspects of the narrative, and so does not offer a complete portrait of the character of the Lukan Jesus. Nevertheless these three narrative agents are chosen to show the promise of such an approach.

This chapter begins with a consideration of character and characterization in the Gospels, goes on to introduce the Lukan text which is used, then sets out two complementary descriptive analyses of the Gospel and concludes with a discussion of how the character discourses will be analysed.

Chapter 9 begins with a reading of the narrator's characterization of Jesus. In Chapter 10 there is a reading of Jesus' self-characterization, and in Chapter 11 is a reading of the contribution of the minor character 'the demons' to the characterization of Jesus. These different perceptions of Jesus are then discussed in Chapter 12.

Character and Characterization in the New Testament Gospels

New Testament literary-critical studies draw upon secular literary theory and criticism for their interpretative tools. In the study of character and characterization this is not easy, for in secular studies there is still much work to be done.[1] At present (at the end of the 1990s) there is no generally accepted theoretical treatment of character, but instead a range of disparate approaches to the subject.[2]

The spectrum of conceptual possibilities for character ranges from literary character as 'textual function' to literary character as a '(fictional) person'.[3] At one end of the spectrum, character as 'textual functionary' draws on the analytical work of narratologists such as Bal and endeavours 'not to *determine* (define) the characters (*who* are they?), but to *characterize* them (*what* are they and how do we find out?)' (Bal 1985: 80; her italics). For Bal, whose roots include structuralism, literary characters are not like real people because they are

---

1.   'It is remarkable how little has been said about the theory of character in literary history and criticism' (Chatman 1978: 107); 'The elaboration of a systematic, non-reductive but also non-impressionistic theory of character remains one of the challenges poetics has not yet met' (Rimmon-Kenan 1983: 29). In his recent survey of narrative theories, Martin claims that even the achievement of Chatman and Rimmon-Kenan 'needs to be supplemented by more radical theories that redefine the very idea of character (1986: 120). John Frow comments that 'the concept of character is perhaps the most problematic and the most under-theorized of the basic categories of literary theory' (Frow 1986: 227). Writing in 1990, John Knapp agrees, for 'until quite recently, the construct in various hermeneutic theories and literary criticism known as character has been neglected in literary studies (1990: 349).

2.   In the discussion of literary character, one spectrum ranges from character as textual feature to character as representation of real people. 'Proceeding along a scale which extends from signifier to signified or textuality to representation, one can distinguish four theoretical models of literary character in current poetics, each of which serves as an explication of one aspect of our intuitions in this area. The four are (A) character as topic entity of a discourse, (B) character as artificial construct or device, (C) character as thematic element, and (D) character as non actual individual in some fictional (possible) world' (Margolin 1990: 454). Fishelov offers a different spectrum of 'types' to account for a similar range of possibilities (1990: 422-39).

3.   The spectrum ranges between points sometimes described as the 'purist' and 'realist' positions (Burnett 1993: 3).

'imitation, fantasy, fabricated creatures: paper people without flesh and blood' (1985: 80).

Structuralist characters are functional elements of the narrative, and characterization means the construction of the character from 'repetition, accumulation, relations to other characters and transformations' (Bal 1985: 86). However, Bal concedes that 'characters resemble people...[and that] no one has yet succeeded in constructing a complete and coherent theory of character is probably because of this human aspect' (1985: 80).[4]

The other end of the spectrum is typified by the descriptive approach that developed in North American literary criticism and is represented by Chatman's eclectic 'open' theory of character. Chatman drew upon structuralist thought in most of *Story and Discourse*, apart from his discussion of character. Contrary to the functional approach of structuralist analysis, Chatman proposes that 'a viable theory of character should preserve openness and treat characters as autonomous beings, not as mere plot functionaries' (1978: 119). 'I argue—unoriginally but firmly—for a conception of character as a paradigm of traits; 'trait' in the sense of 'relatively stable or abiding personal quality' (1978: 126).

In New Testament studies, which tend to lag behind their secular literary sources, it is even more the case that discussions of character and characterization are at a preliminary stage.[5] In the various journals, work on Mark and Matthew is under way[6] and Lukan studies are

4.   Bal's own attempt to do this by mapping 120 structural possibilities of combinations of characteristics is neither simple enough to be workable, nor particularly illuminating. It is interesting to note that she moved away from this position and in her work on biblical narratives used an approach that was more 'realist'.

5.   In 1993, the journal *Semeia* devoted Issue 63 to the topic of 'Characterization in Biblical Literature'. 'One common theme of these essays is that the theory of characterization is underdeveloped and underutilized, both in literary studies generally and in biblical literary criticism in particular. Several of the authors declare a need for more sophistication in the theory of characterization, and together these...essays contribute to that goal' (Fowler 1993: 97).

6.   The literary interest in character in New Testament studies began with Weeden's, *Mark: Traditions in Conflict* (1971) and was taken up again in the work of Best which culminated in his *Following Jesus: Discipleship in the Gospel of Mark* (Best 1981). A specifically narrative-critical interest began with Tannehill's article 'The Disciples in Mark: The Function of a Narrative Role' (1977). Tannehill's article is a descriptive approach, indebted to New Criticism. Malbon published very useful papers on characters in Mark between 1983 and 1989 (see Bibliography). Kingsbury published works on characters in Matthew, including the

increasing as is evident in the Bibliographies. The more extensive work on characterization in the Hebrew Bible has not yet made much impact upon New Testament studies.[7] In 1992 the first full-length Lukan study appeared, written by John Darr, *On Character Building: The Reader and the Rhetoric of Characterization in Luke–Acts.*[8]

There are two extra aspects that come into play in a theological reading of the character Jesus, which both extend and qualify the contribution from literary-critical studies. One of the expressions of the theological 'respect for the text' is the recognition that there is a relationship between the world of the text and the first-century Middle Eastern world in which the text was produced. In that world there were literary conventions for the representation of character in literary discourse. The lack of interest in the context of production typical of recent synchronic literary-critical approaches means that this resource has hardly been tapped by New Testament students interested in a literary reading of a Gospel.[9]

The second aspect is the claim by the Christian reader that he or she already has an experience of Jesus Christ which they have interpreted, at least in part, in 'personal terms'. I have only traced Frei's preliminary discussion of this complex area in *The Identity of Jesus Christ*. Within the Christian community of interpretation, Jesus is held to be at least a person as well as more than that. The consequence of these claims is that there is an extra dimension to be considered in a Christian theological reading of the Gospel narrative, for the literary character Jesus who lives in the world of the Gospel text is held to be related in some way to the Jesus who is encountered today in the life of the Christian com-

clash with Hill over the literary-critical probe into the figure of Jesus (Kingsbury 1984, 1985; cf. Hill 1984).

7.   Adele Berlin, in her descriptive work on the Hebrew Bible, suggested that for biblical characters it is better to consider them across a spectrum 'as points on a continuum: (1) the agent, about whom nothing is known except what is necessary for the plot...(2) the type, who has limited and stereotyped range of traits, and who represents a class of people with these traits; (3) the character, who has a broader range of traits...and about whom we know more than is necessary for the plot' (1983: 32).

8.   Tannehill's study of the narrative unity of Luke–Acts chooses 'to focus on major roles in the narrative...I will be standing on the borderline between character and plot' (Tannehill 1986a: 1). After an introductory chapter 'Previews of Salvation', Tannehill traces the development of the character Jesus through the Gospel of Luke.

9.   Malbon considers that this resource is now being used increasingly (1992a).

munity. More work is needed on the implications of contemporary Christian experience for a theological reading of the Gospels, but not here. Meanwhile I adopt an eclectic, provisional and interrogative approach to character and characterization, in which the character Jesus is primarily a literary character who is also sometimes quite similar to a real person.

The Lukan Text

This study employs the third edition of the United Bible Societies Greek Text published in 1983 which is widely used today. The New Revised Standard Version (NRSV), published in 1989, is used when an English translation is useful, for it is based upon the United Bible Societies' Greek text (third edn). Occasionally I offer an alternative translation, as explained in Appendix E.

Happily, the following analysis of the semiotic subjects within the narrative world of the text is equally clear in the NRSV English translation as in the reading of the Greek text. As the English translation brings increased accessibility, Chapters 9 and 10 are presented as studies of the NRSV (with minor alterations) even though the preparatory work used the Greek text. The NRSV fails to represent the distribution of Jesus' name and so for this, recourse to the Greek is necessary.[10]

Chapter 11 looks at the minor character 'the demons', which appear relatively infrequently, and so the material which treats them is limited. This provides the opportunity to discuss passages in more detail. For each appearance of the demons, I provide a translation of the Greek text which also serves as a preliminary commentary.

Descriptive Analyses of the Gospel of Luke

The Gospel of Luke may be divided up in many ways; even commentators working with similar approaches offer different schemes. Two

---

10. There are two areas where a reading of the NRSV text is inadequate. The first area is that of the style and vocabulary of the Greek text, and the second area is the contribution of the name Jesus to the narrative exposition. The NRSV simply fails to represent the situation in the Greek text with regard to the name Jesus. The Greek text both distinguishes between ὁ Ἰησοῦς and Ἰησοῦς and also uses the name relatively sparingly. Presumably in the interest of clarity the NRSV often supplies the name when it is absent in the Greek, and does not differentiate between the two forms of the name.

complementary analyses are offered and used in this study. The first scheme divides the Gospel narrative into a preface and a sequence of seven acts, whose divisions respect thematic aspects of the narrative. The second scheme analyses the narrative into 184 smaller 'narrative units', which are then critically read for the narrating subjects and their communication within the narrative. The 'sweep' of the acts in the first analysis is argued below, which is then followed by a brief introduction to the five classes of narrative unit employed in the second analytical scheme, the details of which are set out in Appendix C, 'Tables of Analysis of the Narrating Subjects'.

Analysis One: The Gospel as Preface and Seven Acts
In this study the Gospel is treated as a single work comprising a preface and seven acts. This analysis is based upon a descriptive study of the themes which emerge as the text is read and the stories unfold. The divisions are introduced below and then used in the following narrative-critical reading. These 'simple' divisions are useful in a preliminary though limited way, but they are not 'prescriptive' and have been revised already in the process of reading and re-reading.

Title	*Reference*	*Units*
The Preface	1.1-4	1
Act 1: The Arrival of the Character Jesus	1.5–3.20	18
Act 2: The Introduction of the Character Jesus	3.21–4.44	9
Act 3: A Narrative Exposition of 'Who Jesus is'	5.1–9.50	39
Act 4: Jesus in the Shadow of Jerusalem	9.51–19.44	74
Act 5: Jesus Reclaims the Temple	19.45–21.38	16
Act 6: The Suffering and Death of Jesus	22.1–23.56	22
Act 7: The Triumph of the Risen Jesus	24.1-53	5

The Preface (1.1-4). The preface is an example of narrative commentary in which the narrator addresses the narratee Theophilus before beginning the story. The preface constitutes one narrative unit and comprises one long classical sentence whose periodic structure contributes to its possible meanings. My translation draws this out more clearly than the NRSV:

> Inasmuch as many have set their hand
> > to arrange in order a narrative about the events which have been
> > > fulfilled among us
> > just as they have been handed down to us by those who from the
> > beginning were eyewitnesses and ministers of the word

So it seemed good to me also who have carefully followed all these things
        for some time now
    to write an orderly account for you, most excellent Theophilus
    so that you may be completely certain about the things which you have
        been taught.

Act 1: The Arrival of the Character Jesus (1.5–3.20). The proposed first
act includes the infancy narrative material, which has long been considered a homogenous unit together with the story of the preaching of John
which is not usually associated with the infancy narrative.[11]

The act comprises 18 narrative units which are written in a style
reminiscent of the Septuagint and quite different from the style of the
preface. A different style again characterizes the second act. Act 1
covers the period from the first angelic appearance through to the birth
of Jesus and on to his childhood, and finishes with the preaching of
John.

The thematic structure of this act is the juxtaposition of the stories of
John and Jesus, which succeeds in demonstrating their intimate relationship while at the same time making clear to the reader the superiority of Jesus. The pattern of arrangement suggested here is informed by
the analysis of Raymond Brown, without recourse to the redaction-
critical hypothesis of a two-stage production of the present text (Brown
1977: 252-53).[12]

Act 2: The Introduction of the Character Jesus (3.21–4.44). Act 2
stretches from Lk. 3.21 to Lk. 4.44 and comprises six scenes and three
narrator's reports. It is suggested that the function of this act is to introduce Jesus to the narratee before the disciples arrive on the scene. The
literary structure comprises overlapping sections with the form of
'statement followed by a narrative exposition of the statement'. Each

11. Many commentators (e.g. Marshall, Fitzmyer) include the preaching of John
(3.1-20) as the beginning of the next act, and in so doing they allow the opening
sentence of Lk. 3.1 to serve as an introduction to the next stage of the story. This
division is certainly possible, but it fails to give sufficient weight to the thematic
distinction between John and Jesus which is signalled by the juncture of 3.20 and
3.21. The argument for this proposal is supplemented by the cogency of the
integrity of the next act.

12. Of the Lukan infancy narrative, Brown writes that 'there is common agreement today that Luke arranged these chapters with careful artistry, even though
scholars do not agree in their analyses of that arrangement' (Brown 1977: 250).

scene contributes to the narratee's construction of the character Jesus.

The act opens with the baptism of Jesus and closes with Jesus' itinerant proclamation of the kingdom of God in the synagogues of Judaea. There has been much discussion about the literary structure of this section and there are a range of options on offer to the contemporary reader. This variety is unnecessarily extended by the mistaken introduction by modern readers of two extratextual notions which have confused the picture.

The first notion is the supposed distinction between the 'public' and 'private' ministry of Jesus, which has led commentators to suggest a division of the material at 4.14. There is no narrative warrant for such a distinction and so Lk. 4.13 and 4.14 may be reunited and await further consideration.

The second area of confusion arises from the modern fascination with chronological sequence and this has led some readers to consider that the events in the narrative discourse must represent a historical sequence. The narrative plainly subverts this in Lk. 4.23 when Jesus refers to things that he had already done in Capernaum, which the narratee has never heard of. The relaxation of the chronological presumption creates the methodological space for the consideration of other possibilities at work in the ordering of the material.

The literary pattern proposed to illuminate the present material is a simple scheme of 'statements followed by narrative expositions'. This simple scheme is developed in the light of criteria identified by Talbert in his ground-breaking study *Literary Patterns, Theological Schemes, and the Genre of Luke–Acts* (1974). The proposal is principally 'descriptive', and so its appropriateness will be established in the process of reading the text. The pattern is:

Statements	Narrative Expositions of Initial Statements			Summary
The Baptism 3.21-22	The Genealogy 3.23-38	The Temptations 4.1-13	The Synagogue 4.14-39	'A Typical Day' 4.31-44
(1) Jesus Lineage	The Genealogy of Jesus			Jesus combines these three aspects
(2) Anointed One			The Spirit upon Jesus	
(3) Declared Son		The Temptation of the Son		

The genealogy is the first exposition of the character Jesus which takes the form of narrative commentary. The second and third expositions are narrative expositions proper, in which the story begins to make plain the significance of the two events which occur at Jesus' baptism.

Act 3: A Narrative Exposition of 'Who Jesus Is' (5.1–9.50). The third act is a narrative sequence of 39 narrative units loosely structured around the relationship between Jesus and his disciples. The Act begins with the call of Peter, James and John (5.1-11) and closes with the disciple's confusion over the inclusivity of Jesus' discipleship (9.49-50).

The recurring *leitmotif* in this act is the continuation and development of the key question from act 2: 'Who is this Jesus?' Both acts 2 and 3 display an orchestration of questions about the identity of Jesus, with act 3 extending the range of characters who pose this question.[13] Toward the end of the act, the best efforts of the disciple Peter at answering the question of Jesus' identity (9.20) are 'corrected' by the voice from heaven, who specifically addresses the three disciples (9.35).

In act 3 the narrator introduces the 12 apostles who enter the story from time to time, and usually earn a rebuke.[14] The 12 are commissioned and sent out to 'proclaim the Kingdom of God' (9.2), yet the narratee and readers never discover what they accomplish on their mission. Could it be that what they did would not bear directly upon the

---

13. Comments about the identity of Jesus in act 2 of Luke are found in many character discourses, including: the voice from heaven (3.22); the narrator (3.23); the devil (4.3, 9), the people (4.22) and the demons (4.35). In act 3 the range of characters' comments or questions widens: Peter (5.8), the Pharisees (5.21), the crowd (5.26), Jesus himself (6.1, 46), the centurion (7.6), John the Baptist (7.20, repeated for emphasis), the Pharisee (7.39), mother and brothers (8.21), the disciples on the Lake (8.25), the Gerasene demoniac (8.28), Herod (9.7), the crowds (9.18), Peter (9.20), and the voice from heaven (9.35). This great array of character questioning and comment is bracketed by the voice from heaven (3.22; 9.35). Altogether this signals that the central theme of these two acts is the search for the identity of Jesus.

14. The disciples panic in the storm on the lake (8.24), they prevaricate at feeding the 5000 (9.13), they fail to exorcise a demon when asked (9.40), they misunderstand the nature of greatness (9.46) and they forbid others to exorcise in Jesus' name (9.49); each time Jesus rebukes them.

question of the identity of Jesus (9.1-17)?[15]

While this drama is unfolding, other aspects of the story of Jesus are introduced and developed. The characterization of Jesus as a teacher is emphasized through his extended discourses (6.20-49) and the introduction of the 'story parable'.[16] The Pharisees are introduced as important characters in a long and virtually uninterrupted sequence (5.17–6.11). The act also includes a Gentile dimension, through Jesus' interest in Gentiles who live in Galilee and those who live outside Galilee in Gerasa.

Jesus introduces the enigmatic figure of the Son of Man, initially in controversies with the Pharisees. Eventually the disciples have a sufficient understanding of who Jesus is for him to introduce the further dimension of the *suffering* Son of Man. This figure functions as a prelude to Jesus' ministry in the shadow of Jerusalem.

Act 4: Jesus in the Shadow of Jerusalem (9.51–19.44). There is a marked change in the narrative as Jesus enters act 4.[17] The material in act 4 is famously difficult to analyse for a structure, with no consensus yet reached by New Testament scholars. The uncertainty includes unre-

---

15. A striking fact that is developed in the discussion of the narrator in Chapter 9 is that the narrator alternates naming Jesus with the presence of the disciples, but never has the two together in a scene. The three disciples who are called to follow Jesus in Lk. 5.1-11 (and who will become apostles) accompany Jesus only twice in the whole act. This happens when Jairus's daughter is raised and at the Transfiguration.

16. The first parable that Jesus introduces tells of sewing new cloth onto old garments (5.36). The word παραβολή is used on one earlier occasion at 4.23, where the NRSV correctly translates it as 'proverb'.

17. The four types of narrative unit are distributed within each act as follows:

Narrative Unit Type	Act 3	(Proportion)	Act 4	(Proportion)
Narrator's Report	4	10%	3	4%
Scene with Speech and Action	19	49%	13	18%
Scene with Speech and Dialogue	9	23%	27	36%
Speech Units	7	18%	31	2%

The great disparity in distribution of types of material between these two acts undermines Kingsbury's claim that 'the ministry Jesus discharges on the journey to Jerusalem is not fundamentally different from the ministry he previously discharged within Galilee' (Kingsbury 1991b: 55).

solved debate about where this narrative section ends.[18] The opening to this act is disingenuous for the narrator states that 'when the days drew near for him to be taken up, he set his face to go to Jerusalem. And he sent messengers ahead of him' (9.51, 52). The narratee reasonably expects the account of a journey toward Jerusalem, and yet as he or she reads or listens to the subsequent story they find a large collection of material, in which the narrator offers few reminders of the destination. Furthermore, the few geographical places named do not fit into any logical sequence for a journey to Jerusalem.[19]

At the same time, the length of this long section demonstrates its importance within the narrative.[20] 'Clearly the journey section is of central importance to Luke, but the geographical itinerary by which Jesus reaches Jerusalem is scarcely important at all' (Grant 1989: 39). So unimportant is the itinerary that Schmidt concluded that 'although Jesus is travelling to Jerusalem all the time, he never really makes any progress' (Schmidt, quoted in Conzelmann 1960: 61).

I suggest that the 'journey motif' has been overworked, and that the *significance* of *Jerusalem* is the key to the literary analysis of the section.[21] Accordingly, this act is entitled 'Jesus in the Shadow of Jerusalem'.[22] If the contemporary reader still has expectations of the itinerary of a journey, there is still no consensus about an appropriate

18. As well as the standard commentaries, see Moessner's useful survey (1989: 1-44) in which he classifies the approaches to this problem into 4 options which have developed in the last 40 years or so. Also useful is Nolland's brief discussion (1993a: 525-31).

19. Jerusalem is mentioned as the destination by the narrator in 9.51, 53 (the beginning of the act), 13.22 (the middle of the act), and 17.11, 18.31, 19.28, 41 (the end of the act). Jesus speaks of going to Jerusalem in the middle of the section (13.33-34) and toward the end (19.11). Jericho is the only other city mentioned (18.35 and 19.10). Samaria and Galilee are mentioned at 17.11 and Samaritans are mentioned in 9.52, 10.33 and 17.6. Galileans are mentioned at 13.1, and Jews and Judaea are not mentioned at all.

20. This act comprises 74 narrative units out of a total of 184, which is 40.2% of the Gospel.

21. Similarly Conzelmann: 'The discrepancy between form and content does not lead us to "reject" the journey, but helps us discover what is Luke's Christology' (Conzelmann 1960: 62).

22. Bailey offers a similar suggestion: 'The title "Travel Narrative" is a misnomer...we prefer to call it the "Jerusalem Document"' (1976: 82).

way to involve this intermittent aspect of the section. The narrative is sufficiently marked as a journey to be important, but insufficiently developed for this to be of much use hermeneutically. Accordingly, the 'journey' is treated as an organizational device which is subsumed with varying degrees of integration within a literary structure.

The minimal journey motif assists in the identification of the end of the section as 19.44. At 19.45 Jesus is in the Temple within Jerusalem, and so 9.51–19.44 includes all the material narrated between Jesus setting his face to Jerusalem, and the entry of Jesus to Jerusalem.[23]

I adopt with minor adjustments the literary chiastic pattern proposed by Talbert in *Reading Luke* (1982: 111-12),[24] which is in turn a modest revision of the ground breaking proposal of Bailey in *Poet and Peasant* (1976: 79-85).[25] The pattern of references to Jerusalem at the beginning and middle and end of the act marks out the literary 'chi' pattern, and within each half of the act there are ten elements which usually mirror each other in the pattern of a typical chiasmus.

The material is grouped in a way different from the previous act. 'With the Journey we breath a freer air…to a greater extent than hitherto, the pericopae seem to be linked together in *topics*' (Goulder 1989: 456). This arrangement includes a surprising number of scenes or sections grouped together in 'threes'. All this 'should alert us to the author's literary intent' (Grant 1989: 40). The arrangement may be set out as follows:

23. Goulder argues that if Luke is a redaction of Matthew and Mark, then the journey motif need not be collapsed into mere theological construction (*pace* Conzelmann), for 'in writing a biography it is a different matter to keep events in sequence from keeping the sayings in sequence' (Goulder 1989: 454). Nevertheless, Goulder does not find literary-critical arguments for the location of the end of the section, and the attraction of seeing the Gospel divided into lections does not explain Goulder's 'the end of the journey is not clearly marked because it is not very significant' (1989: 456).

24. Talbert's proposal is developed from his earlier work on *Literary Patterns, Theological Themes, and the Genre of Luke–Acts* (1974) and the work of Bailey in *Poet and Peasant* (1976).

25. Bailey considers his work as 'a revision and extension of Goulder's suggestion…of a chiastic structure' (Bailey 1986: 79). Goulder's suggestion is made in his article 'The Chiastic Structure of the Lucan Journey' (1964).

A	The beginning of the 'public' Journey to Jerusalem	9.51-56
B	Following Jesus: the conflict of mission; the mission of the 70	9.57–10.24
C	Eternal Life: The Lawyer (Good Samaritan); Mary and Martha	10.25-42
D	Prayer: the Lord's Prayer and further teaching	11.1-13
E	Signs of the Kingdom: (1) Beelzebul (2) Sign of Jonah	11.14-36
F	Conflict with Pharisees and conflict with lawyers: 6 Woes	11.37–12.34
G	Teaching for Disciples: Beware (1) Enemy (2) Mammon; the Kingdom; the time of the coming of the Son of Man	12.35–13.9
H	Healing/exorcism on the Sabbath: the crippled woman	13.10-17
I	Messianic Banquet: inclusion/exclusion	13.18-30
J	Impossible for prophet to be killed outside Jerusalem	13.31-33
J´	Jerusalem, the city that kills the prophets	13.34-35
I´	Healing on the Sabbath—the man with dropsy	14.1-6*
H´	Messianic Banquet—inclusion/exclusion; the Lost/Found	14.07–15.32*
G´	The Kingdom—shrewd preparation in order to serve God	16.1-13
F´	Conflict with Pharisees—wealth	16.14-31
E´	Signs of the Kingdom—Healing Lepers; Days of the Son of Man	17.1-35
D´	Prayer—Importunate Widow; Pharisees and Tax Collector	18.1-17
C´	Eternal Life—The Rich Ruler; The Eye of the Needle; Disciple's query	18.18-30
B´	Following Jesus—The third Passion Prediction; blind beggar; Zacchaeus	18.31–19.10
A´	To Jerusalem—Parable of Pounds; Welcome on Mount of Olives	19.11-44

*If these units are reversed the thematic symmetry is improved.

Act 5: Jesus Reclaims the Temple (19.45–21.38). Act 5 comprises 16 narrative units which portray Jesus in the Temple precincts teaching and debating with the people and their leaders. The act is bracketed by the literary *inclusio* 'then he entered the temple' (19.45) and 'all the people would get up early in the morning to listen to him in the temple' (21.38). The Temple location is reinforced for the narratee by the triple reiteration (19.45, 47; 20.1); by the link between Jesus' teaching and the Temple (21.1-19); by the absence of any other place name and the comment 'every day he was teaching in the temple...' (21.37). In fact,

Jesus never leaves the Temple during this section. Furthermore, Jerusalem is only mentioned in Jesus' discourse about the future (21.20, 24), and so the narrative 'structuring' of the teaching material is intimately related to the spatial location of the Jerusalem Temple.[26] The act moves through two related phases. The first phase traces the cumulative defeat by Jesus of those who are his controversialists. This sequence of narrative units concludes with a scribe conceding 'Teacher, you have spoken well' (20.39). The absence of the Pharisees and the virtual absence of the disciples is striking.[27] This victory of Jesus is accompanied by the account of those who plot to kill him which is described explicitly for the first time (19.47; 20.19).

The second phase describes Jesus teaching freely once he has vanquished his opponents. The theme of the future destruction of the Temple provides the occasion for other teachings about the future. Jesus explains that 'wars and insurrections' and persecution of his followers 'must take place first, but the end will not follow immediately' (21.9). Eventually some will see the coming of the Son of Man (21.27).[28] With warnings to the people to be on their guard, the act draws to a close.

Act 6: The Suffering and Death of Jesus (22.1–23.56). The action of this act (commonly entitled the Passion narrative) unfolds through 22 narrative units all set in Jerusalem, which is where prophets are killed (13.34).[29] However, now that Jesus has reclaimed the Temple, the final

26. Conzelmann is partially correct when he comments that in Luke's scheme 'there are before the Last Supper only two places in which Jesus is found: in the Temple by day, and on the Mount of Olives by night' (Conzelmann 1960: 125). In fact the Mount of Olives is not mentioned until the final summary report (Lk. 21.37), for the narrative is concerned only with Jesus in the Temple, which he cleanses and reclaims, in order that he might teach and warn the people.

27. Carroll offers a possible explanation in narrative terms for the absence of the Pharisees (1988).

28. The teachings in Jesus' discourse in Lk. 21 separate the elements of persecutions, wars and insurrections, and the end of the Temple from the cosmic events which precede the coming of the Son of Man. Contra Conzelmann, this separation, which creates the space for the mission of the early church, does not 'lift eschatology out of any historical context, and remove [it] from all events which take place in history' (cf. Conzelmann 160: 128).

29. Fitzmyer usefully discusses Jerusalem as the place where the prophets were killed (1986: 1359-69).

conflict has to take place elsewhere in the city. The conflict is introduced with the plotting of chief priests and scribes while Satan enters
into Judas (22.1-3).[30]

The standard commentaries have discussed at length the Passion
narrative in Luke. The act portrays Jesus the innocent who submits to
the Father's will, endures four hearings in which his innocence is
reiterated, and then dies a martyr's death.[31] The significance of his
death is expounded for the only time in the Gospel in the scene of
Jesus' last Passover meal.[32]

The narrative scenes of Jesus in the Garden praying to his father and
the death of Jesus on the cross both echo the temptations in the wilderness at the beginning of Jesus' story. Even in his death, the talk of Para-
dise (23.43) suggests a positive outcome; Jesus still has a Father to
whom he returns.

The slowing of the pace of the narrative in these tightly related
scenes signals their importance for the narrator as Jesus moves towards
his 'exodus'. The exhortation to endure suffering in the previous act is
now demonstrated in the way Jesus conducts himself through his
sufferings, and so Jesus becomes a model for those who follow him (cf.
Talbert 1982: 213-14).

Act 7: The Triumph of the Risen Jesus (24.1–24.53). The last act comprises just five narrative units. The act opens with the scene of the
women at the empty tomb. Jesus is absent, thus emphasizing the empti-
ness of the tomb. The second scene is 'The Road to Emmaus' which is

---

30. Conzelmann suggests that 'when Jesus was alive was the time of salvation;
Satan was far away and it was a time without temptation. Since the Passion, however, Satan is present again and the disciples of Jesus are again subject to temptation' (1960: 16). Conzelmann mistakenly restricts Satan's activities to the temptation of the disciples (cf. Judas [22.3]; and Jesus' prayer for Simon 'whom Satan had
demanded to sift' [22.31]). Satan plays a part in the narrative world in both an association with the rule of the demons (cf. context and comment of Jesus [10.18]) and
explicitly in the affliction of the crippled daughter of Abraham (13.16).

31. Fitzmyer recalls Dibelius's conclusion that 'Luke presents the Passion as a
martyrdom' (Fitzmyer 1986: 1367).

32. Talbert's exposition of Jesus as martyr gives insufficient weight to the narrative of the Last Supper which precedes and explicates the death of Jesus as *more*
than martyrdom (cf. Talbert 1982: 206-25). Jesus' discourse at the Last Passover is
discussed in Chapter 10.

the longest of all the narrative units.[33] Significantly, within this scene the longest discourse is that of the disciples as they rehearse their questions to Jesus. The third narrative is a scene in which Jesus appears to the disciples, which leads into the fourth narrative unit which is a discourse of Jesus. Much of this discourse reiterates the substance and language of the discussion on the road to Emmaus. The narrator completes the Gospel with a summary in which for the first time the disciples are described as 'worshipping Jesus' (24.52). The Lukan narrative closes in the temple where the narrative began, and this time it is the disciples of Jesus who praise God.

These five narrative units are juxtaposed in such a way that it appears to the narratee that these events all happen on the same day—the first day of the week. Significantly, all these 'hopeful' events happen in or around the city of Jerusalem.

Analysis Two: The Gospel of Luke as 184 Narrative Units
At a more detailed level, this study analyses the Gospel into 184 narrative units, each of which displays a discrete thematic integrity.[34] In a descriptive analysis, the actual number of units makes a limited contribution until different acts are compared with each other.

There are three basic categories of narrative unit. There is the *report*, which can be shortened to a summary, the *scene*, in which action takes place, and the *speech* or character discourse. There are two qualifications that extend this classification to five types of unit, and these may be grouped according to their narrative function in the following types of discourse.

---

33. The distribution of narrative time in ch. 24 is represented approximately by the word count of the Greek text. The five narrative units are demarcated by the verse numbers:

Verse	Narrative Unit	Title	Words	% of Act
1-12	Scene	The Women at the Tomb	176	22
13-35	Scene	The Road to Emmaus	386	48
36-43	Scene	Jesus Appears to the Disciples	101	12
44-49	Discourse	Jesus Explains what the Scriptures Teach	101	12
50-53	Summary	Jesus Leaves the Disciples	49	6

34. This use of 'narrative unit' is different from the concept of narrative unit employed by Funk in his New Critical *The Poetics of Biblical Narrative* (1988) which concentrates upon the development of action for his analysis.

The narrator and the primary discourse. The primary discourse is the product of the narrator's voice and may report an activity or a conversation. There is no embedded discourse. The following abbreviations enable the contemporary reader to distinguish the distribution of action and speech in the narrative units: 'Report of an Action', RpA; 'Report of a Character's Speech', RpSp.

The primary discourse and the character discourses. If a story character has a voice they provide their own discourse and this can be embedded within the primary discourse. This combination is labelled a 'scene'. As well as speech within the scene there may also be action providing two kinds of narrative unit: 'Scene with Embedded Speech of One or More Characters', ScSp; 'Scene with Embedded Speech and Description of Action', ScA.

The character discourses. Occasionally the narrator retires and hands over the narration to a character (or characters) for a period of narrative time. This narrative unit comprises the character discourse. In some cases there is a minimal contribution of the narrator (e.g. 'he said to them') which barely interrupts the character's discourse, and so this type of unit is grouped with those units which are pure character discourse: 'Character Discourse of Speech', Sp.

The Discourses of the Narrator and the Character Jesus

The preliminary reading in the next three chapters identifies three narrative agents in the text and traces their contributions to the answer to the question 'Who is Jesus?' Jesus and the demons both act in the narrative and contribute their own discourses, while the narrator provides the primary discourse. As the narrator and Jesus provide extensive discourses, the following discussion draws upon a longer preparatory analysis of these discourses. The discourses of the demons are few in number and are treated individually in Chapter 11.

In studies of the New Testament Gospels there is a long history of attending to the titles which are used of Jesus in the texts, often with little awareness of the importance of which voice is speaking and in what narrative context. To demonstrate the usefulness of the present approach in contrast to these more familiar studies, the names and titles applied to Jesus are treated once again.

In this preliminary analysis the discourses which are embedded within Jesus' discourse are treated as part of his discourse. This is true both for the parables which include their own story characters and also for the moments when Jesus quotes another character. The one exception is when Jesus quotes Scripture, for that is considered to have a voice of its own. Interestingly, the degree of Jesus' revision of Scripture is a clue to the characterization of Jesus.

This analysis uses these two descriptive analyses of the Gospel. The Greek text of Luke is analysed for the various discourses within each narrative unit, and then particular aspects of each discourse are investigated. These results are set out in the Tables in Appendix C.

Chapter 9

THE NARRATOR'S CHARACTERIZATION OF JESUS

Jesus said: 'Return to your home and declare how much has been done
for you *by God.*'
So he went away, proclaiming throughout the city how much had been
done for him *by Jesus.*

Lk. 8.39 (NRSV)

An Introduction to the Lukan Narrator

The opening quotation from Lk. 8.39 displays the difference between
the narrator's discourse and the character Jesus' discourse as they treat
the same event—a contrast underlined by the similarity in the syntax of
the two discourses. This chapter is a preliminary study of the narrator's
characterization of Jesus, and Chapter 10 is a study of Jesus' self-characterization. Both studies employ the multi-semiotic subject model of a
narrative text in the production of a theological narrative-critical reading. The question addressed in this chapter is 'Who does the narrator
portray Jesus to be?'[1] The reader is invited to trace how the narrator
'characterizes' Jesus for the narratee, and through this exercise the
reader may construct his or her own perception of the Lukan Jesus.

It is a commonplace in current New Testament literary studies that
the narrator is reliable, omniscient and authoritative.[2] These three char-

---

1.   The name 'Jesus' is used generally to denote the narrative character Jesus in
this English language discussion. This convention is clearly separate from the
discussion of the distribution of the name in the Greek text.

2.   In New Testament narrative-critical studies Culpepper is typical: 'the narrator is established not only as omniscient and omni-communicative but also as
entirely reliable' (1983: 32). In narrative studies of the Gospel of Luke, Gowler is
typical when he writes that 'the voice that tells the story is the voice of an
omniscient, reliable narrator' (1989: 55); cf. Darr, 'Like other biblical narrators, the
narrator of Luke-Acts is omniscient, omnipresent, retrospective and fully reliable'
(1992: 50).

acteristics are imported from the world of general literary criticism where they were developed in the study of mainly fictional works. While the narrator is usually conceived to be a narrative agent, in recent literary studies there is no requirement for this agent to be reliable, omniscient or authoritative. Yet the first generation of narrative critics displayed an ideological commitment to this position, *which seems to have been adopted independently of any detailed study of the narrator in the text*. In the present discussion, no such assumption is made and 'the narrator's future...[is] open' (Gunn 1990: 60). Instead of a *presumption*, the critical reading commended here enquires 'what kind of authority and reliability is claimed by the Lukan narrator within the narrative?'

In 1986 Robert Tannehill published Volume 1 of *The Narrative Unity of Luke–Acts* as the first major narrative critical work on Luke.[3] In the same year James Dawsey published *The Lukan Voice* as the first major study of the Lukan narrator. Dawsey's study identifies the Lukan voices 'that are peculiar to the narrative world of Luke' (1986b: 2) and concentrates on the voices of the narrator and Jesus. Dawsey analyses the vocabulary, the style and the substance of the Greek text of these two voices and proposes that the narrator and Jesus have different perceptions of who Jesus is (as I also will demonstate); Dawsey concludes that the narrator is confused. These differences between the portrayals of Jesus require the reader to puzzle out who Jesus really is, with the result that 'the narrator's misunderstanding of Jesus [is] the bridge that allowed for full participation [of the reader] in the story and led to decision' (Dawsey 1986b: 155).

The present study considers Dawsey's description of the 'confused narrator' to be a misreading which is due to two fundamental mistakes in his methodology.[4] First, Dawsey fails to grasp the narrative form of

3.   Despite a wide-ranging study, Tannehill does not discuss the narrator as a distinct narrative voice. In a generally appreciative review, Charles Talbert, who pioneered the literary approach to Luke (cf. Talbert 1974), comments that 'Tannehill's approach is closer to the old "New Criticism"...than it is to the newer "narrative criticism", which focuses more on narrator, implied reader, narrative time etc.' (Talbert 1988b: 137).

4.   Dawsey's conclusions and his methodology have not won much support. The unconvinced include Darr 1993: 44-46; Sheeley 1992: 154 and Tannehill 1986a: 7 n. 4. 'Despite Dawsey's literary insight and an admirable willingness to look at the text from novel and unorthodox perspectives...Dawsey lacks a consistent literary methodology, and indeed appears blissfully unaware of the voluminous

the Gospel, and so his analyses lack an appreciation of narrative dynamics and so depend upon word counts and analyses based upon the whole of the Gospel text rather than the changing world of different acts. Second, although Dawsey usually correctly identifies the different voices, he lacks an appreciation of the distinction between narrating and focalizing and so he mistakenly attributes to the narrator every view which the narrator reports.[5] Nevertheless, Dawsey's analyses serve as a stimulus for the present study because there is the shared conviction that 'the characters and the narrator of Luke are in dialogue with each other and with us. Meaning arises out of the conversation' (Dawsey 1986a: 13).[6]

The next monograph to treat the Lukan narrator is Steven Sheeley's *Narrative Asides in Luke–Acts* published in 1992.[7] This modest work treats a particular kind of narrative commentary which Sheeley labels 'narrative aside'. Sheeley studies this kind of 'aside' in other ancient narratives and offers a functional classification of such asides. Sheeley concludes that their principal role is to 'reinforce and affirm the authority and reliability of the narrators' (1992: 175). Sheeley's study is moderately useful but lacks theoretical rigour. There is no discussion of the criteria for the identification of narrative asides and no explanation of how he selects his short and eccentric list of examples.[8] The present

work on narration in secular literary theory' (Darr 1993: 44). In contrast Moore gives qualified approval (1989a: 30-34).

5. Dawsey's confusion arises from 'the monologic of classical structuralism based on one speaker equals one subject identification' (Bal 1991a: 1).

6. Dawsey's starting point is very similar to the starting point of the present thesis. 'The different characters in the story...refer to Jesus in different ways and give different interpretations to what they see occurring with Jesus. The reader, in turn, plays off one view against the other, sorting through and interpreting the story at a different level' (Dawsey 1986a: 145).

7. In 1989, David Gowler published an article entitled 'Characterization in Luke: A Socio-Narratological Approach'. He begins with a narrative-critical study and argues that the 'presentations of characters in Luke can be evaluated upon scales of descending reliability and explicitness' (1989: 55). He goes on to propose that the modern reader must study the 'cultural codes of the world of these scripts' to interpret correctly these narrative presentations.

8. A further contribution to the discussion of the Lukan narrator has been made by John Darr in his article 'Narrator as Character: Mapping a Reader-Oriented Approach to Narration in Luke–Acts' (1993). Darr builds upon his general study of Lukan characterization in *On Character Building* (1992) and develops an approach which is 'based on two interrelated observations about the production of literary

study of the Lukan narrator engages with Dawsey's and Sheeley's studies when they are relevant to reading for the narrator's characterization of Jesus.

The narrator's characterization is the sum of the contributions of the narrating and the focalizing semiotic subjects. The principal contribution is made through the focalizing activity, and this is identified when the reader attends to the aspects of the discourse that reveal the ideological interests of the focalizing subject. These aspects are principally the ordering of the narrative material, the management of narrator and character discourses and the relative allocations of narrative time.

The narrating activity supplements this contribution through the choice of the language and style of the Greek text, the selection and distribution of the names and titles for Jesus, and the occasional example of narrative commentary. Of these three, the distribution of the names and titles makes most contribution, albeit still a modest one.[9] By attending to the changing approach to the characterization of Jesus as act succeeds act, this study breaks new ground in the narrative-critical study of the Lukan narrator.

The surprise for the present writer is that *the narrator does not emerge as the most authoritative voice in the Lukan narrative.* Yet neither is he the confused and ironic narrator of Dawsey's imaginings. Instead, the narrator is a disciple who came later than the eye-witnesses and invites readers who are like him to learn from the characters who were involved in the events at that time.

The Characterization of Jesus in the Preface (1.1-4)

The preface to Luke (1.1-4) has long puzzled students of the New Testament and generated a large and expanding literature. The preface

character: readers build characters, and critics build readers' (1993: 46). The contribution of Darr is discussed in the present study.

9.   This narrative-critical discussion of the names and titles used of Jesus has the further attraction that it contrasts clearly with the usual historical-critical studies of the same names and titles. It does seem that with modern Western interest in character, the significance of Jesus' titles in New Testament studies is over-emphasized. An advantage of the narrative-critical approach is the central place given to the *story* of Jesus, which contextualizes the distribution of the name and titles for Jesus. For example, standard historical-critical commentaries do not comment upon the way in which the name Jesus appears 30 times in 14 of the 39 narrative units in act 3, in contrast to only 20 times in 10 of the 74 units in act 4.

comprises 1 sentence of 42 Greek words which could be 'the most carefully constructed period in the New Testament' (Cadbury 1922: 492).
Yet it promises more than it delivers, for it is extraordinarily brief,
anonymous and elliptical about its theme.[10] Furthermore, it employs
vocabulary which occurs only here in whole of the Lukan narrative.[11]
Even those who look to the history of Greek literature receive little help
from genre studies of contemporary literature.[12]

   In the present study, the preface is considered to be an example of
narrative commentary which displays some features of the narrator's
literary strategy, even though it cannot display the range of literary features which are found in the acts that follow. Sheeley correctly observes
that the preface 'builds the relationship between the narrator and
Theophilus, the narratee' (1992: 175).[13]

   The preface includes no character discourse and so is an example of

---

   10. The absence of Jesus is the prime example which puzzles the Christian
reader. Furthermore, 'the prologue is very sparing in the use of specifically Christian conceptions' (Brown 1978: 102). Although there is classical Greek vocabulary
(e.g. ὑτόπται) there are also phrases which have Christian associations (e.g. ὁ λόγος
ὑπηρέται γενόμενοι τοῦ λόγου), which led Giblin to suggest ambitiously that
'Luke is writing a religious history' (1985: 14). Nolland's comment is more
judicious: 'Only the absolute use of ὁ λόγος betrays the deeply religious content to
come' (1989: 5).
   11. The literature upon the brief preface to Luke is large and growing, which
confirms that its interpretation is problematic. There is little consensus about which
type of literary preface it is. Cadbury's comments about the 'difficulties which its
terse and ambiguous language raises' (1922: 489) are echoed by Evans: 'As the history of interpretation shows, the meaning is hardly anywhere clear and incontrovert-
ible' (1990: 120).
   12. Talbert lists the minimal inferences that can be drawn about the preface
from studies of the genre of 'ancient prefaces': (1) The preface cannot be used to
deduce the genre of Luke–Acts. (2) We cannot determine Luke–Acts' historical
accuracy from the claims made in the preface. (3) The preface's statement about the
purpose cannot guarantee the aim of what follows (1982: 11). Talbert's conclusions
reinforce Cadbury's observation that 'it is in the bare fact of his using a preface
rather than in its details that Luke's relation to literature is apparent' (Cadbury
1927: 196).
   13. Theophilus will be referred to as 'narratee' and not by name in the following
reading, in order to emphasize his function. The name 'Theophilus' 'is a proper
name commonly used from the third century B.C.E. on...by both Gentiles and
Jews' (Fitzmyer 1981: 299).

the narrator's primary discourse in the form of narrative commentary; thus it offers limited resources for a critical reading.

The Contribution of the Language and Style
The choice of vocabulary and the elevated style of the preface have an indirect bearing on Lukan characterization. Initially, the narratee is reminded by the preface of a range of contemporary and public literary works.[14] Although the genre of the Lukan Gospel is still debated, the text will have circulated in wider circles than those of Theophilus.[15]

The language of the preface implies that other narratives have failed to produce the assurance the narratee seeks and now the Lukan narrator will redress the matter.[16] In this way, the narrator begins to establish himself as a 'reliable' narrator whom the narratee may trust.

The Lukan text is described as another *narrative* (διήγησις [1.1]) and so possibly a *historical* narrative, although the debate is unresolved.[17] The reference to 'the events that have been fulfilled among us' (1.10) points to a historical dimension, although with a short preface at the head of a long narrative work, a reading of the complete narrative must be conducted before any sure estimate of the preface is made.[18] Whether history or biography, the relationship between the discourse world and the events of the narrator's world is clearly one of its themes.

The preface is an 'orderly account' (1.3), yet the meaning of καθεξῆς

14. 'The Third Gospel from its very outset betrays the author's intention of relating his work consciously to contemporary literature of the Greco-Roman world' (Fitzmyer 1981: 288).

15. Theophilus already has an acquaintance with Jesus, whereas the wider public may not have this knowledge. 'The double tendency in Luke does seem to presuppose two circles of readers' (Brown 1978: 108).

16. The Greek verb ἐπεχείρησαν (which I translate as 'have set their hand to') can be a neutral description of what the many others had done, or it may convey the sense that these other efforts have failed, and a new narrative is required. The thrust of the preface supports the latter interpretation.

17. Talbert argues that Luke is closer to the genre of Greco-Roman βίοι (Talbert 1977); but contrast Aune's response to Talbert (Aune 1981).

18. The preface is so brief and the Gospel narrative sufficiently distinctive that a description of it as 'historical narrative' is provisional and should be refined in the light of the detailed study of the Gospel. It is not impossible that Luke's preface heralds a new genre of literature—a possibility still under discussion. For example, Callan suggests that Luke's two-volume work is an example of a genre of history writing emerging in the first century BCE, whose principal emphasis is 'to present a true account of something' (Callan 1985: 581).

is still debated. In a narrative reading, the meaning of a word is primarily decided by its narrative context, so the rest of the Lukan text is the key to the 'order' which is claimed. Thus Tannehill's suggestion that 'the order in question may be an order appropriate to narrative' (1986a: 10) can be formulated more precisely: the 'orderly account' is that which follows in the narrative of the Gospel.

The phrase 'the events that have been fulfilled among us' (1.1) suggests a continuing dimension to the story of Jesus which engages with the time of the narrator. This impression is supported by the tenses of the Greek verbs, with the perfect tense used of 'fulfilled'.[19]

The preface is a single discourse in which the narrator *reports* other narrative voices rather than allowing them to speak for themselves. In the preface, the two kinds of voice present are the narrator, and in a reported form, the 'first eye-witnesses and servants of the word' who function as a single voice.

The narrator makes a key distinction between himself and these 'eye-witnesses and servants of the word' (1.2). The authority which this carefully researched narrative attracts arises from its ability *faithfully to represent those who were there as the events occurred.*[20] This distinction suggests that the narrative voices in the preface function within a *'hierarchy of authority'*. The narrator claims no divine anointing, and so does not speak with the authority of Spirit-anointed characters. Instead, his more modest authority springs from the rather pedestrian claim of having 'investigated everything carefully from the very first' (1.3).[21]

---

19. The verb πεπληροφορημένων is in the perfect tense which includes a sense of continuing relevance, and also the verb is in the passive voice, not unlike the literary convention of the 'divine passives'. The verb is used of prophetic fulfilment, and so this word succeeds in conveying that God has brought to pass things in the story-world which are still relevant for the narrator (cf. Schweizer 1984: 10-11).

20. Luke 'was concerned to hand on tradition, rather than be a *littérateur*' (Marshall 1978: 40). The same feature is noted but interpreted differently by Plummer: 'The modest position claimed by the writer is evidence of his honesty' (1901: 2).

21. The narrator is a Christian who never knew Jesus. 'Because a person was not with Jesus and the twelve by no means allows rejection of his ministry (cf. Luke 9.49-50); both types were commissioned by Jesus, so both are legitimate. Yet those who were "with him" function as a control on those who "were not"' (Talbert 1982: 101).

This distinction between the narrator and the eye-witnesses is typical of the Gospel narrative. There is a 'hierarchy of authority' of voices which is respected and never overturned by the narrator. This hierarchy may explain why at times the narrator chooses to embed the discourses of eye-witnesses rather than report their discourses, for the narrator is not the most authoritative voice in the narrative: instead he is a *disciple*, learning of Jesus from those who knew him. This respect for the authority of the eye-witnesses may even help explain the anonymity of the preface of the Gospel.[22]

This hierarchy of voices involves a temporal distance between the eye-witnesses and the narrator, but the narrator speaks in the preface of 'events that have been fulfilled among *us*' (1.1), which suggests a *hermeneutical* dimension to this story. There is a marked contrast between the cultural horizons associated with readers of texts which are introduced by classical Greek prefaces, and the cultural horizons of Palestinian eye-witnesses of an itinerant Jewish rabbi. Thus, the narrator has to engage in a hermeneutical exercise in order to introduce the rabbi Jesus to the narratee. This possibility will be examined in the following discussion.[23]

The Deployment of the Name and Titles of Jesus
The preface does not mention Jesus at all. Even in a preface which is so brief and elliptical, this omission is surprising.[24] Although the significance of this omission is not discussed in the standard commentaries, in a narrative-critical reading the omission of a name is significant.[25]

22. The anonymity is unusual, although the other Gospels are also anonymous. 'When they had a dedication, ancient works were not anonymous' (Nolland 1989: 5). Marshall's suggestion that the anonymity arises from Luke being 'content to be seen as a member of the church which he serves, like the servants of the Word before him' (1978: 40) is unsatisfactory, because it does not spring from the analysis of the narrative, but a from an unverifiable conjecture about Luke.

23. 'Luke is addressing precisely the problem of how the past events of Christ's life are appropriated for salvation by successive generations of believers...as Schürmann correctly states: "in the apostolic paradosis the redemptive events retain their imperative contemporaneity" [Schürmann 1969: 269; translation Childs].' (Childs 1984: 106). 'Luke clearly sees the problem of tradition, that is, how to link events of the past with the message of today' (Schweizer 1984: 14).

24. 'No Preface for a published work distributed in the public book market in antiquity would reveal so little of the intention of the work' (Nolland 1989: 5).

25. Nolland comes closest: 'the Preface is very noncommittal about the subject

I suggest that under the convention of a hierarchy of authority, the narrator *cannot* introduce Jesus—because the narrator is not a sufficiently authoritative voice. Instead, the introduction of Jesus to the narrative world properly falls to a Spirit-anointed (and thus 'reliable') character who is also Jesus' contemporary. Consequently, Jesus' introduction has to be deferred until a suitable character comes along. The more modest task of the narrator is to marshal the eye-witnesses who will in due course introduce the character Jesus.

The Narrator's Characterization of Jesus in Act 1 (1.5–3.20)

The narrative proper opens at Lk. 1.5. In contrast to the earlier limitation due to the absence of embedded discourses, the narrator can now display the repertoire of literary devices which togther signal the semiotics within the world of the text. Now the reader can trace the semiotic focalizing and narrating that are 'located' within the descriptive narrative agent of the narrator.

The Contribution of the Narrator's Focalizing in Act 1
The narrator's focalizing of this act creates an elaborate literary scheme in which Jesus is contrasted with John.[26] The two characters are related through family connections in the story-world (1.36) and also through an ordering of their two stories which emphasizes both the common unity of their task and, at the same time, the superiority of Jesus in contrast to John (Tannehill 1986a: 19).[27]

The scene of Jesus' birth is briefly reported with no embedded discourse or narrative commentary, all of which suggest that it is relatively unimportant. In contrast, the longer narrative units which follow introduce a panoply of characters who speak of Jesus. The narrative time accorded to these discourses and the presence of embedded discourses

---

matter of the work, beyond saying that Theophilus already knows what it is about... [Luke's] Christian conviction has been kept out of sight' (Nolland 1989: 11-12). Talbert's genre studies lead him to observe that 'subjects treated [in the prefaces] were sometimes quite alien to the contents of the main work' (1982: 11).

26. The literary relationship between John and Jesus is discussed in Brown 1977: 250-53; cf. Tannehill 1986a: 47-73.

27. When the narratee reaches Lk. 7.28, this superiority will be retrospectively enhanced by Jesus' discourse that 'among those born of women no one is greater than John'.

demonstrate a narrative emphasis. Their common theme is *who* Jesus is to be, rather than *how* he arrived.[28]

While the narrator's focalizing establishes that Jesus is the help which 'God promised to our ancestors, to Abraham and to his descendants for ever' (1.55), the narrator does not instance a single Hebrew prophecy to confirm this fulfilment. The Lukan narrator often *alludes* to the Hebrew Scriptures in speaking of Jesus, while generally *avoiding* the quotation of them. Yet curiously, the narrator is content to introduce John the Baptist with a Hebrew Scripture (3.4).

In Jesus' case, a collection of story characters produce 'canticles' instead of scriptural quotation, which form 'the chief medium for the central expanding symbols of the birth narrative' (Tannehill 1986a: 20).[29] These 'canticles' function by integrating the past into the celebration of the present. The narrator emphasizes *Jesus in his present story*, who transforms Jewish prophecies as he fulfils them. Consequently for the narrator the detail of these prophecies is unnecessary.[30] This is one feature of the hermeneutical transformation at work in the narrator's characterization of the Jewish character Jesus.

The narrator portrays Jesus as a 'King to be' through the ordering of the material concerned with Davidic descent.[31] Bethlehem is included because it is David's city, rather than a fulfilment of prophecy.[32] How-

28. Apart from the opening scene, the presentation of Jesus in the Temple is the longest scene in this act, and includes much comment about Jesus from reliable characters.

29. The view is mistaken which considers that the Lukan narrator 'finds God's purpose revealed in Scripture, particularly in certain key texts of the Septuagint which appear repeatedly in Luke-Acts...Jesus' quotation from Isaiah in Luke 4.18-19 is an obvious example' (Tannehill 1986a: 21). As Tannehill fails to distinguish between narrative voices in his analysis, he misses the fact that it is story characters and not the narrator who instance Hebrew prophecy.

30. The manner and consequent significance of the Lukan narrator's employment of the Hebrew Scriptures is discussed further in the treatment of act 7 later in this chapter. Already it is clear that there is a christological conviction at work.

31. The narrator's discourse describes Joseph as 'of the house of David' (1.27); the angel's discourse to Mary which includes 'the Lord God will give to him the throne of his ancestor David' (1.32); Zechariah's discourse about the 'mighty Saviour in the house of his servant David' (1.69); the narrator's repetition of Joseph's lineage 'descended from the house and family of David' (2.4); and the angel's description of Bethlehem as 'the city of David' (2.11).

32. Unlike Matthew, where Bethlehem is an example of the fulfilment of Hebrew prophecy (Mt. 2.5-6). Talbert curiously claims that Bethlehem is 'an

ever, the narrator risks subverting this Davidic descent in the genealogy 'Jesus was the son (*as was supposed*) of Joseph' (2.23).

The final focalizing is of Jesus the boy in the Temple, bracketed by a literary *inclusio*. Although not the longest scene in the act, it is important because it is the first time that Jesus speaks. The setting is the Temple, which is at the very heart of Jewish religion. Through this story the narrator presents Jesus as the one who makes a claim upon the Temple as 'my Father's house' (2.49). At this point, the conflict may be considered to have begun.[33]

The Contribution of the Narrator's Narrating in Act 1
The contribution of language and style. Act 1 opens with a new range of vocabulary and a different style as it enters a world reminiscent of the Jewish stories in the LXX and leaves behind the Graeco-Roman world of the preface.[34] Such a change of style is striking, but not unusual.[35] The change 'makes the reader aware of the characterization of the...narrator' (Dawsey 1986b: 19), but more importantly, contrives a link between the Graeco-Roman world and the Jewish traditions.[36] The change in style also anchors Jesus' origins within the Jewish traditions for a non-Jewish narratee.[37]

A narrative-critical reading that distinguishes between narrative voices attends to the language and style *peculiar to each voice or dis-*

allusion to prophecy, though it is not made explicit by the evangelist, most likely to Micah 5.2' (1982: 31). There is no textual evidence to support this suggestion. .

33. Frei overlooks this scene and mistakenly concludes that in the infancy narratives the person Jesus is identified wholly in terms of the identity of the people of Israel. He is not the individual person Jesus, not even of "Nazareth"' (1975: 128).

34. There is 'a shift both from literary Greek to heavily Semitic Greek and from studied secularity to a tone of intense Jewish piety' (Nolland 1989: 17). Schweizer considers that the Gospel is written in the modern language of educated and demanding contemporaries (1984). Dawsey presents a recent detailed discussion of this change in style (1986b).

35. 'Intended as they were to provide a semblance of literature to quite prosy compositions, the prefaces were often in marked contrast with the style of the technical books to which they were attached' (Cadbury 1927: 197).

36. Any further significance of the change in style has proved to be a continuing enigma, for if the narrator can write in good Attic Greek, why did he not? 'It will undoubtedly remain a mystery' (Fitzmyer 1981: 109).

37. '[Luke] can count on Greco-Roman auditors to appreciate the antiquity of the Jewish scriptures, and the quaint style of his work would invite further attention' (Danker 1987: 5).

course.[38] Such an analysis of the language of the narrator's discourse is found in Dawsey (1986b), developed from the work of Moulton and Cadbury.[39] The present discussion enquires how the narrator's language and style contribute to the characterization of Jesus.[40]

The deployment of names and titles of Jesus. In act 1, Jesus is named by the narrator in only 4 of the 15 narrative units which mention him (2.21, 27, 43, 52) and the narrator never uses a title for him.[41] The deployment of the name Jesus is significant in that Jesus is 'unnamed' more frequently than he is named, and this feature continues with minor variations throughout the Gospel. Moreover, the scenes in which he is named are not the longest. Therefore the narrator demonstrates that Jesus is portrayed *principally through the medium of the story* and names (and titles) play a subsidiary role in his characterization.

The way that the name 'Jesus' is introduced into the primary discourse is also significant. The name first appears in Gabriel's discourse (1.31), and is *subsequently* adopted by the narrator (2.21) with the justification that it is 'the name given Jesus by the angel' (2.21). The

---

38. Historical-critical analyses of the language and style of various elements within the text are constructed upon distinctions between the Lukan redactor and pre-Lukan material. In a narrative-critical reading, the distinctions are between the various narrative voices in the text, which provide a completely new kind of analysis. This is particularly useful in Luke, for the narrator varies his Greek style for the voices of the different characters, as well as 'steeping his style in Biblical phraseology...as long as his narrative moves in Palestinian circles' (Moulton 1929: 7).

39. Dawsey fails to distinguish between the narrator's Greek in the infancy narratives and the rest of the Gospel and so the details of his conclusion have been checked before being adopted here. It turns out that his analysis is sufficiently representative of the Greek of the third and longest part of the Gospel.

40. Dawsey enumerates the characteristics peculiar to the Greek of the narrator's discourse. These include 'the use of short sentences, the lack of variety in his use of function words, the small number of vocables in his average word, his avoidance of precise numerical terms, his tendency to generalise'. Dawsey concludes that the style is an affected style of its own unlike both Attic and koine Greek. The style lends itself for reading aloud, and that the language and style evoke the ambience of worship, which suggests that the 'narrator's language has as its locus the community of faith' (Dawsey 1986b: 240).

41. The one case of an indirect ascription of a title is when the narrator describes Simeon who is waiting to see the Lord's Messiah. This description is focalized from Simeon's perspective, and not that of the narrator (2.26). The narrator first uses the title 'Messiah' on his own account in the next act (4.41).

narrator emulates the anarthrous form Ἰησοῦς used by Gabriel, which confirms the hierarchy of narrative voices identified in the preface. This hierarchy is also evident in the contrast between the virtual absence of narrative commentary by the narrator and the range of story characters who do comment upon Jesus, often in canticles. Most of these characters are associated in the narrative with God,[42] and so what they say is authoritative and reliable.[43]

In act 1, apart from Gabriel (1.31), no other character mentions the name Jesus. A study of the whole Gospel narrative reveals that of the 83 uses of the name Jesus in Luke, 77 examples occur in the narrator's discourse. Furthermore, apart from Gabriel, the remaining characters who use the name are minor characters.[44]

This narrator's virtual monopoly of the name Jesus imposes continuity in the unfolding presentation of Jesus, which counters the differences which the story characters contribute. In this, the narrator is constructing a unity in the text which is demonstratively of his own making.[45] In addition, the name Jesus is theologically insignificant for

42. The angel Gabriel 'stands in the presence of God' (1.19). Elizabeth speaks of Jesus as 'my Lord' when 'filled with the Holy Spirit' (1.41). Zechariah speaks of the Saviour from the House of David when 'filled with the Holy Spirit' (1.67). The angel who speaks to the shepherds is an 'angel of the Lord' (2.9); Simeon, who recognizes Jesus as the Lord's Messiah, is 'guided by the Spirit' (2.26). Anna, who speaks of Jesus as the Redeemer of Jerusalem, 'never left the Temple but worshipped there with fasting and prayer day and night' (2.37).

43. 'Consider how the portrait of Jesus is initially painted…these statements are made by reliable characters…The impression made upon the reader by these early portrayals will be reinforced throughout the entire narrative. Jesus, even though he encounters great opposition, will remain the hero of the story' (Gowler 1989: 57).

44. The name Jesus is employed by six story characters. Gabriel names the child Jesus (1.31); the Demons address Jesus as 'Jesus of Nazareth' (3.34); the lepers address Jesus as 'Jesus, Master' (17.13); the crowd describe Jesus as 'Jesus of Nazareth' (18.37); the blind man addresses Jesus as 'Jesus, Son of David' (18.38); and the criminal on the cross addresses Jesus as 'Jesus' (23.42). The Greek text of Lk. 18.37 can be either a narrator's report of the crowd's words to the blind man, or it can be translated as a separate and embedded discourse. In this discussion the Greek is construed as a separate discourse for the crowd (as Fitzmyer 1985: 1215, NRSV, contra Nolland 1993b: 897).

45. The sense of continuity generated by the repetition of the name Jesus is unwittingly magnified in some English translations of the Lukan text, which due to the ambiguity of successive Greek pronouns, replace many of them with the name 'Jesus'. NRSV (1989) inserts 'Jesus' for 'he' 34 times.

the narrator, which opens the way for its meaning to be primarily determined by the story of Jesus.[46]

The narrator uses the title 'Messiah' for Jesus twice in this act (2.26; 3.15) and once in the next act.[47] The first occurrence is a phrase from the Jewish Scriptures with 'messianic overtones'.[48] The second occurrence is the narrator's report of the crowd's question about John the Baptist. Both uses are only obliquely related to Jesus, which suggests that the narrator does not find 'Messiah' to be a useful category with which to identify Jesus.

Narrative commentary about Jesus. There are just two 'evaluative' narrative comments about Jesus in this act which form the *inclusio* of the scene of the boy Jesus in the Temple.

(1)   'The child grew and became strong...*and the favour of God was upon him*' (2.40).

(2)   And Jesus increased in wisdom and in years, *and in divine and human favour* (2.52).

Such evaluations can logically only be made by God, and so although the narrator writes the comments, they are focalized from God's perspective. The notion of 'God's favour coming upon people' has already appeared in the angel's discourse (1.30; 2.40) and so the narrator may now take it up.

These evaluations are *general* in form and not obviously shaped by the Hebrew Scriptures. This would fit with the narrator's conviction that Jesus transcends the particularities of Hebrew prophecies. Instead

46. Even when Gabriel in the Lukan narrative introduces the name Jesus, there is no etymological comment from either Gabriel or the narrator, as there is in Matthew: 'you are to name him Jesus, for he will save his people from their sins' (Mt. 1.21). For the Lukan narrator, the name Jesus awaits a narrative exposition.

47. The title Messiah appears just 12 times in the whole Gospel spread among at least 8 story characters of varying stature (2.11, 26; 3.15; 4.41; 9.20; 20.41; 22.67; 23.2, 35, 38; 24.26, 46). The narrator employs it only three times (2.26; 3.15; 4.41). The modest number of occurrences and the spread of voices demolishes the views of Fitzmyer (and others) who maintain that 'though not the most frequently used title for Jesus in the Lukan writings, *christos* has to be regarded as the most important' (Fitzmyer 1981: 197).

48. ' "The Lord's Messiah" is an Old Testament expression (1 Sam. 24.7, 11; 26.9) but is used here in a messianic sense' (Nolland 1989: 119).

of the Scriptures, the narrator prefers the 'living voice' of Spirit-anointed characters.[49]

These two narrative comments illustrate the narrator's re-shaping of Jesus' dismissal of his parents' concerns, which might seem harsh to the narratee. The description of God's approval functions as a literary 'counter-balance' to this possibility. The narrator's 'approval' of Jesus is further conveyed by the inclusion of the report that 'all that heard him were amazed at his understanding and answers' (2.47). This use of narrative commentary suggests that the narrator 'tones down' the conflict in which Jesus is involved.

The Narrator's Characterization of Jesus in Act 2 (3.21–4.44)

The Contribution of the Narrator's Focalizing in Act 2
The focalizing of these scenes is most evident in the ordering of scenes and in the allocation of narrative time. The act is a narrative exposition of the descent of the Spirit and the declaration of the voice from heaven which accompanied Jesus' baptism. Whereas the baptism itself is described in one Greek participle (3.21), the two events are described at greater length and their narrative expositions constitute the two longest scenes in the act.[50]

The voice from heaven declares to Jesus that 'he is his beloved son' (3.22) in the only embedded discourse in the scene. The importance of the discourse is further emphasized by its relative length (10 of the 43 words of the scene). The 'voice *from heaven*' is a periphrasis for the 'voice *of God*', who is the most reliable of narrative agents.

---

49. There is a large literature on the use of the Old Testament (or Hebrew Bible) in the Gospel of Luke. Cf. in particular Tiede 1980, Childs 1992. Such studies are useful, although they have to be recast to engage with a narrative-critical analysis of the different textual voices.

50. The distribution of narrative time is a function of the word count of each the narrative units together with the number of embedded discourses.

Narrative unit	Baptism	Genealogy	Temptation	Journey	Nazareth
Words	43	165	203	31	271
Embedded	1	0	2	0	2

Scene	Capernaum	Healing	Evening	Departure
Words	118	38	52	54
Embedded	3	0	1	1

The sonship the voice speaks about is developed in a narrative exposition of the temptations of Jesus by the devil, who begins 'If you are the Son...' (4.3). The authority of Jesus is underlined by his brief dismissal of the devil (26 out of 203 words of the scene).[51] Jesus' obedience is to the will of God, which is expressed through the Deuteronomic Scriptures. This story is what sonship is about.

The second event is the descent of the Holy Spirit, which is developed narratively in the visit of Jesus to the Nazareth synagogue—the longest (and so probably the most important) scene in the act (271 words). Jesus speaks at length for the first time which takes up half the scene (137 words).

A preliminary reading of the different narrative voices might conclude (as does Dawsey) that there is a significant difference between the narrator's report that 'all (the people) spoke well of him' (4.22a) and Jesus' perspective which does not trust the people's response and challenges it.[52] The question 'is not this Joseph's son?' (4.22b) does not seem to merit Jesus' aggressive response. When Jesus is almost killed by those who spoke well of him, the narrative dissonances pose questions of the narrator's reliability.[53]

---

51. When a discourse is an example of the exercise of authority, brevity emphasizes authority. When a discourse is teaching, the length of it is a pointer to its importance within the narrative. The authority of Jesus is emphasized by the contrast between the length of his and the devil's discourse, together with the increasing length of the devil's discourse as he fails:

Temptation 1:	Devil's discourse	12 words;	Jesus' response	9 words
Temptation 2:	Devil's discourse	28 words;	Jesus' response	10 words
Temptation 3:	Devil's discourse	34 words;	Jesus' response	7 words

52. Dawsey reads the narrator's characterization of Jesus as 'a misunderstood but well liked Messiah' (Dawsey 1986b: 82). Such confusion arises if the reader assumes that the narrator is speaking for himself when he reports that the people 'all spoke well of him' (4.22). The narrator clearly attributes the comment to the people, and so the narrator's words are focalized *from the people's perspective*. It is a mistake to assume (without other evidence) that if a narrator reports a view then he must subscribe to it.

53. 'Even the most unsophisticated reader is likely to be caught short by the shocking contrast of the two halves of the story... The juxtaposition is so sharp that it tests the adequacy of any considered attempt to explain, expound or interpret the text' (Tiede 1980: 20). Tiede concludes that 'The passage does not "explain" why Jesus was rejected, nor does it "explain" why the prophet turns against his audience.' (Tiede 1980: 55).

The focalizing of the discourses permits the people one brief discourse (4.22b) and then all else about them is reported by either the narrator (4.22a) or Jesus (4.23). In Jesus' discourse the camouflaged truth about the people is laid bare and the subsequent attempt to kill him offers confirmation of Jesus' discernment.[54] The allocation of so much narrative time to Jesus' discourse makes clear that the narrator *approves* of Jesus' discourse; the narrator considers Jesus to be an anointed prophet who is rejected as were the prophets of old.[55]

The presence of this scene early in the narrative signals its programmatic function.[56] From now on, when the 'people' stand in awe and amazement, the narratee will be cautious about what weight to give to what they say.

The act ends with four scenes woven into a 24-hour period and includes the third longest scene in the act when Jesus confronts the man with the spirit of an unclean demon. The focalizing of the scene displays the importance *for the narrator* of the demon's contribution and the people's responsed because the demon is only silenced *after* it has declared who Jesus is.

The words of the people express the development in their perception of Jesus as one who exercises authority *and power* (4.36, cf. 4.32). In the healings at sunset the focalizing is tightened by refusing a discourse to Jesus and the people, but allocating one to the demons (4.41)—who are silenced, again *after* they speak. The discourses of the demons are clearly important for the narrator and these are discussed in Chapter 11.

The Contribution of the Narrator's Narrating in Act 2
The contribution of language and style. The Greek style of the second act is similar to act 1, but without the archaic features of the style of the LXX. Jesus now moves onto the public stage and leaves behind the world of his childhood and its Jewish piety.

54. A possible narrative logic of these swiftly moving events is proposed by Sanders, after studying the history of the midrash upon Isa. 61. Sanders suggest that Jesus raised the expectations of the hope with his '*Today...*' (4.21), and then dashes the listener's hope by explaining that outsiders would benefit instead of the Jews, and that this outcome is completely acceptable to God (1993: 67-69).

55. Jesus' discourse is discussed at length in the next chapter.

56. This thematic re-ordering of the chronicle material is clear from the discourse of Jesus in which he refers to 'works which he did at Capernaum' (4.23) which have not yet appeared in the text.

The narrator prefers 'non-theological' language. When Jesus heals people, the narrator uses the verb θεραπεύω (4.40) and never uses σῴζω (cf. Dawsey 1986b: 83).[57] To the narrator, Jesus' works are demonstrations of power (δύναμις [4.14]), rather than aspects of salvation. This avoidance of 'theologically nuanced' language, which recurs throughout the Gospel, is part of the narrator's characterization of Jesus as *the man for the Gentile world*.

The deployment of the names and titles of Jesus. Jesus is named in four of the eight scenes of the act, in contrast to the anonymity of most of the other characters in this act.[58] The narrator develops his portrayal of Jesus through the modification of Jesus' name. In the first three scenes the character Jesus is denoted by the anarthrous form Ἰησοῦς, which is also used of Jesus in act 1. When Jesus addresses the devil with authority, the narrator denotes him as ὁ Ἰησοῦς (4.4; 4.8; 4.12), which signals 'the authoritative Jesus'.[59] This development is also found in the contrast between perceptions of Jesus before and after the temptations (4.1 'full of the Holy Spirit'; 4.14 'filled with the power of the Spirit').[60]

When Jesus addresses people, the narrator does not use Jesus' name to denote Jesus, even in the longest scene in the act in the Nazareth synagogue. This suggests that the narrator perceives Jesus as *less* authoritative in his interaction with the people than with the demons.

For the last time in the Gospel the narrator employs the title Messiah in a report of the demon's knowledge (4.41). I suggest that the narrator

57. There is a difference between the narrator and Jesus, as will become clear in the next act when Jesus does use σῴζω to describe a healing (Lk. 8.48).

58. Jesus is named eight times by the narrator (3.21, 23; 4.1, 4, 8, 12, 14, 35) and once by the demon (4.34). Otherwise, only the hitherto unknown Simon (4.38 [twice]) and the prophet Isaiah are named (4.17). The description 'the Devil' is considered a generic description; the name 'Satan' is reserved until later in the narrative.

59. It is usual for proper names not to include the definite article in New Testament Greek, but in the Synoptics, Ἰησοῦς takes the article as a rule (Funk 1961: 136). It is significant that the article is omitted in every use before the temptation scene, and that the name attracts and generally retains the article from then on.

60. The suggestion is confirmed by the contrast in perception of Jesus before (he spoke with authority' [4.32]) and after the exorcism in the synagogue at Capernaum ('with authority and power he commands the unclean spirits' [4.36]), and where ὁ Ἰησοῦς denotes Jesus.

relinquishes this concept because Jesus also relinquishes the category by refashioning it in his own story. The result is that the title is not retained: it is obsolete for the Lukan narrator.

The use of 'Messiah' is problematic in this scene for another reason. The narrator employs it in when reporting a view of the demons—who declare Jesus to be the 'Son of God' and *not* the Messiah. The title 'Son of God' is related to the title Messiah only here in all the Gospel.[61] If this is a literary parallelism to redescribe Messiah in terms of the Son of God, it further supports the suggestion that the narrator deliberately relinquishes the title 'Messiah'.

Narrative commentary about Jesus. There are two examples of narrative commentary that contribute to the characterization of Jesus. First, the narrator recounts that Jesus went to the synagogue as *was his custom* (4.16), which functions in an evaluative way, presenting Jesus as the faithful Jew.

The other example is the first occasion that the narrator presents an 'inside view' of the mind of Jesus.[62] The narrator explains that Jesus rebukes the demons 'because they knew he was the Messiah' and so the narrator reports Jesus' point of view—or does he?

Since W. Wrede, many redaction critics have argued that the Markan 'messianic secret' has been adopted by the Lukan evangelist.[63] Dawsey presents a literary-critical version of the 'Lukan messianic secret' based on the assumption that the narrator always speaks only for himself. A narrative-critical reading of this scene is attentive to the difference

61. A difficulty acknowledged in the commentaries: Marshall refutes the suggestion that Luke has 'down-graded "Son of God" to become merely an attribute of "Messiah" (1978: 197); Fitzmyer fails to explain the difficulty with the suggestion that 'this last part is obviously written from the standpoint of the evangelist... several generations after the ministry of Jesus itself' (1981: 554). Nolland offers the theological possibility that 'a right knowledge of Jesus Christ and redeemer is only to be had in connection with the cross' (1989: 214).

62. Sheeley curiously does not consider that this example of 'inside view' fits the criteria of his 'narrative aside', even though he explicitly includes 'inside views of characters' (1992: 98).

63. In Luke, the pattern is more accurately described as occasions when 'silence is commanded'. The repeated commands to silence encompass more activities than the occasions when Jesus is referred to as Messiah by another narrative voice (4.41). More usually, these refer to Jesus' healings and exorcisms. Cf. Danker's discussion of a 'silence motif' (1987: 90-92).

between narrating and focalizing and notices that the narrator reports Jesus silencing the demons who have *already* declared him to be the Son of God *before* they *also* declare him to be the Messiah.[64] A better reading then construes the narrator presenting Jesus as seeking to avoid the title Messiah, albeit without explanation.[65]

The Narrator's Characterization of Jesus in Act 3 (5.1–9.50)

For a reader interested in the identity of Jesus, act 3 is the most important of all the acts because within it the greatest attention is given by various narrative agents to the question of who Jesus might be. This is particularly true in the case of the narrator.

The Contribution of the Narrator's Focalizing in Act 3

The narrator focalizes the sequence of narrative units to offer two expositions in response to the question 'who is Jesus?' The first exposition actually begins in the synagogue at Nazareth in the previous act and runs on to the moment when the disciples of John ask 'are you the one who is to come?' (7.19, exact repetition for emphasis in 7.20). Jesus' answer (7.21-23) is framed in language which evokes the quotation from Isaiah in the synagogue (4.16-21).[66]

The focalizing of this sequence between Lk. 4.16 and 7.21 makes clear that the narrative exposition is 'ordered' to fit not the list from Isaiah which is mentioned at Nazareth but the *list of events which Jesus rehearses*.[67] This feature expresses the narrator's conviction that the

---

64. Jesus' hesitation about the title Messiah is discussed in Chapter 10.

65. The literary-critical version of the redaction-critical argument for a so-called 'messianic secret' is found in Dawsey's *The Lukan Voice*, where he concludes that the narrator's 'idea of secrecy in no way corresponds to Jesus' open proclamation of who he is and what he is all about' (1986b: 94).

66. The similarity between Lk. 4.18-19a and Lk. 7.22 is often recognized. 'Without quoting, Jesus' words echo the terms of Isaiah 61.1' (Nolland 1989: 330). The sequence of Jesus' ministry between these two scenes constitutes the narrative exposition with these passages as the *inclusio* (contra Talbert 1974: 39).

67. *Nazareth List*	*List for John*	*Narrative Scenes*
sight to the blind	blind receive sight	7.21 (singled out in summary)
—	lame walk	5.17-36 'man through roof'
—	lepers cleansed	5.12-16 leper healed
—	deaf hear	—
—	dead are raised	7.11-17 son of widow at Nain 4.44?
good news to poor	good news to the poor	—

character Jesus both fulfils and definitively transforms the prophetic hopes of the Hebrew Scriptures. Jesus is the one whose story interprets Scripture, rather than the other way round.

The second narrative exposition is the story of the change in the disciple Peter as he moves from a view of Jesus as 'Master' (5.5) to view Jesus as 'Messiah' (9.20). Even this recognition by Peter needs the further correction which is given in the Transfiguration scene which follows, when the voice from heaven addresses the disciples (including Peter), and describes Jesus as 'my Son' (9.35).

The Transfiguration scene is the narrative hinge between the questions of 'who is Jesus?' which repeat through this act and the journey to Jerusalem which informs the next act. The focalizing of this scene emphasizes Jesus as the obedient Son through the inclusion of an embedded discourse for the voice from the cloud, and also through the silence of Jesus throughout the scene.[68]

The longest discourse comprises six thematic units (commonly known as the 'Sermon on the Plain') which emphasize Jesus as a teacher. It is in this act that Jesus introduces the parable as a teaching device (5.36).[69]

The longest scene in the act occurs at Gerasa (8.22-39) and includes the longest dialogue in which Jesus is involved. This the only scene in the whole Gospel in which Jesus travels to a Gentile region.[70] Jesus commissions the man who is exorcised to 'return home and declare how much God has done for you' (8.39)—and this in a Gentile region. As in Nazareth, the first response to Jesus' ministry is rejection, this time by Gentiles, which underlines the irony of the welcome that Jesus receives upon his return to Galilee (8.40).

release to captives	—	These general categories
set free the oppressed	—	may include the exorcisms
proclaim the year of the	—	
Lord's favour		

68. Even in the narrator's report, Moses and Elijah are talking to Jesus, who says nothing. The response to Peter's foolishness is given by the Voice from the Cloud. This pattern is the 'prayerful silence of acquiescence' which also features in Jesus' baptism.

69. The narrator first describes Jesus as telling a παραβολή at 5.36. In Jesus' discourse in the Nazareth synagogue (4.23) the range of meaning of παραβολή is clear when it correctly describes a 'proverb' (NRSV).

70. Commentators agree that although Nain (7.11) geographically is not within traditional Galilee, the narrator considers that it is.

Jesus' discourse to the man with leprosy includes a brief narrator's report that Jesus 'ordered him to tell no one' (5.14a).[71] This focalizing of embedded and reported speech raises again the question of a literary pattern of 'commands to silence'. This healing is in a sequence of events which are *necessarily* public, because the narrator requires them for Jesus' answer to John's disciples (7.18-23). It is therefore unlikely that the narrator's comment is a *general* command to silence, but rather that he should be silent until he has shown himself to the priest.[72] In fact, four of the five examples of 'commands to silence' are found in the narrator's discourse.[73] In a narrative-critical reading the audience

71. Despite Dawsey's hesitation that the shift in voice may have resulted from some sort of stylistic quality of the writer (Dawsey 1986b: 90), Marshall's observation (informed by redaction criticism) seems more to the point, even if the explanation is unconvincing: 'Luke turns Mark's direct command into indirect speech, but is unable to keep up this style, and relapses into direct speech almost immediately' (1978: 209).

72. 'The retention of the counsel [to keep silent] is vestigial in the Lukan account, since it has none of the Markan messianic-secret motif. Later on, Luke will omit the mention of the leper's failure to comply' (Fitzmyer 1981: 575); cf. Nolland 'the injunction to silence serves merely to underline Jesus' concern here for compliance with the Old Testament law: a public claim to cleansing from leprosy was inappropriate prior to priestly investigation...cf. Leviticus 14.1-32' (1989: 228).

73. Apart from the first command to silence, the four other commands are in the narrator's discourse, and with varying audiences, which means they need to be read separately and not simply counted together.

(1) The audience of the Demons—who shout out the identity of Jesus:
    4.35 Jesus rebuked [the demon], saying 'Be silent, and come out of him...'
    4.41 But he rebuked [the demons] and would not allow them to speak...
(2) The audience of the healed people—who have been changed by their encounter with Jesus:
    5.14 And he ordered [the healed man with leprosy] to tell no one...
    8.56 ...but he ordered her parents to tell no one what had happened...
(3) The audience of the disciples, once they have reached the point of partially understanding who Jesus is:
    9.21 He sternly ordered and commanded [the disciples] to tell no one...

Dawsey mishandles this theme by uncritically mixing redaction-critical and literary-critical insights, and by imprecision in his reading of the text. Dawsey correctly identifies that Jesus purposefully keeps his identity secret in Lk. 4.41; 5.14 (though he misses 8.56 and 9.21, and hesitates about the key example in 4.35 [Dawsey 1986b: 90 n. 7]). Mistakenly he inflates the occasions when this is sup-

and occasion of example are significant, and once the three different audiences are identified, it is clear that there is no general imposition of secrecy in the narrative by the narrator.[74]

The Contribution of the Narrator's Narrating in Act 3

The contribution of language and style. As the style of the Greek according to Cadbury is relatively uniform (1920: 39), discussion of the style of this section and future sections will concentrate upon the language employed by the narrator.

For the first time the narrator uses the phrase εὐαγγελιζόμενος τὴν βασιλείαν τοῦ Θεοῦ (8.1) to describe Jesus, and so repeats Jesus' earlier description of his own ministry (4.43). The verb εὐαγγελίζομαί is used twice of Jesus in the Gospel in two summary reports (8.1; 20.1) This minimal use of the verb is surprising, for it soon became part of Christian vocabulary; could it be too Jewish, and so unimportant for the narrator?[75]

The phrase 'the kingdom of God' is taken up by the narrator from Jesus' discourse, and is used three times in the act in summary reports of Jesus' activity (8.1; 9.2, 11). As the narrator never comments or develops the phrase it seems that it is another part of the Jewish world which the narrator leaves behind.[76]

posed to happen by including a further curious list of vaguely related scenes: Lk. 7.37-50; 8.37-39; 9.7, 45; 11.14-26; 18.34; 20.26.

74. The narrator treats at length Jesus' commission to the disciples to *announce* that the kingdom is coming (9.1-6), and to *announce* that Jesus is coming (9.52-56; 10.1-12). Furthermore, the narrator repeatedly records (without criticism or qualification) the growth in interest in Jesus from among the crowds (e.g. 5.15). The focalizing of the events in this act which gives large amounts of narrative time to *public* events of Jesus precludes any generalized concern by the narrator for Jesus' silence.

75. The verb εὐαγγελίζομαι is used four times by the narrator (3.18; 8.1; 9.6; 20.1), while the noun εὐαγγέλιον is never used. The verb is also used twice by the angel Gabriel (1.19; 2.10) and four times in Jesus' discourse (4.18; 4.43; 7.22; 18.16). The narrator always uses the verb with a positive association—even when describing John the Baptist, for the verb relates to the promise about the baptism of the Spirit (3.18).

76. Jesus introduces the phrase 'the kingdom of God' in his discourse at the end of act 2 (4.43) and mentions it a further four times in act 3 (6.20; 7.28; 8.10; 9.27). The contrast between Jesus' use of the phrase and the narrator is seen more plainly in the next act, where Jesus mentions the kingdom of God 17 times, and the narrator just twice. The significance for Jesus is discussed in Chapter 10.

The Names and Titles for Jesus. The narrator names Jesus 30 times in 14 of the 30 scenes in which he appears, yet 15 of the 30 occurrences of the name Jesus are concentrated in just 3 scenes of healing/exorcism (7.1-10; 8.29-39; 8.40-56). Only two examples are anarthrous.[77] The narrator employs the form ὁ Ἰησοῦς when Jesus acts authoritatively in dealing with sickness and the demons, as in the last act, and introduces this convention into controversy with the Pharisees, in which Jesus is portrayed as a *teacher* with authority.[78]

The analysis of the omission of the name 'Jesus' in the narrative scenes reveals a surprising feature. The key is the presence or absence of the disciples.[79] Jesus is rarely named when the disciples are mentioned as present. Through this literary device the narrator presents Jesus as *constrained* by the presence of his disciples, which fits the Lukan characterization of the disciples as slow to understand and in continual need of correction and teaching.[80] Jesus rarely exercises

77. There are variant readings in Lk. 8.41; this discussion follows *UBSGNT*, 3rd edn, and includes the article.

78. The Pharisees are introduced to the narrative in a sequence of five virtually consecutive controversies with Jesus. On each occasion Jesus is denoted as ὁ Ἰησοῦς (5.17-26; 5.29-32; 5.33-39; 6.1-5 and 6.6-11). This 'concentration' suggests the importance of Jesus' *teaching* authority.

79. The distribution *in relevant scenes* of the presence of (1) the named character Jesus and (2) the disciples:

Scene	3.01	3.02	3.03	3.04	3.05	3.06	3.07	3.08	3.09	3.10	3.11
Jesus	*yes*	yes	yes	no	yes	yes	*yes*	yes	no	no	no
Disciples	*yes**￼*	no	no	*yes**￼*	no	no	*yes*	no	yes*	yes	yes

Scene	3.17	3.18	3.19	3.20	3.21	3.22	3.23	3.24	3.25	3.26	3.28
Jesus	yes	no	no	no	yes	no	no	—	no	no	yes
Disciples	no	yes	no	no	no	yes*	yes	—	yes	yes	no

Scene	3.29	3.30	3.31	3.32	3.33	3.34	3.35	3.36	3.37	3.38	3.39
Jesus	*yes*	no	—	no	no	no	*yes*	*yes*	no	*yes*	no
Disciples	*yes**￼*	*yes**￼*	—	*yes**￼*	*yes**￼*	yes	*yes**￼*	*yes*	yes	*yes*	*yes**￼*

(1) * signifies an equivalent word (e.g. the 'twelve'); ** signifies the presence of 'named' disciples.

(2) The scene reference numbers (3.01, etc.) are those used in the analysis given in Chapter 8.

(3) The columns in italics are the six cases where a 'named' Jesus and disciples are present.

80. 'Although Jesus' major conflict in Luke's gospel story is with Israel, whether people or authorities, he must also struggle with the disciples' (Kingsbury

authority over his followers, but teaches them as disciples. The imma-
ture disciples are ineffective in Jesus' ministry of power and are often
literally 'absent' from these scenes of Jesus acting with power.

The narrator offers an elliptical contribution in his literary juxtaposition of Jesus and God (8.39).[81] A careful reading recognizes that there
are two discourses in play rather than the single discourse of traditional
Hebrew parallelism, and so this feature is a contrived parallelism,
though not without effect. It will be reconsidered in the discussion of
act 7.

The narrator denotes Jesus as 'the Lord' (ὁ κύριος) for the first time
(7.13).[82] A second example is Lk. 7.19, which is focalized from the perspective of John. The narrator continues the pattern of taking up that
which authoritative voices in the narrative have already introduced and
so legitimized.[83] The title denotes Jesus when he raises to life the son of
the widow of Nain, and so an association begins (but is not developed)
between the title 'Lord' and Jesus' power over death.[84]

Narrative Commentary about Jesus. The three examples of narrative
commentary that relate to Jesus are all examples of a limited 'inside

1991b: 109; cf. Tannehill 1986a: 203-74).

81. The closeness of the parallel is most clear in the Greek text:

Jesus: Ὑπόστρεφε εἰς τὸν οἶκόν σου, καὶ διηγοῦ ὅσα σοι ἐποίησεν ὁ θεός.
Narrator: καὶ ἀπῆλθεν καθ' ὅλην τὴν πόλιν κηρύσσων ὅσα ἐποίησεν αὐτῷ ὁ
Ἰησοῦς (8.39).

The words 'Jesus' and 'God' are emphatic, and there is a strikingly close textual
parallelism.

82. The narrator shares with other subjects the ability to use ὁ κύριος to denote
God. The narrator restricts this use to the 12 occurrences in the early chapters (1.6;
1.9; 1.11; 1.58; 2.9 (2×); 2.22; 2.23; 2.24; 2.26; 2.39 and 5.17). The narrator then
begins his 12 examples which are distributed through the rest of the Gospel when at
Lk. 7.13 he uses ὁ κύριος to denote Jesus. The narrator never uses 'Lord' as a
respectful way to address or describe men.

83. The title 'Lord' is used of Jesus by Elizabeth (1.43), the angel (2.11), Peter
(5.8), an anonymous leper (5.12) and Jesus has used it of himself (6.46).

84. At the lexical level, Nolland is correct: 'despite the passive form of the verb
ἐγέρθητι (Lit. be raised up), no special resurrection connotation should be discerned: the passive of this verb is often used with intransitive active (middle) force'
(Nolland 1989: 323). At the narrative level, however, the appearance of the title 'the
Lord' on this one occasion is significant. This conclusion must be qualified by the
fact that the title is not employed in the account of the raising of Jairus's daughter
(8.49-56).

view' into his mind. The narrator explains that Jesus 'knows the inner thoughts of those with whom he is engaged' (opponents 5.22, 6.8; helpers 9.47) and this contributes to the stature of the character Jesus.

The Narrator's Characterization of Jesus in Act 4 (9.51–19.44)

Act 4 presents Jesus on a journey in the central and longest act of the Gospel.[85] The narrator's presentation of Jesus as teacher develops significantly in this act, as Jesus engages in controversies with opponents and with the disciples. Jesus is the controversialist who no one can confound. The way that the narrator focalizes the material also provides the opportunity for the narratee to hear what Jesus teaches.[86] The shadow of Jerusalem falls over the whole of the act, for the narrator knows that Jerusalem is the place where the conflict will be resolved—even if it is hidden from the disciples (18.34).

The Contribution of the Narrator's Focalizing in Act 4

The journey of Jesus displays no clear temporal or geographical structure.[87] In contrast to the vagueness of geographical indicators, Jerusalem is mentioned 12 times.[88] Jerusalem is the place where the events *will take place*, but not until the time for Jesus' death.[89] The chiastic the-

85. In Chapter 8 the Gospel is analysed into 184 narrative units. Act 4 is 74 units long, which equals 40.2%.

86. Chapter 10 is devoted to a reading of Jesus' discourses and so the present discussion concentrates upon the significance of aspects of the presentation of Jesus as teacher.

87. Conzelmann is correct when he observes that the 'scheme of a journey' in the narrative, with its attendant difficulties for the reader of reconciling the material and the scheme, displays a 'deliberate intent', such that 'Luke is determined to carry it out at any cost' (1960: 61 n. 6). The omission of a clear geographical structure to the 'journey', which is in marked contrast to the preceding and succeeding narrative sections, is a feature of great importance.

88. Jerusalem is mentioned at Lk. 9.51, 53; 10.30; 13.4, 22, 33, 34; 17.11; 18.31; 19.11, 28; and 19.41.

89. One curious feature of the act is that the narrator occasionally reminds the narratee where events are leading, but never provides a location for where the present events are taking place. In the whole of this narrative section, there is no geographical precision until the mention of Jericho in ch. 19. This explains why the narrative confuses those readers who endeavour to construct itineraries for the 'so-called' journey. Their failures help explain comments such as 'obviously there is no travelling done at all' (Bailey 1976: 82).

matic pattern created by the narrator's focalizing identified in ch. 8 places literary emphasis upon Jerusalem, and also subverts the hope of tracing a temporal sequence to this journey.

The focalizing of the character Jesus is principally conveyed through the two stratagems of the management of narrative time and the ordering and deployment of different discourses.[90] Moessner suggests that the Lukan narrator's representation of the Jesus material in this act is akin to the Deuteronomic re-presentation of the story and discourses of Moses (Moessner 1989).[91] Even if that is to claim too much, it is the case that the selection of the events places much more emphasis upon Jesus the teacher/prophet than upon his activity as healer or exorciser.[92] For example, in the exorcism in Lk. 11.14-26, the exorcism is described briefly (in contrast to the detail of earlier scenes), while most of the narrative time is allocated to the controversy.

The focalizing allocates much more narrative time to Jesus' discourses than to the discourses of the narrator or any character.[93] In this act the narrator usually retires into the background and hands over the stage to Jesus.[94] The teaching role of Jesus is further emphasized by the appearance in this act of 24 of the 30 parables in the whole Gospel, and

90. In this act, attention to narrative time is particularly important as other characteristics which assisted in the recognition of focalizing in earlier acts are rarely present.

91. 'Far from a random collection of disjointed material sewn together only by virtue of common themes or catchwords, the Central section discloses a very specific, fourfold plot based on the Prophet like Moses of Deuteronomy' (Moessner 1989: 292).

92. Out of the 71 narrative units of this act, only 13 portray an activity of Jesus, and of these only 5 scenes portray Jesus healing or exorcising (11.14-23; 13.10-17; 14.1-6; 17.11-19; 18.35-43).

93. Jesus has his own discourse in 68 of the 71 narrative units. In 44 of these 68 occasions, Jesus is the only character to have an embedded discourse. In 20 of these 44 narrative units, Jesus' discourse is presented without the narrator present, and a further 11 narrative units comprise Jesus' discourse with the presence of the minimal narrator. The combination of these last two categories means that in 31 narrative units (44% of the act), Jesus is presented as (virtually) the only voice speaking.

94. This may be illustrated in various ways. One striking example is that in 25 scenes which comprise just the narrator's primary discourse and the discourse of the character Jesus, Jesus speaks for longer than the narrator in 24 cases, and in 10 of these 24 cases the narrator is reduced to merely signalling the discourse subject.

the longest narrative unit in the act is the parable of the Lost Son.[95]

The authority of Jesus' teaching is characterized by the cumulative narrative description of controversies in which he always has his own discourse and in which he is never confounded. There are nine occasions when Jesus engages with the Pharisees, and only once does he not engage them in controversy (13.31-35). At the same time, the disciples continue to learn from Jesus the teacher, while Jesus does less and less.[96]

The teaching of Jesus is not tied to particular places, and so the narrator leads the narratee beyond the particularities of the occasions to Jesus' teaching.[97] The omission of temporal and spatial signifiers together with the frequent absence of audiences 'decouple' the scenes from their rootedness in the story-world and construct the narrative effect of Jesus teaching *the narratee*.

The Contribution of the Narrator's Narrating in Act 4
The contribution of the names and titles of Jesus. The name Jesus appears in only 10 of the 39 possible reports and scenes in this act. These ten narrative units are either healings/exorcisms or discussions about the salvation associated with Jesus, and always display the form ὁ Ἰησοῦς.[98] Jesus is not named in the remaining 29 occasions, and the

---

95. For this preliminary reading, this analysis adopts Jeremias's identification of 31 'story' parables in Luke, though it can be argued that there are more than 31 (Jeremias 1972: 247-48). Four are found in act 3, 25 in act 4 and 2 in act 5. The importance of parables in act 4 is also suggested by the allocation of the longest amount of narrative time to the parable of the Lost Son (391 words). This parable and the road to Emmaus scene (also 391 words) are the longest narrative units in the Gospel.

96. Even the achievements of 'the 70' on their missionary tour are omitted from the narrative.

97. This change in emphasis is illustrated in the Beelzebul controversy. In contrast to the detail of the exorcisms in the earlier act, the exorcism is summarized briefly in 16 words, which precipitates the long debate about the significance of Jesus' exorcisms, in which Jesus' discourse is 172 words long.

98. The name 'Jesus' appears in 10 of the 71 narrative units. There are only four scenes of healing or exorcism, and in every case Jesus is named (13.10-17; 14.1-6; 17.11-19; 18.35-43); there is also one brief report of an exorcism, in which Jesus is not named (11.14). The common theme shared by the remaining six scenes is the salvation *associated with Jesus*: the 'would be' disciples (9.57-62); the lawyer's question about eternal life (10.25-37); children as models of the reception of the kingdom (18.15-17); the rich ruler's question about eternal life (18.18-30); the

disciples are not usually mentioned either. The emphasis is upon the teaching rather than the teacher, an impression confirmed by the fact that there is only one occasion when Jesus' identity is directly in question (11.15-23).[99]

The narrator employs ὁ κύριος in 8 of the 39 possible reports/scenes. The title is introduced by the disciples (9.54) before the narrator takes it up (10.1).[100] One scene illuminates the relative significance of the title 'Lord' for the narrator. In a healing controversy, Jesus is first named as ὁ Ἰησοῦς (13.12) and then as controversy deepens he is described as ὁ κύριος (13.15), which suggests that for the narrator the title 'Lord' conveys greater authority than the name 'Jesus'.

The title 'kingdom of God' is almost irrelevant for the narrator, appearing only twice (17.20; 19.11) in his reports of the comments of others.[101] Surprisingly, at key moments in the narrative, Jesus remains both nameless and title-less, as when he sets his face to Jerusalem, laments over Jerusalem or weeps over Jerusalem. Jesus the character seems to retire in order to give emphasis to the discourses of Jesus.

Narrative commentary about Jesus. There are just three examples of narrator's commentary which might assist in the characterization of Jesus. Two reiterate the ability of Jesus to know what people are thinking, while the third explains why Jesus introduces a parable (19.11).

arrival with Jesus of salvation at the house of Zacchaeus (19.1-10); and the ride into Jerusalem (19.29-40). In 61 narrative units, Jesus is simply unnamed.

99. This is in marked contrast to the previous two acts in which the narrator deploys character after character to reiterate versions of the question 'who is Jesus?'. In act 4 the question is posed directly only once (11.15-23) and indirectly only three times (10.17; 12.13-14; 13.10-17).

100. The pattern of the narrator taking up ways to denote Jesus occurs at a micro-level within individual scenes:

(1) In 10.38-41, an unnamed Jesus enters the scene and meets Martha, who calls him 'Lord' (10.40). The narrator then describes Jesus as 'Lord' as he introduces Jesus' response (10.41).
(2) In 12.41-48, Peter enquires of a unnamed Jesus 'Lord, is this parable for us?' (12.41) and the narrator introduces Jesus' reply as 'the Lord said' (12.42).

101. This is in marked contrast to Jesus, who employs the title 'kingdom of God' 17 times in his discourses in act 4, distributed among 12 distinct occasions, and usually (10 of the 12) when he is not named by the narrator. On these occasions the focus of interest for the narratee is the kingdom of God, and not the person Jesus who speaks of the kingdom.

These narrative comments make a modest contribution to the increasing stature of the character Jesus.

The Narrator's Characterization of Jesus in Act 5 (19.45–21.38)

At this stage of the story, the character Jesus needs no further explicit comment from the narrator and so the focalizing of the story now 'shows' who Jesus is.

The Contribution of the Narrator's Focalizing in Act 5
The act begins as Jesus cleanses the Temple and claims it as his own.[102] The emphasis upon the Temple and not the city of Jerusalem is surprising after the importance of Jerusalem in the previous act.[103] The reclaimed Temple becomes a setting for Jesus' eventual unrestricted freedom to teach, in contrast to the growing power of the opposition associated with Jerusalem.

Jesus neither heals nor exorcises anyone, but engages in controversy in the place where he first spoke (2.41-51). Once Jesus reaches the Temple the Pharisees play no further part in the story, which signals the end of genuine controversy and the start of moves to trap Jesus (20.20).[104] The scenes are ordered to portray the increasing authority of Jesus as his opponents gradually disappear, and Jesus is left undis-

---

102. Conzelmann correctly observes the narrative order of cleansing/teaching in the Temple through which Jesus takes possession of the Temple (1960: 76). However, it is doubtful that this exhausts the narrative importance of the cleansing of the Temple, as Conzelmann goes on to argue (1960: 78).

103. Jerusalem is only mentioned once by the narrator during the whole of this act, when he explains that Herod was in Jerusalem at that time (23.7). The narrator does not comment on or develop the significance of 'Jerusalem'. The three other references to Jerusalem in this act are found in Jesus' discourse (21.20, 24; 23.28). Conzelmann correctly portrays the journey of Jesus from 'Galilee to the Temple' (1960: 17).

104. Carroll suggests that the omission of the Pharisees from the plot to kill Jesus allows them later to speak in defence of Paul the Pharisee (Acts 23.7-10) and so legitimize the mission of the church (1988: 618). The hypothesis is possible, but needs more discussion to distinguish whether it is likely to be a consequence of their omission, or a reason for that omission. Within the Gospel narrative the omission fits with the characterization of the Pharisees as a complex character group, who at times can oppose Jesus and at other times can welcome him to dine with them and who can warn him of Herod's intent.

turbed to teach as he wishes.[105] The people 'get up early in the morning to listen to him' (21.38).

Jesus speaks much more than other characters and, with one exception, always has the last word. Significantly, that exception is the scribe who concedes that Jesus speaks well (20.39).[106] The focalizing locates Jesus' warning about the future of the Temple within the Temple precincts.

The Contribution of the Narrator's Narrating in Act 5

The contribution of the language used. The narrator describes Jesus as εὐαγγελιζομένου (20.1 'telling the good news'; NRSV). The only other use of the verb is to describe an earlier period of itinerant ministry (8.1) where it is also a summary report.[107] When Jesus reclaims the Temple, he recalls it to its proper function and it becomes the place of the proclamation of the Good News.[108] The intensity of opposition to Jesus is conveyed by the verb which describes the plan to *destroy* Jesus (19.47).[109]

---

105. This sequence makes clear the growing impotence of Jesus' opponents. First the question of Jesus' authority leaves the religious leaders unable to answer him (20.7); the parable of the Wicked Husbandmen leaves the opponents impotent due to the crowd (20.19); the spies sent on behalf of the opponents are reduced to silence (20.26); after the controversy with the Sadducees, one of the scribes acknowledges that Jesus speaks well (20.39). At this point in the narrative the opponents disappear altogether and leave Jesus teaching daily and unhindered in the Temple for the rest of the act. 'At this point [Jesus'] conflict with the religious authorities intensifies dramatically... At every turn, however, Jesus outwits them, and so they finally fall silent (20.40). Leaving the Temple for the time being to Jesus, they henceforth concentrate on one objective, to bring about his death' (Kingsbury 1991b: 106).

106. Of the 16 narrative units, 14 include a discourse of Jesus. 4 of these units are Jesus' discourse alone, and of the remaining 10, Jesus' discourse is longer than that of the narrator in 8 cases. This pattern of focalizing builds Jesus as an authoritative teacher for the narratee.

107. Fitzmyer mistakenly suggests that 'it seems unlikely that Luke intends the verb to be understood in its etymological sense of announcing/preaching the good news...the verb normally means no more than "preach"' (1981: 148). The distribution of the verb only at key points in the narrative suggests that there is more involved (cf. Nolland 1993a: 943).

108. 'When the sheep are not fed, others may be expected to come to remedy the deficiency. Jesus' teaching in the Temple daily appears to be in response to the failure of the Jewish leaders' (Talbert 1982: 188).

109. The narrator employs the verb ἀπολέσαι (to destroy) rather than ἀποκτείνω

The names and titles of Jesus. The narrator names Jesus twice in the nine scenes of the act (20.8, 34) when he exercises his authority in direct confrontation with the religious leaders and the Sadducees; otherwise Jesus is nameless and title-less.

The contribution of narrative commentary. There is more narrative commentary in this act but it all contributes to the characterization of Jesus' enemies, and none relates to Jesus.

The Narrator's Characterization of Jesus in Act 6 (22.1–23.56)

The focalizing activity continues to contribute most to the narrator's characterization of Jesus as the character in control of events at the very time Jesus becomes increasingly powerless.

The Contribution of the Narrator's Focalizing in Act 6

As Jesus has reclaimed the Temple, the next stage of the conflict occurs elsewhere in Jerusalem.[110] The allocation of extended narrative time to these two days in the story-world attracts attention and thus gives emphasis to this part of the story.

The act opens with the report of the religious leaders' impotence and the return of Satan who can overcome their powerlessness.[111] The act moves to the 'Last Passover' which is the longest scene in the act.[112]

(to kill), which places emphasis upon the intensity of opposition (19.47). The verb is used by the demon voice when under threat from Jesus (4.34) and Jesus himself uses it to denote the options for his ministry: ψυχὴν σῶσαι ἢ ἀπολέσαι (6.9). This is the only occasion in the whole Gospel narrative that the narrator uses the verb 'to destroy'. The nuance is lost in NRSV, which translates it as 'to kill him'.

110. After Jesus has ascended his disciples will return to the 'cleansed' Temple with great joy, and will be continually found there blessing God (24.53).

111. The chief priests and scribes were looking for a way to put Jesus to death (22.1), and after Satan enters Judas, he begins to look for a way (the same Greek verb used for both subjects). 'Luke has brought together the stories of the priests' and scribes' plot and the betrayal by Jesus into a unified account' (Marshall 1978: 787).

112. The allocation of most narrative time in the act to this scene raises questions about the commonly held assumption that 'there is no trace of any Passion mysticism, nor is any direct soteriological significance drawn from Jesus' suffering or death. There is no suggestion of a connection with the forgiveness of sins' (Conzelmann 1960: 201; cf. Talbert 1982: 212). On the contrary, Jesus' death is important

The interpretation of Jesus' death is restricted to his own lengthy discourse, which both illustrates the hierarchy of narrative voices and also signals the importance to the narrator of what Jesus says. The focalizing employs the 'report and embed' convention, so that only Jesus speaks in this scene, and speaks in the longest discourse of the whole act.

Jesus on the Mount of Olives is a 'model' of how to pray (*inclusio*: 22.40, 46) in contrast to the disciples. Once the Son embraces the Father's will, the arrest quickly follows, initiated by Judas—who never kisses the Son of Man.

The focalizing allocates considerable narrative time to Satan's sifting of the representative disciple Peter in his denial of Jesus.[113] The following sequence of four hearings portrays Jesus as increasingly powerless as he gradually retires into silence, and is not even present at the last hearing.[114] The focalizing orchestrates the characters to reiterate that Jesus 'has done nothing to deserve death' (23.15).[115] Talbert is partly correct to suggest that the narrator 'portrays the death of Jesus as a martyrdom, the unjust murder of an innocent by the established powers' (1982: 212).[116] In fact, by giving so much narrative time, the narrator's

for the narrator, and sufficiently important that Jesus himself is the appropriate voice which may interpret it.

113. At 142 words, this scene is the third longest in the act, surpassed only by Pilate's final hearing (23.13-25) and the Last Passover (22.14-23). This unexpected attention is not discussed in the standard commentaries, which at this point are mostly taken up with source-critical debates. Since Jesus is presented as a model for the disciples (cf. Talbert 1982: 213), the failure of Peter forms an important literary counterpoint to Jesus' example of obedience. Peter functions as a *representative* disciple because Jesus' prophecy is that 'Satan has demanded to sift *all of you*' (22.31). The scene shows that Jesus' prophecy and prayer come true (22.32), and that 'the martyr Jesus is concerned to return straying disciples' (Talbert 1982: 215). This return is confirmed in the report of Jesus' appearance to Peter (24.34).

114. The four hearings are unlikely to be patterned on the four hearings of Paul in Acts as suggested by Talbert (1982: 215), because the literary dependency is the wrong way round. It is more likely that the Gospel will influence Acts, which is probably written subsequently.

115. In a narrative analysis the interaction between the characters is an important contribution to the characterization. The primary narrative function of Pilate's threefold dismissal of the charges (23.4; 23.15; 23.22), together with the inscription on the cross which he commissioned (23.38), is to place emphasis upon Jesus' innocence, rather then exonerate the Roman authorities.

116. One of the criminals and the centurion on duty reiterate the theme that 'certainly this man was innocent' (23.41; 23.47).

focalizing also commends the link between Jesus' death and the new covenant of Jesus' discourse; Talbert's literary-critical approach is unable to recognize what a semiotic analysis can illuminate.

The Contribution of the Narrator's Narrating in Act 6
The contribution of the language used. The narrator reports but does not develop the phrase 'the kingdom of God' in his description of Joseph of Arithmathea (23.51), but there is no special vocabulary used of Jesus in the narrator's primary discourse.

The contribution of the names and titles. The name Jesus appears 11 times in 6 of the 22 scenes of the act, with 4 of these occurrences in the scene of Judas' betrayal.[117] The name with the article is employed to denote Jesus exercising authority, and for the first time, authority over the disciples (22.51). The narrator reintroduces the anarthrous Ἰησοῦς on three occasions when Jesus yields to his opponents in the form of Judas (22.48) and the religious leaders (22.52). The third example is when the helpless Jesus, on his way to the place of the skull, addresses the daughters of Jerusalem.[118] Through the omission of the article, the narrator portrays the authority of Jesus ebbing away.

The powerlessness of Jesus is reinforced by the use of 'Lord' on two occasions in one scene when Jesus deals with the disciple Peter: 'ὁ κύριος turned and looked at Peter' (22.61).[119]

The contribution of the narrative commentary. Of the seven examples of narrative commentary in this act, only one refers to Jesus: 'he went

117. There are 22 narrative units in act 6 which comprise 1 speech unit, 5 narrator reports and 16 scenes. The name Jesus appears in Lk. 20.8; 20.34; 22.47, 48, 51, 52; 23.8, 20, 25, 26, 28, 46, 52. In addition, Lk. 23.34a is bracketed in *UBSGNT*, 3rd edn, and NRSV as one of the 'later additions to the text, but which are retained because of their evident antiquity' (*UBSGNT*, 3rd edn: xii). As the *UBSGNT* commentary acknowledges the secondary status of this text, rather than a variant in early MSS, the present discussion omits the verse. The only other narrative agent to use the name Jesus in this act is the criminal on the cross (23.42).

118. There is a variant reading with the article at Lk. 23.28 when Jesus is denoted as addressing the daughters of Jerusalem. The tenor of the scene is the character Jesus yielding to what is inevitable, and as such is similar to the other two anarthrous examples, and so in this discussion, Lk. 23.38 is considered as anarthrous.

119. The poignancy is deepened by Peter's earlier discourse in which he addressed Jesus as Κύριε (22.33).

out, *as was his custom*, to the Mount of Olives to pray' (22.39). The absence of further commentary suggests that the narrator's story of Jesus must now be its own 'commentary'.

The Narrator's Characterization of Jesus in Act 7 (24.1-53)

This last act comprises four scenes and one discourse of Jesus, all of which take place in or just outside Jerusalem on the first day of the week (24.1).

The Contribution of the Narrator's Focalizing in Act 7

Only the angels are permitted their own discourse in the opening scene at the empty tomb. When the women notice the absence of the body, the angels tell them that Jesus is risen *according to Jesus' own words*. The primary datum for interpreting the story of Jesus does not lie in the Hebrew Scriptures, but in the words of Jesus himself.

This aspect consolidates the narrator's view that Jesus interprets the Hebrew Scriptures, rather than the other way round. It also helps explains why throughout the Gospel the narrator does not discuss specific scriptural passages relating to Jesus, and also why he does not include the substance of Jesus' discourse explaining the Scriptures to the disciples (24.27). The 'report and embed' pattern (24.25-27) underlines the narrator's focalizing that scriptural detail is simply unnecessary. For the narrator it is important that Jesus is the fulfilment of the Jewish Scriptures (24.27, 32, 44), but the detail of how this occurs is irrelevant because Jesus transcends the Scriptures through these events.

The focalizing of the first three scenes sets out to persuade the narratee that Jesus is risen. The disciples' difficulties with the resurrection are acknowledged by the distribution of the discourses in the road to Emmaus scene.[120] This scene is given narrative emphasis through its length, for it lasts for almost half of the whole act and is also one of the

---

120. The comments of the various disciples attract attention due to their embedded discourse form and also their length (165 out of 391 words [42.2%]). The general substance of these discourses is the doubt about whether Jesus is risen, and what answers the doubt and gives rise to faith. The length (112 words) of Cleopas's list of difficulties is striking and quite unusual. Schweizer correctly comments that 'the help that is given is not a response to faith in Jesus, but the gift of faith itself' (1984: 368).

longest scenes in the Gospel.[121] In the three scenes taken together, the focalizing marshals seven different grounds for the assurance that Jesus is risen.[122]

The final scene when Jesus is carried up to heaven explains why the narratee cannot replicate the experiences of the eye-witnesses. The narratee is invited to weigh the 'evidence' of these who were 'from the beginning eye-witnesses' (1.2).

The focalizing of this act reveals that the principal significance of the resurrection *for the narrator* is the reality of the risen Jesus; he is not a spirit ($\pi\nu\epsilon\hat{\upsilon}\mu\alpha$ [24.37]; NRSV 'ghost') for he may be touched and he eats fish. However, the narrator does not develop the theological implications of the resurrection beyond this reality of Jesus' victory over death.[123]

As Jesus completes his exodus journey, the narrator's focalizing ensures that the last two narrative units contain only Jesus' discourse. In these, Jesus commissions the disciples (vouched safe by Scripture [24.46-47]), and takes to himself the sending of the 'power from on high' (24.49). As Jesus completes his journey, another story is set to begin.

The Contribution of the Narrating in Act 7
The contribution of the language. The language chosen to describe Jesus blessing the disciples is very similar to the account in Ben Sirach of the blessing of the people by the high priest Simon. The debate continues about the possible significance of this parallel.[124]

---

121. The length of the act is 818 words, and the road to Emmaus scene takes up 391 words, which is 47.9% of the length of the act.

122. The grounds include: (1) the empty tomb; (2) the angel's words; (3) the previous explanations of Jesus; (4) the appearances of Jesus; (5) the marks on Jesus' hands and feet; (6) Jesus eats some fish in the disciples' presence; and (7) the prophecies in the Hebrew Scriptures. The recognition of Jesus by the disciples as he took, blessed, broke and gave them the bread (24.30) is an occasion of recognition and not the means of recognition; the disciples recognized Jesus not because of his action, but because 'their eyes were opened'.

123. Jesus' victory over death 'is not to be understood as an escape from this perishable frame but a transformation of it; it is not a transformation into a purely spiritual angelic being, because Jesus remained flesh and bones...it is no more the immortality of the soul while the body decayed than it is the survival of his "shade"' (Talbert 1982: 229).

124. The raising of hands in blessing is only found once in the Hebrew Testa-

A new aspect of the narrator's characterization of Jesus is conveyed in the report that the disciples' last response to Jesus was that 'they *worshipped* him...'(24.52).[125] The Greek construction portrays this worship as the response to Jesus' ascension. The disciples worship one who is now in heaven, and may therefore be worshipped by *subsequent* generations of disciples.

Jesus' exodus journey is completed as he ascends to heaven, from where he will send the Spirit to clothe the disciples with power for Christian mission.

The deployment of names and titles of Jesus. Jesus' name appears twice in the narrator's discourse, and in unexpected ways. The narrator uses the name in the phrase 'the body of the Lord Jesus' (24.3), which the women could not find.[126] This conjunction with 'Lord' occurs only once in the Gospel. However, its significance is qualified because it is used in a report of the women *before* they knew that Jesus had risen.

The second employment of the name Jesus is to identify for the narratee the stranger on the road to Emmaus in narrative commentary.[127] The narrator employs the anarthrous form which recalls times when Jesus does not exercise his authority.[128] This is part of the literary evidence for the development of the narrator into a reliable and authoritative voice.[129] The narrator informs the narratee that the traveller is Jesus

ment. Nolland is uneasy with the priestly associations (1993b: 1227), while Talbert considers that 'with a priestly Act the risen Jesus puts his disciples under the protection of God before he leaves them' (1982: 233).

125. The narrator has chosen the verb προσκυνήσαντες to represent this act, and it is the first time that the narrator has described worship offered to Jesus. The verb is only used elsewhere in Luke in the temptation scene where the devil invites Jesus to worship him, and Jesus replies Γέγραπται, Κύριον τὸν θεόν προσκυνήσεις (4.7, 8). Luke 'appears to have deliberately avoided the word until this point, conscious that recognition of the divinity of Jesus by men did not precede the resurrection' (Marshall 1978: 910).

126. *UBSGNT*, 3rd edn, includes 'of the Lord Jesus' (24.3). Two other standard works also include this, contra NRSV (Fitzmyer 1985: 1544; Marshall 1978: 884).

127. The Greek καὶ αὐτὸς Ἰησοῦς is intensive.

128. *UBSGNT*, 3rd edn, does not follow the weakly attested variant reading καὶ ὁ Ἰησοῦς...

129. The grounds for this suggestion include the fact that the narrator contributes almost half of the Emmaus scene (190 words of 391 words), in which his discourse is far longer than Jesus' discourse (190/36 words respectively). Each of the three discourses of Jesus is cast in the interrogative mood, whereas the narrator provides

(24.15). At the literary level this adds interest to the reading, but at the level of narrative communication, the narrator has done what only God can do—he has opened the eyes of the narratee to Jesus. With this simple literary device, used for the first time in the Gospel, the narrator finally functions as a fully reliable and authoritative witness. And so the apprenticeship is complete and the Lukan narrator is one who may now speak reliably *in his own right*.

Narrative commentary about Jesus. The last act is replete with narrator's commentary upon the disciples, but in only one case does it directly refer to Jesus. As the disciples walk along the road to Emmaus with the unrecognized Jesus, 'he interpreted to them the things *about himself* in all the scriptures' (24.27).[130] The principal function of the comment is to reinforce for the narratee that Jesus is the one of whom 'all the scriptures speak' (24.27).

Two other narrative comments bear indirectly upon the characterization of Jesus, for they explain to the narratee that Jesus can only be recognized when God 'opens the eyes or the minds' of people. The 'divine passive verbs' through which story characters do or do not understand Jesus reappear (24.16, 31). Jesus is the one whom God reveals, and without God's help, even the eye-witnesses who journeyed with Jesus cannot see who he is.[131] The final 'opening of the minds' is achieved by Jesus, acting as if he is God, and he does it through the blessing and breaking of the bread (24.45).

The Narrator's Characterization of Jesus

This preliminary narrative-critical reading of the literary narrator in Luke is a preparation for the construction of the narrator's characterization of Jesus. This reading reveals both the fundamental assumptions of the narrating voice, together with hermeneutical and theological contri-

the explanation in the indicative mood.

130. Although the phrase '*about himself*' is not in the form of a parenthesis, it is treated as commentary because it momentarily reinforces the bond between the narrator and narratee. This description of what Jesus did could not be appreciated by Cleopas and his companion at that moment. If the narrator wished only to describe what was happening, then his report would have stated that 'he interpreted to them the things about the Messiah in all the scriptures'.

131. The narrative plays upon the three characters who see differently as Jesus dies on the cross (the centurion, the crowds and the disciples [Lk. 23.44-49]).

butions generated through an 'interrogative reading for the narrator'.

The first assumption of the Lukan narrator is that *Jesus is the Jesus of his own story*. The assumption prioritizes the story form as a fitting exposition of the identity of the Lukan Jesus. This insight is then adopted by the narrating voice who duly produces the narrative discourse *which is also in story form*. The narrating voice retells the story for the narratee, and so may be described as one of the earliest 'narrative theologians'.[132]

The second assumption is that communication in the narrative world of the Gospel is governed by the convention of a hierarchy of narrative voices. Under this convention, the narrator and others who are not eye-witnesses defer to those reliable characters in the story-world who are eye-witnesses. There is an interaction between a mixture of narrative voices of various degrees of authority.

This narrative convention has a practical consequence. Some matters may require a more authoritative voice than the narrator, and so the absence of such matters from the narrator's primary discourse can mean that either they are not important to the narrator or that they are too important for the narrator to handle! The focalizing activity by the narrator within the discourses in the narrative offers an illumination that other literary-critical readings miss and consequently confuse their appreciation of the Lukan narrator. The refusal of the narrator to tackle a subject in his discourse and then grant generous narrative time to a reliable character to address the subject actually signals the modesty of the Lukan narrator, and not his lack of interest!

The Hermeneutical Aspects of the Lukan Narrator's Characterization of Jesus
The inadequacy of alternatives to 'the story' of Jesus. The narrator refuses to adopt any 'figure' or title for Jesus. Even the name Jesus is a mere indicator to denote the character, with no further significance. The focalizing of the discourses makes plain that none of the 'figures' or 'titles' which the disciples or even Jesus employ is acceptable to the narrator.[133] At the end of the Gospel, the ascended Jesus is character-

---

132. 'The model of Luke–Acts as a "translation" from one context to another seems appropriate; Luke is attempting to explain Christianity in such a way that it might be more fully understood by hellenized Christians' (Squires 1993: 191).

133. The nearest that any story character comes to a 'figure' which embraces the identity of Jesus is discussed in Chapter 11.

ized through the *story* of how the disciples worshipped him.[134] The minimal commentary about the character Jesus also confirms this commitment to the category 'story' as the form of the exposition of the identity of Jesus.[135]

Historically, the inadequacy of particular Jewish figures or types is likely to be shared by those figures in the Hellenized world of the narratee. Just as Jesus is not sufficiently understood by considering him as a 'Son of Man', so he is also not sufficiently understood by accommodating him to the Greek notion of the 'Great Benefactor' (Danker 1987).[136]

The Lukan Jesus and the Jewish past. The Lukan narrator is clear that Jesus is the one who fulfils the prophecies of the Jewish traditions. However, Jesus achieves this in a way that both fulfils and transcends the prophecies at the same time; the era of the prophets is now complete, and a new era has begun with Jesus. The clearest voices who speak of 'who Jesus is' are story characters and not the prophecies in the Scriptures.[137]

The deployment of 'eye-witnesses' rather than the sacred writings of a Jewish religious tradition which has been left behind is a 'non-religious' strategy which would resonate in the Gentile world.

The narrator is able to 'leave behind' much of the Jewishness of the story of Jesus *because it has been superseded*. This brings a degree of freedom in the hermeneutical process, together with the responsibility to 'represent' the new era in terms with which the narratee (and readers like him or her) can engage. Thus the absence of many Jewish motifs in the Lukan narrator's retelling of the story of Jesus has theological as

134. At the end of the Gospel the narrator does not 'sum up' with explicit commentary in the way that is true of the Johannine narrator (Jn 20.31).

135. The commitment to 'story' is not peculiar to the narrator, for the preface contrasts the narrator's story with those produced by others (1.1).

136. Danker suggests that in the light of Acts 10.38, where Jesus is described as εὐεργετῶν (which he translates as 'benefactor'), 'modern studies that focus on the social context for biblical interpretation do not permit evasion of Luke's own statement and the manner in which throughout Luke–Acts, his two-volume work, he interprets Jesus as the uniquely Great Benefactor' (1987: v).

137. The narrator employs various characters to function as reliable voices in the narrative, which functionally take the place of the Hebrew Scriptures as comments upon Jesus. For example, in the infancy narratives, the narrator employs angels and prophets to speak for God rather than Scripture, and the clearest declaration of who Jesus is comes from the voice from heaven.

well as hermeneutical implications. This development is illustrated in the narrator's relinquishment of many Jewish categories of thought. Messiah and kingdom of God are dropped, while the figure of the suffering Son of Man employed by Jesus remains undeveloped.[138]

On the other hand, the principal characteristic of the new era is encountered in the story of Jesus, as is made clear in Jesus' discussion with the disciples of John the Baptist (7.22-23). It is this story which the narrator sets out to retell in his 'orderly account'.

The Lukan Jesus and those who come later. The 're-presentation' of the story of Jesus for the narratee is an example of theological hermeneutics. The principal key to appreciate the internal dynamics is the concept of the 'hierarchy of narrative voices' which informs the production of the represented story. The narrator defers to the reliable characters in the story-world, and so ensures that when possible they make their own contribution through their action and particularly their discourses. The narrator's responsibility is to allocate sufficient time for these contributions.

The hermeneutical task begins with the parameters which are set out by the reliable characters in the story-world and comes to fruition in the rewriting of the stories by the narrator in a world characterized by the Gentile narratee. This narrative convention becomes a formal tool for the development of new versions of the story of Jesus.

The narrator's management of differences about the character Jesus. The convention of a 'hierarchy of narrative voices' inculcates a respectful and largely uncritical narrator, for who is he to argue with Jesus? However, it is possible to trace dissonance between different aspects of the narrator's presentation of Jesus and the discourses of Jesus himself.[139] One area of unease is the aggressiveness of Jesus, as he lives out his prophetic role. The narrator retells the story of the boy in the Temple and casts Jesus in a more sympathetic light.

The story of Jesus is focalized as if he were a prophet, but the story is

---

138. Conzelmann's analysis of the Lukan reworking of the eschatology of Mark is the result of a redaction-critical analysis (1960: 95-136). In a narrative-critical reading the contrasts that generate insight are *between narrative voices within the narrative world*.

139. See the further comment in Chapter 12 upon the dissonances between the narrator and Jesus.

narrated as if Jesus is a teacher. It is significant that the narrating voice elects to include uncongenial aspects and supplement them with narrative commentary (to 'draw the sting') instead of omitting the aspect in question.

The Theological Aspects of the Lukan Narrator's Characterization of Jesus
Jesus as the One Obedient to the Will of God. The recurring feature of the focalization of Jesus is the presence of the divine will as the guiding influence within the narrative.[140] Act 1 succeeds in making plain that the coming of Jesus was the initiative of God in accordance with what the Israelite prophets foretold (Squires 1993: 26-32). The focalizing of the acts presents Jesus at key moments seeking the will of God. The recurring references to 'journeying to Jerusalem' within act 4 remind the narratee of Jesus' obedience to his earlier 'setting of his face to Jerusalem'.

For the narrator, the suffering of Jesus up to and including the cross is primarily an expression of obedience to the Father. Any further significance is explained by Jesus himself—at the invitation of the narrator.

Jesus as the one in whom god is at work. The narrator dispenses with the Jewish notion of the kingdom of God, but retains the activities which Jesus in his discourse associates with the kingdom of God. In this way the kingdom of God is still present, while the story is not restricted to the Jewish traditions. Thus Jesus continues to conduct healings, give forgiveness and carry out exorcisms.

The Beelzebul controversy functions in the narrative to make clear that it is what Jesus does 'by the finger of God' that is equivalent to the kingdom of God. Consequently for the narrator, the story of what Jesus does constitutes 'the kingdom of God', and so replaces the phrase.

It is also the case that the resurrection for the narrator is not an eschatological event in Jewish categories but rather the demonstration that what God has done in raising Jesus from the dead is what the Scriptures foretold.

---

140. The theme of the 'divine will' is so clearly present that scholars can claim that it is the central theme of the Gospel.

Jesus is god's ambassador to the gentiles. The Lukan narrative makes plain that the narrator characterizes Jesus as the man for those beyond the Jewish world. The absence of Jewish concepts and scriptural exposition, together with the inclusion of occasional commentary within the primary discourse, suggest that the narrator is retelling the story for those who are not Jews. This is further confirmed by the narrator's focalizing which gives a modest but significant emphasis to Gentiles and Samaritans within the narrative, and allocates a relatively generous narrative time to the trip Jesus makes to Gerasa.

Jesus as the one who speaks for the way of god. Jesus is frequently reported as 'teaching in their synagogues' and many of his teaching discourses are included in the narrative. The long central section is the narrator's presentation of Jesus as a teacher or prophet, possibly after the style of the Deuteronomic recasting of the prophet Moses. This central section is presented in a way that allows Jesus to address the two audiences of the story characters and the narratee by the focalizing stripping away the geographical detail. When Jesus reclaims the Temple, he teaches the people, and when he is raised from the dead, he teaches the disciples. The narratee is invited to listen to Jesus the teacher, for he speaks for the way of God.

Jesus as the one who is now worshipped as god. The exodus journey of Jesus is finally completed in the last act when Jesus 'is carried up to heaven' (24.51), and the disciples worship him. In this event the blindness of the disciples is finally removed, and Jesus is worshipped as God is worshipped, and in the place where God is worshipped.

The narrator knew this all along, but has used the Gospel narrative to eventually make it plain. Even now, the narrator employs the story of what the disciples did to describe who Jesus is. The recurring theme of the blindness of the disciples now plays its part, for it explains why what has been true about Jesus throughout the narrative was not appreciated by the disciples until now. The ascension is the final revelatory moment in the narrative exposition of who Jesus is.[141]

---

141. The possibility that Jesus *became* the Son of God at the ascension is unlikely, but not excluded (cf. Acts 2.36), and only a careful re-reading of the Lukan narrative will clarify the situation.

Jesus as the one whom god makes present in his story. The narrator's story of Jesus is recounted to help the narratee reach a certainty about what he had been taught earlier. The story of Jesus functions as the exposition of who Jesus is and it also functions as the ground for confidence. The narrator considers that this juxtaposition forms the hermeneutical bridge from the world of the text to the world of the narratee. The story ends with the disciple's worshipping the ascended Lord. This is only possible because he has been raised to life and lives on. The worship of the risen Lord by Theophilus leads to the recognition of the presence of the Lord in the reading of his story. Jesus is both the literary character in the Lukan world and the one who can be present for the Christian reader.

Chapter 10

THE SELF-CHARACTERIZATION OF JESUS

> When the men had come to him, they said 'John the Baptist has sent us
> to you to ask "Are you the one who is to come, or are we to wait for
> another?" ' Jesus had just then cured many people of diseases, plagues
> and evil spirits and had given sight to many who were blind. And he
> answered them 'Go and tell John what you have seen and heard.'
>
> Lk. 7.20-22 (NRSV)

Preliminaries for a Reading of the Self-Characterization of Jesus

The character Jesus presents different characterizations of himself to
the various audiences he addresses in the Gospel of Luke. For example,
the traditional Jewish categories of 'prophet' and 'kingdom of God'
appear principally in Jesus' dialogues with the Pharisees and the
crowds, and are virtually ignored when Jesus addresses the disciples.
Conversely, Jesus introduces the enigmatic figure of the 'suffering Son
of Man' only to the disciples and then expounds *through the medium of
his life* what this might signify. The reader faces the interesting critical
task of respecting these different self-characterizations and enquiring
(but not presuming) how these different characterizations relate to each
other in the construction of Jesus' self-characterization.

The following reading for the self-characterization of a story character rests on the assumption that a literary character is a narrative agent
who can make three context-specific semiotic contributions to their
characterization. The first two aspects are the 'focalizing' and
'narrating' within the character's discourses which are read in the same
way as the narrator's discourse in Chapter 9. In contrast to the narrator,
a story character possesses the extra dimension of communication when
he or she *acts* in the story-world; thus 'acting' is the third semiotic
subject activity.

These three semiotic activities of the character are context specific, and, in an analysis based upon a communication model of the text, the receptor or audience is the most influential aspect of the context of reception. *What* the character communicates is a function of *whom* he or she addresses, with the result that the audience of a story character functions as the prime contextual 'qualifier' of the contributions of each of the three semiotic subject activities.

This contribution of the audience is particularly significant in the 'acting' mode of communication, for the activity itself unfolds and awaits interpretation in the world of the text. The audiences—either in their own discourse, or in a report—proffer their interpretations of Jesus' action, which Jesus may or may not then affirm.

A character engages with a variety of audiences in the world of the text which is in marked contrast to the activity of the narrator who is assumed to address the same narratee throughout the narrative. In the Gospel of Luke, this range of audiences accounts for the range of self-characterizations which Jesus displays.

Narrative-Critical Studies of the Lukan Character Jesus
Jesus is the central character of the Gospel of Luke and so has attracted increasing narrative-critical treatment in articles and monographs. The works which have contributed most to the present discussion begin with Tannehill's *The Narrative Unity of Luke–Acts*, I (1986a), which structures its treatment of Jesus in the light of his various audiences. Although the book is heavily indebted to New Criticism, it is useful for the present study because of its sensitivity to the different audiences which Jesus addresses.

Dawsey's *The Lukan Voice* (1986b) analyses the Gospel narrative into distinct voices, and then studies at length the two voices of the narrator and the character Jesus. As well as what seem to me to be mistakes (as noted earlier), Dawsey fails to recognize the major extra dimension that a character's *acting* brings to narrative communication, and so he treats narrator and character alike, as if they can only speak. Nevertheless Dawsey's book contains useful preliminary material for the present discussion.[1]

Kingsbury's brief, popular study *Conflict in Luke* (1991b) is useful in a preliminary way for it traces three different storylines through the

---

1. 'What Dawsey fails to comprehend, however, is that one cannot isolate and concentrate on a single kind of datum—voice, choice, actions, names or whatever... without skewing those characters' (Darr 1993: 51).

Gospel. In addition to these works, the present discussion engages with the standard English language historical-critical and literary-critical commentaries, and with Conzelmann's seminal *The Theology of Luke*, still insightful after 40 years.[2]

The Conventions of This Preliminary Reading
There are three preliminary issues to be addressed and resolved before beginning the reading of the Gospel.

The structure of this study. The major importance of the 'context-specific audience' raises the possibility of structuring the reading by tracing the encounter between Jesus and his principal audiences through the Gospel, as is done in Tannehill's study (1986a). The attraction of this arrangement is that the reader begins to appreciate the narrative development in these relationships, and its influence upon Jesus' unfolding self-characterizations. Although the decision is finely balanced, this approach is not adopted. The principal reason is that there are long periods when a particular audience fails to appear, and the reader risks losing the overall sense of the narrative development. Instead, the analysis into a preface and seven acts is retained; within each act, attention is paid to Jesus' principal audiences and the point the story has reached.

The quotation of the Hebrew Scriptures. When Jesus quotes the Hebrew Scriptures, the quotation is treated as an embedded discourse within Jesus' discourse. If the quotation has not been revised by the character Jesus, then the focalizing subject of the quotation is considered to be God, for that was the convention of first-century Jewish tradition. If the quotation has been revised or edited, it is considered that Jesus thereby becomes the new focalizing subject, and his ideological position is appreciated by the contrast between the revision and the original form of the Scripture. In this preliminary study, these two focalizings are simply described and incorporated into the reading.[3]

2. The present discussion engages with recent English language commentaries: Marshall 1978; Fitzmyer 1981, 1986; Nolland 1989, 1993a, 1993b; Goulder 1989; and Evans 1990; together with Schweizer 1984. Schürmann 1969 is occasionally consulted. From a narrative-critical perspective it is striking how much time in these commentaries is taken up with questions of source and redaction criticism, and how little attention is devoted to the final form of the text.

3. The way that the Old Testament Scriptures are employed in the Gospel of Luke is a large field of study. The present discussion is cast in narrative-critical

Identification of the missing audiences. In the Gospel narrative Jesus speaks to a variety of characters and his discourses are tailored to his audiences. When an audience is either described but not named or is not mentioned at all, the substance of what Jesus says may make clear which audience he is addressing. If it is still not clear, then the narrative convention adopted here treats the discourse as addressed to the most recently mentioned audience prior to the discourse.

The Self-Characterization of Jesus in Act 1 (1.5–3.20)

The first occasion when the character Jesus contributes to his self-characterization is when he stays in the Temple (2.41-51). Both this act and the discourse of the young Jesus which accompanies the incident are significant. This is the very first time in the Gospel that Jesus speaks. A preliminary analysis of every discourse of Jesus in the Gospel narrative is provided in Appendix C and underlies the discussion in this chapter. The following reading for Jesus' self-characterization proceeds through a series of steps which illuminate how this approach proceeds.

The 'Focalizing' within Jesus' Discourse

Jesus' brief discourse (15 words in a 180-word scene) ends with the question: 'Did you not know that I *must* [δεῖ] be about my father's business?' (2.49). The word 'must' disguises the nuance of a literal translation, 'it is necessary that…', which introduces a separate authoritative narrative agent, although un-named. A study of all the character discourses in the Gospel reveals that of the 18 occurrences of cognate forms of this Greek verb, 15 of them are in Jesus' discourse.[4] The

categories, as it enquires about the way particular character discourses employ Old Testament Scriptures which properly require an extended treatment in their own right. The scriptural focalizing position is actually dual, for it incorporates the textually expressed position and the canonically informed position, which may be quite different. Although this is not the place for such a study, particular assistance is acknowledged from the collection of essays of Evans and Sanders 1993. In addition, the work of Childs upon canonical approaches to the Christian Bible has also proved illuminating (1984, 1992).

4.   The character Jesus employs δεῖ 12 times in the Gospel. Ten of these are when Jesus addresses audiences about his own future, and in 8 of these 10 examples (2.49; 4.43; 9.22; 13.33; 17.25; 21.9; 22.37; and 24.44), the contexts confirm that the word carries the sense of 'the purpose of God' regarding Jesus' ministry and suffering. Occurrences 11 and 12 are when Jesus speaks of going to the house of

narrative deployment of the verb 'must' may be treated as a periphrasis
for 'God's purpose is...' or 'God's will is...'[5] So the reader concludes
that at these moments Jesus' discourse is focalized from God's
perspective.

The 'Narrating' within Jesus' Discourse

Jesus' discourse in this scene includes the phrase 'my father' which
implies that Jesus is the son of the father. By describing him as 'my'
rather than 'our' father, Jesus distinguishes his sonship from the sonship
of others. The distinctiveness of the character Jesus is also stressed by
the emphatic position of the Greek pronoun in the phrase: 'Did you not
know that *I* must be...'[6]

The rest of the phrase may be translated as 'about my Father's
business' (NRSV margin: 'about my Father's interests').[7] This 'narrating

---

Zacchaeus (19.5) and the assurance that the Holy Spirit will teach the disciples what
to say (12.12).

Jesus also employs four of the five examples of ἔδει (11.42; 13.6; 15.32 [parable
character]; 24.26) which continues the sense of the 'purpose of God'. Finally, Jesus
includes the only example of δεῖν (18.1) when encouraging the disciples to pray
and not lose heart.

This sense of 'the purpose of God' is also found in the reliable voice of the
angels who repeat Jesus' words to the disciples (24.7). The ruler of the synagogue
is the only other story character to use the term and he clearly uses it as a periphrasis for 'what God decrees' (13.14).

5.   The phrase 'the purpose of God' is adopted as a shorthand for a 'variety of
thematic strands...woven together to emphasize the certainty and consistency of the
plan of God as it is worked out in the life of Jesus and the early church' (Squires
1993: 1). The phrase 'the purpose of God' is a translation of Ἡ βουλὴ τοῦ θεοῦ
(7.30). Although not sensitive to the different voices at play in the narrative, by a
consideration of the occurrences of δεῖ in Luke, Marshall (1970: 106-111) effec-
tively dismisses Grundmann's suggestion that δεῖ is a narrowly defined eschatological term reserved for 'the End' (Grundmann 1965: 21-25). Conzelmann's alternative proposal that Luke has eliminated an imminent eschatology, and so δεῖ is properly associated with salvation history, also falls when the use of the verb is traced
(1960: 95). 'Rather, the term δεῖ 'brings to expression the fact that the course of
history, including those events which may be termed eschatological, is dependent
upon the will of God, so that what he decides becomes as a result of his decision
something that "must" happen' (Marshall 1970: 111).

6.   'In Luke the first word spoken by Jesus is a reference to the God who is
above him yet with whom he is associated as with no other' (Schweizer 1984: 64)

7.   The relevant part of the phrase ἐν τοῖς τοῦ πατρός μου δεῖ εἶναί με may be
translated literally as 'to be in the things of my Father'. This awkward construction

aspect' of Jesus' discourse makes clear that God is Jesus' father in a particular way, with the corollary that Jesus is God's son in a particular way.[8] The narratee awaits the narrative exposition of what is involved in this 'particular' kind of sonship.

The 'Acting' of Jesus in the Narrative

The literary character Jesus communicates through his activity—even when he says nothing. In this scene Jesus separates himself from his parents and attends to his father's business in his father's house. In this way the character Jesus lives out his commitment to one with a greater claim upon him than his natural parents.

The semiotic significance of this action is that Jesus at 12 years old lives out a new kind of sonship. The way in which this semiotic statement is congruent with Jesus' discourse reinforces the narratee's impression of the integrity of Jesus.

The Contribution of Jesus' Audience

Jesus communicates with two audiences in this scene. The encounter with the teachers (2.46) is mediated to the reader by the narrator and portrays Jesus as a boy wise beyond his years who astonishes all who hear him in conversation with the teachers. The narrator does not include discourse from Jesus, the crowd or the teachers. Consequently Jesus' self-characterization is only conveyed through his actions, and these offer this modest contribution.[9]

However, when Jesus engages with his parents, he makes a significant claim for himself. Jesus' activity in separating himself for his Father is clear but not understood by his parents. Jesus rebukes them

---

with little support from contemporary literary parallels may refer to the activities which go on in the Temple rather than just the place itself. NRSV margin captures the inclusive nuance in the Greek with 'be about my Father's interest', which at least embraces what the standard commentaries prefer: 'in my Father house'. 'About my Father's business seems the more natural' (Moule 1959: 75).

8. The theme of Jesus as a son of God develops what has been introduced by the reliable character of the angel who described Jesus as 'the Son of the Most High' (1.32; Most High is a circumlocution for 'God'). For pious Jews, the location of the Temple for Jesus' discourse also makes clear that God is the Father of Jesus, for the Temple was known as God's house.

9. The meeting with the teachers is not very significant within the narrative, for it is brief and includes no discourse within it. The response of the teachers is also quite general (they were astonished [2.47]).

for not appreciating who is his true Father, and how important is his
Father's business. In this way Jesus characterizes himself as the son of
his Father *before Mary and Joseph*. In the *contrast* with his natural parents, Jesus makes plain the distinctiveness of his sonship.[10]

The narrator frames this incident in the Temple with the favourable
commentary about Jesus, his wisdom and his good standing (2.39-40;
2.51-52). These comments contrast with the character Jesus who in this
scene is in conflict with those closest to him, his parents.[11]

*The Significance of the Stage within the Development of the Lukan
Narrative*
Jesus portrays himself as the Father's son, and a son whose father is
God. This is the first contribution of Jesus to his self-characterization
and is therefore a fundamental key to the unfolding characterization of
Jesus. The subsequent narrative may expound more precisely this sonship, and may also offer different perceptions of who Jesus is, yet all
these subsequent contributions of Jesus are read in the light of this
initial self-characterization. Even before his baptism, Jesus characterizes himself as the Father's Son.[12]

The Self-Characterization of Jesus in Act 2 (3.21–4.44)

The brief baptism scene releases Jesus into Judaea and Galilee. The
scenes that follow the baptism scene then function as narrative commentary upon that scene. The following discussion treats the principal
scenes in turn.

The Temptations of Jesus by the Devil (4.1-13)
The devil is the first character in this act to raise questions about Jesus'
identity, searching out *what kind* of son of God Jesus might be in the

10. There are resonances in the Greek text between the understanding of Jesus
(2.47) and the understanding (knowledge) of his parents (2.49). There is the contrast between the different houses where Jesus must be.

11. Commentators exercise themselves whether Jesus is surprised by his
parents' concern or whether he reproaches them for their lack of understanding. The
tendency to 'lighten' the reproach is an example of the reader 'constructing a unity'
when the text displays a clear difference in the two discourses.

12. I am unpersuaded by Conzelmann, who implies that Jesus' sonship awaited
the moment when 'God proclaimed or anointed him as Son at the Baptism' (1960:
174).

light of the declaration at the baptism of Jesus.[13] Jesus replies in a discourse which upon closer inspection turns out to ignore the devil's question and does not mention himself.

In response to three questions, Jesus' discourses are quotations from Deuteronomy (8.3a; 6.13; 6.16), which he knew as Scripture. The focalizing of Scripture in Jesus' discourses is deemed to be from God's perspective unless the text is reworked by Jesus. Here, Jesus quotes two passages exactly, and the third almost exactly from the LXX.[14]

Who is the audience? Although the discourses are addressed to the devil, the focalizing from God's perspective together with the substance of the quotations tends to imply an audience where faith is to be found, which in this case is Jesus; thus Jesus is the real audience of his own discourse![15] Jesus' *activity* is seen in his response to these Scriptures. Jesus *submits his life* to the God of the Scriptures.[16] This section can be read as the narrative exposition of what the voice from heaven meant when it declared Jesus to be 'the Son of God'.

The submission to God is made before the audience of Satan, who functions as the antithesis of the one to whom Jesus submits. So Jesus' sonship as 'the way of obedience' is reinforced by the contrast with Satan, who militantly opposes such a view.

Jesus in the Synagogue at Nazareth (4.16-30)
This is the longest and most important scene in the act, and contains Jesus' first long discourse.[17] Jesus' audience is the synagogue congre-

---

13. The two preceding narrative units include declarations of who Jesus is, first by the voice from heaven (3.22) and then in the genealogy (3.23-38). The temptation scene is the first occasion that the identity of Jesus is questioned. The Greek construction 'if you are the son of God...' is a conditional taunt (cf. Lk. 23.37).

14. The first quotation is the exact wording of the LXX Deut. 8.3a. In the second quotation, the LXX verb φοβέομαι in Deut. 6.13 is replaced by προσκυνέω in an assimilation to Lk. 4.7 (Marshall 1978: 172), and the Scripture is intensified by the insertion of μόνῳ. The third quotation is the exact quotation of Deut. 6.16. Jesus introduces it with the third person impersonal verb εἴρηται, which does not involve Jesus.

15. 'Each one of the temptations is answered in terms of right human piety. The stands taken by Jesus are those proper to every man' (Nolland 1989: 180).

16. The authority of Scripture is also recognized by the devil who invokes Ps. 91.11 during the last temptation in Jerusalem. Jesus' response emphasizes that it is submission to the Lord of Scripture which is the mark of sonship, rather than submission to the mere text of Scripture itself.

17. This scene lasts for 271 words which is significantly longer than any other

gation in his home town, and their astonishing switch from approval to opposition within the scene requires a careful reading of Jesus' two-part discourse which precipitates this reversal.[18]

The discourse opens with a reading from Isaiah which is a conflation of two LXX passages.[19] This conflation is an example of Jesus' freedom to revise the Scripture which alerts the reader to look for the ideological perspective (or focalizing) at work.[20] This refocalizing of Isaiah 61 makes clear that *Jesus is able to interpret the Jewish prophecies*, rather than vice versa.[21]

The principal quotation (Isa. 61.1-2) concerns the anointing of a prophet who will proclaim good news. By the time of Jesus this passage

narrative unit in this act, and of these 271 words, Jesus' discourse lasts for 137 words (cf. the analysis in Appendix C).

18. A recent survey of the options for coherence or otherwise in the discourse is Nolland (1989: 191-95).

19. The conflation is not completely surprising for 'Jesus availed himself of various phrases then associated with Isaiah 61.1 'in a manner generally reminiscent of Targumic practice' (Chilton 1981: 166).

20. The quotation is a conflation of the LXX form of Isa. 61.1-2 and Isa. 58.6:

Lk. 4.18	Πνεῦμα κυρίου ἐπ' ἐμὲ	Isa. 61.1	Πνεῦμα κυρίου ἐπ' ἐμέ,
	οὗ εἵνεκεν ἔχρισέν με.	(LXX)	οὗ εἵνεκεν ἔχρισέν με·
	εὐαγγελίσασθαι πτωχοῖς,		εὐαγγελίσασθαι πτωχοῖς
	ἀπέσταλκέν με,		ἀπέσταλκέν με,
	[ἰάσασθαι τοὺς συντετριμ-		ἰάσασθαι τοὺς συντετριμ-
	μένους τὴν καρδίαν]*		μένους τῇ καρδίᾳ,
	κηρύξαι αἰχμαλώτοις ἄφεσιν		κηρύξαι αἰχμαλώτοις ἄφεσιν
	καὶ τυφλοῖς ἀνάβλεψιν		καὶ τυφλοῖς ἀνάβλεψιν
Isa. 58.6	ἀποστεῖλαι τεθραυσμένους ἐν ἀφέσει		—
Lk. 4.19	κηρύξαι ἐνιαυτὸν κυρίου δεκτόν	Isa. 61.2	καλέσαι ἐνιαυτὸν κυρίου δεκτόν
	—		καὶ ἡμέραν ἀνταπο- δόσεως

* *UBSGNT*, 3rd edn, brackets the phrase due to weak attestation, and it is not adopted in this discussion.

21. 'In Luke the point is not the identification of the speaker as a new messianic figure, but rather that the functions of this Old Testament figure are now fulfilled in Jesus' (Marshall 1978: 183). This 'interpretative reversal' is developed as the narrative unfolds.

had attracted future eschatological associations.[22] Jesus modifies the quotation by the insertion 'to let the oppressed go free' (Isa. 58.6), which expands the prophet's activities to include both the proclamation of these things *and playing a part in bringing them to pass.*[23]

Jesus' quotation stops at Isa. 61.2a, and so strikingly omits 'the day of vengeance' together with the future great reversal when Jews expected to be served by foreigners (Isa. 61.2b-5). In this way the Lukan Jesus dispenses with Jewish particularist hopes of salvation and by implication opens up the future for Jew and for Gentile.[24]

Jesus declares that 'Today this scripture has been fulfilled...' (4.21), which implies that he is the prophet foretold by Isaiah.[25] As Jesus has the freedom to *revise* the prophecy, he further implies that he is more than the prophetic figure foretold.[26] The emphatic 'Today' makes clear

22. Isa. 61.1-3 appears in rabbinic traditions and in various manuscripts from Qumran. These develop the eschatological dimension, and in Qumran, the association with the eschatological hope of the year of Jubilee (Evans and Sanders 1993: 48-57).

23. The interpolation from Isaiah 58.6 within Isaiah 61.1-2 is important: 'Jesus not only announced forgiveness and freedom (like the Baptist) but brought them' (Schweizer 1984: 89). 'This interpolation underscores the significance of Jesus' (Nolland 1989: 196).

24. The language of the conflated quotation will become typical of Jesus and his mission. The verb εὐαγγελίσασθαι in Isa. 61 is applied to Jesus for the first time in the narrative. Jesus also replaces the LXX καλέσαι (Isa. 61.2a) with κηρῦξαι (4.19) which links the text to the vocabulary which will describe Jesus' ministry, and the ministry of the disciples (9.2) (cf. Marshall 1978: 629; Tannehill 1986a: 78).

25. The narrator's description of the Spirit coming ἐπ' αὐτόν (3.22) is related to the Isaianic description of the Spirit coming ἐ' ἐμέ (4.18) in Jesus' discourse. This suggests the narrative link between the scene in Nazareth and the descent of the Spirit at Jesus' baptism (so also Fitzmyer, contra Tannehill's suggestion that the Nazareth scene explains what Son of God means [Fitzmyer 1986: 63]).

26. Kingsbury among others argues that the verbal link between ἔχρισέν (4.18) and Χριστός allows the possibility that this story declares Jesus as Messiah (Kingsbury 1991: 45). This is unlikely, for the context points to Jesus as prophet, and prophets are anointed by the Spirit as Isa. 61 makes clear (cf. Marshall, Fitzmyer, contra Tannehill and Schürmann. Nolland wants both messianic and prophetic associations, but concedes that at least 'in the immediate pericope the prophetic thought is predominant' [1989: 196]). The prophetic role of Jesus is also recognizable in his discourses. In his analysis of the style of Jesus' discourses, Dawsey builds upon the analyses of Bultmann and others and observes that 'for the most part, Jesus' sayings are pronouncements...in that they initially appeal to

that the salvific 'end time' begins now (Goulder 1989: 301). The narrative combination of the revision of the prophecy and the emphasis upon
'today' in Jesus' discourse contributes to his self-characterization: Jesus
is the prophet whom the traditions and the people await, but *on his own
terms.*[27] The synagogue is the setting where the Jewish faith and its
practical wisdom is taught to the faithful. The narrative locates Jesus
the 'reviser' of the scriptural tradition in the place of the teaching of the
tradition. Jesus is a truly radical prophet. From now on, conflict is
inevitable.

The audience whom Jesus addresses is significant. The narrator portrays the audience in the most general of terms with no mention of any
leaders, scribes or Pharisees. The audience is never described, but
seems to comprise the pious, ordinary people. Jesus is the prophet primarily concerned for the people and not the religious establishment.
Indeed, the very fickleness of the people's response reveals their need
of help. Jesus, the people's prophet, introduces himself first to the
people.

The people's incredulous question—'Is not this Joseph's son?'—precipitates a long discourse in which Jesus declares what the congregation
think—just as earlier prophets could do—and recalls the failure of
ordinary people to welcome prophets in earlier times. This suggests that
Jesus is a kind of a prophet; yet Jesus speaks with more than prophetic
authority when he says: ἀμὴν λέγω ὑμῖν (4.24).[28] Jesus refers to himself obliquely through the aphorism that 'no prophet is accepted in his
home town' (4.24). Even the disconcerting verbal aggression toward the
audience is typical of the Hebrew prophetic tradition.[29] The audience in

Jesus' own authority for their truth claims. In this sense, Jesus' speech in Luke is
more prophetic than didactic' (Dawsey 1986b: 39).

27. 'The actual fulfilment had begun, and nowhere in the Second Testament is
this more sharply put than in this hapax in Luke 4.21' (Evans and Sanders 1993:
61). σήμερον is found in Jesus' discourse for 9 of its 11 occurrences in the Gospel
(4.21; 13.32; 12.28; 13.33; 19.5; 10.9; 22.34; 22.61; 23.43). Six of these uses convey the association with God's salvation, which is also true of the angel's use of the
term (2.11).

28. The phrase 'Amen, I tell you' and minor variations on it are typical of Jesus'
discourse. The phrase builds a sense of prophetic authority both within the story
world and for the narratee. 'Amen' is the only Semitic word retained in the Gospel
(cf. Fitzmyer 1981: 536; Nolland 1989: 200).

29. Tannehill draws the parallel with John's prophetic preaching. 'The response
of the people to both prophets is favourable... But John greets them with scorching

the synagogue unwittingly re-enacts the rejection by Israel of the prophets of old, *and thus confirms Jesus' self-characterization*. The consequence of this rejection is that Jesus does not do any works in Nazareth, and never returns there.

Jesus and the Demons at Capernaum (4.31-37)
Jesus' exorcism at Capernaum is the first 'saving event' in the Gospel—hitherto he has taught in the synagogues. On the sabbath, Jesus is teaching again in Capernaum. The people are astounded because of Jesus' authority—as the narrator explains. The encounter with the spirit of the unclean demon opens a new dimension of characterization. Just the presence of Jesus as he teaches with authority is construed by the demon as an attack (4.34)! Through this 'activity', the character Jesus has developed his sense of 'authority'.

Jesus responds in a brief discourse: 'Be silent, and come out of him' (4.35)—a mere five Greek words. Jesus uses the commonly used verb 'Be silent' but with no exorcism ritual, which contrasts markedly to other exorcists of that time.[30] The reason for Jesus' command to silence is not clear, for it comes too late to preclude the demon addressing Jesus in public as 'the Holy One of God' (4.35). Could it be that the narrator deliberately allows the demon to speak *before* the command to silence, in view of the contribution made by the demon's discourse? This possibility is discussed in more detail in Chapter 11. As far as Jesus' self-characterization is concerned, the demon does not speak again and comes out as commanded (4.35).

There are two audiences present in this scene, each allocated its own discourse. The people before whom the events unfold interpret the activity of the exorcism as a display of power and authority beyond their experience, which they attribute to the authoritative word of Jesus, rather than Jesus himself (4.36). Jesus does not comment upon their questions. The people's comments suggest that they have not heard the demon's discourse about Jesus.

Jesus' second audience is the spirit of an unclean demon (4.35) which

---

words "offspring of vipers!" John does not confuse superficial religion with real repentance, and Jesus does not confuse wondering admiration with openness to his mission' (1986a: 70). In a Gentile setting, would such language be better 'toned down'?

30. The Greek verb is used 'extra-biblically' for stifling evil spirits with a magic spell (Fitzmyer 1981: 546).

had initiated the conflict with him in its opening discourse. To the demon, Jesus characterizes himself in word and as the one who has authority over them. An audience of powerful demons is a suitable context in which the power of the Holy One is manifest. Jesus' authority is clearly great, which is underlined by his need of no further assistance from ritual or prayer.

Interestingly, Jesus does not approve or deny the demon's description of him as the 'Holy One of God', though the command to silence could be a tacit agreement. At this stage of the narrative, whereas the demon is interested in who Jesus is, the people are still endeavouring to interpret what he does.

Jesus goes on to heal and exorcise at sunset in the presence of people in need. The narrator's inclusion of 'and heal' expands the scope of the authority of Jesus. The demons speak the only discourse in this scene and Jesus rebukes them so that they cannot speak further. The lack of a denial from Jesus leaves open the possibility that he might be the Son of God—the kind of Son with authority over the demonic realm.

Jesus and the Crowd in Act 2 (4.40-41)
The act concludes with the crowd wanting Jesus to remain with them, which provides Jesus with the occasion to interpret his activity as 'the proclamation of the good news of the kingdom of God' (4.43).[31] This is the first time the 'kingdom of God' is introduced, and significantly it is found in the discourse of Jesus. The retrospective use of the phrase allows the preceding scenes to function as the narrative exposition of this new kingdom.[32] Significantly Jesus chooses *what he does* rather than Jewish tradition to give meaning to this Jewish concept.[33]

31. The verb εὐαγγελίσασθαι in the summary of Lk. 4.43 is the same verb in Lk. 4.18 which suggests a literary *inclusio*. The NRSV translation loses this continuity by translating εὐαγγελίσασθαι as 'bring the good news' (4.18) and 'proclaim the good news' (4.43). These two summaries also share the verb ἀπεστάλην.

32. The description εὐαγγελίσασθαί με δεῖ τὴν βασιλείαν τοῦ θεοῦ (4.43) evokes the later Christian language of evangelism. Jesus portrays himself as the 'proclaimer of the good news of the kingdom of God'.

33. This manner of 'retrospective description' for the introduction of the phrase the 'kingdom of God' is similar to the hermeneutical convention of the narrator discussed in Chapter 9. Fitzmyer has completely missed the point in his comment that 'surprisingly, no attempt is made at this first occurrence of the expression in the Lukan Gospel to define what the kingdom of God is' (1981: 557); the story up to

The audience for Jesus' discussion of the kingdom of God is yet another crowd of local Jews, which in the Gospel of Luke is a corporate character which displays continuing interest but little understanding. As will be seen, Jesus uses the phrase 'kingdom of God' principally with the crowd, which suggests that the kingdom of God is unlikely to be a major aspect of the Lukan Jesus' self-characterization.

Jesus combines the Greek δεῖ with the clause 'for I was sent for this purpose' (4.43), which is another 'theological passive' Greek verb (Fitzmyer 1981: 557). Jesus makes his final semiotic contribution in this act by leaving Capernaum despite the requests of the crowd, and so demonstrates that his first allegiance is to the will of God.[34]

Jesus' Self-Characterization in Act 2 of the Lukan Narrative
Jesus develops his earlier self-characterization as the Father's son in two ways. First, he demonstrates more of the obedience associated with sonship of his Father—which was introduced during the last act. Now this obedience is acted out in the face of temptation to disobedience, in the acceptance of the prophetic commission and in the 'prioritizing' of the claims of God and the people. Second, Jesus demonstrates a powerful authority over the demons which is associated with the figure of the Son of God. The demons are an important audience in Jesus' self-characterization, as is discussed in Chapter 11. As powerful influences which cannot be tamed by people, their subjugations in this act are narrative expositions of one aspect of Jesus, the Son of God.

Jesus introduces a major new aspect when he characterizes himself as a prophet to the Jewish people. The response of the faithful both confirms the category and also limits what Jesus can develop from this figure. By choosing a Jewish audience for this aspect of his self-characterization, Jesus takes up the Jewish tradition of the prophets sent from YHWH. Jesus portrays himself as one who is a prophet and as one who is more than a prophet. The story of Jesus' activities provides the narrative resolution of this ambiguity. For example, Jesus develops the prophetic figure by associating it with the 'one who will proclaim good news'.

this point is the narrative definition Fitzmyer seeks (cf. discussion of the kingdom of God later in this chapter).

34. The compound verb ἦν κηρύσσων is an imperfect which portrays the continuous action. The sentence has no direct object and so a better translation is: 'he continued preaching in the synagogues of Judaea' (4.44).

The narrative link between the figures of 'son' and 'prophet' is found in the life of the character Jesus, and in particular at his baptism. Jesus' commitment to God is the obedience of a Son, which takes the form of the life of a Spirit-anointed prophet.

The Self-Characterization of Jesus in Act 3 (5.1–9.50)

Jesus contributes most to his self-characterization in the interchanges within this act as a steady stream of story characters pose the question 'who is this Jesus?'[35] The disciples and the Pharisees form two new and important audiences. The following discussion traces Jesus' self-characterizations with the four principal audiences in this act: the disciples, the crowd, the Pharisees and the disciples of John the Baptist.[36]

In this act the character Jesus develops his two strategies of self-characterization. First, he lives out his ministry while saying very little about himself. Those who encounter him construct their perception of him as events unfold and they express it in an address or response to Jesus, which he then may accept or correct. In this way, the *activity* of Jesus determines the meaning of the descriptions of him in 'retrospective self-characterization'.

Second, Jesus introduces the enigmatic figure of the Son of Man before the crowds, and a slightly different suffering Son of Man figure when alone with his disciples. Jesus does not unequivocally adopt any one figure or description as a correct representation of himself, with the implication that none can sufficiently embrace who Jesus is. Thus the reader is left with the narrative itself: *the stories about Jesus constitute Jesus' narrative identity.*

Jesus and the Disciples in Act 3

Jesus calls disciples to follow him in this act, and the developing relationship between Jesus and the disciples provides the principal narrative

35. In act 3 there are nine moments that address the question of Jesus' identity (5.21; 7.19 reiterated in 20, 39, 49; 8.25; 9.9, 18, 20, 35), together with an indirect question about his family (8.19). There are three further occasions when Jesus' identity is declared, although not understood (9.20, 35, 44).

36. The Pharisees are considered in their own right, although they have a wider significance in the narrative. On each of the eight occasions that the religious leaders as a composite character are named in this Act, the Pharisees are always part of the group, while other members vary (cf. 5.17, 21, 30, 33; 6.2, 7; 7.30, 36).

opportunity for Jesus to disclose more of who he is, for unlike other story characters, to the disciples 'has been given to know the secrets of the kingdom of God' (8.10). The 'divine passive' construction which occurs in the text suggests that it is God rather than Jesus who gives or withholds this understanding.

In this act Jesus reveals himself to his disciples principally *through what he does*. Apart from his introduction of the figure of the 'suffering Son of Man' at the end, Jesus does not refer to himself at all directly or indirectly when speaking with the disciples. The narrative dynamic unfolds Jesus' activity before the disciples, followed by their suggestions of what this might signify.

The enigma of the act is that the disciples are not mentioned (and so may be considered literally as not present) during many of the key activities of Jesus in the act![37] The disciples miss all but one of the healings and exorcisms,[38] and when they are present, they do not place themselves in a flattering light.[39] The only two occasions when they may form a view are the controversies and the calming of the storm (8.22-25).[40] Jesus offers the disciples a limited view of himself in

37. The five longest (and so most significant) scenes are:

Scene	Word Count	Disciples Present
Exorcism of the Gerasene demoniac	294	None
Two women in need	287	Peter, James, John
The woman with the ointment	273	None
The healing of the man let down through the roof	214	None
Jesus speaks of John	202	None

38. The analysis of Jesus' healing and exorcising in this act:

Ref.	Scene	Presence of Disciples
5.12-16	Healing of the man with leprosy	No
5.17-26	Healing of man let down through the roof	No
6.6-11	Healing of the man with the withered hand	No
7.1-10	Healing of the slave of the centurion	No
7.11-17	The raising of the widow's son at Nain	Yes
8.26-39	The exorcising of the man from Gerasa	No

39. The characterization of the disciples is discussed by Tannehill 1986a and Kingsbury 1991. The present discussion is interested in their role in the self-characterization of Jesus.

40. There are 39 narrative units in this act, which comprise 4 narrator's summary reports, 28 scenes and 7 speech units. The disciples appear in all 4 narrator's summary reports, but in only 14 of the 28 scenes.

action, and yet this becomes the basis for his question: 'who do you say that I am?' (9.20).

Jesus exercises authority over natural events by calming the storm, which raises the question for the disciples 'who it is that even the winds and water obey him?' (8.25). No explanation is offered by Jesus, though for Peter it is possible that the stilling of the storm enlarges his understanding of what 'Lordship' might include (5.8).

Jesus lives the life typical of a first-century rabbi, and so *during this act alone*, the disciples (and only they) address him as the 'Master', [41] which is the translation of 'rabbi'.[42] Jesus goes beyond the role of a typical rabbi when he commissions the 12 to be apostles and go out to proclaim the kingdom of God (9.1, 2), which is only the second time Jesus speaks of the kingdom of God to the disciples.[43] The kingdom is associated with the same kind of ministry that Jesus demonstrated in the previous act. The new dimension is the 'devolved authority', which poses the question 'who can give such authority to others?' The 70, upon their return, recognize that it is one who is 'the Lord' (10.17). Jesus only employs 'Lord' twice in his discourses in this act and both times when speaking to non-disciples (6.5; 6.46). This suggests that it is not a major feature in Jesus' self-characterization because the audience is unable to develop its significance.

After a period of ministry, Jesus questions the three disciples about his identity. Peter volunteers that Jesus is 'the Messiah of God' (9.20), which the crowds had not suggested. The importance of Peter's answer is in part what it elicits from Jesus. Instead of confirming or denying the possibility, Jesus commands silence and then introduces the figure of a Son of Man, who 'must undergo suffering...and be killed, and on the third day raised' (9.21). The absence of a more direct response from Jesus, together with the command to silence evokes the interactions between Jesus and the demons, who had also explicitly characterized Jesus.

---

41. In this act, Jesus is addressed as 'Master' (ἐπιστάτα) five times and only by the disciples (5.5; 8.24, 45; 9.33, 49). The title is used once more in the whole of the Gospel, when it is found on the lips of the ten men with leprosy (17.13).

42. The absence of 'rabbi' in the Lukan narrative contrasts with the other three Gospels (Matthew 4×; Mark 4× and John 8×), and illustrates the Lukan hermeneutical concern for a Gentile reader.

43. Jesus mentions the kingdom of God 4 times in this act compared to 17 in the next act.

For Jesus, this contrast between 'Son of Man' and 'Messiah' is significant. The figure of the 'Messiah' seems inappropriate for him—perhaps because it does not adequately represent who Jesus considers himself to be?[44] At the very least, it seems that Jesus is not the popular Messianic figure the disciples imagine. At the same time, the disciples do not comment upon the figure of the suffering Son of Man, which suggests that at this stage the figure awaits explanation.

With the three disciples on the mountain, the prayerful Jesus is surrounded by Moses and Elijah and is momentarily transfigured by the glory which Jews associate with God himself. The transfiguration is for the benefit of the disciples. This time the voice from the cloud addresses them and interprets Jesus' identity *for the sake of the disciples*: 'This is my Son, the Chosen' (9.35; evoking 3.22). Jesus is acting out the submission of the Son, and the heavenly commentary confirms it to the disciples.[45]

Jesus and the Crowds in Act 3
Jesus exercises a teaching ministry principally before the crowds and anonymous characters, who in return address him as 'Teacher'.[46] Jesus proclaims his first extended teaching discourse in the Sermon on the Plain, and introduces the teaching device of the story parable in this discourse. Jeremias suggests that Jesus employs 30 parables in the

44. The need for 'correction' of the disciples' understanding is also expressed in the narrative juxtaposition of the present scene with the adjacent scene of Jesus on the mountain of Transfiguration, when the voice from heaven addresses *the disciples*.

45. Tannehill suggests that 'it is doubtful that we should understand the transfiguration as an event simply staged for the three apostles. Probably it has meaning for Jesus as well' (1986a: 225). This is true to the extent that the different communicative acts within the scene are distinguished by identifying the different audiences. The voice from heaven addresses the disciples, whereas Moses and Elijah address Jesus and discuss the way he is to go.

46. Jesus is perceived and addressed as a teacher by those who are not disciples: Simon the Pharisee (7.40), Jairus's friend (8.49) and the man in the crowd (9.38). This characteristic is also true for the rest of the Lukan narrative: cf. a lawyer (10.25), lawyers (11.45), someone in the crowd (12.13), a certain ruler (18.18), some of the Pharisees (19.39), those who wanted to trap Jesus (20.21), some Sadducees (20.28), some who spoke of the Temple (21.7) and the owner of the room where the Passover was held (22.11). The disciples never address Jesus as 'Teacher'.

Gospel. Jeremias's list is adopted and the distribution between the different acts and different audiences is set out in Appendix D.

Jesus' phrase 'But I tell you' signals an authority to expound and re-interpret the Jewish traditions which goes beyond the remit of a typical rabbi.

When Jesus does great works, the crowds offer interpretations of their significance. On two occasions Jesus is portrayed as raising the dead, though the significance beyond an expression of compassion is not developed by Jesus.[47] On the first occasion (7.11-17) 'the crowd' offers their interpretation of the event: 'A great prophet has risen among us' (7.16). The crowd is not the most reliable or perceptive of characters and while Jesus never describes himself to them as a prophet,[48] the pattern of his ministry fits the profile of the prophet.[49] Jesus' avoidance of the description 'prophet' raises the possibility that Jesus is in the process of transforming the popular concept of a 'prophet'.

Jesus and the Pharisees in Act 3

The narrator introduces the Pharisees in a sequence of five controversies with Jesus followed by a scene when Jesus dines with Simon the Pharisee (9.36-50). In these scenes, two aspects of Jesus' self-characterization stand out for the narratee.

Jesus is one who forgives sins. As soon as the Pharisees appear there is a controversy about Jesus forgiving the sins of the man let down through the roof (5.17-26), followed by a debate in which Jesus declares 'I have

---

47. Jesus raises the widow's son at Nain (7.11-17) and Jairus's daughter (8.40-56). Jesus' discourse about the daughter being asleep and not dead is 'prognosis and not diagnosis' (Nolland 1989: 421), as the future tense in Jesus' discourse makes clear: 'Only believe and she will be saved' (8.50).

48. The possibility that Jesus is a prophet is brought before the narratee by two story characters of uncertain reliability. The crowd comment that 'a great prophet has risen among us' (7.16) and Simon the Pharisee thought that 'If this man [Jesus] were a prophet he would know who and what woman she is' (7.39).

49. The characteristic of prophets which may be constructed from the Lukan narrative include: (a) anointed by the Spirit; (b) the authority to interpret the traditions; (c) the ability to do signs; (d) the ability to know the hearts of men; and (e) the experience of rejection by God's own people. Although Moessner does not distinguish between Jesus' audiences, he is broadly correct: 'Luke's Gospel...thrusts Jesus onto a stage of prophetic flurry and spotlights Jesus self-proclaimed prophetic career' (1989: 47).

come to call not the righteous but sinners to repentance' (5.32). Later in the act, the controversy reappears in the home of Simon the Pharisee when Jesus forgives the sins of the woman who anointed his feet (7.36-50).[50] These are the only occasions in the Gospel when Jesus actually declares sins forgiven.[51] On both occasions the Pharisees are the audience.[52]

Might Jesus forgive sins in the presence of the Pharisees because this audience is best able to recognize the implications of his declaration? Although the Pharisees eventually reject Jesus, their response 'who can forgive sins but God alone?' (5.21; 7.49?) supports this suggestion; the effectual declaration of forgiveness can only be made by (i.e. focalized by) God. So Jesus' forgiveness of sins is a narrative declaration of who he is; for the religious Jew (Pharisee or disciple) this revelation is more important than the forgiveness itself. When Jesus responds to the Pharisees, the issue is clearly the question of his identity.[53] In the next act Jesus tells parables of the joy when a sinner repents (Lk. 15), and the Pharisees are the audience again, together with the scribes (15.2).

50. The forgiveness of sins is included in Jesus' commission to the disciples in Lk. 24.47, which confirms that the matter is a proper aspect of Jesus' identity, and is not just a concern within the Pharisaic tradition.

51. Tannehill overplays the forgiveness of sins when he suggests that 'Jesus' mission to proclaim "release of sins" has thematic importance' (1986a: 108). There is an insufficient number of explicit treatments of the issues. It could be argued that Jesus lived out a forgiveness of sins by mixing with sinners.

52. Jesus teaches about sin and repentance on five occasions in the Gospel, which is relatively infrequent (contra Fitzmyer 1981: 223-24): the three controversies with the Pharisees (5.17-26; 5.30-32; 7.48-49), followed by advice to the disciples about forgiving one another (17.1-4) and finally Jesus includes repentance and forgiveness of sins within his commission to the disciples (24.4). There is a possible allusion to the forgiveness of sins in the language of Isa. 61.1-2, but it is not the obvious meaning, despite using the word ἄφεσις (4.18). Tannehill correctly suggests that 'release (ἄφεσις) for the captives has a broader meaning which can include the forgiveness of sins (1986a: 103). The description by the angels of Jesus as 'Saviour' (2.11) is neither mentioned again nor developed in the narrative, and the Gospel does not include the etymological comment upon the name Jesus—'for he will save his people from their sins' (Mt. 1.21).

53. 'The structure of the story places emphasis upon the fact that Jesus forgives (5.21), and thus assumes the prerogative of God' (Marshall 1970: 138; cf. Carroll 1988: 608). Nolland misses the focus upon who Jesus is when he suggests that the forgiveness of sins 'renders explicit the challenge to the religious leaders of Jesus ministry to call sinners' (1989: 232).

The effectual forgiveness of sin by Jesus is reinforced when he 'acts' out the forgiveness of sins by mixing with and eating with those who are 'sinners' (5.30-32; 7.33-34; 7.36-39). This is observed by the Pharisees and forms a ground for complaint.[54]

Jesus' association with the son of man. Jesus introduces the figure of the Son of Man into the narrative world in disputes with the Pharisees, beginning with the argument about the authority on earth to forgive sins (5.24). Jesus clearly aligns himself with the Son of Man who has authority to forgive sin and to heal through both Jesus' discourse and through his 'acting' in the dispute.[55] The Son of Man recurs when Jesus debates the requirements of the Sabbath with the Pharisees and declares that the Son of Man figure exercises authority over the Jewish traditions (6.5).[56] The narrator emphasizes the authority of Jesus by ensuring that the Pharisees do not reply and so seem to be silenced by his teaching.

The Pharisees contribute the appreciation of the claim to authority implicit in Jesus' activity, but they do not comment upon the figure of the Son of Man, and this lack of response reduces the narrative potential

---

54. The contrast between Jesus and the narrator is sharply drawn. Although the narrator retains the stories of Jesus forgiving sin and mixing with tax collectors, the narrator only mentions a cognate of 'sin' three times in his discourse in the complete Gospel (3.3; 7.37; 15.1). (The distribution of the cognates of the word 'sin' within the discourses is: Jesus 20×; Pharisees 5×; narrator 3×; and other single uses: Peter 1×; crowd 1×.) This distribution suggests that for the narrator, 'sin' is a concept within a peculiarly Jewish scheme of thought, which can be supplanted by other aspects of the salvation which Jesus brings. Hermeneutically, the forgiveness of sins is negotiable. This view is supported by the narrative treatment of the death of Jesus, which the narrator does not construe as achieving forgiveness of sins; only Jesus develops this interpretation when he is with the Jews who were his disciples. Tannehill recognizes this picture, but without narrative-critical tools is unable to develop his insight (1986a: 106-108). See further discussion in Chapter 12.

55. In a narrative-critical analysis the significance of a title such as the Son of Man depends in part upon its context. In this act the Son of Man is always found in Jesus' discourse, twice when he addresses the Pharisees (5.24; 6.5), once when he addresses the crowd (7.34), and the remaining four examples are addressed to the disciples. Each relationship is the occasion of a different emphasis.

56. The claim that what Jesus does 'is not lawful' (6.2) accords with the audience of 'Pharisees and teachers of the law' (5.17; 6.2). The freedom to dispense with the Jewish Sabbath traditions has already been demonstrated by Jesus' healings on the Sabbath.

of the Son of Man figure. Jesus' actions stir them to a fury which emerges in the next scene when Jesus breaches their law (again) and heals in a synagogue on the Sabbath (6.6-11). Jesus exercises an authority (as the Son of Man) over the law and the traditions, which the Pharisees and the teachers of the law do not have. Jesus' discourse refashions Sabbath practice in line with its original intention. Unlike the act of forgiving sin, the Pharisees do not develop the implications of who could properly do these things.

Jesus and the Disciples of John the Baptist in Act 3
The disciples of John meet Jesus once (7.20) and provide the perfect occasion for Jesus to demonstrate his stratagem of self-characterization. John had looked forward to 'the one who is to come' (3.16), and now is uncertain whether Jesus is that person. John's disciples put the question to Jesus (repeated in the narrative twice for emphasis). Jesus does not answer directly, but replies 'Go and tell John what you have seen' (7.22).

The first significance of Jesus' response is the emphasis he places upon his deeds. This is typical of Jesus' handling of the question of his identity and is subsequently taken up by the Lukan narrator as he constructs the Gospel narrative. Comparisons with other figures or the attribution of previously known titles to Jesus are unable to capture the unique and unsubstitutable aspects of Jesus. Only Jesus himself can do this through his activity which becomes a narrative exposition of who he is. As Frei recognized, the Gospels are basically ascriptive stories in which all the comparisons employed to illuminate the identity of Jesus are firstly self-referential, and avoid slipping into circular tautology by the narratives of the life of Jesus himself.

The second significance of the discourse Jesus addresses to the disciples of John is that the list of the deeds does not match exactly the list set out in the Isaianic quotation which Jesus employed in the Nazareth synagogue.[57] Clearly Jesus considers the list which he offers these enquirers to be 'definitive', which is a reinterpretation of the Isaianic text. The narrator recognizes this and uses the second list as a guide when constructing the sequence of Luke 4–7.

---

57. The narrator recognized this and focalized the narrative contents in the light of Jesus' discourse and not Isa. 61, as is discussed in Chapter 9.

Jesus displayed the freedom to rework the Isaianic text in Luke 4 and now he reinterprets it. In so doing Jesus transforms John's expectations; instead of 'winnowing in judgment' as John foretold (3.17), Jesus ensures that the climax of his discourse is that 'the poor have good news preached to them' (7.22).[58] Jesus is the eschatological prophet, and the one who is greater than John—and he is these figures *on his own terms*, and these terms are revealed in the narrative of his activity.

Jesus' Self-Characterization at This Stage of the Lukan Narrative
Amid all the questioning of this important act, Jesus reveals who he is principally *by what he does*. Jesus employs Scripture to begin to interpret what he does as a prophet (4.18) and then lives out the narrative exposition of this prophetic call. The narrator's unfolding of these events is clearly 'shaped' by the discourses of Jesus. Jesus also uses the phrase 'the kingdom of God' to describe retrospectively what he does (4.43). Jesus refuses to be 'restricted' to particular figures, particular Scriptures or particular expectations. Instead, Jesus is who he is in his story—what he says and does, and it is a peculiarly Jewish story at that. As argued in Chapter 9, the narrator considers it possible to tell the story of who Jesus is without further development of these Jewish aspects.

This 'characterization by story' is developed further toward the end of this act when Jesus alludes to two aspects (authority and suffering) of the 'Son of Man'. This figure is sufficiently undefined as to excite little comprehension amid Jesus' audiences, and is therefore ripe for a fuller exposition by Jesus.

The Self-Characterization of Jesus in Act 4 (9.51–19.44)

There is a marked development in Jesus' self-characterization in act 4. As the journey to Jerusalem begins, the narrative changes in style and the type of material included. Jesus spends much more time teaching, and includes in this act 24 of his 30 parables in the Gospel (as set out in

58. What puzzled John is likely to be this absence of judgment and this difference 'is sometimes construed as a rejection of the Baptist's expectations' (Fitzmyer 1981: 667-68). But 'the judgment motif is not absent from Jesus' ministry, and in the Lukan frame we should think rather of the Lukan "two-stage" eschatology: what John expects will come later on' (Nolland 1989: 330).

Appendix D).[59] Jesus' discourses are frequently cast in the form of pronouncements which resemble the oracles of the Hebrew prophets.[60] In contrast, Jesus heals or exorcises only five times in this long act. The question of 'who is the Lukan Jesus?' now appears less frequently.[61] The rejection of Jesus by the religious leaders deepens as the narrative unfolds, in ways analogous to what happened to the prophets of old.[62]

The narrative structure of this act is not altogether clear, and so this discussion is structured about a preliminary analysis of the interaction between Jesus and four of his principal audiences, each of which provides a distinctive context for Jesus' further self-characterization.[63]

59. Twenty-four of the 30 story parables in the Lukan narrative are found in this act, addressed to three principal audiences in an interesting distribution. Further details are found in Appendix D.

(1) 'The disciples', 'little flock', 'apostles'	7
(2) The crowds, unspecified 'they', anonymous members of crowd	9
(3) The Pharisees, their guests	6
(4) A lawyer	1
(5) those who are confident and 'who trust in themselves'	1

60. Characteristics of Jesus' discourse include (1) the use of 'Blessings and Woes'; (2) the authoritative tenor; (3) the lack of interest in persuasion; (4) the rhetorical function of most of Jesus' questions; (5) the 'pronouncement' form of much of his discourse. Dawsey argues this case in general and concludes that 'the form of Jesus' speech was prophetic' (1986b: 43). I suggest that this is most clearly the case in this act.

61. In the 74 narrative units of this act, Jesus discusses himself either directly or indirectly (through references to the Son of Man) in 28 of the narrative units. This is 41% of the material.

62. It is sufficient for this study to demonstrate that the relationship between Jesus, the people and the religious leaders mirrors the relationships of earlier prophets. These fit within Steck's scheme (Moessner 1989: 84). Moessner proposes a further and more precise parallel in this central section in which Jesus is a prophet like Moses, which is more difficult to establish. In the present discussion, it is sufficient to establish Jesus' general role, for I argue that whatever tradition he finds himself in, Jesus transforms it in his own story.

63. Act 4 comprises 74 narrative units, 3 of which are narrator's summaries addressed to the narratee. The remaining 71 narrative units portray Jesus addressing various audiences. The distribution is as follows: disciples 28; crowds 13; Pharisees 13; anonymous individuals 7; cities 3; God 1; miscellaneous 6.

Jesus and the Disciples in Act 4

The relationship between Jesus and the disciples develops intermittently in this act, except in the middle period when the disciples are completely absent (12.53–16.1).[64] Jesus gives the disciples 'guidance on the way' (Talbert 1982) as he teaches about the life of their new community, about prayer and warns of Pharisaic influence. Seven of Jesus' parables are addressed to the disciples. Jesus' discussion of the kingdom of God with the disciples is minimal,[65] although 'the kingdom of the Father' is used three times and only with the disciples.[66] Five scenes with the disciples are particularly important.

The mission of the seventy. Jesus' mission charge declares that the harvest belongs to God, and then Jesus commissions the disciples as if he is the Lord of that harvest (10.3).[67] Jesus, the Lord, gives authority to the 70 to heal the sick, and to explain that the kingdom of God has drawn near to their audiences.[68] The narration of the 70's success confirms that Jesus has acted to bestow such authority upon men and the 70 now address Jesus as 'Lord' (10.17). On the lips of this larger group of disciples, of whom the narrative tells the narratee very little, the significance of the vocative 'Lord' awaits clarification. At the very least Jesus' lordship is literal for he exercises a lordly authority. Once

64. The disciples play a part in 16 of the 40 scenes in this act.

65. Jesus speaks of the kingdom of God to the disciples twice: to reprove them for excluding children (18.16, 17) and to encourage Peter about those who have made sacrifices for the kingdom of God (18.29).

66. 'Father, hallowed be your name. Your kingdom come...'—to the disciples (11.2); 'your Father knows that you need them. Instead, strive for his kingdom...'—to the disciples (12.31); 'Do not be afraid little flock, for it is your Father's good pleasure to give you the kingdom' (12.32).

Jesus does speak of the kingdom of God to 'would-be followers' in Lk. 10.60, 62; 18.24, 25.

67. 'Pray to the Lord of the Harvest that *he sends* (ἐκβάλλω) workmen to harvest. 'Go, see, *I am sending* you out (ἀποστέλλω) like lambs among wolves' (10.2). The narrator appreciates this identification by employing 'Lord' to denote Jesus in Lk. 10.1.

68. The analysis of the audiences with whom 'the kingdom of God' is used is most illuminating. Jesus charges the disciples to use the phrase 'the kingdom of God' in the same way that Jesus most often uses it, which is to employ the concept to help the crowds understand what he is doing. This convention is discussed at greater length in the next section of Jesus and the crowds.

again, Jesus docs not respond directly, and turns to his vision of the fall of Satan.

Tannehill's suggestion that 'the Sonship of Jesus, confirmed to Jesus at his baptism and revealed to the three apostles at the transfiguration has been revealed to the seventy (two?)' fails to persuade because the language of sonship is absent in this scene, and Lord and Son are not previously linked in the narrative and have distinctive characteristics (1986a: 237). What would be more illuminating is reading the range of characters who address Jesus as 'Lord' in comparable contexts of response to what Jesus has done and determining the focalizing going on in these encounters.

The narrative context of Jesus' vision of Satan's fall suggests that exorcisms in the Lord's name (10.18) are particular examples of the wider defeat which Jesus saw in this vision.[69] If this is the case, Jesus is not the one whose authority is ultimately responsible, for Jesus does not claim to have thrown down Satan—rather, Jesus saw it happen. This qualifies the significance of the address 'Lord' on the lips of the returning 70.

The vision Jesus experiences seems similar to those visions typical of the Hebrew writing prophets, and worthy of further study.[70] Certainly, Jesus is the prophet to whom God gives visions and in whose ministry these visions becomes reality—which is the scriptural confirmation of an authentic prophet.

The discourse about fire on earth (12.49-53).[71] Jesus clearly denotes himself as 'the one who has come to bring fire on the earth', evoking

69. The preferred translation of the Greek text is 'I saw Satan fall from heaven like lightning', and not 'I saw Satan fall like lightning from heaven'. The most likely explanation of this passage is that this is a vision of Jesus which he had earlier (the Greek imperfect serving as a simple past tense), the realization of which will be worked out in Jesus' ministry. Each exorcism constitutes another occasion of the expulsion of Satan (cf. standard commentaries).

70. The theme of the fall of Satan is alluded to in Isa. 14.12: 'How you are fallen from heaven, O Daystar, son of the Dawn', and may lie behind Lk. 10.15. Satan is named in Job 1.6 as one of the heavenly beings who came before the Lord. Nolland disagrees with the link to Isaiah, and suggests that the fall motif is closer to the *Testament of Solomon* 20.16-17 (Nolland 1993a: 563; cf. Goulder 1989: 478).

71. This passage is replete with difficulty (cf. Marshall 1978: 545; Fitzmyer 1985: 993) and is discussed here strictly in the light of the question of its contribution to Jesus' self-characterization.

for the narratee the discourse of John the Baptist (3.16) and also the misplaced zeal of the disciples (9.54).[72] The phrase 'from now on' (12.52) suggests that the fire comes *before* the final judgment and that divisions are its consequence (Conzelmann 1960: 109; contra Tannehill 1986a: 251). This is Jesus' first association of himself with eschatological judgment before the disciples and contrasts with the discourse in the synagogue at Nazareth before the religious people where Jesus is the prophet of peace. The key to this difference is the change of audience; these differences become clearer as the narrative continues.

The discourse about the coming Son of Man (17.22-25). For the second time in the Lukan narrative Jesus speaks in the third person of a future Son of Man figure (12.8; cf. 9.26). The relationship between Jesus and the Son of Man is still unresolved and leaves open the question of who is focalizing this aspect of Jesus' teaching.[73] This future figure will come at an unexpected hour, as illustrated in the parable of the Unexpected Thief (12.39-40).

When Jesus speaks to his disciples alone of the coming of the Son of Man (17.22-37) he includes a comment upon the suffering Son of Man, which succeeds in suggesting a narrative relationship between the suffering Son of Man (whom the narratee recognizes as Jesus) and the future Son of Man figure. This reiterates the first narrative link between these two figures set out in act 3 (9.22-25).

Jesus' passion prediction (18.31-34). Towards the end of this act, Jesus returns to the 'suffering Son of Man' figure in discourses when alone with the disciples.[74] In the longest discourse, Jesus explains to the 12

---

72. The principal narrative resonance is with John, for whom baptizing with fire is a characteristic of 'the one who is to come' (3.16). This narrative link is reinforced by the immediate mention of baptism within Jesus' discourse. The options of what 'fire' might symbolize in Lk. 3.16 are discussed in Fitzmyer 1981: 473-74. In this discourse, the link between fire and division suggests the eschatological judgment (cf. Nolland 1993a: 708).

73. The tendency to identify the Son of Man figure with Jesus can be premature, and it collapses the semantic potential of the curious construction. Nolland correctly observes that 'the text does not assume an immediate identity between Jesus himself and this Son of Man' (Nolland 1993a: 679).

74. The suffering Son of Man is introduced toward the end of act 3 (9.22, 44). The theme reappears toward the end of the present act in the comment amid the

that what will happen to the Son of Man will take place in Jerusalem (18.31-33). In this conflation of the narrative theme of 'Jerusalem' and 'the suffering Son of Man', Jesus foretells that the frequent Israelite rejection of the prophets is to be re-enacted for the prophet Jesus in the form of the sufferings of the Son of Man in Jerusalem.[75] The narrator's later commentary on the parable of the Wicked Husbandman (20.19) makes clear that the narrator includes the death of Jesus as part of this rejection.

Jesus uses the verb 'to hand over' as a description of his future (18.32) and does not provide any explanation of how this death might be of wider significance—a theme which is briefly discussed later in this chapter.

Jesus recalls the expectation that 'he will rise again' (18.33; cf. 9.22). This is so unexpected that in the narrative no response is allowed to the disciples; instead they are silent, 'understanding nothing' (18.34). Here is one of the tests of a prophet of God—will his words come true? The narratee (and reader) have the rest of the Gospel to answer this question.

Jesus' ride into Jerusalem (19.37-40). The ride down the Mount of Olives is a significant action of Jesus, yet he does not comment upon it directly. When arranging for the collection of the colt Jesus describes himself as 'Lord' to its anonymous owners. The word 'Lord' is reiterated for emphasis, but nothing is developed from this.[76]

A possible significance of the ride into Jerusalem is supplied by the crowd of disciples, and is not refuted by Jesus (19.40).[77] To them, Jesus is the pilgrim king (the first time Jesus is so described in the Gospel) and the multitude of disciples welcome him in that light (19.37; cf.

proclamation of the future coming of the Son of Man (17.5) and in the present passage under study (18.31-33).

75. 'The title "prophet" says something positive and important about Jesus. In particular, it enables the narrator to comprehend, through relating Jesus' life to a scriptural pattern, the combination of powerful word, mighty deeds *and* rejection by God's people.' (Tannehill 1986a: 97).

76. It is possible that the owners are disciples and 'Lord' would be an appropriate form of address (cf. Peter in Lk. 5.8), or possibly 'Master'. It is more likely that they are not, for the two disciples sent by Jesus seem not to know them. In this case the ambiguity of the meaning between the general, respectful 'Master' and the description of God himself serves well the narrative context.

77. The multitude of disciples refocalize the pilgrim greeting in Ps. 118.26, by the replacement of 'the one who comes' with the phrase 'the King who comes'.

13.35) employing a revision of Ps. 118.26b (substituting the specific title 'king' for the general phrase 'one who comes'). The narrative does not make clear that this is a scriptural quotation or develop the significance of the revision, for as usual the narrator does not directly link Jesus' activity with a particular Jewish Scripture. The quotation evokes the discourse of the angels to the shepherds (2.14) and so introduces an element of 'reliability'. Nevertheless the silence of the narrator and the silence of Jesus are ambiguous and leave Jesus' actions to speak for him—and await future clarification!

Jesus and the Crowd in Act 4
Jesus unfolds more self-characterization to the crowd, which is usually an audience that displays little insight. Nevertheless, Jesus' activities before them include his teaching in parables, his acts to heal and exorcise and his teaching about the kingdom of God.

Jesus teaches in parables. Jesus' discourses to the crowd and to anonymous people include 10 of the 24 parables in this act. These contribute significantly to the self-characterization of Jesus *as a teacher*, but the substance of these parables does not illuminate the character of Jesus any further. Among the various themes addressed, Jesus teaches the crowds about the kingdom of God (13.18-21; 24-30) and about the demands of discipleship (14.28-32).

Jesus acts to save. There are five healings and exorcisms in this act.[78] When on two occasions the person healed breaks out into praise of God, Jesus' discourse employs what was to become salvific language (e.g. the verb σέσωκέν)(17.19; 18.42).[79] The only other use by Jesus of such language is found when he describes the salvation which came to the house of Zacchaeus (19.10).[80] Significantly, each time Jesus

---

78. These include (1) the exorcism of the mute demon (11.14); (2) the healing of a crippled woman (13.10-17); (3) the healing of a man with dropsy (14.1-6); (4) the cleansing of the 10 lepers (17.11-19); (5) the healing of the blind man near Jericho (18.35-43).

79. This pattern echoes the pattern in the earlier act when Jesus describes his activity as 'salvific' (σέσωκέν) for the people (7.50, 8.48). In those cases the recipients are women, and in this act two men.

80. Jesus employs the noun σωτηρία only once (19.9), and in conjunction with '*Today*, salvation has come to this house'.

employs this language, it is the presence of Jesus which brings salvation near.

Jesus and the kingdom of God. Jesus speaks most frequently of the kingdom of God in this act[81] and includes three parables to illuminate what the kingdom of God is like.[82] Jesus speaks of the kingdom of God to four audiences, most commonly to the crowd.[83] Since the crowds require assistance to understand the kingdom of God, Jesus charges the 70 to heal in his name and explain the healings as the coming near of the kingdom of God (10.9, 11).[84]

Jesus' rhetorical question about analogies for the kingdom of God which prefaces the parables is accompanied by the activities which

81. A narrative-critical analysis enquires which narrating subject uses the phrase and who is addressed by the subject voice. The phrase 'kingdom of God' is found 32 times in the Gospel text and is used by just 3 voices.

Act	Voice	to Disciples	to Crowd	to Pharisees	to Others	Total
2	Jesus	—	1	—	—	1
	Narrator	—	—	—	—	0
3	Jesus	2 + (1 joint)	1 + (1 joint)	—	—	4
	Narrator	—	—	—	—	3
4	Jesus	3*	5	3	6	17
	Narrator	—	—	—	—	2
	Anon	(Jesus)	—	—	—	1
5	Jesus	—	1	—	—	1
	Narrator	—	—	—	—	0
6	Jesus	2	—	—	—	2
	Narrator	—	—	—	—	1
7	Jesus	—	—	—	—	0
	Narrator	—	—	—	—	0

*Jesus commands the disciples to use the phrase *with the crowd*, who thus form the audience.

82. Lk. 13.18-19: the parable of the Mustard Seed; Lk. 13.20-21: the parable of the Yeast in the Flour; and Lk. 13.24-30: the parable of the Closing Door.

83. The kingdom of God is included in Jesus' discourse 17 times in this act, (9.60, 62; 10.9, 11; 11.20; 13.18, 20, 28, 29; 16.16; 17.20, 21; 18.16, 17, 24, 25, 29), and *only once* is the phrase used in a discourse addressed to the disciples (18.29). In the commissioning of the 70 Jesus refers to the kingdom of God twice more (10.9, 11), but only to instruct the disciples to say that the kingdom of God has drawn near.

84. The narrator makes a further contribution by including the comment that Jesus sent them 'to where he intended to go' (10.1). When the pairs healed in Jesus' name, that constituted the drawing near of the kingdom—which also presages the drawing near of Jesus.

Jesus does and which form the narrative exposition of the kingdom of God. Thus Jesus takes up the concept and fills it with his own particular significance.

Jesus' clearest exposition of the kingdom of God is provided in the Beelzebul controversy (11.14-23). If the exorcism of the demon from the mute man is by the finger of God, then Jesus explains 'the kingdom of God has come to you' (11.20).[85] The phrase 'the finger of God' comes from the priestly tradition of Exod. 8.15 and describes the battle between the power of God and Pharoah's magicians, who in later Jewish tradition were interpreted as serving demonic powers.[86] In a similar way, Jesus defeats the demons with the power of God.

In this discussion, the 'action' and 'discourse' of Jesus reinforce one another to make clear that Jesus' exorcisms constitute the *arrival* of the kingdom. What is peculiar to this exorcism performed by Jesus? It is not the exorcism itself, for others also performed exorcisms (11.19). It is not the power by which the demons are cast out, for both Jewish exorcists and the 70 on their missions invoke the power of God. The peculiar feature is simply that these exorcisms are performed *by Jesus in person*. When Jesus exercises authority over the demons the kingdom—or the reign of God—arrives.

In contrast the exorcisms performed by the disciples in Jesus' name signal that the kingdom *draws near* (10.9).[87] The 70 were sent out 'to every town and place where he himself intended to go' (10.1). Could it be that the drawing near of the kingdom in the disciples' ministry is a preparation for the arrival of the kingdom when Jesus arrives and acts as the King? Jesus' own exorcisms *are the present presence of the kingdom,* for where Jesus reigns, there God reigns, with all the implications that ensue. That Jesus in his ministry *enacts and so constitutes* the

85. The phrase ἔφθασεν ἐφ' ὑμᾶς has occasioned debate. C.H. Dodd understandably welcomed the emphasis upon realized eschatology, but Campbell suggests that it is better rendered 'drawing near to completion'. The classical use of the verb with preposition is 'to reach' and this sense is found in LXX (e.g. Dan. 4.20, 'the tree top reached to heaven') So this discussion follows Kümmel 1957: 107: 'it can therefore be said with certainty that...Lk 11.20. must be translated "the kingdom of God has come upon you"'.

86. Discussed in Ellis 1974: 166, noting the caution that these texts are at least a century later (cf. Vermes 1983; and Str–B: iv, 532-35, quoted in Marshall 1978: 475).

87. The Greek verb ἤγγικεν is literally translated as the kingdom of God '*has drawn near*' (10.9, 11).

kingdom of God illuminates my translation (already preferred on separate grounds) of Jesus' retort to the Pharisees: 'the kingdom of God is among you' (17.21).

Jesus and his Father in Act 4

For the first time in the Gospel the narrative includes the discourse of a prayer of Jesus.[88] There is uncertainty about which audiences are addressed within the discourse of Jesus. The prayer is usually considered to be 10.21-22, with v. 23 addressed to the disciples privately. The first part (10.21) is clearly addressed to Jesus' father, but the change in substance and style in v. 22 make the audience unclear.[89] The most likely audience is the crowd, which would include the disciples.[90]

Jesus' prayer is offered when the Spirit is present (10.21a), which in the narrative is a device which bestows 'divine reliability' upon what is said. Jesus employs the familiar vocative πάτερ to address God for the first time in the Gospel. Although used to address a human father by the prodigal son (15.12, 18, 21) and to address Abraham by the rich man in Hades (16.24, 27, 30), πάτερ is only used of God by Jesus (10.21; 22.42), and at his invitation, by the disciples (11.2). This use evokes for the narratee the discussion of the boy Jesus with his parents when in the Temple.[91]

88. Jesus is portrayed as a man of prayer throughout the Gospel narrative, but his prayers are only given twice (10.21-22; 22.42—this analysis follows the *UBSGNT*, 3rd edn, decision to treat as secondary Jesus' prayer on the cross [23.34]).

89. This difficulty has provoked historical-critical suggestions of separate logia redacted into this text. In contrast, the narrative critic seeks to make sense of the present form of the text. Nolland correctly observes that in v. 22 'the content becomes decidedly didactic' (1993a: 573).

90. The audience is unlikely to be God because of the change from the vocative to the didactic. The implication of the comment 'then turning to his disciples he said to them privately' (v. 23) is that in the world of the text, Jesus' audience prior to his turning to the disciples is larger than just the disciples. This possibility is supported by the following: (1) the presentation of the 70 leaving and returning suggests that Jesus delivered his woes to the Galilaean towns before a crowd while the 70 were away (10.13-16); (2) immediately after the private word to the disciples a lawyer stood up to test him, which suggests the presence of a crowd (10.25); (3) the clause 'know who the Father is' (10.22) is appropriate for an audience of non-disciples.

91. This accords with Jeremias's historical-critical study of the Aramaic vocative *abba* which is lies behind the Greek πατέρ. 'When Jesus addresses God as

Before the audience of the crowd and disciples, Jesus clearly implies that he is the Son of the Father, Lord of heaven and earth (10.22). The implication is not taken up by the audience, and Jesus spells out the importance of the revelation for the disciples, because the appreciation of this revelation is given by the Father 'to those whom the Son chooses to reveal him' (10.22). Immediately Jesus takes the disciples aside privately and explains more. In this, Jesus develops the preceding discourse, but more importantly he confirms that he considers himself to be the Son, because he is doing exactly what he describes the Son as doing.

Jesus and the Pharisees in Act 4

Jesus encounters the Pharisees 13 times in this act, including twice sharing table fellowship with them. However, every meeting but one ends in controversy. The debates revolve about the interpretation of the law and the relationship between piety and God's interest in the sinners and outcasts.[92]

The parables addressed to the Pharisees emphasize the 'joy in heaven over one sinner who repents' (15.7, 10). Jesus' parable of the Pharisee and the tax collector (18.9-14) underlines the contrast between the Pharisaic way of condemning sinners and Jesus' way of forgiving sinners and welcoming them back, which reaches its peak in this act (Carroll 1988: 611).[93] Jesus' self-characterization takes place in the extended narrative *contrast* between himself and the Pharisees, in which the Pharisees provide the necessary foil to make clearer Jesus' approach to the law and sin and to the sinner.[94]

---

abba (πατέρ) the word is by no means simply an expression of Jesus' familiarity in his converse with God. At the same time it shows complete surrender of the son in obedience to the Father' (Jeremias 1967: 62).

92. The parable of the Owner compelling the poor, crippled and lame to come to dinner (14.15-24) and the parable of the Prodigal Son (15.11-32) are addressed to Pharisees.

93. Tannehill's comment about the scribes and Pharisees applies particularly to the Pharisees: 'The story strongly emphasises the tension between the scribes-Pharisees and Jesus...Study of the references to scribes and Pharisees in Luke shows that these groups are mentioned almost entirely in pronouncement stories or similar scenes in which they interact with Jesus by objecting, posing a testing enquiry, or taking a position which Jesus corrects' (1986a: 170).

94. The Pharisees' hostility to Jesus arises from their conception of the demands God makes of the pious man, which is mediated through the Law. Carroll is par-

Jesus develops his self-characterization in two particular scenes. When the Pharisees warn Jesus that Herod wants to kill him (13.31), Jesus responds that 'it is impossible for a prophet to be killed outside of Jerusalem' (13.33b, cf. 11, 47-52).[95] This impossibility arises from the divine purpose (cf. 13.33a), for Jesus' life is ordered by God.[96] In this scene Jesus identifies himself to the Pharisees as a prophet who will suffer, but without implicating them.[97]

As the conflict deepens the Pharisees and Jesus clash over the issue of wealth, for some of the Pharisees 'were lovers of money' (16.14). This precipitates Jesus' second self-characterization: 'the law and prophets were in effect until John came; since then the kingdom of God has been proclaimed, and everyone tries to enter it by force' (16.16).[98] Jesus reiterates that the kingdom of God supersedes John (cf. 7.28 to the crowds), and emphasizes that his own ministry constitutes the proclamation of that kingdom (16.16).[99] In the translation 'everyone is

tially correct in identifying these demands with the demands of the kingdom of God, but the Pharisees rarely use this phrase, and disputes about the Law would be a more accurate description. 'Luke's narrative, therefore employs Jesus' encounters with Pharisees to display competing understandings of the kingdom of God. At stake in Jesus' controversies with the Pharisees, expressly within the travel narrative, although the battle lines are drawn already in 5.21–6.11; 7.29-50, is the nature and composition of God's *basileia* (kingdom or reign)' (Carroll 1988: 612).

95. No evidence of a tradition to this effect has been discovered, but there are many examples of prophets dying at Jerusalem (cf. Fitzmyer 1985: 1032).

96. The third-person saying about the prophet echoes the periphrastic anonymity in the treatment of God as a narrative agent. The saying is introduced by a clause which includes the 'divine' δεῖ (13.33). This proposal is supported in ch. 24 when Jesus relates the third-person 'Son of Man' sayings to the Scriptures (24.26, 46).

97. Jesus speaks of his death as a prophet *to the Pharisees* as a response to Herod's plan to kill Jesus. The Pharisees are not implicated in this death, and disappear from the narrative as Jesus enters Jerusalem.

98. Jesus speaks of the kingdom of God to the Pharisees on three occasions. Jesus responds to a comment about the kingdom of God at a dinner with a Pharisee (14.15); once when he argues about the Law and the Prophets (16.16) and once when a Pharisee enquires about how the coming of the Kingdom may be recognized (17.20).

99. Lk. 16.16 serves as 'the key to the topography of redemptive history. According to this passage there is no preparation before Jesus for the proclamation of the kingdom of God...it is only through (Jesus') proclamation of the Kingdom that John's preaching, and only through the Spirit that John's baptism, are raised to a level appropriate to the new epoch' (Conzelmann 1960: 23). 'In this sense John is

urgently invited into the kingdom'[100] there are implications of urgency for Jesus—could it be that now he is on the way to Jerusalem time is running out?

Jesus' Self-Characterization at This Stage of the Lukan Narrative
Jesus develops his self-characterization before the audience of the Pharisees both as a prophet and as one who forgives sin. The crowds recognize that Jesus brings in the kingdom of God as they observe the healings and exorcisms which Jesus performs. The disciples recognise the growing authority of Jesus, but are perplexed by his discourse about suffering. Jesus acts as the 'son' of his Father, and so formally claims sonship for himself. The 'tone' of this act is the new perspective of the future events at Jerusalem. The self-characterizations which Jesus offers will be developed further in what happens in Jerusalem.

The Self-Characterization of Jesus in Act 5 (19.45–21.38)

Jesus returns to the Temple in act 5 and reclaims it as the place in which to teach the people. As this happens the Lukan narrative returns to the place where it began. There are four audiences whom Jesus addresses: the traders, the religious leaders, the people in the temple, and the disciples, although it is not usually possible to distinguish the last two groups.

Jesus and the Traders
When Jesus arrives in the Temple, his first audience comprises the traders who are selling what the faithful need for their sacrifices and exchanging money needed for the Temple tax. Jesus' encounters with

a precursor of Jesus, not as a Christian or a Kingdom preacher himself, but the Jewish reform preacher who prepares Israel for the preaching of the Kingdom' (Fitzmyer 1985: 115).

100. The verbal construction εἰς αὐτὴν βιάζεται is difficult; 'few sayings in the Gospels are so uncertain in interpretation as this one' (Marshall 1978: 630). There are three possibilities, each with an active and passive option. For discussion see the standard commentaries. The preferred meaning for the verb is to 'invite urgently', for it is used in this way in Acts 16.5, 24.29. The passive form is preferred for it parallels the passive form of the proclamation of the kingdom of God (16.16b), and fits the thrust of the discussion. So also Fitzmyer, 'everyone is pressed to enter it' (1985: 1114).

the traders as he starts to drive them out is the context for further self-characterization (19.45). To begin, this 'driving out' of the sellers is a 'prophetic' kind of act.[101]

Jesus' discourse begins with a revision of Isa. 56.7 in which 'shall be called' is replaced by the 'shall be': 'My house shall be a house of prayer'. This refashioning makes the Scripture more of a legal stipulation (Nolland 1993b: 937) and so inaugurates judgment upon the present practices. Jesus also omits the last phrase in Isaiah, 'for all peoples', and so restricts the focus of the saying to the Temple.[102] The description of a 'den of robbers' is taken from Jer. 7.11. Jesus' revision of Scripture refocalizes the texts so that they become the justification for his activity. The narratee may well ask: 'could it be that the Temple is now *his* house?'

In the narrative the controversy in the Temple opens up the act's principal focus upon Jesus' activity—he teaches and 'all the people are spellbound' (19.48b).

Jesus and the Religious Leaders
Jesus' encounter with the religious leaders develops through this brief time in the Temple.[103] Through clever debate Jesus distances himself from these leaders, while their public options are constrained by the support for Jesus by the people who visit the Temple. The one occasion to ask a pertinent question about Jesus' authority is missed when the religious leaders refuse to acknowledge John. As Jesus answers the other questions of the religious leaders they are gradually reduced to silence and finally acknowledge that 'he has spoken well' (20.39). Then

---

101. 'Jesus arrives as a King (19.38) acts as a prophet (quoting the prophets of old) and takes possession of his Father's house' (Fitzmyer 1985: 1265). However, 'it is not clear whether Luke regards the action as having any deeper significance. The cleansing of the Temple was expected in the end time (Malachi 3, 1ff; Zechariah 14.21)...but Luke makes so little of the incident that it is hard to believe that he saw this significance in it' (Marshall 1978: 721).

102. The discourse has replaced Isa. 56.7b 'My house shall be called a house of prayer for all peoples' with 'My house shall be a house of prayer' (19.46) for 'no very obvious motive' (Marshall 1978: 721). Nolland wonders whether it is altered to read as if it is a legal stipulation, which would give Jesus more authority (1993b: 937).

103. The members of this group are variously described, but in narrative functional terms, they all act as a single corporate character.

Jesus is free to teach the people who come to the Temple to hear him. The semiotic contribution is that as he teaches the word of God, so Jesus is 'at home' in his Father's house.

Jesus, the Disciples and the People in the Temple

Apart from one explicit discourse, the people and the disciples function as a single combined character, as when 'in the hearing of all the people he said to the disciples' (20.45).[104] To this audience Jesus tells the parable of the wicked tenants (20.9-18) which while making a point about religious leaders (20.19) also suggests a father–son relationship which illuminates Jesus and his Father. This is done through the medium of parable and awaits the hearers' response.

Jesus speaks of two other related matters before the people and disciples. First, the exploration of why the Messiah must be more than David's son, for did not God say to 'my Lord...sit at my right hand' (20.42). The second matter touches on why 'you will be hated by all because of my name' (21.17), and develops a range of visions of the future, some cast in apocalyptic terms. 'On account of my name' raises the status of Jesus for the disciples and for the narratee.[105]

The only unambiguous narrative unit in respect of the disciples is the warning to 'beware of the scribes...'(20.45). The adjacent context is the argument about the Messiah and David. The irony is that when Jesus teaches in the proper 'seat of learning', neither the disciples nor the people appreciate what this signifies about him.

Jesus' Self-Characterization at this Stage of the Lukan Narrative

Jesus develops his role as the authoritative teacher before the crowds. The stature of Jesus grows as he makes clear in apocalyptic terms that he is greater than the Temple and, in a preliminary way, makes clear that he is associated with the future.

---

104. The disciples are only mentioned once in their own right (20.45), but the discourse about suffering on account of the name of Jesus seems also addressed to the disciples (21.17).

105. Jesus' name is used in three ways in the narrative: first, 'on account of my name' (21.17) is an extension of the person (9.48); second, the name is the power to do mighty works (9.49; 10.17); third, allegiance to Jesus is introduced as the occasion of persecution.

The Self-Characterization of Jesus in Act 6 (22.1–23.56)

Jesus contributes most to the characterization of himself in the scenes of the last Passover, the arrest, the hearings and the crucifixion.

The Last Passover

In Jesus' initial discourse, he describes himself to an anonymous character as 'the teacher' who wishes to eat the Passover with his disciples' (22.11). The room is available, just as Jesus had said (22.13), which reinforces his reliability as a character for the narratee.

The scene of the Passover is the longest in this act, and two-thirds of the scene comprise Jesus' discourse, interspersed by the narrator's brief descriptions of Jesus' actions.[106] The discourse is addressed to the apostles (22.14) but they are not allowed a discourse to respond— possibly because they miss the point (22.23)?

Jesus speaks of his sufferings, the Passover and the kingdom (56 words in the Greek text), then of the disciples and the Passover (29 words) and finally the betrayal (30 words).[107] This is not a typical 'farewell discourse' for they usually open with an announcement of imminent death followed by an exhortation.[108] The betrayal at the end involves Judas and prepares for the following scene. The allocation of narrative time places most emphasis on the first theme, which is further emphasized by the inclusion of the authoritative phrase 'I tell you' in this section alone (22.16, 18).

Jesus 'eagerly desires to eat this Passover before he suffers' (22.15), but it is not clear that he does eat for he is not described as eating anything; could it be that he awaits the fulfilment of the kingdom of

---

106. The scene lasts for 168 Greek words, and Jesus' discourse takes up 115 Greek words (68%).

107. The thesis follows *UBSGNT*, 3rd edn, and includes vv. 19b-20. The words of Jesus in this discourse have been the subject of extensive redaction-critical study, as traced in a recent review of scholarship (Nolland 1993b: 1040-49). Within the constraints of a preliminary reading, the present discussion highlights the particular contributions of a narrative-critical reading of this discourse. The first contribution is the recognition that the discourse is in three parts, and not the usual two-part division into 'Passover' and 're-interpretation' (e.g. Fitzmyer 1985: 1391).

108. A 'farewell discourse' begins with the announcement of death which is followed by the exhortation to friends and disciples (Talbert 1982: 207).

God?[109] Even if Jesus is not portrayed as eating, he does feed the disciples. The implication of the narrative is that Jesus' death and resurrection *is an aspect of the coming of the kingdom*, and thus illuminates
'who Jesus is'. This thematic juxtaposition links the Passover meal with
the messianic banquet in the future kingdom of God, which accords with
the choice of the verb 'fulfilled'. [110] The repetition of the phrase the
'kingdom of God' emphasizes its importance, while the variation in the
parallelism of 'until the kingdom of God comes' (22.18) opens 'the
possibility that the kingdom will come *in the future experience of
the apostles*; in both cases the eschatological fulfilment is stressed'
(Schweizer 1984: 335).[111] This interest in the kingdom accords with
earlier discourses of Jesus, in contrast to its minimal presence in the
discourse of the Lukan narrator.[112]

In the shorter middle part of the discourse, Jesus develops the eschatological significance of this Passover and speaks of himself in lan-

109. The present discussion follows *UBSGNT*, 3rd edn, which omits οὐκέτι, and
so the translation omits 'again' in 'I will not eat it [again] until it is fulfilled in the
kingdom of God' (22.16). (cf. *UBSGNT*, 3rd edn, 'Critical Apparatus' and Nolland
1989: 1041). Furthermore the syntax of λέγω γάρ ὑμῖν means that 'the logic of
Luke's "for" (γάρ) is not too plain because of the compressed style: he means I
wanted very much to eat this Passover with you because it will be our last meal
together until we eat it fulfilled in heaven' (Goulder 1989: 725). However, there is
the fact that Jesus does not eat or drink in the account. Perhaps Jesus awaits the
Kingdom to be fulfilled before he will eat the Passover? Jeremias's suggestion that
Jesus 'desire to eat was an unfulfilled wish' (1966: 208) is persuasive, for the
phrase ἐπιθυμεῖν plus infinitive can mean 'unrequited desire' (as when the prodigal
son was hungry 15.6); contra Nolland 1993b: 1041.
110. Nolland conjectures that 'It is likely that already in the time of Jesus,
Passover did not only look back to redemption from Egypt but also on to eschatological redemption to come—this is clear enough for the post New Testament
period' (1993b: 1050). Without further evidence, it is more certain that 'Jesus thus
gives a new eschatological dimension to the Passover meal being taken with the
apostles' (Fitzmyer 1985: 1397).
111. 'Lk 22.18 is sufficiently general that it could be fulfilled in the references to
the post-resurrection appearances where Jesus ate and drank with the disciples (Lk
24.1-2)' (Talbert 1982: 207).
112. The contrast is clear in the language of the discourse. Nolland concedes this,
though cautiously because he is engaged in a historical-critical debate about the
traditions: 'the language is nowhere notably un-Lukan, but it does at points involve
idiom that cannot be shown to have come spontaneously from Luke's pen' (1989:
1050).

guage which evokes the Paschal lamb which has been killed (the narrator's commentary, 22.7).[113] Jesus gives out bread and describes it as 'my body which is given for you' (22.19), a phrase which 'adds a vicarious dimension of meaning' (Fitzmyer 1985: 1391). The choice of language in 'the cup that is poured out for you is the new covenant in my blood' (22.20) reinforces the parallel between Jesus and the lamb.[114] The phrase 'New Covenant' evokes Jer. 31.31, and the verb 'poured out' echoes the Sinai pact (Exod. 24.8).[115]

Jesus' discourse is the only time in the Gospel that any character or the narrator offers an interpretation of Jesus' suffering and death. Until this point, suffering has been just one aspect of the way of obedience. The significance of the death of Jesus is interpreted by its juxtaposition with the death of the Passover lamb, which long ago effected the deliverance which led to the exodus and a new life for the children of Israel.[116] Jesus' discourse makes clear that the link is between himself and *the story* of the Paschal lamb rather than particular Scriptures.

After the explaining that the bread is his body given for (ὑπὲρ) them, Jesus instructs the apostles to 'do this in remembrance [ἀνάμνησις] of me' (22.19) in the way that the Jews 'remembered the day of their

---

113. '[Jesus] is the *eschatological paschal lamb*, representing the fulfilment of all that of which the Egyptian paschal lamb and all subsequent paschal lambs were the prototype' (Jeremias 1966: 223; Jeremias' italics).

114. The Greek text is

τοῦτό τὸ ποτήριον ἡ καινὴ διαθήκη
ἐν τῷ αἵματί μου
τὸ ὑπὲρ ὑμῶν ἐκχυννόμενον

115. The vocabulary of the Greek phrase clearly conveys that Jesus will be a vicarious sacrifice for the disciples. The Greek preposition ὑπέρ is equivalent to 'on your behalf', and the verb διδόμενον is used to describe that which is sacrificed (e.g. Exod. 30.14 LXX). Talbert maintains that the expression 'should not be understood in terms of an atoning sacrifice' (1982: 209). The confusion arises from Talbert's general approach which is 'a type of redaction criticism heavily influenced by nonbiblical literary criticism' (1982: 2), and which fails to distinguish the different narrative voices. For the narrator, Jesus is the innocent martyr (which is the position that Talbert holds for the whole of the text), but for Jesus himself, he is the Paschal lamb whose sacrifice is the means of salvation.

116. The Greek construction places emphasis upon the possessive pronoun in the phrase: 'the new covenant in *my* blood' (22.20) which sharpens the contrast with the Passover.

departure' (Deut. 16.3).[117] The parallels and literary contrast between the first and second sections of Jesus' discourse suggest that he is offering the eucharistic body and blood to *replace* the Passover lamb and cup (cf. Nolland 1993b: 1049).

The narrator in the primary discourse makes clear the later eucharistic significance of this middle section through the choice of language, but does not develop the soteriological dimension.[118] What has primary significance for the character Jesus is the desire to eat this meal when the kingdom of God has come, which allows that the fulfilment of his suffering is an aspect of the coming of the kingdom.

The third section of Jesus' discourse returns to the theme of his exodus journey, with the emphasis for the narratee on the 'divine necessity' of the way which Jesus travels.[119] The discourse displays literary parallelism which confirms Jesus as the suffering Son of Man figure (22.21 // 22.22) and which correlates with the opening of the discourse where Jesus speaks of his own suffering (22.15). The devastation among the disciples is simply reported rather than given a voice.

The discourse that Jesus addresses to the disciples (now described as apostles) elicits only a report of a discussion about which one would betray Jesus (22.23). This contrast highlights Jesus' discourse. The disciples understand little, but they are the audience whom Jesus can now address about himself. Talk of suffering precipitates no rebuke now. The new link between Jesus and the coming of the kingdom of God (22.16; 22.18) lies undeveloped, but the apostles can return to it.

Prayer and the Arrest
The scene on the Mount of Olives is arranged by the narrator to portray prayer amid temptation, bracketed by the *inclusio* of 'pray not to come into the time of trial' (22.39, 46). The scene includes the contrast

---

117. The symmetry between Lk. 22.19 and 22.20 is lost when Jesus expands upon the 'New Covenant' instead of reiterating 'do this in remembrance of me'.

118. The choice of the four verbs 'taking', 'giving thanks' (εὐχαριστήσας), 'breaking', 'giving' (20.19) is 'a piling up of verbs which evokes solemn eucharistic practice' (Nolland 1993b: 1052).

119. Although the discourse does not use the verb δεῖ (22.22), the passage conveys the same sense of the necessity of the divine will. Schweizer correctly observes that 'v.22 speaks of what has been determined (by God) instead of Scripture' (1984: 336).

between the disciples and Jesus, and all within a chiastic structure (Nolland 1993b: 1081).[120]

Jesus addresses God with the familial vocative 'Father' in the central discourse which once again signals Jesus as 'son'. Jesus' Father is his audience, and this is emphasized by the disciples falling asleep![121] Before God, Jesus acknowledges plainly his sonship.

Within the son's commitment to the Father are the twin desires to escape this 'cup', and to please his Father. Jesus' discourse reinforces that *Jesus is the obedient son*. In contrast to Jesus' discourses in the Temptation scene (4.1-13), Jesus turns to his Father and not to Scripture for help to resolve his dilemma, and uses language which refers to the will of a personal Father.[122] The decision to prefer the Father's will is underscored by the emphatic position of the Greek verb in the phrase 'let your will be done' (22.42). As the story continues, it is clear that Jesus acts out his surrender to his Father's will. This discourse is the turning point in the act, for here the sonship of Jesus is most plainly revealed.[123]

As Jesus returns to the disciples, the crowd come to arrest him. In his discourse to Judas who is still a disciple, Jesus describes himself again as the figure of a suffering Son of Man (22.48). In his last discourse to the crowd, Jesus declares that 'this is your hour' and refers for the first time to the 'power of darkness' (22.53), echoing the prophecy of Zechariah (1.79). By implication, Jesus characterizes himself as 'light'.

---

120. This discussion follows *UBSGNT*, 3rd edn, in the omission of Lk. 22.43-44 as not part of the original text.

121. As the disciples are asleep, this scene has posed difficulties for some historical-critical scholars who cannot explain how the narrator knows these things. In a literary-critical reading of a fictional work, the question is inappropriate; in a literary reading of a historical narrative such as a Gospel, although not necessary for the reading, it is sufficient to posit how the story may have been passed on. As with the temptations, a simple possibility is that Jesus subsequently told the apostles.

122. 'Father if you wish' employs βούλει to denote the Father's wish (or 'plan'; Squires 1993) and echoes the description of the faithful who accepted the baptism of John as the 'purpose' (NRSV) of God (7.30). What the Father wishes is described as his θέλημα, which is 'not a capricious whim of the Father...but the Father's plan of salvation' (Fitzmyer 1985: 1442). The impersonal third-person δεῖ is not used.

123. 'As for Jesus himself, it may be fair to say that the real struggle takes place here rather than later: as martyr, Jesus here faces up to his fate, and having done so, he is able to go through what lies ahead with comparative equanimity' (Marshall 1978: 828).

The Four Hearings

Jesus appears before three different audiences in four hearings.[124] Jesus speaks at length in the first dialogue with the Sanhedrin, and not at all thereafter.[125] There is underlying opposition to Jesus among the Sanhedrin, which wants to trap him rather than learn from him. In response to an enquiry whether Jesus is the Messiah, Jesus prophesies that they will see the Son of Man in glory, which for the narratee is reminiscent of Jesus' discourse at the recent Passover meal.

The second discourse in this first hearing acknowledges that these opponents only listen to themselves and their plottings (22.3). Jesus recognizes that there is no receptivity, and retires into silence.

The narrator's chiastic arrangement of the second hearing pivots around Jesus' enigmatic words 'You say so', which returns the onus to the interlocutors.[126] This time the audience is Pilate and there is no discussion of Jewish visions for the future. After this response, Jesus falls silent for the remaining two hearings. The hearing before Herod is simply reported and no character speaks. In the last and longest hearing, Jesus is not even described as 'present'.

The narrative sequence represents various ways of describing Jesus dependent upon the different audiences involved. Through his interaction Jesus clearly distances himself from the expectations of the different Jerusalem parties. The figure of the Son of Man is sufficiently

---

124. The debate continues about the legal status of the different hearings. The position adopted in the present discussion is that the two hearings before Pilate constitute the legal trial hearings. The Sanhedrin, which was unable to exercise the death penalty, conducted a pre-trial hearing, and Herod's hearing could be a quasi-legal hearing (cf. Nolland 1993b: 1105-1109).

125. The distribution of words in the respective Greek discourses is as follows:

Hearing	Audience	Unit	Narrator	Jesus	Opponent
1. (22.66-71)	Sanhedrin	94	35	33	26
2. (23.1-7)	Pilate (1)	118	72	2	44
3. (23.8-12)	Herod	91	91	—	—
4. (23.13-25)	Pilate (2)	163	92	—	71

126. The narrator arranges the discourses to place emphasis upon Jesus' discourse:

A	The Sanhedrin	16 words	
	B	Pilate		6 words
		C	Jesus	2 words
	B´	Pilate		7 words
A´	The Sanhedrin	15 words	

imprecise or unknown to elicit any response, and awaits Jesus' activity as its narrative exposition.[127] In these four hearings Jesus takes leave of the Jerusalem establishment and what they represent. The disciples have already gone. In his silence Jesus characterizes himself as the one who depends upon God alone.

The Cry on the Cross
As Jesus dies he cries out in his third and last prayer.[128] Jesus addresses God with the familial vocative Πατέρ (23.46) as he begins a short prayer of just eight Greek words. Jesus' discourse is a quotation from the Psalms which he refocalizes and makes his own. The Psalmist entrusts himself to God for a better future, and Jesus revises the quotation into a more intimate expression of faith and expectancy.[129] Jesus then acts out what he has prayed, and hands over his spirit as he dies.

Jesus characterizes himself as the son who trusts his Father God with his life, which leads him to Jerusalem and the cross. Jesus is the son who demonstrates that sonship is expressed in self-giving.

Jesus' Self-Characterization at This Stage of the Lukan Narrative
The first important aspect of Jesus' self-characterization is as the Paschal lamb slain for all. Jesus' death will bring life through the eating of bread and drinking of wine in remembrance of him. There is much in this dimension of Jesus' self-characterization that awaits development;

---

127. The question 'Are you then the Son of God?' (22.70) seems to be a response to the second part of Jesus' discourse: 'seated at the right hand of God' rather than the phrase 'Son of Man' (22.69).

128. The narrator describes Jesus 'crying with a loud voice' (φωνῇ μεγάλῃ), which is striking for the usually measured style of this narrator. Talbert, bemused by the partial insight that Jesus is presented as a 'model martyr', mistakenly comments that 'Jesus dies quietly, full of trust, a model for Christian martyrs to follow' (1982: 225).

129. This prayer is closely based upon the LXX of Ps. 31.5a (NRSV):

> into your hand I commit my spirit;
> you have redeemed me. O Lord, faithful God.'

Jesus adds 'Father' to v. 5a, changes the tense of the verb from future tense to the present tense and omits the phrase looking back to a past redemption (Ps. 31.5b). The psalm originally did 'not refer to impending death, but to the preservation of the life of the Psalmist. [It] is not an expression of "acquiescent fatalism", but an affirmation of faith and trust' (Anderson 1972: 248; cf. Nolland 1993b: 1158).

its significance is emphasized by only appearing once in the whole
Gospel narrative, and only in Jesus' discourse.

The second thrust of Jesus' self-characterization is the living out of
his peculiar 'sonship' as submission to his Father. Jesus speaks less and
less as the plot unfolds, but his actions speak louder and louder, and
louder than any words: Jesus is a true son of the Father.

The Self-Characterization of Jesus in Act 7 (24.1-53)

The story of the resurrection of Jesus is so fundamentally unbelievable
that the disciples only grow to appreciate it retrospectively. In ch. 24
the narrator recognizes these difficulties and allows Jesus to address
them in the following key scenes.

The Angels at the Tomb

Jesus is absent in the first scene in this act. If Jesus' absence is due to
his initiative, then it makes a semiotic contribution to his self characterization; however, if the absence is due to God's activity, then it does
not strictly contribute to Jesus' self-characterization. It is clear from a
reading of the whole Lukan narrative that Jesus' resurrection is
attributed to God's activity, and so the absence of the body would be a
statement of God's activity. However, the discourse of the angels describes *the living Lord* who is not here (24.5). The risen Lord presumably may decide where he wishes to be, and so if this analysis is correct,
the absence of Jesus is another contribution to his self-characterization.

Two men in dazzling clothes declare that 'he is not here, but has
risen' (24.5 NRSV).[130] The Greek verb is in the passive form and can be
translated intransitively (as NRSV) or as a simple passive 'He has been
raised'. It is suggested that the intransitive translation is slightly more
likely, which would treat Jesus as the active subject: 'He is risen and he
has gone on his way'.[131] The confirmation of this unusual reading is that

---

130. This discussion follows *UBSGNT*, 3rd edn, text and includes the phrase 'He
is not here, but has risen' (24.5c) (so also NRSV, contra RSV).

131. The translation proposed is difficult because of the consequences it brings;
in particular the contrast with the God who raises Jesus from the dead, as set out in
Acts. Nevertheless 'he is risen' seems preferable: (1) when Jesus speaks of the Son
of Man rising he uses another verb in the future middle, which functions reflexively:
ἀναστήσεται (18.33); however, in 9.22 Jesus uses the passive ἐγερθῆναι which is
translated 'on the third day be raised'; (2) the other two examples of the aorist
passive ἠγέρθη are intransitive and not passive in sense; (3) the thrust of the angel's

the issue addressed by the two men is 'where the living Jesus may be found' and not 'how he came to be alive again'.

Part of the discourse of the two men evokes Jesus' earlier discourses to the disciples (principally 9.22; cf. 9.44; 18.31-33). The men's conflations and development of Jesus' discourses signify that the focalization has been revised, and the absent Jesus can only make an indirect contribution within this scene.[132] The men's discourse does not use the passive verb, and so is well translated 'and on the third day rise again' which would support the earlier proposal 'he is risen' (24.5).[133] Jesus' absence together with his minor contribution through the men's declaration combine to make it clear that Jesus has risen—and that this is in accordance with his earlier words to the disciples. Significantly, this

---

message does not attribute what has happened to God. The proposed translation is adopted by NRSV, NIV, but not REB (cf. discussion in Fitzmyer 1985: 1545).

132.

Jesus' discourse (Lk. 9.22)	The Men in Dazzling Clothes (Lk. 24.7)
Δεῖ τὸν υἱὸν τοῦ ἀνθρώπου	τὸν υἱὸν τοῦ ἀνθρώπου
πολλὰ παθεῖν καὶ ἀποδοκιμασθῆναι	ὅτι δεῖ παραδοθῆναι
ἀπὸ τῶν πρεσβυτέρων καὶ ἀρχιεπέων	εἰς χεῖρας ἀνθρώπων ἁμαρτωλῶν
καὶ γραμματέων	
καὶ ἀποκτάνθῆναι	καὶ σταυρωθῆναι
καὶ τῇ τρίτῃ ἡμέρᾳ ἐγερθῆναι	καὶ τῇ τρίτῃ ἡμέρᾳ ἀναστῆναι

The first significant revision is the introduction of '*sinful* men' for the list of Jewish leaders. Jesus rarely uses the description 'sinful' in Luke, and when he does it is either general (6.32, 33, 34) or a compassionate warning accompanied by a call to repentance (5.32; cf. 13.2). This pejorative use is focalized from a different perspective (probably from God, as the men are portrayed as angels from God, who elsewhere are reliable spokesmen). The second alteration is the introduction of 'be crucified': this verb only occurs after the passion and resurrection, although Jesus' earlier discourses include 'taking up the cross' (9.23; 14.27). The third change is the introduction of the aorist ἀναστῆναι for the future middle ἀναστήσεται (18.33), which reflects the post-resurrection viewpoint. It is methodologically unsatisfactory to conjecture that Luke is drawing on unused parts of the Markan tradition (Nolland 1993b: 1190). The focalizing of what the angels say is the key: it is from a post-resurrection viewpoint, when all is clear; it describes the Jewish leaders as sinners, and the discourse is uttered by reliable characters. Hence this discourse is focalized from God's point of view, and thus it is God who speaks.

133. The discourse runs καὶ τῇ τρίτῃ ἡμέρᾳ ἀναστῆναι (24.7). The verb is intransitive (so also Fitzmyer, 1985: 1546), which is best translated 'will rise' (contra Nolland 1989: 1190).

event is not related to the fulfilment of Scripture; instead, Jesus fulfils his own words of prophecy—and God himself authorizes this approach by ensuring that Jesus' rising comes about.

The Road to Emmaus

This long scene is the key to the whole act, for the disciples' difficulties are narrated at length, and Jesus' discourse is a direct response to these. As the two men are disciples of Jesus, Jesus' response is typically explicit. When the disciples portray him as a prophet, Jesus responds in a brief discourse and for the first time talks of the *Messiah* figure who has to suffer (24.25, 26).[134]

The introduction of 'Messiah' into Jesus' discourse is a surprise (24.26, 46), and has led to suggestions that Jesus *becomes* the Messiah through his suffering.[135] It is more likely that Jesus employs the title to represent the disciples' understanding of 'the one who was to redeem Israel' (24.21). The difficulty for the disciples is not whether Jesus is Messiah, but whether the Messiah (or redeemer) should suffer, which is reminiscent of an earlier discussion with Peter (9.20).[136] Jesus is concerned not to assure the disciples that he is risen, but rather that it was necessary (ἔδει) that he should suffer. Could this suggestion also explain why Jesus does not identify himself to the disciples?[137]

---

134. Jesus' discourse is remarkably brief at 36 words in a scene of 391 words; compare the disciples' initial discourse which lasts for 112 words.

135. In the light of the distribution of the descriptions 'the prophet' and 'the Messiah' in Jesus' discourse, Dawsey concludes that 'the Christ is not the Christ until he dies on the cross and is raised from the dead; until such time he is a prophet' (1986b: 49). This superficial suggestion is apparently buttressed by the fact that in Luke's Gospel, Jesus is presented as growing and developing—particularly when he is young. Dawsey's suggestion is mistaken for two fundamental reasons: (1) it attributes undue importance to the descriptions/titles of Jesus which appear very rarely; (2) the principal thrust of a narrative is that the *story* is the exposition of who the characters are, and provisional descriptions by other characters function as foils to be revised by the reader in the light of the story. 'Messiah' is just such a foil.

136. 'Only an issue of urgency and importance deserves the amount of attention given in Luke 24 to the revelation to the disciples of the necessity of Jesus' suffering and resurrection' (Tannehill 1986a: 278).

137. The narrator employs another 'divine passive': 'their eyes were kept from recognizing him' (24.16). Jesus implies that the disciples' failure to understand what has happened (and thus their lack of expectation about meeting Jesus again) is

Jesus makes clear that his suffering is part of the divine will, which he later makes plain is set out in the Scriptures (24.46).[138] The fundamental thrust of Jesus' discourses is that Jesus has lived as a suffering Son of Man figure and that this accords with the divine will, which the Scriptures confirm. The absence of a discussion of particular Scriptures is illuminating, for it is consonant with the narrator's portrayal of Jesus as a character who transforms the traditions as he fulfils them.[139] Consequently the detail of the Scripture is unnecessary.

The second moment of Jesus' communication in the Emmaus scene is when he sits at supper and takes, blesses, breaks and distributes the bread (24.30).[140] The function of the scene in the narrative is the disciples' recognition of Jesus, and the occasion is the recurring motif of Jesus at a meal.[141]

---

due to their foolishness: 'Oh, how foolish you are, and how slow of heart to believe all that the prophets declared' (24.25).

138. One of the principal emphases in the Lukan story is that Jesus suffers according to the divine will. The Scriptures function as an expression of that will, but do not constitute it. Thus Jesus suffers according to Scriptures to the extent that they are an expression of the divine will. In Lk. 24.26, Jesus' discourse makes clear that it was the divine will which ordered events in this way, and it is the narrator who adds that this was explained in terms of the fulfilment of Scripture (24.27), probably in the light of Jesus' later discourse (24.44-49).

139. In this type of narrative analysis, the narrator chooses the point at which to end an embedded discourse and return to his own discourse. It is also the case that the narrator has no particular interest in the Old Testament Scriptures. Hence, '[Luke] gives no specific references to the *Torah* or to the *Nebi'im* and the modern reader will look in vain for the passages in the Old Testament to which the Lukan Christ refers...this is the Lukan way of casting Old Testament data; it is his global christological use of the Old Testament' (Fitzmyer 1985: 1558).

140. This moment in the scene takes the form of a narrator's report, and so the focus falls upon the activity of Jesus, for he has no separate discourse.

141. Although Jesus frequently attends the meals of others (5.29; 7.36; 11.37; 14.1; 19.5) he only hosts three meals in the Lukan narrative. Each time there are marked similarities:

(1) 'taking the loaves and fishes, he looked up to heaven and blessed and broke them, and gave them to the disciples to set before the crowd' (9.16).
(2) 'then he took a loaf of bread, and when he had given thanks, he broke it and gave it to them, saying...' (22.19).
(3) 'he took bread, blessed and broke it and gave it to them...' (24.30).

Jesus in Jerusalem

Jesus appears to the disciples in Jerusalem, speaks of the reality of his appearance (24.38-43) and eats some fish. Jesus' discourse with the disciples is explicit: 'everything written about me in the law of Moses, the prophecies and the psalms must be fulfilled' (24.44). Jesus is the one who fulfils these Scriptures, even though many Jews could not accept this and it was a group of Jews who instigated Jesus' death.

The sharing of food communicates to the narratee the reality of the resurrection. The 'acted' demonstration together with the discourse invitation to 'touch me and see' (24.39) despatches suspicions of ghosts; here is a proper respect for the material. Jesus communicates that he has not been simply 'raised into a new and different life' but rather he is raised in a way which includes the life experienced by the disciples.

Jesus considers his sufferings as the way to glory, a theme which has recurred throughout the narrative. Initially, the Son of Man will be raised (9.22, passive ἐγερθῆναι). At the transfiguration, Jesus, is seen in his glory (9.32) which is associated with his departure (ἔξοδος). By the time of Jesus teaching in the Temple the future is more than rising from the dead—it includes 'becoming the cornerstone' (20.17) which includes sitting 'at the right hand of God' (20.42). Now in the Emmaus dialogues, Jesus summarizes the future as 'entering into his glory' (24.26). The association of glory with God is worked out at the end of Luke, for at the ascension, the narrator records that the disciples *worship Jesus* (24.52).[142]

Jesus' Self-Characterization at This Stage of the Lukan Narrative

Jesus declares in his activity and discourse that he is the Messiah in whom all the Jewish traditions find their fulfilment (24.44b), albeit not often in the way expected. The resurrection of Jesus now opens a new

---

142. The suggestion that 'glory' (24.26) is restricted to the past event of the resurrection does not embrace all the significance of the term 'glory', nor does it accord with the narrative climax in Lk. 24.52. (cf. Tannehill's discussion of Dillon's suggestion [Tannehill 1986a: 284 n. 13]) Talbert's summary is useful if overstated: 'In earliest Christianity the resurrection of Jesus encompassed three different realities: (i) Jesus' victory over death; (ii) his removal from human time and space into another dimension; (iii) his new function as cosmic Lord.' In Luke–Acts the unity of these three realities is broken and they become three separate events on a chronological time line' (1982: 226). I do not adopt Talbert's detailed exposition of these three aspects.

chapter in which 'repentance and forgiveness of sins' are to be proclaimed in Jesus' name not to Jews alone, but *to all nations* (24.47). Jesus the risen Lord is now a universal figure, who as Son of his Father may bestow what his Father promised.

The Development of Jesus' Self-Characterization

Jesus' perception of his significance is constructed by the narratee from the different self-characterizations which Jesus offers to the audiences he addresses. Any composite characterization must respect these particularities and not endeavour some simple synthesis or integration. In this narrative-critical reading of the character Jesus, this 'tendency to synthesis' is recognized and deliberately suspended, in order that the ambiguities and dissonances in the narrative may be given their full weight.

This very preliminary critical reading of Jesus' self-characterizations builds the impression that Jesus is one in whom the Jewish traditions are fulfilled, transformed and transcended. Within his discourses there is an interest in typically Jewish concepts such as Messiah, Son of Man; Prophet, kingdom of God; sin and repentance; and the Temple. This 'Jewish dimension' is in marked contrast to the narrator's characterization of Jesus.

In general, Jesus' discourse and activity engage in a multifaceted set of relationships which approximate to the pattern of relationships of the Jewish prophets and Israel. Jesus in his relationship with the Father, with the people, with the religious establishment and with his own disciples comes nearest to this kind of prophetic figure of the Jewish traditions. All of these aspects are developed in interaction with audiences which are Jewish.

Yet the provisionality of such a sketch is spelt out by Jesus himself, who considers the time of his ministry as the time of the kingdom of God, a time which supersedes the time of the prophets (16.16). Jesus portrays himself as a 'prophet who is more than a prophet' in the new era introduced by John the Baptist. For those who are not yet disciples, this period is presented as the period of the kingdom of God, However, the kingdom of God is not an architectonic concept for the disciples, and is not mentioned in the resurrection scenes. The kingdom is an interim conceptuality to represent who Jesus is, and in due course Jesus defines it and eventually transcends it and dispenses with it.

For the disciples, Jesus makes it clear that the new era is the period in which the figure of the Son of Man suffers. In this era the familiar Messianic expectation is unable sufficiently to represent who Jesus is, and so in Jesus' discourse 'Messiah' is superseded by the enigmatic concept of a Son of Man figure, whose imprecision allows the character Jesus the freedom to develop its significance through his own story.

Jesus' characterization of himself is a complex of images and figures which gather about the story of a person whose life is lived in the service of another. Through Scripture fulfilment, though times of prayer, through the anointing of the Holy Spirit and through the heavenly voices, Jesus lives the life of a son of his Father. 'Sonship' is used in the Jewish traditions to describe the obedience involved in being a son of God. In literary-critical terms, Jesus is not the most authoritative voice in the story-world; rather, it is God. Jesus' self-characterizations build a character who is the son of the Father God.

The Lukan narrative develops the sonship of Jesus beyond that general concept through the particularity of Jesus' story. In this story Jesus lives his life, and points away from himself to God for the interpretation of his story. The shock of the way of the cross as Jesus' 'exodus' and the completely new fellowship meal shared with his disciples fundamentally subvert all the expectations of Jesus associated with the characters in the world of the text. As a consequence, it becomes even more critical for the narratee (and readers who come later) to accord a breadth of imaginative space to the Lukan Jesus and the astonishing story of his life.

The principal way that Jesus conveys self-characterization is through the medium of his life, about which he is his own best interpreter, both in the things he did and interprets and also in the way he invites others to interpret what he does. *The unsubstitutable feature of Jesus is his unfolding activities, and all interpretations of him must make some sense of the way he lived, died and rose again.* 'Go and tell John what you have seen and heard' (7.22) is the hallmark of Jesus' style of self-characterization. Jesus fulfils, transforms and leaves behind the shape of people's hopes and expectations, for although related to them, he is more. This is why his life story is the key to who he is and is a non-negotiable when considering alternative readings of the character Jesus in the Lukan narrative.

Chapter 11

THE DEMONS' CHARACTERIZATION OF JESUS

> But if it is by the finger of God that I cast out the demons, then the king-
> dom of God has come to you.
>
> Luke 11.20 (NRSV)

'The Demons' as a Narrative Agent

The demons are a surprisingly significant narrative agent in the Lukan narrative which appear in the first half of the Gospel and then disappear completely. Nevertheless, because when present they militantly oppose Jesus, their characterization of Jesus is of particular interest. Further-more, the encounters between Jesus and the demons occur at significant narrative moments, which increases the importance of the contributions of this minor character. The surprise for the reader is that the demons turn out to be completely *reliable* characters in all that they say about Jesus. Even so, the demons in the Lukan narrative have received little attention in recent literary studies of the Gospel.[1]

The demons are described as both singular or plural narrative agents and sometimes both descriptions are used of the same demon in the one scene. In the narrator's discourse the demons are often described as τὰ δαιμόνια (4.41), whereas in the discourse of the Jewish characters the demons are more typically described as ἀκαθάρτον πνεῦμα (11.24) or πνευμάτα πονηρα (8.2).[2] In this study the phrase 'the demons' is used

---

1. Literary and narrative studies have concentrated upon characters with higher profiles such as 'the Religious Leader' and 'the Pharisees'. Historical-critical studies of the narratives describing the demons have little to say after working through the complex discussion of the history of the traditions; occasionally Jesus' exorcisms are compared with reconstructions of Jewish exorcisms of the time.

2. These descriptions are occasionally combined to describe the same narrative agent as in ἄνθρωπος ἔχων πνεῦμα δαιμονίου ἀκαθάρτου (4.33). There is also a description which appears only once: γυνὴ πνεῦμα ἔχουσα ἀσθενείας (13.11). The

to denote the demons, whether or not the Greek text uses τά δαιμόνια, and the contribution of alternative descriptions are noted when appropriate. This convention springs from the recognition that, functionally, the activities of the various demons in the Lukan narratives are sufficiently similar to treat them as a single narrative agent in the Gospel, however they are denoted and whether they are single or plural. Therefore in this literary analysis, I treat the demons as a 'single character'.

The demons appear 14 times in the first half of the Gospel narrative, and on 13 of these occasions there is a conflict between the demons and Jesus.[3] Some argue for two further incidents to be attributed to demonic activity, but these are not included here.[4] The last mention of the demons is found in Lk. 13.31-35, after which they are neither seen nor discussed again.

The appearances can take one of three forms: (1) scenes in which an exorcism takes place; (2) reports of exorcisms; and (3) scenes in which the demons are discussed. These appearances of the demons may be grouped temporally into three successive phases, each of which is thematically distinct. In the first and longest phase, the common theme is the ability of Jesus to engage with the demons and defeat them. In the second phase, the theme is the devolution of authority to exorcise in Jesus' name, together with the accompanying difficulties that devolution brings. The theme of the final phase is the significance of the exorcisms

value of a narrative-critical approach may be appreciated by the usefulness of distinctions between discourses in character studies. For example, in the report of the return of the 70, the disciples describe demons as 'demons', while Jesus describes them as 'spirits' (10.17-20).

3. The 14 occurrences of the demons are distributed as follows:

Act 2: 2 occurrences (4.31-37; 4.40-41);

Act 3: 8 occurrences (6.18; 7.21; 7.33; 8.2; 8.26-39; 9.1-2; 9.37-43; 9.49-50);

Act 4: 4 occurrences (10.17-20; 11.14-26; 13.10-17, 13.31-35).

4. The appearance of the verb ἐπιτιμάω in two further scenes is considered to be evidence of a conflict between Jesus and the demons, because the verb is used to describe Jesus' exorcisms: καὶ ἐπετίμησεν αὐτῷ ὁ Ἰησοῦς λέγων, Φιμώθητι καὶ ἔξελθε ἀπ' αὐτοῦ (4.35). The argument is that the use of the verb to rectify the situation in the scenes of the healing of Simon's mother-in-law (4.38-39) and the calming of the storm on the lake (8.22-24) implies the presence of a demon. I am unpersuaded, and follow Fitzmyer who suggests that the use of the verb acts as a 'catchword bond' (Fitzmyer 1981: 550) which draws together different activities within the ministry of Jesus to display his authoritative power.

for the characterization of Jesus. Although these distinctions are not precise, the division is sufficiently useful to order the following discussion.[5]

This chapter employs the narrative-critical theological reading practice developed earlier to trace all the contributions made by the demons to the narratee's understanding of Jesus. The discussion of each appearance of the demons begins with a literary appreciation of the narrative unit in which they appear, and is followed by an enquiry into the semiotic 'subjectivity' at work in the narrative.

In the case of those narrative units that are scenes, the discussion is prefaced by a translation of the Greek text that keeps as close to the NRSV text as possible; my occasional alternative translations are italicized and explained in Appendix E.[6]

Phase One: Jesus Defeats the Demons

The first phase of Jesus' confrontation with the demons demonstrates his authority and power over the demons. The phase opens in the synagogue at Capernaum (4.31-37) and finishes in the region of Gerasa (8.26-29). There are three scenes and a group of three summary reports in these six encounters. In the three scenes the demons speak to Jesus and the outcome of the encounters is the same—Jesus triumphs over the demons.[7]

---

5.   The division of the narrative into seven acts is based upon an analysis of the stages in *Jesus'* activity. The three phases of demonic activity do not follow the seven-act structure, but instead cross the boundaries between the acts. The reason is that the analysis into three phases is based upon a different set of criteria, which attend to the variety of narrative functions of demonic appearance. This is expressed in the use of the new term 'phase' to signify these narrative sections.

6.   This study uses as far as is possible the NRSV translation (1989) of the third edition of the *UBSGNT*, 3rd edn (1983). At times, however, the NRSV translation is considered unsatisfactory and I offer my preferred translation. The places where I do not follow the NRSV are italicized in the text and the reasons are given in Appendix E.

7.   Six of the seven occurrences of the demons in this first phase involve encounters between Jesus and the demons. The seventh mention is Jesus describing an allegation about John the Baptist (7.33).

	Scene		*Summary*
4.31-37	118 words	6.18	7 words
4.40-41	52 words	7.21	13 words
8.26-39	294 words	8.2	20 words

Phase 1.1: Jesus Exorcises an Unclean Spirit at Capernaum (4.31-37)

> [31]He went down to Capernaum, a city in Galilee, and was teaching them,
> *Sabbath by Sabbath.* [32]They were astounded at his teaching, because his
> *word* had authority. [33]In the synagogue there was a man who had the
> spirit of an unclean demon, and he cried out with a loud voice, [34]'Let us
> alone. What have you to do with us, Jesus of Nazareth? *You have come
> to destroy us!* I know who you are, the Holy One of God!'[35]
>
> But Jesus rebuked him, saying: 'Be silent and come out of him!'
> When the demon had thrown him down before them, he came out
> without having done him any harm. [36]They were all amazed and kept
> saying to one another, 'What kind of *word* is this? For with authority and
> power he commands the unclean spirits and out they come!'
> [37] And a report about him began to reach every place in the region.

A Literary Appreciation. Jesus encounters demons for the first time in
the Gospel narrative in the synagogue at Capernaum. Jesus' exorcism
of the demon is striking because the synagogue is the place for teaching, and so nothing prepares the narratee to expect an exorcism (4.31).[8]
The immediate literary context of the scene comprises two further
scenes forming a tightly constructed sequence which together portray 'a
day at Capernaum' (Goulder 1989: 311-12). The day commences with
the exorcism in the synagogue, goes on to the healing of Simon's
mother-in-law,[9] and ends with further exorcisms when the Sabbath ends
at sunset.[10] The following day is then marked by Jesus' departure early

---

8.   Some commentators suggest that the teaching of Jesus precipitates this
encounter. This seems unlikely on three grounds: (1) there is no narrative suggestion that Jesus' teaching is linked to the flushing into the open of the demon, for v.
33 introduces this particular occurrence after a general introduction; (2) the
response of the crowd suggests that the exorcism is not linked to Jesus' authority,
but to his power. This is shown in the response of the crowd after the exorcism
when they describe Jesus' word as having authority and power (v. 36), in contrast
with the earlier comment about Jesus' teaching as a word 'with authority' (v. 32);
(3) the other encounters in the Gospel between Jesus and the demons are not
directly linked to his teaching.

9.   The recognition that the verb ἐπιτιμάω is employed in each of these three
scenes within the narrative unit has limited usefulness. The literary links which
integrate the three scenes and the subsequent scene are clear and specific.

10.   'As the sun was setting' translates Δύνοντος δὲ τοῦ ἡλίου (4.40), which is
often assumed to signify the ending of the Sabbath, although the end of the Sabbath
is not until sunset.

the next morning to the cities of Judaea (4.42-44).[11]

The literary structure of the exorcism in the synagogue focuses the narratee's attention upon Jesus through two related patterns. The first pattern is a literary *inclusio*:

> ὅτι ἐν ἐξουσίᾳ ἦν ὁ λόγος αὐτοῦ (v. 31-32b)
> Τίς ὁ λόγος οὗτος, ὅτι ἐν ἐξουσίᾳ καὶ δυνάμει (v. 36b)

Second, the *inclusio* brackets a narrative scene which displays a chiasmus literary pattern which is ordered by the narrative agents:

A The narrator describes him (Jesus) 'going down' to a specific place: Capernaum
  B They (the crowd) were astounded at the authority of his word
    C A man was in the synagogue
      D who had a spirit of an unclean demon—who cries out in a loud voice
        E Jesus rebukes him and commands him to be silent and come out of him
      D´ the demon threw the man down, and then comes out
    C´ The man is not harmed
  B´ They (the crowd) were amazed at the authority of his word
A´ The narrator describes a report of him (Jesus) spreading out to the whole region

The chiasmus leads the narratee to focus upon Jesus at point E as the turning point in the scene. This is also the moment when the character Jesus is named, and the moment when Jesus speaks. Jesus' word is effectual and the demon is defeated. Jesus' authority and power is then reiterated by the crowd in the *inclusio* (4.36).

The narrator (4.33) and Jesus (4.35) both refer to the demon in the singular, but the demon's discourse divides into two parts in which it refers to itself as first a plural subject and then a single subject:[12]

Type of Discourse	Text of the Discourse
(a) The request	Let us alone
The enquiry	What have you to do with us, Jesus of Nazareth?
The declaration (1)	You have come to destroy us
(b) The declaration (2)	I know who you are, the Holy One of God

The distinction between (a) and (b) is apparent in the content of the

---

11. The *UBSGNT*, 3rd edn, followed by NRSV reads 'Judaea'. This is surprising as the setting of the early part of Jesus' ministry is Galilee. However, as well as referring to southern Palestine, the term Judaea is also used in the Gospel 'for the wide sense for the whole of Jewish Palestine as at 1.5, 6.17, 7.17, 23.5 and in Acts' (Nolland 1989: 216; cf. Marshall 1978: 199).

12. The plural form is taken up by in the discourse of the crowd (4.36).

discourse. In part (a) the demon speaks of matters which concern the demon, whereas in part (b) the demon speaks about Jesus.

The Analysis of the Semiotic Subjects. The focalizing position for part (a) of the demon's discourse is that of the demon, for the question expresses demonic self-interest. Thus the narrating and focalizing subjects coincide in the demon character in a realistic manner when it declares 'You have come to destroy us' (ἦλθες ἀπολέσαι ἡμᾶς). In the narrative, however, the demon is not destroyed, but simply 'comes out of him' (v. 35) and no mention is made of where it went. What the demon fears does not happen.

The verb ἀπολέσαι is usually used in the world of the narrative to signify a destruction which is an eschatological event.[13] Consequently the first part of the demon's discourse is focalized by the demon from an eschatological point of view. Associated with the 'end time', every demon will be destroyed, and so by extension, it is the whole realm of the demonic which is under threat. Might this be the explanation for the introduction of the plural form in the discourse? The demon perceives Jesus as the eschatological figure who brings the judgment of the 'end time'.

In Jesus, the victor in the cosmic struggle has come, and so the demons can only submit—they have no other option. The demon's defeat is further emphasized because although the demon knows the name of Jesus from Nazareth,[14] the knowledge of the name brings the demon no advantage.[15]

Part (b) of the demon's discourse is different. The narrating subject of the discourse is still the demon, but the focalizing subject changes.

---

13. Nolland correctly comments: 'you have come to destroy us, [the demon] rightly declares, and thus expresses the cosmic scope of Jesus' battle against the demonic. More is involved than relief by exorcism for the individual demoniac' (1989: 209). Fitzmyer offers a slightly different slant: 'It reflects the belief that the demonic control of human beings would come to an end before the eschaton or the Day of the Lord, when God's control would be established over all on behalf of those faithful to him' (Fitzmyer 1981: 545-46).

14. The NRSV translation follows the *UBSGNT*, 3rd edn, in adopting Ναζαρηνέ which means 'from Nazareth' and not 'a Nazirite'. For discussion see the commentaries.

15. There is no evidence that Jewish exorcism required the name of the demon in order to compel it to come out, although the practice is found in some contemporary exorcisms.

Also, the substance of the discourse also changes as attention focuses upon Jesus and not demonic self-interest.

The focalizing subject is constructed by a study of the discourse. The narratee attends to the substance and the style of the discourse, and the response it elicits. These aspects are then contrasted with similar discourses elsewhere in the narrative in order to identify the conventions of that particular focalizing subject. This process allows the narratee to identify the ideological position of the focalizing subject, which may lead to the identification of the focalizing subject. As contemporary readers, we emulate the moves which the narratee makes and so construct our perception of the focalizing subject.

The substance of this part of the discourse is the identity of Jesus as the Holy One of God, and the style of the discourse is one of 'unequivocal declaration'. The discourse elicits no response, for no one acknowledges what the demon says. In fact there is no sign that this declaration is heard by any narrative agent—even Jesus does not comment upon it. Furthermore, the narrative of the events 'works' whether this declaration is present or not, for Jesus' command to silence is sufficiently explained by the shouts of the demon in the first part of its discourse. It seems that this declaration serves no clear function within the exorcism scene.[16]

An inspection of the Lukan narrative finds a similar set of literary features when the voice from heaven speaks at the baptism and when the voice speaks at the transfiguration. In those two cases the narrating subject and the focalizing subject are one and the same, unlike the case of the demons. The similarity in the literary features suggests that the focalizing position of the voice from heaven and the second part of the demon's discourse *is the same*. This declaration of the demon is made from the focalizing position which in the narrative is attributed to God. Hence in this second part of the demon's declaration, the focalizing subject is God. The demon's discourse becomes a vehicle whose task is

---

16. Schürmann's suggestion that this is a piece of flattery with a view to the avoidance of exorcism does not explain the absence of response (1969: 248). From a literary perspective, an absence of response or 'uptake' can occur when narrator's discourse is presented as part of a character discourse. No character can 'hear' what the narrator says because the narrator addresses the narratee. In this particular case, the narratee does seem to be the audience for the declaration about Jesus, but the declaration is not consonant with other aspects of the narrator's strategy. It is therefore better to consider the declaration as part of the demon's discourse which was not taken up at the time.

to declare verbally what God sees from his own perspective. This is the ultimate submission of the demons—that God requires them to speak for him, and they cannot refuse. So the demon speaks 'truthfully' just as God wishes.

The demon's description of Jesus as 'the Holy One of God' is not used by anyone else in the narrative, and is virtually absent from the relevant literature of the first century (Nolland 1989: 207). The description evokes the angel's description of Jesus as 'the Holy One' (1.25) who will come as a king, and whose reign will never end. In a narrative reading, the principal meaning(s) of the discourse arise from the context in which it is used. In this case, the reign of the King is actualized in the exorcism of the demons. Thus the possible meaning of the description is expounded by the story: Jesus is the one from God, who comes to reign and to banish evil from his kingdom.

The theoretical distinction between the narrating subject and the focalizing subject produces an analysis which explains the strange feature of an evil, self-serving and demonic character speaking truly and 'reliably' about who Jesus is.[17] This reading of the second part of the demon's discourse throws new light upon the focalizing of the first part.

In the first part of the discourse, attention is paid to demonic self-interest. On closer inspection, it is clear that the apprehension expressed in the discourse springs from the assumption that Jesus *is* the one who will destroy the demons. The demons object to that which they assume to be true. Within the narrative world, Jesus is the agent who brings the reign of God with its ultimate destruction of evil. Consequently, the first part of the demon's discourse is also based on a true perception of Jesus—in this case, what he will do.

The third semiotic contribution is the activity of the demon. The narrator lays out the sequence of events involving this semiotic subject: 'The demon is in residence / the demon is rebuked by Jesus / the demon

---

17. This proposal has been suggested in an intuitive way by commentators, who consider that the demon is 'supernaturally aware of the identity of Jesus as the holy one of God' (Nolland 1989: 209). The usefulness of the semiotic subject distinction between narrating and focalizing activities is that it can relate these two perspectives without prejudice to each other. Earlier analyses, which assumed that the narrating agent approximates to a personal agent, struggle formally to accommodate the truth or reliability of the character's discourse when uttered by an unreliable character.

leaves.' This constitutes another narrative statement that Jesus is the one with authority over the demons. As the demon leaves, it throws down the man but cannot harm him, which emphasizes the impotence of the demon before Jesus. Jesus has authority over the demon and the power to render it powerless.[18] There is also a further subtle contribution. The demon initiates this sequence of events and knows the name of his opponent, yet even with these advantages, the demon is completely defeated.[19]

Phase 1.2: Jesus Exorcises Demons at Sunset in Capernaum (4.40-41)

[40]As the sun was setting, all those who had any who were sick with various diseases brought them to him; and he laid his hands on each of them and cured them [41]*Out came* demons from many, shouting, 'You are the Son of God!'

But he rebuked them and would not allow them to speak, because they knew he was *the Christ*.

A literary appreciation. The account of the exorcisms at sunset is too brief to display any developed literary pattern. The narrator includes only one discourse and, significantly, selects the demons to speak for themselves (4.41). In contrast, Jesus' command for silence is merely reported, and, importantly, only *after* the demons have spoken. As far as the narratee is concerned, Jesus does not silence the demons until they have played their part in the narrative. And curiously, when the injunction to silence is reported the narrator's explanation does not obviously accord with the shout the demons had just issued (4.41).[20]

The analysis of the semiotic subjects. The importance of the demon's discourse is signalled by the fact that it is the only discourse in the scene.[21] In this brief discourse, the demons do not argue, bargain or

---

18. The syntax of the Greek text underlines the impotence of the demon by the emphatic position of ἐξῆλθεν ἀπ' αὐτοῦ μηδὲν βλάψαν αὐτόν (4.35).

19. In an actantial analysis, as the demon initiates the conflict, Jesus would be classified as the opponent, yet as the narrative unfolds, the reverse is the case.

20. This difference between the narrator and Jesus is discussed in Chapter 12.

21. The character Jesus does not speak within this scene. This is an eloquent narrative comment upon his authority, for it seems that Jesus does not need to speak to ensure that demons submit and go. The presence of Jesus is enough. The omission of any discourse of command suggests that the principal interest in Jesus is elsewhere. The 'laying on of hands' suggests that his concern is the healing of the

protest; their discourse is a simple declaration addressed to Jesus: 'You are the Son of God' (4.41). The demons as narrating subject declare Σὺ εἶ ὁ υἱὸς τοῦ θεοῦ. The focalization of this description may be traced as before by consideration of analogous declarations within the Lukan narrative. The combination of literary features and the response elicited suggest that this declaration is focalized from God's perspective, as on a previous occasion (4.31-37). Furthermore the description of Jesus as 'the Son of God' evokes for the narratee other similar descriptions, which are also focalized from God's perspective.[22] In this scene, the demons shout their description of Jesus *as they come out* (4.41).[23] Thus for these demons, the Son of God is the one who has power over them.

The narrator unfolds the sequence in which the demons make their third semiotic contribution. The narration opens with the summary of Jesus' healing ministry, and includes the 'laying on of hands' by Jesus

---

sick, and that the encounter with the demons is accidental. The suggestion is confirmed by the narrative which makes clear that Jesus healed *all* the sick who were brought to him, by the laying hands on *each* of them. The corollary is that the demons have an incidental role within an overarching concern of Jesus, which succeeds in reducing the importance of the demons.

22. The demons shout out Σὺ εἶ ὁ υἱὸς τοῦ θεου. It is illuminating to trace the narrative subjects which use this phrase elsewhere in the Gospel. The exact phrase ὁ υἱὸς τοῦ θεοῦ is only found as part of a question on the lips of the people at the trial (22.70). The voice from heaven at the baptism declares Σὺ εἶ ὁ υἱός μου ὁ ἀγαπητός (3.22) and the voice at the transfiguration states: Οὗτός ἐστιν ὁ υἱός μου ὁ ἐκλελεγμένος (9.35). 'Both voices employ the definite article, and are clearly focalized from God's perspective. Without the definite article, the angel Gabriel states of Jesus that κληθήσεται, υἱὸς θεοῦ (1.35). This is similar to the earlier υἱὸς ὑψίστου κληθήσεται (1.32). In both these cases the focalization is clearly from God's perspective.

The Devil, during the temptations of Jesus, enquires Εἰ υἱὸς εἶ τοῦ θεοῦ (4.3, 9). The narrative sequence suggests that 'the devil is not doubting Jesus' messiahship...[but] challenges his filial status' (Fitzmyer 1981: 515), and so the phrase could be translated 'Since you are Son of God...' The substance of the temptations suggests that the Devil is convinced that Jesus is the Son of God. The narrative context of the scene of the temptations suggests that they form a narrative exposition of the declaration of the voice at Jesus' baptism (cf. ch. 8).

Consequently, the use of the phrase ὁ υἱὸς τοῦ θεου is a description from God's perspective.

23. In Lk. 4.41, the Greek verb is in the imperfect tense text ἐξήρχετο δὲ καὶ δαιμόνια ἀπὸ πολλῶν, and 'the bringing forward of the verb may accentuate Jesus' victory' (Marshall 1978: 196). 'The demons identify their experience as an encounter with the Son of God' (Nolland 1989: 214).

for the first time in the narrative. Jesus does this for each sick person (4.40), including 'the many' from whom demons came out (4.41). These demons come out without even needing a command to do so. When Jesus lays on his hands, it is sufficient. The demons leave, accompanied by great shouting which is abruptly silenced. All this signifies the absolute authority of the character Jesus over the demonic world. Is this not a characteristic of the one who is the Son of God?

Phase 1.3: Jesus exorcises Legion in Gerasa (8.26-39)

²⁶They *sailed* to the country of the Gerasenes, which is opposite Galilee. ²⁷When *he* stepped out on land, a man of the city who had demons met him. For a long time he had worn no clothes and he did not live in a house but in the tombs. ²⁸When he saw Jesus, *he shouted out*, fell down before him and said at the top of his voice, 'What have you to do with me, Jesus? Son of the Most High God. I beg you, do not *start tormenting* me!'
²⁹(For *he was about to* command the unclean spirit to come out of the man. For many times it had seized him *violently*; he was kept under guard and bound with chains and shackles, but he would break the bonds and be driven by the demon into the wilds.) ³⁰Jesus then asked him, 'What is your name?'
He said 'Legion', for many demons had entered him. ³¹They begged him not to order them to go into the Abyss. ³²Now, there on the hillside a large herd of swine was feeding there; and the demons begged Jesus *for permission* for them to enter these. So he gave them permission. ³³Then the demons came out of the man and entered the swine, and the herd rushed down the steep bank into the lake and was drowned. ³⁴When the swineherds saw what had happened, they ran off and told it in the city and in the country.
³⁵Then the people came out to see what had happened, and when they came to Jesus, they found *sitting there at the feet of Jesus* the man from whom the demons had gone, clothed and in his right mind. And they were afraid. ³⁶Those who had seen it told them how the one who had been possessed by demons had been *saved*. ³⁷Then all the people of the surrounding country of the Gerasenes asked Jesus to leave them, for they were seized with great fear. So he got into the boat and returned. ³⁸ The man from whom the demons had gone begged that he might be with him; but Jesus sent him away, saying, ³⁹'Return to your home and declare how much *has been done for you by God.*'
So he went away, proclaiming throughout the city how much *had been done for him by Jesus.*

A *literary appreciation*. The exorcism of the man in the region of Gerasa is the only occasion in the Lukan narrative when Jesus moves into Gentile territory. Yet when Jesus encounters a demon, he exorcises it just as he did in the Jewish region of Galilee.[24] The literary similarities between this exorcism and the exorcism in Capernaum underline that both scenes signal a new initiative within their particular context.[25]

The exorcism at Gerasa is the longest exorcism scene in the Lukan narrative which is a measure of its importance. The scene falls into two parts—the exorcism itself and the response it elicits. The exorcism takes place in the Gentile region of Gerasa which the narrator describes as ἀντιπέρα τῆς Γαλιλαίας (8.26), with the association of 'over against' and therefore 'the opposite' of Galilee.[26]

The narrative displays features of literary patterning which develop the range of meanings the narratee can construct. These include the repetitions of the phrases 'what had happened' to underscore the achievement of Jesus (8.34, 35), and the repetition of 'to give permission' (8.32a, 32b) to emphasize the authority of Jesus. When the demons have gone, the narrator describes the man as καθήμενον τὸν ἄνθρωπον (8.35) which is the position of a disciple and is in marked contrast to his earlier condition when ἐν οἰκίᾳ οὐκ ἔμενεν (8.27).

The narrative unit closes with the literary parallelism between Jesus' charge to 'declare how much has been done for you by God' (8.39a), and the narrator's description of the man declaring 'how much has been done for him by Jesus'. This contrast is underscored by the emphatic position of the name Jesus at the end of the sentence (8.39b).[27]

The selection of particular words and phrases makes a further literary contribution. At the *sight* of Jesus, the demon throws down the man, which the narrator portrays as ἰδὼν δὲ τὸν Ἰησοῦν...προσέπεσεν αὐτῷ (8.28). This may evoke an association of worship, although the verb is

24. 'Luke's point here is more than just the universality of Jesus' concern: it is rather the universal scope of Jesus' power. That is why a miracle story is used' (Talbert 1982: 98).

25. Similarities include the use of similar phrases, and the structuring of the narratives. Both exorcisms occur at the beginning of a period of ministry, and in each exorcism the demons speak their own discourse. These two scenes are the only two occasions in the Gospel when the demons engage in apparent dialogue with Jesus.

26. The textual difficulty about whether the place is Gerasa or Gadara is of little significance in this narrative reading, for it is the *kind* of place which is significant, and that is made plain by the narrative.

27. This literary feature is discussed in detail in Chapter 9.

also used to convey reluctant submission.[28] In the second part of the story, the narrator uses such vocabulary with definite associations with the mission of the early church.[29]

The literary structure places emphasis upon Jesus. He enters the scene anonymously amid the sailors (8.26), yet while still unnamed he is singled out as the only person to disembark (8.27). Eventually when he is seen by the demon, Jesus is named (8.28), and the action proper begins.[30] The demon initiates the conflict with its first discourse. Upon questioning by Jesus the demon acknowledges its name as Legion, after which the demon refers to itself in the plural.

The demon's first discourse comprises three elements:

	Type of Discourse	Content of the Discourse
(a)	The enquiry:	What have you to do with me, Jesus?
(b)	The declaration:	(you who are) Son of the Most High God
(c)	The request:	I beg you, do not start tormenting me

The second discourse is the one-word statement of the name of the demon.

An analysis of the semiotic subjects. While the one narrating subject produces all three elements in the first discourse, the narrative critical reader seeks to identify which are the focalizing subjects in play. The focalization of 'the enquiry' is from the perspective of the demon, as also is 'the request'. 'The declaration' is a different matter, for it is in the indicative and not the interrogative mood and the subject matter is quite different.

The declaration that Jesus is the 'Son of the Most High God' evokes no response from any of the characters involved, and so seems superfluous to the narrative development of the story. Even Jesus does

---

28. Fitzmyer's suggestion that the verb could be translated as 'lunged' at Jesus (1981: 738) is not borne out by its use elsewhere in the Lukan discourse. For example, Peter falls at Jesus' feet—and asks him to leave: ἰδὼν δὲ Σίμων Πέτρος προσέπεσεν τοῖς γόνασιν Ἰησοῦ (5.8) (cf. Nolland 1989: 408).

29. The man's deliverance is described as ἐσώθη (8.36) and Jesus' command to proclaim his story (διηγοῦ) results in the description of the man's activity as κηρύσσων (8.39b).

30. The frisson of this encounter is underlined by the fact that the narrator introduces the name Jesus for the first time when Jesus comes into range of vision of the demon (v. 28a), in contrast to the earlier description 'when *he* stepped out on land' in v. 27a.

not comment upon the declaration. This pattern is similar to earlier declarations about Jesus by demons, and so the narratee concludes that this 'declaration' is focalized from the same perspective as the declarations at Jesus' baptism and at the transfiguration.[31]

The phrase the 'Son of the Most High' reiterates the description that the angel Gabriel gave to Mary, which was accompanied by a clear attribution to God himself.[32] The phrase 'Son of the Most High' may be considered as equivalent to the 'Son of God'.[33] For the demons, the meaning of this phrase is a function of the occasion of its use. The demon recognizes the Son of the Most High God in the *presence* of Jesus who has power and authority over the demonic. In this scene, Jesus is recognized even before he acts.[34] The demon's perception of Jesus as the Son of the most High God is in broad agreement with the readings of the earlier exorcisms.[35]

The demon's second discourse comprises the single word 'Legion' which is given in answer to Jesus' enquiry. The demon's name is made public—a name which is hitherto unknown to all in the story. Once Jesus elicits the name, he neither refers nor responds to it. Some commentators consider that the function of the name is to make clear the

31. The suggestion that 'Son of the Most High God' is a title for Jesus which would have particular resonances within Gentile culture is unlikely to be the case: (1) the expression 'Most High' is a Jewish circumlocution; (2) 'Most High' is used elsewhere in the Gospel in the discourses of the angel (1.32, 35), Zechariah when anointed with the Spirit (1.76), and Jesus himself (6.35). Nolland correctly argues against the proposal (1989: 408). However, the most cogent reason for disconnecting the form of address from the Gentile setting is a literary observation. Not one of these three comments engages with the story-world. To a marked degree, these are decoupled from the particulars of the occasion of its use. *The sayings are rooted in the encounter and conflict between Jesus and the demons*.

32. The phrase is found on the lips of Gabriel who says to Mary that her son will be the 'Son of the Most High' (1.32; cf. 1.35), and Gabriel is introduced as one 'who stands in the presence of God' (1.19). When Zechariah is filled with the Holy Spirit, he speaks of Jesus as the 'prophet of the Most High' (1.76).

33. Jesus employs the phrase in this general sense in Lk. 6.35.

34. The fact that Jesus is declared to be the Son of the Most High God *before* he acts is made clear partly by the translation of 8.28 (see Appendix E) and partly by the fact that there is still a dialogue to ensue before the demons leave the man.

35. The ability of the demon to speak truly of Jesus is puzzling if the narrative is read as a simple, realistic text. However, if the narrative is read as a 'web of semiotic subjects' in 'realistic' dress, the analysis identifies the focalizing subject at this point as God himself.

multiple nature of the demon, but this is unlikely for that fact has already been established (8.27).[36] The significance of the revealing of this name becomes clearer when the demon's activity makes its third semiotic contribution.

The sequence of events functions as a semiotic 'exposition of the demon's perception of Jesus' power and authority'. The sequence opens with Jesus' arrival, after which he does nothing. When the demon sees Jesus, it is violently upset, shouts out and throws the man down before Jesus. The demon pleads with Jesus not to torment it. Jesus asks for the demon's name, and *then ignores it.* The demons seek an alternative destination and permission to go there, which further underlines Jesus' authority. The demons enter the pigs and precipitate the destruction of the pigs and presumably themselves.

Through this sequence in which the demons are always subject to him, Jesus' authority is made plain. Ironically, the demons destroy their chosen alternative to the abyss. The narrator portrays Jesus as *doing* nothing throughout, which further emphasizes his stature as the authoritative Son of God. The demon's naming of itself is a demonstration of Jesus' authority, underscored by the irrelevance of this name for Jesus' exorcism. Jesus does not need any assistance from the demon, and so the secret name is redundant in the presence of Jesus, the Son of the Most High.

The exorcism at Gerasa develops the characterization of Jesus because the demons display that the authority of Jesus over them is not limited to Judaea. Furthermore, the manner of the exorcism moves the emphasis towards Jesus' authority rather than his power, for Jesus does nothing—it is enough for him to be there, and the demons are defeated.

Phase 1.4: A Group of Three Reports of Jesus' Exorcisms (6.8; 7.21; 8.2)

> [A great multitude] had come to hear him and to be healed of their diseases; and those who were troubled with unclean spirits were cured (6.18).

36. 'Legion' is a name from which *the narrator* develops the fact that the demons are multiple: εἰσῆλθεν δαιμόνια πολλὰ εἰς αὐτόν (v. 30b). There do not seem to be persuasive grounds for Fitzmyer's suggestion that 'Legion' is offered *instead* of the real name of the demon (1981: 738). Nolland is closer to the meaning of the narrative: 'The possessing power is already at the mercy of Jesus. He can do no other than answer the question, and would gain nothing from frantic attempts to conceal the name' (1989: 409).

[Jesus] had just then cured many people of diseases, plagues, and evil spirits, and had given sight to many who were blind (7.21).

Some women who had been cured of evil spirits and infirmities: Mary, called Magdalene, from whom seven demons had gone out... (8.2).

A literary appreciation. These three summary reports by the narrator reiterate Jesus' success as an exorcist by placing emphasis upon the outcome of the exorcisms rather than upon the acts of exorcism. In this way the summaries contribute to the demons' cumulative characterization of Jesus as the one in whom resides complete authority over them: the activity of the demons is always obedient withdrawal.[37]

The emphasis upon the changed condition of those whom Jesus helped is also conveyed by the narrator's choice of the verb θεραπεύω (NRSV 'to cure'), for it subsumes the exorcism of the demons within a wider healing activity.[38]

The analysis of the semiotic subjects. The semiotic activity of the demons is the only contribution they make, for they do not speak their own discourse within the summaries. The first two occasions present the defeat of the demons upon a wide scale and without the mention of any resistance.

The third exorcism extends the characterization of Jesus by mentioning that seven demons came out from Mary Magdalene, which 'implies the severity of the possession' (Fitzmyer 1981: 698; Nolland 1989: 366); this illuminates further the authority of Jesus.[39]

---

37. The convention adopted in this thesis is that the third semiotic subject which communicates through 'acting' is mediated to the narratee through the narrator's discourse, unless the experience of critical reading raises a question about the reliability of the narrator in this respect.

38. This construction is typical of the narrator:

6.18   καὶ οἱ ἐνοχλούμενοι ἀπὸ πνευμάτων ἀκαθάρτων ἐθεραπεύοντο
7.21   ἐθεράπευσεν πολλοὺς ἀπὸ...πνευμάτων πονηρῶν
8.2   ἦσαν τεθεραπευμέναι ἀπὸ πνευμάτων πονηρῶν

39. The warning which Jesus will later give about making room for more demons confirms the suggestion that the seven signal the severity of her condition (cf. 11.24-26).

Phase Two: The Devolved Exorcisms

The second phase of the story of the demons unfolds as exorcisms are performed by others using the authority of Jesus' name. These four occurrences come just before and just after the end of the third act when Jesus' own identity is less of an issue, and when the shadow of Jerusalem begins to fall across the story. Three of the occasions involve some or all of the apostles while the fourth involves 'the seventy'.[40] One of the four occurrences is a scene which is discussed in more detail.

Phase 2.1: Jesus' Commission to 'the Twelve' to Exorcise (9.1-2)

[1]Then he called the twelve together and gave them power and authority over all demons and to cure diseases, [2]and he sent them out to proclaim the kingdom of God and to heal.

A literary appreciation. Through the device of literary parallelism, the narrator makes clear the association of the exorcism of the demons and the proclamation of the kingdom of God:

[Jesus] gave them power and authority over all demons [A][41]
and to cure diseases [B]
he sent them out to proclaim the kingdom of God [A]
and to heal [B]

40. The narrator in Luke describes a larger group of disciples from whom 12 apostles are chosen (6.13), and it is members of this group who constitute the narrative agent 'the apostles' (so called in 6.13; 9.10; 11.49; 17.5; 22.14; 24.10; cf. discussion of 'the Wisdom of God' use of 'apostles' in 11.49 [cf. Marshall 1978: 502-504]). The narrator also describes the apostles as 'the twelve' (6.13; 8.1; 9.1; 9.12; 18.31; 22.31; 22.47). In the three passages instanced here, three different voices describe the same narrative agent in various ways:

(1)   The narrator describes them as 'the twelve' (9.1).
(2)   The distraught father, unaware of the distinctions within the group, uses the general term 'your disciples' to describe the disciples/apostles who were without Peter, John and James (9.40).
(3)   John (one of the disciples) speaks for all of them: 'We saw someone...who does not follow with us' (9.49).

41. The narrator's clause ἔδωκεν αὐτοῖς δύναμιν καὶ ἐξουσίαν ἐπὶ πάντα τὰ δαιμόνια (9.1) recalls the crowd's comment ὅτι ἐν ἐξουσίᾳ καὶ δυνάμει ἐπιτάσσει τοῖς ἀκαθάρτοις πνεύμασιν (4.36).

The devolution of the authority to exorcise the demons is an extension of Jesus' authority, given to the 12 after the exorcism at Gerasa and after the healings when Jesus returned to Galilee. The novelty and significance of this devolvement by Jesus and its ensuing implications escape many recent commentators; Jesus' authority over the demons has been established, but what kind of person can give such authority to others?[42]

Jesus' commission to the 12 includes 'the power and authority over all demons and to cure the diseases' (9.2). The narrator does not include either a scene of the 12 in action or an account of any exorcisms when they return (9.10). The literary symmetry with the later narrative of the mission of the 70[43] is in effect a statement of the disciples' failure; it seems that the disciples never achieve a successful exorcism, neither here nor in the rest of the Lukan story-world.[44]

42. Geldenhuys perceptively notes the uniqueness of this action by Jesus, but rather overstates his conclusion: 'An ordinary human leader no matter how wonderful he may be, cannot communicate to his followers physical or spiritual powers to do what he is doing. But Christ Jesus does it, and thereby we see yet again his divine greatness' (1950: 264).

43. The narrative device of patterning is used quite frequently in the Gospel of Luke (e.g. Zechariah and Mary). The literary relationship between the mission of the 12 and the mission of the 70 is made even clearer by the symmetry in the detail of the two accounts:

(1) The 12 are commissioned with power over demons; on their return there is no mention of exorcism
(2) The 70 are commissioned with no mention of exorcism on their return; there are reports of exorcism

44. Ellis, Fitzmyer, Goulder, Marshall, Nolland, Talbert, Tannehill and Schweizer do not discuss the significance of this 'silence' in the narrator's description of the return. Creed simply assumes that 'the apostles return from their journey and report their success' (1930: 126). It falls to Plummer to acknowledge the possibility that this silence signifies failure, even though he disallows it: 'It is strange that anyone should infer from Luke's not expressly mentioning...the casting out of the demons that Luke wishes us to believe that they had failed in this respect. Luke records the success of the seventy exorcising demons (10.17); why should he wish to insinuate that the twelve had failed?' (1901: 242). Instead of an argument to close the discussion, Plummer's rhetorical question is actually the starting point of a narrative enquiry. A further argument in favour of the reading of the narrator's omission as signifying the 'failure of the disciples' is that the next account (the feeding of the 5000) is also an account of the failure of the disciples.

An analysis of the semiotic subjects. After the encounter with Jesus at Gerasa, the demons do not speak again in the Lukan narrative, which leaves their activity as their only medium of communication. Jesus' commission to the 12 anticipates prospective encounters with the demons.

The absence of successful exorcisms by the disciples is a declaration that Jesus alone has the authority to exorcise. The failure of the disciples rightly to deploy this authority when devolved to them is curious but it is not developed as a commentary upon the character Jesus.

Phase 2.2: The Failure of the Disciples' Exorcism (9.37-43a)

[37]On the next day, when they came down from the mountain, a great crowd met him. [38]Just then, a man from the crowd shouted *and implored*:

'Teacher, I beg you to look at my son *with compassion*, for he is my only child. [39]Suddenly a spirit seizes him and all at once he shrieks. It convulses him until he foams at the mouth; It mauls him and will scarcely leave him. [40]I begged your disciples to cast it out, but they could not.'

[41]Jesus answered, 'You faithless and perverse generation, how much longer must I be with you and bear with you? Bring your son here.'

[42]While he was coming, the demon dashed him to the ground in convulsions. But Jesus rebuked the unclean spirit, healed the boy and gave him back to his father. [43]And all were astounded at the greatness of God.

A literary appreciation. The principal characters in this encounter are the man from the crowd and Jesus. The man's importance is signalled by the extended discourse allowed him.[45] Jesus speaks his own discourse but the demon character does not speak at all. Jesus is given further literary emphasis by the narrator by the fact that although the group comes down the mountain, the crowd is only interested in *him* (9.37).

The disciples' impotence seems to be shared by the crowd, for Jesus addresses 'this generation'.[46] However, Jesus does not address the

---

45. The discourse of the distressed father comprises 43 words within the total of 124 words in the Greek text of this exorcism.

46. The words of Jesus are addressed to what is typical of that generation. The criticism does not address the failure of the disciples specifically, as if they ought to have been able to accomplish this exorcism. There is a strange aspect to the earlier account in the narrative of the disciples 'at work'. Although the charge to the 12

demon when the young boy arrives.[47] This suggests that the crowd is the more pressing problem for Jesus, and that Jesus can deal relatively easily with the demon.

The scene comprises elements which form a chiasmus pattern which is ordered around the different narrative agents:

A   A great crowd meet him (Jesus).
  B   A man who is a distraught father cries out
    C   A son, the only child, is introduced
      D   A demon seizes him and convulses him
        E   The disciples fail to help
          F   Jesus speaks
        E′   'O faithless and perverse generation' is addressed (at least) to the disciples
      D′   The demon throws the son to the ground in convulsions
    C′   The boy is healed by Jesus
  B′   The father receives his son
A′   All were astounded at the greatness of God

The literary pattern stresses the person of Jesus who acts at the centre point F and who is named for the first time at the same point within the scene. This literary arrangement leads the narratee to appreciate that the whole affair hinges upon Jesus and his authority.

The literary form of this exorcism evokes the literary form of the account of the raising of the son of the widow of Nain (7.11-17), although there is no involvement of the demons in that incident.

An analysis of the semiotic subjects. As the demon does not speak, the semiotic contribution of the demon is conveyed through its activity, which includes the convulsive effect upon the child, the indifference to the disciples' entreaties and its yielding to Jesus without a great conflict. When summoned to Jesus the demon throws down the child

includes δύναμιν καὶ ἐξουσίαν ἐπὶ πάντα τὰ δαιμόνια καὶ νόσους θεραπεύειν (9.1, 2) the narrative does not include any discussion of what they achieved (cf. 9.10). This is in marked contrast to the account of the return of the 70: Ὑπέστρεψαν δὲ οἱ ἑβδομήκοντα μετὰ χαρᾶς λέγοντες, Κύριε, καὶ τὰ δαιμόνια ὑποτάσσεται ἡμῖν ἐν τῷ ὀνόματί σου (10.17). Within the world of the narrative, the request of the distraught father is the first time that the disciples tackle an exorcism.

47. The focalization of the remarks of Jesus is from God's perspective. Jesus speaks of Ὦ γενεὰ ἄπιστος καὶ διεστραμμένη (9.41) which evokes the LXX of Deut. 32.5 in which Moses as God's prophet speaks of the people as γενεὰ σκολιὰ καὶ διεστραμμένη.

while on the way—but still the demon cannot escape.[48] Once the child arrives in the presence of Jesus, the convulsions stop.

There is a distinction between the influence of the demon and the sickness.[49] The demon is portrayed as a tyrant who exploits the weakness of a sick boy, which portrays further the evil inherent in the demon. However the demon is not solely responsible for all of the boy's sickness, and so healing is also required.

The scene serves to reiterate the authority of Jesus over the demons, particularly through the literary contrast between Jesus and his impotent disciples.

Phase 2.3: The Unknown Exorcist (9.49-50)

> [49]John answered: 'Master, we saw someone casting out demons in your name, and we tried to stop him because he does not follow with us.'
> [50]But Jesus said, 'Do not stop him; for whoever is not against you is for you.'

A literary appreciation. News reaches the disciples that someone else is exorcising in Jesus' name, and that this man is not even a disciple (9.49). The disciples try to stop him, but Jesus forbids them. Could it be

48. Contra Nolland: 'For Luke, the attack occurs while the child is still coming to Jesus. [Luke] probably understand this as simply one of the sudden attacks, not specifically as a response to the sight of Jesus' (1993a: 510).

49. The distinction between the power of the demon and the sickness is missed by many recent commentators, with comments like 'This is another case of demon-sickness' or 'the failure to distinguish clearly between a healing and an exorcism' (Fitzmyer 1981: 810). The case for such a distinction is that (1) the narrator portrays Jesus conducting three distinct activities in v. 42b, each distinguished by the conjunction καὶ:

ἐπετίμησεν δὲ ὁ Ἰησοῦς τῷ πνεύματι τῷ ἀκαθάρτῳ,
καὶ ἰάσατο τὸν παῖδα
καὶ ἀπέδωκεν αὐτὸν τῷ πατρὶ αὐτοῦ.

(2) the verb which describes the healing (ἰάσατο) has a precise range of usage in Luke, in which it describes healings of sicknesses and weakness which are *not* associated with demonic influence (5.17; 7.7; 8.47; 9.2,11; 14.4; 17.15; and 22.51); and (3) when demons and sicknesses are linked together as in 6.18, the verb is used *in contrast* to the verb to exorcise:

οἳ ἦλθον ἀκοῦσαι αὐτοῦ καὶ ἰαθῆναι ἀπὸ τῶν νόσων αὐτῶν·
καὶ οἱ ἐνοχλούμενοι ἀπὸ πνευμάτων ἀκαθάρτων ἐθεραπεύοντο (6.18).

that the concern of the disciples was not so much that exorcisms were being done in Jesus' name without authority, but that this man was able to exorcise—*when the disciples could not?*

An analysis of the semiotic subjects. The disciple John speaks his own discourse, which is focalized from the perspective of the 12 who follow Jesus.[50] The language of his discourse is full of the associations of discipleship which confirms this focalization.[51]

In contrast, the stranger is not a disciple, and yet is able to exorcise 'in the name of Jesus'.[52] There are two occasions when the name of Jesus is the explanation of successful exorcisms (9.49; 10.17).[53] Clearly it is not the status of the exorciser, but the authority of the name which is effectual.[54] In the world of the narrative, the 'name' seems to function as a powerful representation of the character Jesus, which poses

50. This is suggested by the repeated use of 'we', together with the description 'who does not follow with us' (9.49). Furthermore, the narrator characterizes John as a spokesman for the disciples, and thus able to focalize their views reliably. The narrator names the disciple John upon eight occasions in the narrator's discourse (5.10; 6.14; 8.51; 9.28, 49, 54; 11.1; and 22.8). John is part of the inner core of disciples [John and James were partners of Simon 5.10], and accompany Simon Peter to the healing of Jairus's daughter and Jesus onto the mountain of transfiguration). John only speaks his own discourse twice: here at 9.49 and with his brother James in indignation at the refusal of the Samaritans to welcome Jesus (9.54). Thus the narrator characterizes John as able to speak for the 12.

51. In the Lukan narrative the vocative form Ἐπιστάτα is addressed only to Jesus (5.5; 8.24, 45; 9.33, 49; and 17.13) and always in the discourse of a disciple: Peter (3×); John (1×); 'disciples' (1×) and the '10 lepers' (1×). Furthermore, the verb used for the self-description of the disciples ἀκολουθεῖ μεθ' ἡμῶν (9.49) is first employed in 5.11 when they left their nets and ἠκολούθησαν αὐτῷ.

52. The discourse is addressed to Jesus and so the name is described as ἐν τῷ ὀνόματί σου (9.49). This phrase is only used twice in the whole Gospel narrative. In this example it is in the discourse of John, the representative disciples, and in the other examples it is in the discourse of the 70 addressed to Jesus upon on their return: ' even the demons submit to us [ἐν τῷ ὀνόματί σου]' (10.17).

53. The phrase ἐν τῷ ὀνόματί is an 'instrumental dative', and should be distinguished from the phrase ἐπὶ τῷ ὀνόματι, which although it may be the literary 'catchword bond' (Fitzmyer 1981: 820) between 9.46-48 and 9.49-50, is a phrase found only in Jesus' discourse (9.48; 21.8; and 24.47).

54. The brief discourse forms a narrative commentary upon the failure of the disciples to exorcise while Jesus and Peter, James and John were away on the mountain of transfiguration.

searching questions for the narratee about this man Jesus.[55] As before, the authority and power of Jesus which are vested in his name successfully vanquish the demons.

Phase 2.4: The Successful Exorcisms of 'the Seventy' (10.17-20)

[17]The seventy returned with joy saying, 'Lord, in your name even the demons submit to us.'

A literary appreciation. The 70[56] are appointed by Jesus to go ahead of him to the different places through which he plans to go (10.1). Jesus' discourse to the 70 includes the commission to cure the sick (10.9) and he says to them that they shall proclaim that 'the kingdom of God has come near' (10.9).[57] The narrator pays no attention to the departure of the 70, but takes care to recount their return. Full of joy, the 70 speak in their discourse: 'Lord, in your name even the demons submit to us' (10.17).

The demons had clearly submitted to the authority of Jesus' name when it was invoked by the 70.[58] The 70 return with joy and the qualification '*even* the demons submit…' signals that the experience of exorcism has surprised and delighted the 70, and in so doing, has elevated Jesus to the status of their 'Lord',[59] even within the pre-resur-

55. The 'name of Jesus' is also invoked to represent Jesus (9.48; 21.8, 12, 17) and in association with the forgiveness of sins (24.7).

56. This translation follows the NRSV and adopts '70' rather than '72'. For discussion of this choice, see Metzger 1958: 299-306; Marshall 1978: 414-15.

57. The phrase Ἤγγικεν ἐφ' ὑμᾶς ἡ βασιλεία τοῦ θεοῦ is to be distinguished from the later discourse of Jesus about himself in which he describes ἄρα ἔφθασεν ἐφ' ὑμᾶς ἡ βασιλεία τοῦ θεοῦ (11.20). See the discussion of the kingdom of God in Chapter 10. I would argue that the command to announce the nearness of the kingdom is the equivalent of a command to exorcise demons.

58. The verb ὑποτάσσεται is used in Greek magical papyri (cf. Fitzmyer 1985: 861).

59. The absence of an explicit command to exorcise in 10.1 has led some to suggest that the force of '*even*' is that the 70 tried out exorcisms, even though unbidden (Evans 1990: 453), and were surprised and delighted that 'it worked'. This is not impossible, although as argued above the kingdom (10.9) is associated with exorcism. It seems more likely that the use of Κύριε is a consequence of the experience of seeing Jesus' name at work, and that it is the scale of the authority of the name which surprises them.

rection period.[60] The literary contrast with the return of the '12' contributes to the characterization of the 12.

An analysis of the semiotic subjects. In this brief passage, the semiotic contribution is appreciated in the focalization of the discourse of the 70, which is that of the disciples. The use of Lord in the vocative (Κύριε) is typical of other disciples who followed Jesus throughout his ministry.[61]

Phase Three: The Significance of Jesus' Exorcisms

In these last three occurrences of Jesus' exorcisms, the emphasis moves to the significance of the acts.[62] These comments are not strictly the demons' characterization of Jesus, but are comments of other characters which are occasioned by the exorcisms of the demons. These offer a useful collateral perspective upon what the demons have already contributed to the characterization of Jesus.

Phase 3.1: The Beelzebul Controversy (11.14-26)

> [14]Now he was casting out a demon that was mute; when the demon had gone out, the one who had been mute spoke, and the crowds were amazed.
>
> [15]But some of them said, '*It is by Beelzebul*, the ruler of demons, that he casts out demons.'
>
> [16]Others (to test him), kept demanding from him a sign from heaven.
> [17]But he (knew what they were thinking and) said to them, 'Every kingdom divided against itself becomes a desert and house falls on house.

---

60. It is attractive but inaccurate to suggest that 'in this triumphant moment Jesus is addressed by his title as ruler of the church' (Evans 1990: 453). Even the argument that ὁ κύριος is the form of the title which Luke has 'time and again retrojected into the phase of Jesus' earthly ministry' (Fitzmyer 1981: 202) needs careful investigation. In the resurrection narratives the longest discourses are given to Jesus, and there is no 'disciple discourse' addressed to Jesus. The only example of a post-resurrection use of any form of ὁ κύριος is the disciples report that ἠγέρθη ὁ κύριος (24.34).

61. Κύριε is found on 19 occasions upon the lips of a variety of disciples. It is clearly the form of address of those who have seen more in Jesus than 'Master', and involves the submission to the one who is 'the Lord'. In the narrative of Jesus directing Peter to fish again, Peter begins by calling Jesus 'Master' (5.5), but when the fish have been caught, Peter addresses him as Lord (5.8) and asks him to depart.

62. For example, in the Beelzebul controversy, the exorcism itself and its consequence are described in 20 words while the controversy employs 139 words.

[18]If Satan also is divided against himself, how will his kingdom stand? for you say that I cast out demons by Beelzebul. [19]Now if I cast out demons by Beelzebul, by whom do your *people* cast them out? Therefore, they will be your judges. [20]But if it is by the finger of God that I cast out demons, then the kingdom of God has come upon you.

[21]'When a strong man, fully armed, guards his castle, his property is safe. [22]But when one stronger than he attacks him and overpowers him, he takes away his armour in which he trusted and divides his plunder. [23]'Whoever is not with me is against me, and whoever does not gather with me, scatters.'

[24]'When the unclean spirit has gone out of a person, it wanders through waterless regions looking for a resting place, but not finding any, it says 'I will return to my house from which I came'. [25]When it comes, it finds it swept and put in order. [26]Then it goes and brings seven other spirits more evil than itself, and they enter and live there and the last state of that person is worse than the first.'

A literary appreciation. The exorcism of the man who was mute and the subsequent controversy occur early within the longest Act which unfolds 'under the shadow of Jerusalem'. In this scene, Jesus gives his longest discourse in the Gospel on his exorcisms and their significance. As the practice of exorcism disappears from the narrative world soon after Jesus 'sets his face to go to Jerusalem' (9.51), this scene functions as a narrative climax and commentary upon all the previous encounters with the demons.[63]

There are two distinctive features of the appearances of the demons in this period 'under the shadow of Jerusalem' which are not found elsewhere. The first feature is that Jesus now speaks explicitly about the demons and the significance of his exorcisms *for his own identity*. The second and related feature is that the name Satan is introduced and appears in every one of Jesus' discourses concerning the casting out of demons.

The narrator anchors the controversy within the account of the exorcism by the use of the imperfect tense 'Now he was casting out a demon'.[64] The account of the Beelzebul controversy displays no distinctive literary structure.

---

63. In contrast, the two remaining encounters with demons which come after this controversy (13.11-17 and 13.31-35) function as elements within a separate argument about the Sabbath and about Jesus' identity.

64. 'The use of the periphrastic ἦν ἐκβάλλων is slightly odd. It is probably meant to set the scene for the saying in v. 15' (Marshall 1978: 472).

An analysis of the semiotic subjects. Continuing the assumption that the demon (11.14) and the unclean spirit (11.24) are functionally the same character,[65] the demon as a semiotic subject contributes indirectly in two places within this narrative unit. First there is the narrator's summary of the exorcism (11.14) and then Jesus' discourse about unclean spirits.[66]

In the narrator's summary report the demon character does not allow the dumb man to speak, nor does it speak itself. The Beelzebul controversy is the last of the unambiguous exorcisms in the Gospel narrative. There is a marked contrast between this last example and the first of the exorcisms in which the unclean spirit shouted with a loud voice (4.31-37). In this case, the irony is that when the demon of silence goes, so the man speaks again. The demon 'communicates' by its actions. In response to Jesus who was casting out demons, the demon goes out. The authority of Jesus is acted out once more.

The warning about homeless, unclean spirits provides the occasion for the demon's discourse, which this time is not linked to an exorcism. The discourse of Jesus represents the perspectives of the demons who have been ordered out of the healed person,[67] and wander about through waterless places (the traditional home of the demons)[68] in possession of a degree of freedom and in search of a resting place.[69] If this search fails, then these demons are able to go back and re-inhabit their original home, and this time the demon will bring seven other spirits which 'symbolize the totality of evil' (Fitzmyer 1985: 925).[70] This reiterates

---

65. This is argued earlier in the chapter, and supported by the similarity between he description τὸ ἀκάθαρτον πνεῦμα (11.24) and the description πνεῦμα δαιμονίου ἀκαθάρτου (4.33).

66. Typically the narrator refers to this entity as δαιμόνιον, while those voices representing characters who are Jews (in this case Jesus) tend to employ τὸ ἀκάθαρτον πνεῦμα or πνεύματα πονηρότερα.

67. The demon considers the experience of being exorcised as merely a 'leaving': Ὅταν τὸ ἀκάθαρτον πνεῦμα ἐξέλθῃ ἀπὸ τοῦ ἀνθρώπου (11.24), and continues to display a freedom to return to the house (contra Plummer who correctly observes but misinterprets the absence of the mention of exorcism. [1901: 304]).

68. For a discussion of the background to this conviction cf. Fitzmyer 1985: 925.

69. This portrayal bears a marked resemblance to the activities of the demons in the exorcism at Gerasa.

70. The Greek syntax makes the number 'seven' emphatic: τότε πορεύεται καὶ

that people are unable to resist these demons, and so underscores the authority of Jesus.

The demon speaks for itself when it says 'I will return to my house from which I came' (11.24). The demon perceives exorcism as a mere 'leaving'.[71] Furthermore, the demon considers that the house belongs to him (οἶκος μου). In this way the demon makes clear the hierarchy of power within the narrative world. People are impotent when a demon finds its way into them.[72] On the other hand, Jesus exercises power (as the strong man [11.21-23]) which demons must obey.

Phase 3.2: The Woman Crippled by a Spirit (13.10-17)[73]

[10]Now he was teaching in one of the synagogues *Sabbath by Sabbath.* [11]And just then there appeared a woman *who had had a spirit of infirmity* for eighteen years. She was bent over and was *completely* unable to stand up straight. [12]When Jesus saw her, he called her over and said, 'Woman, *from now on you are released* from your *infirmity.*'

[13]*And* he laid his hands on her and immediately she stood up straight and began praising God. [14]But the leader of the synagogue, indignant because Jesus had cured on the Sabbath, kept saying to the crowd, 'There are six days on which work ought to be done; come on those days and be cured, and not on the sabbath day.'

[15]But the Lord answered him and said, 'You hypocrites! Does not each of you on the sabbath untie his ox or his donkey from the manger, and lead it away to give it water? [16]And ought not this woman, a daugh-

παραλαμβάνει ἕτερα πνεύματα πονηρότερα ἑαυτοῦ ἑπτα (11.26).

71. Jesus describes the demon as ἐξέλθη, and now the demon describes the same event using the same verb: τὸν οἶκόν μου ὅθεν ἐξῆλθον.

72. Marshall suggests that the discourse might be 'a criticism of the Jews who practise exorcisms, but do not take the side of Jesus and thereby make the situation worse' (1978: 479). There is no suggestion of criticism of the Jewish exorcists. It is much more likely that any 'disastrous conclusion is the result, not of the imperfect methods of the exorcist, but of the misconduct of the exorcised' (Plummer 1901: 304).

73. Some raise the possibility that this story is not an exorcism but a healing (e.g. Evans 1990: 550; Nolland 1993a: 724). Although this is the only example of πνεῦμα ἔχουσα ἀσθενείας, and the way in which Jesus deals with the person is more typical of a healing than an exorcism, on balance it is treated here as an exorcism, because (1) there are literary parallels with the first exorcisms in Capernaum (the location, the source of the trouble—a spirit of uncleanness/ infirmity; the laying on of hands); (2) the reference to the binding of Satan; (3) the phrase 'a spirit of infirmity' is an Aramaism which is used to describe demonic conditions (cf. Fitzmyer 1985: 1012).

ter of Abraham whom Satan bound for eighteen long years, be *untied* from this bondage on the sabbath day?'

[17]When he said this, all his opponents were put to shame; and the entire crowd was rejoicing at all the wonderful things he was doing.

A literary appreciation. The scene is located in a synagogue, the traditional place for teaching (13.10). Synagogues in Luke feature in various ways which cumulatively present them as places of controversy and hostility for Jesus before he goes to Jerusalem.[74] This scene is the last time in the Gospel story that Jesus visits a synagogue, for as Jesus journeys to Jerusalem, Galilee and its synagogues are left behind.[75]

In this exorcism scene, the condition of the woman is spelt out in detail. Jesus has compassion upon her, calls her to him and declares a permanent release from her condition and lays hands on her. The woman stands up, and immediately praises God. As far as this spirit is concerned, the second part of the scene makes clear the link between the spirit which oppressed her and Satan.[76]

An analysis of the semiotic subjects. The phrase 'the spirit of infirmity' is used only here in the Lukan narrative, although reminiscent of the similar phrase 'the spirit of an unclean demon' in the exorcism in the Capernaum synagogue (4.33).[77] This 'spirit of infirmity' is functionally

74. There are four accounts of Jesus teaching in a synagogue (Nazareth [4.16]; Capernaum [4.31]; in an unnamed synagogue [6.6]; and in another unnamed 'one of their synagogues' [13.10]). In every case Jesus is portrayed as 'teaching', and in every case there is a controversy and opposition. The synagogues are the courts before which the disciples will be delivered (12.11; 21.12). The synagogues are the places where the leaders of the Jews are found, who 'love the seats in the Synagogues' (Pharisees [11.43] and the scribes [20.46]), but of whom the disciples should beware. This narrative picture contrasts markedly from the initial response described in 4.15: 'He began to teach in their synagogues and was praised by everyone'.

75. Synagogues are mentioned only twice more (20.46; 21.12) and in both cases within the context of a controversy which does not occur within a synagogue.

76. Fitzmyer suggests that 'this is the closest that Luke comes to associating an evil spirit with Satan' (1985: 1013). In fact the earlier debate about whether Jesus exorcises by the power of Beelezebul also clearly suggests a link. See the discussion in the next section of this chapter.

77. The narrating subject speaks of this spirit of infirmity, which is unusual in that the narrating voice often employs the nomenclature of 'the demon'. The phrase 'unclean spirits' is more typical of the Jewish crowd (e.g. 4.36), which suggests that

equivalent to a demon and as it does not speak it makes its semiotic contribution through its activity. The severity of the woman's condition together with the length of her affliction eloquently convey the power of this spirit, which provides the context and contrast for the power of Jesus who effects a full and immediate release—so great that the narrator portrays the woman bursting into praise of God.

The activity of the unclean spirit is the cause for the woman's condition, but beyond this fact, the spirit is of less importance in contrast with earlier scenes. Indeed on this occasion Jesus addresses the woman and not the demon. The spirit of infirmity is dismissed without a word directed to it. Whereas the exorcism is primarily the occasion for the debate about healing upon the Sabbath,[78] this effortless setting free from the spirit's bondage constitutes the spirit's characterization of Jesus as the powerful one before whom even demons must yield— immediately and completely. As Jesus in his discourse attributes this bondage ultimately to Satan, here Jesus is presented as the one who can defeat the greatest of spiritual enemies.

Phase 3.3: Jesus Describes Himself as the One who Exorcises (13.31-35)

> 'Listen, I am casting out demons and performing cures today and tomorrow and on the third day I finish my work' (13.32).

This enigmatic saying of Jesus is addressed to Herod who wants to kill him. Jesus uses language closest to that which he used in the Beelzebul controversy.[79] Jesus' discourse makes clear that exorcisms and healings are two central and distinct facets of his ministry. Jesus' reply is an abbreviated form of his earlier comment to the disciples of John the Baptist, although in that case exorcisms are not mentioned (7.22; however, the narrator does mention it).

For the present discussion it is sufficient to note that Jesus considered the exorcism of demons to be a defining description of his mission. The consequence is that Jesus' encounters with the demons are likely to

the explanation of the woman's condition is focalized from the perspective of the crowd.

78. 'The perfect passive used suggests: "God's release has come for you" (Nolland 1993a: 724).

79. The discourse employs vocabulary which Jesus uses in his controversy with the crowds about Beelzebul: Ἰδοὺ ἐκβάλλω δαιμόνια καὶ ἰάσεις. The present tenses are equivalent to an assured future tense (Moule 1959: 7).

prove important for the characterization of Jesus, and so it has proved.

This is the last time that the exorcism of demons is mentioned in the Gospel. It seems that what these exorcisms can contribute to the characterization of Jesus is now complete, and that both the narrator and the story characters now look elsewhere to develop the characterization of Jesus.

The Contribution of the Demons to the Characterization of Jesus

The demons have the power to take over people and inflict terrible conditions upon them, and as people are impotent to deal with the demons, the tyranny continues. There are occasional deliverances performed by Jewish exorcists, but otherwise, the victims are helpless. Jesus' encounters with the demons allows them to make four contributions to his characterization, by providing the occasion for the demonstration of his authority as the Son of God.

The Demons Represent what Jesus Came to Destroy

The first contribution made by the demons is the immediate apprehension and opposition that they display when Jesus appears. In the two longest scenes, it is the demons who take the initiative in speaking their own discourse to Jesus, because their continued existence is clearly in complete opposition to all that Jesus represents. There is a fundamental conflict, which illuminates Jesus as the figure who has come to destroy the works of evil.

The Demons Are Vanquished Completely by Jesus, the Son of God

The second contribution made by the demons is their total and complete capitulation to the authority of Jesus. Every time the conflict occurs, Jesus is the victor—the demons always yield and are always removed. The only failed exorcism is that conducted by some of Jesus' disciples, and that is remedied by Jesus. Jesus' authority over the demons is absolute.[80]

The quality of Jesus' authority is made clear in several ways. As the demons leave, whatever noise they might generate, the people whom they have tyrannized are not harmed. Jesus' authority is further mani-

---

80. Jesus' exorcism by an authoritative word contrasts with 'the Jewish exorcists [who] had neither δύναμις nor ἐξουσία, and made elaborate and painful efforts, which commonly failed' (Plummer 1901: 239).

fested in the contrast with the procedures used by the Jewish exorcists of the first century. Indeed, the narrator is sufficiently impressed by Jesus' authority that after the account of how Jesus exorcises with an authoritative word, the narrator no longer includes that word, but simply reports the effect.

The authority exercised by Jesus is associated in the narrative with the description of Jesus as the Son of God. There is an eschatological dimension to this defeat, so that the prospect for the demons is their complete destruction. Their defeat at the hands of the character Jesus is the inauguration of their final defeat and destruction, and it is Jesus who begins this process. In Jesus the shape of the demon's end is clear, which signals that Jesus is more than another Jewish exorcist—he is the judge of the end time.

The Ultimate Defeat: The Demons Are Recruited to Serve God's Ends
The third contribution made by the demons is unexpected. The demons are able to make statements about Jesus which are focalized from the perspective of the voice from heaven. It follows that within the story world these statements about Jesus are true in the way that the statements about Jesus by the voice from heaven are considered to be true. Furthermore, these statements by the demons elicit the same pattern of response from Jesus—silence, which can be construed as acquiescence.

Jesus' ultimate victory in the encounters with the demons is that they are not just defeated, but that in their defeat they are recruited to serve the cause which they completely oppose.

The Significance of the Exorcisms for the Character Jesus
Finally, these defeats of the demons by Jesus provide the occasion for Jesus to interpret their significance. In the Beelzebul controversy, Jesus explains that the exorcism of the demons is a particular example of what is associated with the presence of the kingdom of God. This interpretation distinguishes the exorcisms of Jesus from those of the Jewish exorcists. The difference lies not in the technique (ritual or authoritative word), nor in the outcome (the expulsion of the demons), but in the person who conducts the exorcism. The *presence* of Jesus is what ensures that his exorcisms are examples of the kingdom of God.

Chapter 12

STORIES OF JESUS IN THE GOSPEL OF LUKE

And Jesus answered them: 'Go and tell John what you have seen and heard: the blind receive their sight, the lame walk, the lepers are cleansed, the deaf hear, the dead are raised, the poor have the good news preached to them.'

Luke 7.22

Résumé of the Argument

What is involved in a theological reading of a Gospel narrative text? Drawing principally upon the early work of Hans Frei, this study argues that a theological reading of a biblical narrative text requires a literary reading of the text as part of the reading practice, and that this need not be tightly constrained by historical questions. At the same time an awareness of the historical context in which the text was produced is necessary to assist the reader construct his or her world of the text.

Theological readers need to be equipped to read literary narrative texts. This study introduces a version of a critical narratology to furnish the categories and the theoretical model which inform the development of the literary-critical tools used in the theological reading of the text.

The theological position adopted in this study is very similar to key aspects of the formal 'respect for the text' commended by Frei. One element of this position is the decision by the theological reader to grant the text priority over the reader and reading, while not prejudicing the critical freedom of the reader. A reading practice has been developed within these guidelines. A further expression of this 'respect for the text' is the decision to keep the reading practice open to revision in the light of the experience of reading the Gospels.

In this study, three narrative agents in the Lukan textual world are considered. Their particular value lies in the contributions they make to the answer to the question 'who is Jesus?' The preliminary reading of these narrative agents produces three distinctive and different perspectives upon the character Jesus. These stories of Jesus cannot be formally synthesized, but they may be appreciated in their context by the reader and so provide the catalyst for the reader's production of their own story of Jesus.

Reading into the World of the Gospel Narrative Text

When a reader reads the Gospel narrative, a world is constructed in the imagination of the reader in which the characters live out their different stories. The critical reader discovers that the text is not a unity in any simple kind of way. Thematically, the Gospel is taken up with Jesus, but who he is and what he signifies is under continuing discussion. Different narrative agents agree and sometimes disagree, and the conversation between these narrative agents is unfinished; there is no final consensus, resolution or closure. The reader is invited into a world in which different agents wrestle with and argue about the question of the identity of Jesus; these characters experiment with historical ideas, figures and traditional categories to illuminate his identity, with varying degrees of success. There is no single story of Jesus; the Gospel offers us stories of Jesus which make up the unfolding activity of the character of Jesus.

The most developed story in the Gospel of Luke is the story told by the Lukan narrator as he offers his version of the story of Jesus. Yet Jesus offers a more authoritative though less immediately obvious story. The differences between the narrator and Jesus signal a debate still in process.

The variety within the world of the text is acknowledged and cultivated by the Lukan narrator, who respects the characters in the narrative sufficiently to offer access to them and their views expressed by the literary device of embedded discourse and through the representation of their activity. There is sufficient internal coherence in these perceptions within particular characters to confirm the openness of the Lukan narrator in his engagement with views other than his own. Various narrative agents offer their own perceptions of Jesus, and these alternatives contribute to the continuing debate.

The Lukan narrator demonstrates a way of living with these differences. His first contribution is the respect for variety which acknowledges that the various stories cannot be harmonized into a single story.

At the literary level, the harmonization of these different stories is impossible because the inevitable adjustment to their narrative form in any synthesis would inevitably change their potential meaning for the reader.

There are some readers who intuitively seek for a resolution of difference and may endeavour to construct such a resolution or closure if they cannot find one as they read the text. However, a reading that 'respects the text' will attend carefully to the significance of the text in its present form. A respectful reader discovers that the debates going on in the world of the text have made some progress, but are not yet finished.

The narrator does not revise these different contributions into a contrived unity, but instead chooses to live with the different stories as they interact, inform and provide the occasion for the revision of each other. Whatever else may be suppressed, the variety in perceptions about the identity of Jesus is quite plain in the world of the text. And it may be that in this lack of harmonization, and in the fragility of our readings, there is a theological insight into the provisionality of the life of faith.

The decision of the narrator to 'preserve difference' is emulated in the Christian church. The decision of the church councils to include four different Gospels in the canon of the New Testament rather than either a single Gospel or a harmonization of all of them springs from the same theological sense of 'respect for the text'. It is more important to respect them in their diversity with the attendant difficulties than to synthesize them into a single narrative.

The Lukan narrator offers further assistance to the reader who seeks to live with this unresolved variety. The narrator makes clear that there is a hierarchical view of the authority of the different narrative agents within the narrative world. The world of the text is not an anarchic world devoid of criteria of discernment. The order within this hierarchy may surprise some readers, because the narrator does not claim first place and defers to the eye-witnesses of the life of Jesus. These eye-witnesses defer in turn to Jesus and Jesus defers to his Father God.

This hierarchy of authority among the narrative agents is accompanied by a second literary 'move' in the recurring recourse of the character Jesus *to the things that he has done*. The *events* in the life of Jesus are the points to which all interpretations must return, and by which their adequacy may be assessed. This stratagem is the interpretative expression of the theological appreciation that the stories about Jesus are ultimately and necessarily literally 'ascriptive'.

A Theological Narrative-Critical Reading Practice

Hans Frei called for a way of reading the Gospel narratives that expresses the theological concerns of the reader. What form might such a way of reading assume for the theologian who is committed to a respect for the final form of the text and who prioritizes the text over the reader? This study has mapped the kind of 'moves' a theological reader can make in the production of a respectful and critical theological reading of a Gospel narrative.

One practical expression of the 'respect for the text' is that the reader's encounter with the text in the act of reading should inform and revise the reading practice. Accordingly, this thesis offers a preliminary reading which includes revisions generated by the activity of reading.

The writings of Hans Frei helpfully open up these issues and form the starting point for the discussion which maps the present proposal; however, Frei's analysis is preliminary and insufficiently critical so a more rigorous approach is required that will continue to work within the same theological constraints that Frei championed.[1]

The critical revision of Frei's work introduced in this study develops in two significant ways. First, the reading practice approximates more and more closely to *the narrator's way of reading and retelling the story of Jesus*. The constraints adopted by the narrator both respect and retain the stories of the character Jesus and his contemporaries while also creating space for the narrator's hermeneutical concern for the narratee. In the narrator's discourse the Gospel story is carefully rewritten for readers who inhabit another world.

The second significance of the present proposal is the possibility for

---

1.   Frei's hermeneutical proposal is 'anti-theoretical' in cast, and this is reflected in the style of his proposal: popular at a serious level without ever being precise enough to be technically or philosophically rigorous, and owing little to thinkers outside the community of faith. Fodor compares Frei's approach with that of Ricoeur and describes Frei's proposal as 'modest, and at times all too meagre biblical hermeneutics' (Fodor 1995: 335). The present thesis has begun with Frei's proposal and its level of 'generality' and developed a revision of his hermeneutical proposal which is more rigorous when treating the theoretical issues, and engages much more with the actual Gospel text when reading them.

rigorous and critical engagement with readers who inhabit late twentieth-century modern and postmodern worlds, informed by a thoroughgoing 'hermeneutics of suspicion'. Dissonance, difference, the absence of
stable and objective meaning and the lack of closure characterize the
fabric of such realities. The recognition of the fundamental role of the
contemporary reader in every reading practice opens up new hermeneutical possibilities for the reading of Scripture in the community of
faith. Furthermore, hard critical reflection can avoid a premature and all
too common collapse into subjectivity or deconstruction.

The postmodern reading practice introduced here displays the following characteristics:

1. A theological decision to accord primacy to the biblical text. This
entails attention to the selected text in its entirety, independent of the
reconstructed history of its production or any subsequent revision
which both risk atomizing the text. This characteristic does not prejudice a critical reading of the text; a literary deconstruction of the text
may be required as it is read, but this deconstruction will begin with the
text—and all of the text.

2. A theologically generated 'respect for the text' entails a respect for
the literary features of the text. For these Gospel texts, this inevitably
ensures that their narrative features are respected.

3. Every reader requires assistance to read the texts well. The two
principal resources are a theoretically informed critical reading practice
and a community of interpretation with whom to discuss and criticize
the various readings produced.

4. Such literary reading is best achieved by the employment of a narrative-critical approach generated from a narrative theory which is
appropriate for this exercise. The study adopts and revises for this task
some of the narratological work developed by Mieke Bal.

5. A theoretically informed reading which accords primacy to the text
will include the encounter with the particular text in the development of
the reading practice. Consequently the discussion cannot proceed without the sustained engagement with the text in question. The experience
of reading the text revises and refines the reading process in a dialectical conversation.

6. The reading practice generates story-worlds in which characters
and events are formed in the imagination of the reader. This 'world of
the text' is crucially dependent upon the contributions of the reader and
so every reader's world of the text will be unique, while including

aspects common to the worlds generated by other readers. Although there may be a great deal of overlap in the worlds so generated, they are not 'objective' in the 'modern' sense, and never can be so. This variety is to be welcomed, as a happy sign that a particular text is able to 'speak' into many different situations.

7. The imaginary world of the text is constructed by the reader whatever the type of narrative text that is read. There is no conceptual difference between the world of the novel and the world of history. The extratextual world referentiality of a narrative text is a separate and subsequent discussion. In a fictional world, there need be no extra textual reference whereas with a historical text, there is a relationship between the reader's story-world and the historical world to which the text is related. The existence of an extratextual reference is not *formally* relevant to the reader's construction of a story-world, although materially the text itself may signal such a reference.

8. Theologically, the story-world of the Gospel narrative represents a dimension of contemporary reality within the horizon of the reader. In the christological reading of the Lukan narrative by a believer or believing community, there is an extratextual reference to the Jesus who is contemporary with these readers. Truthfulness in this case is the correlation between the (possibly unfocused) reader's experience of Christ and the Christ of the story-world.

9. When the text is 'accorded primacy' this includes primacy for the world of the text. This means that the believer's understanding of their own experience is assimilated into and interpreted within the world of the text. The Christian Scripture is ultimately a 'world-absorbing text' (Fodor 1995: 258).

The discernment of how well these different characteristics have been brought into play is the task of those communities of interpretation which work with the same texts and embrace similar hermeneutical concerns.

An Invitation to a Theological Way of Reading the Gospel Narrative

There is no single story of Jesus which the reader can simply rehearse. Instead, the reader is invited to emulate the narrator in the production of his or her own respectful reading of the Gospel. Such a reading is limited because it is a context-specific and reader-specific reading, yet it also has the hermeneutical potential of a responsible engagement by the world of the text with the reader and his world. The readings produced are then offered to the continuing discussion within the community of interpretation regarding the theological reading of the Scriptures.[2]

The narrator offers his example of a hermeneutical reading for the character Jesus, in which emphases and concepts are transformed and reminted in the retelling of Jesus' story in the narrator's narrating. By his example, the narrator thereby commends a hermeneutical reading *or rewriting* of the story of Jesus as the proper responsibility of the theological reader.

Future Possibilities

A critical theological reading practice has been sketched and a preliminary reading conducted of the Gospel of Luke. I suggest that there is sufficient promise in this approach to engage in further reading projects.

There are three areas which would benefit from further work. The first aspect is the concept of 'respect for the text', in which the theological criteria can be more precisely identified and in particular the constraints can be inspected which bear upon the reader's critical freedom within such a reading practice.

The second area which awaits further work is a theologically informed critical reflection upon the reading practice in the light of studies in the neo-formalist area within the field of reader-response criticism. The reading practice developed in this study offers potential for the development of a theological hermeneutics and this possibility awaits critical evaluation.

The third area for further work is the production of an extended reading of the Gospel of Luke which would engage with the full range of literary perceptions of who Jesus is, and explore the possible relationships between these different perceptions. Such a work would be offered to the communities of interpretation for their responses and suggestions for refinement or correction.

During the preparation of this study an interest grew in how others

---

2.   'Can we talk about the Christian story, the biblical narrative? Not without a great many qualifications. Christians learn about a vulnerable God through complex and ambiguous narratives in which no one story overpowers all the others. Partially repressed voices make themselves heard, and honest readers have to struggle with diversity and ambiguity as they think about how these texts make sense and relate to their world' (Placher 1994b: 89).

read the Gospels which led to an interest in the *others* who read the Gospels. Four figures have contributed significantly to the thinking within this study: Frei, Bal, and to a lesser extent, Moore and Jasper. What might be the significance of the fact that all four eventually relinquished their interest in a formalist or neo-formalist literary-critical contribution to a theological reading of the biblical narratives?

Frei's project began with a concern to address the difficulties of the 'modern' situation, which then influenced his revision of that first proposal. Frei's approach has inevitably shaped the strategic development of the present study. Could it be that the first step in any further work is to review whether the shape of the discussion might need a new starting point, where postmodern rather than modern dilemmas face those who would read the Gospels theologically?

Appendix A

THE LIMITATIONS OF CHATMAN'S NARRATOLOGY

Chatman's Interest in Narrative

Seymour B. Chatman was Professor of Rhetoric at Berkeley and first made his name in the area of stylistics, which in the 1970s in the United States drew upon Russian formalism, French structuralism, Hjelmslevian linguistics and the American Schools, including the New Criticism (Chatman [ed.] 1971: ix). Chatman's first venture into narrative theory drew on the structuralism of Roland Barthe in a reading of James Joyce's 'Eveline' (Chatman 1978: 11).

In 1972, Chatman chaired the 'Recent Linguistics and Literary Study' section at the annual English Institute, and edited the collected papers *Approaches to Poetics* (1973).[1] In the foreword, Chatman follows Todorov's suggestion and identifies the field of poetics as a branch of semiology rather than linguistics, and turns his attention to how literary 'structures are meaning-bearing in their own right' (1973: 9). This interest eventually led to the publication of *Story and Discourse* (1978).

Chatman also taught in the film school and maintained that narrative is not just a verbal artefact; the variety of expressions of a narrative suggests that 'common to these artifacts (mime, dance, film, text etc) there must be some substratum' and so *Story and Discourse* addresses the question 'what narrative is *in itself*?' (1978: 9).

Chatman looked to literary structuralism to analyse meaning-bearing structures within a narrative. David Lodge groups structuralist approaches to narrative 'into three categories, according to the depth at which they address the narrative structure' (1980: 25).

First there is 'narratology and narrative grammar' which works with the *langue* of deep structures of narrative, pioneered by European scholars such as Propp, Bremond, Greimas, Lévi-Strauss, Todorov and Barthes. Second are studies in 'poetics of fiction', which work with techniques of fictional representation, and employs the *fabula/sjuzhet* dichotomy, developed by French structuralists as *histoire/discours*, and in Anglo-America writings as *story/discourse*. Chatman's *Story and Discourse* is a 'particularly valuable contribution' in this area (Lodge 1980:

---

1. The English Institute is a prestigous series of annual conferences in the United States which treats contemporary literary themes and debates. Founded in 1943, the Institute held conferences in the late 1960s that addressed aspects of narrative prior to Chatman's chairmanship of the 1972 conference.

28). The third approach is 'rhetorical analysis', which focuses on the surface structures of narrative texts, and draws on the achievements of the close reading techniques of Anglo-American New Criticism.

The wider context of Chatman's work is the change in Western culture as the modern period undergoes dissolution and transformation. Linda Hutcheon, in her *A Poetics of Postmodernism* (1988), describes this change as 'the need to break out of the still prevailing paradigms—formalist and humanist—and to situate both art and theory in two important contexts...the enunciative act...and the historical, social and political context' (1988: 75).

Influences upon Story and Discourse

In the preface to *Story and Discourse*, Chatman mentions three principal influences upon his thought. The largest influence is attributed to the French structuralists, Todorov, Genette, and 'the special inspiration of Roland Barthes' (1978: 12). The organization of the book into sections on 'story' and 'discourse' is drawn from these structuralists, and, as Moore notes, the chapters on plot and character are based principally upon them (1989a: 44). For Chatman 'the most exciting approach to the questions is dualist and structuralist' (1978: 9).

The second contribution comes from Anglo-American narrative study, including the writings of Wayne Booth. The American contribution is 'essentially empirical and text-based, [and] theoretically rather underpowered' (Lodge 1980: 25). This approach contributes principally to the discussion of discourse.

The third influence Chatman includes is Russian formalism, although this seems to make a more indirect contribution.

Chatman's synthesis makes it difficult to characterize his work as belonging exclusively to one tradition. Chatman sees it as primarily structuralist (so also Lodge), typical of 'structuralists [who] are dualists...who burrow for the structures precisely for the sake of the precious surfaces' (Chatman 1980b: 259). However, Chatman's inability to reckon with the deconstructive possibilities of structuralism, which are demonstrated in the later works of Barthes, leads Scholes to suggest correctly that Chatman's work is most nearly formalist (Scholes 1980: 191).

Story and Discourse

In the introduction to the book Chatman defines the task addressed and the basic categories he employs. *Story and Discourse* is an exercise in narrative theory, and is interested in the 'narrative structure' which is independent of any particular concrete expression of a narrative. *Story and Discourse* will 'work out the ramifications of the fundamental story-discourse dichotomy, with attention focussed on the "narrative form" rather than the surface of particular narratives' (1978: 10).

An 'ideal narrative may be studied as a structure because it displays the three characteristics of wholeness, transformation, and self-regulation' (1978: 21). Real narratives will display this kind of coherence to the extent that they are narratives.

Narrative structure comprises different features, which are grouped under the two heads of 'story' and 'discourse'. Chatman is working with fiction and so this is a synchronic study. Narrative structure is a semiotic (meaning-bearing) system 'communicating meaning in its own right, over and above the paraphraseable contents of the story' (1978: 23). Narratives are never encountered directly, but only in particular manifestations of the narrative, such as a book or a dance, and this encounter only occurs 'when the observer experiences the object aesthetically' (1978: 27).

A narrative is a communication as 'narrative-transaction-as-text', that is, *within a text*. Hence the real author and the real reader are bracketed out. Communication occurs between implied author and narrator, and implied reader and narratee by the process of the story-as-discoursed. This happens by employing a range of types of literary or narrative statements (not grammatical) which function as either 'telling' (Plato's *diegesis*) or 'showing' (Plato's *mimesis*). Both of these kinds of statement can convey the impression of narration.

Chatman considers that to 'read out' a narrative is a more sophisticated task than reading a text for it moves between the surface manifestation of a narrative through to the deeper narrative level (1978: 41). *Story and Discourse* is about 'reading out' and so includes an appreciation of the narrative structure as well as the narrative surface of a text.

The Concept of 'Story'

The story aspect of a narrative comprises the elements or the 'what' of the narrative, as distinct from discourse which is 'how' the story elements are assembled and presented. 'Story' includes the 'first order narrative elements—events, characters, props and setting' (Chatman 1978: 280).

Events are either *actions* or *happenings*. Unusually, for Chatman the 'story' includes the temporal relationships of these events, when most, including Genette upon whom Chatman draws, locate the temporal relationships between the elements as one aspect of the discourse.

Chatman notes that there is little 'said about the theory of character in literary history and criticism' (1978: 107) which he attributes to the classical priority of plot over character. Today, characters are more likely to treated in their own right as 'products of what is...required of them to do' (1978: 111).

Chatman rejects this structuralist concept of character, and suggests an 'open theory of character...treating characters as autonomous beings, not as mere plot functions' (1978: 119). Thus character is developed using the notion of a 'trait' which is 'any distinguishable relatively enduring way in which one individual differs from another' (1978: 121).

Settings are more than the narrative space in which characters move, for they include all the elements which 'set the character off' in contradistinction to them, and so include both minor characters and the props.

The Concept of 'Discourse'

The second part of *Story and Discourse* which treats discourse is often considered the more original (e.g. Mosher 1980: 175). Narration requires a narrator, and narrators range from the least visible to those who are clearly present. The narrator tells or shows the story with varying degrees of overtness and reliability. Chatman tackles the difficult concept of the point of view of the narrator which 'has been treated in more detail than any other aspect of narrative technique' (Martin 1986: 129).

There is a confusion in Chatman's treatment of 'point of view' which is eventually resolved in his later work *Coming to Terms* in which his curious concept of non-narrated stories(!) is discarded (1990a).

The Reception of Story and Discourse

Mosher and Nelles suggest that literary historians will classify the period around the 1980s as the 'silver age of narratology' (Mosher and Nelles 1990: 419). After the golden age of the pioneers, they suggest that narratology moved into a period of consolidation and refinement of the application of these theoretical impulses. Such a move could already be discerned in 1977 with Mieke Bal's *Narratologie* and in 1978 with Seymour Chatman's *Story and Discourse*. However as Bal's *Narratologie* was not translated into English until 1985, Chatman's *Story and Discourse* was the only popular synthesis available in English.

There was a need for an introduction to the structuralist approach to narrative for students at colleges and universities in America, and *Story and Discourse* fitted that need perfectly (Scholes 1980: 190). The book is a clear and patient introduction which is both ordered and accessible. In his 1980 appreciative review in *Poetics Today*, Harold Mosher concluded that *Story and Discourse* 'will act as a basic guide to the study of narrative' (1980: 185).

Two types of criticism emerged. The first is represented by Robert Scholes, who in a review in *Poetics Today* (Scholes 1980) wrote that while *Story and Discourse* is 'an excellent introduction to some of the formal features of the narrative structure...the animating force behind most recent continental criticism...has been studiously ignored by Chatman...*Story and Discourse* is still, after all, merely formalism. And there is something beyond formalism, isn't there? Isn't there...?' (1980: 190-91).

Scholes knows the field, having co-written the classic *The Nature of Narrative* with Kellogg (1966) and also written: *Structuralism in Literature: An Introduction* (1974). Scholes argues that the insularity of *Story and Discourse* from those very currents of thought which threaten its approach deceives the readers and does not prepare them for the real debates.

The second area of criticism focused on the 'dualism' adopted by Chatman from the structuralist tradition. Chatman's colleague Barbara Herrnstein Smith offered a 'vigorous critique' of Chatman's *Story and Discourse* in a paper entitled 'Narrative Versions, Narrative Theories' read at the conference 'Narrative: The Illusion of

Sequence' in Chicago in 1979 (published in 1980). This precipitated a 'testy' reply
from Chatman (1980b) and a return to the fray some ten years later in his 'What
Can We Learn from Contextualist Narratology?' (1990b).

If 'usefulness' is a criterion of success, then *Story and Discourse* is a successful
introduction to narrative theory. Not only did it become a classic within the world
of popular literary theory, it became the key work for the emergence of New Testament narrative criticism. Chatman returned to the field in 1990 with *Coming to
Terms*, and made no fundamental changes in approach, apart from the abandonment
of the curious idea of 'non-narrated discourses'.

However, I suggest that *Story and Discourse* is flawed and has misled students
who have used it, including the New Testament critics who chose it as their first
guide as they ventured into the world of literary theory. There are two principal
weaknesses in the work.

Theoretical Incoherence
Chatman claims that the work is a synthesis of the various traditions, but there is no
evidence of an inner theoretical coherence. The book is simply eclectic. Chatman
came nearer (but still fails) to appreciate its theoretical value when he describes it as
'an amalgam of Anglo-American narrative study...and Russian and French literary
semiotics' (Chatman 1980b: 258).

The significance of this point lies in the inability of the book to generate new
theoretical insights. Its clarity and orderliness of exposition makes it accessible for
the new student, but it has limited theoretical usefulness.

An Uncritical Work in a Critical Age
The second criticism is that the book does not stimulate the reader to explore narrative theory. Its style is authoritarian, its ambience is timeless, it introduces concepts
as if they are commonly shared perceptions in the wider world of narratology when
they are not, and it takes too many decisions for the reader. Thus the book is an
excellent introduction of a pragmatic kind, and Chatman avers that 'structuralists
are pragmatic to a fault!' (1980b: 259). It equips the reader with sufficient understanding of narrative theory to make a start at exercises in narrative criticism, but it
does not pose radical critical questions.

The book is written in the style of the 'reliable narrator', subjugating the reader
with its authority. Scholes parodies works which are 'designed to manipulate the
reader into a state of passive consumerism' (1980: 191) and that could be said of
Story and Discourse.

Worryingly, the book lacks self-criticism. It has been argued that the emergence
of any subject into a science is marked by its ability to criticize its own achievements. Chatman evidently considers narratology to be a science which exhibits a
theory of narrative as distinct from the practice of a narrative criticism. However,
within *Story and Discourse* there are no theoretical difficulties, and, what is more
significant, no discussion of the way to proceed should incoherence strike. The
exposition is serene, confident, leaving the reader only to decide to 'try harder' if

his first attempt at understanding narrative theory or the practice of narrative criticism does not work.

Story and Discourse has constructed a narrative theory which is insulated from the actual debates and uncertainties which occur within narratology. Instead, the book has popularized and simplified elements of narratology which suit its purpose, in order to give a confident start to students as they enter a new discipline. There is no 'doubt', there is rarely acknowledgment of alternative options and there is no critical dimension. Consequently objections are neither acknowledged nor addressed.

The final irony is that this flawed work has been a great success, and that for two reasons. First, there was no other text in the English-speaking field at the time. Second, the employment of its eclectic narrative theory enabled many to begin narrative criticism and their first attempts worked so well that (at least initially) they seemed to legitimize the choice of Chatman's narrative theory.

Appendix B

PRELIMINARY STUDIES FOR A THEOLOGICAL READING PRACTICE

The Criteria for the Classification of 'Commentary' and 'Narrative Asides'

In general literary criticism, 'commentary' is a mark of an 'intrusive narrator [who] not only freely reports but freely comments on and evaluates the actions and motives of the characters' (Abrams 1988: 145). The task of the identification of criteria for the recognition and the interpretation of such commentary is difficult, and Abrams merely illustrates the concept. A theoretical discussion of narrative commentary can prepare for the practicalities of its identification in a narrative-critical reading.

Narrative commentary is material which is inserted within a narrative in order that the narratee may follow the narrator's story. When this happens, the narration is momentarily suspended, and the attention of the narratee moves from the story world to the narrator.

The appreciation of 'commentary' depends in part upon the appreciation of the difference between 'description' and 'commentary' and this is not easy, not least because of the great difficulties encountered in theoretical analyses of 'description' within narrative theory. As a consequence, in Bal's *Narratology*, the reader is offered an eclectic collection of observations about commentary (1985: 126-29).

In the light of the failure until now to deal with commentary at a theoretical level, the present discussion adopts a descriptive classification. The narrator's commentary is considered to be communication between the narrator and the narratee which offers the narratee three kinds of assistance: (1) informative commentary, which provides information that improves the narratee's ability to follow the narrator's story; (2) explanatory commentary, which makes plain for the narratee the narrator's explanation for the course of events. This kind of commentary is often given in the form of 'inside views' of a character's thoughts, reasoning or intentions; (3) evaluative commentary, which assists the narratee to adopt an ideological position with regard to the unfolding of the events and the characters involved.

The function of narrator's commentary is to 'recruit' the narratee to the narrator's view of the story. This explains why attention to narrator's commentary is a particularly useful way for the critical reader to 'characterize' the ideological concerns of the narrator. Whereas evaluative commentary and explanatory commentary are both relatively easy to recognise, the difficulty for the reader is the recognition of the informative type of commentary.

Narrative commentary often includes elements of description while not being typical of general narrative description. Description is one of the three fundamental text types, along with narrative and argument.[1] As description is atemporal[2] it has long been considered problematic[3] and held to be secondary or derivative—not just in the service of but positively inferior to narrative (Chatman 1990a: 23). Even in recent narrative theory, description has proved a real challenge to integrate within a theoretical scheme. It is difficult to define, to distinguish, to analyse and to integrate (cf. Bal 1991a: 109).[4]

In the present proposal, a new and simple functional distinction is employed to distinguish between description and commentary. The advantage of this approach is that it distinguishes textual elements not by the range of their grammatical forms—which often confuses the reader because they overlap—but by *the function of that element in the narrative*.[5] Description in general draws the narratee into the story world by filling out the detail of this imaginary world, and making it more concrete. Description which functions as commentary reinforces the distance between the narratee and the story-world. The usefulness of this simple distinction will be assessed as the exposition proceeds.

The distinction produces a practical criterion for the critical reader. Description which reinforces the distance between the narratee and the story-world is character-ized as *that which is in principle unavailable to the story characters at that narrative moment*. The phrase 'in principle' distinguishes between material which can be considered as available to the narratee, even though the narrator may choose not to include it. Two important examples of material which is in principle unavailable to the story character include the inside views of a person's thoughts and motives, and

1.   Chatman distinguishes the three fundamental text types as narrative, description and argument (Chatman 1990a: 6-21), in which only narrative is characterized by an internal time sequence, which Chatman labels chrono-logic in contrast, both description and argument do not have an internal time sequence, and are fundamentally atemporal.

2.   Before the emergence of structuralism, the distinction had been based on the ontological status of the object described. Actions and events belonged to narrative texts; things, places and characters to descriptive texts. A similar distinction was based on the object's mode of existence: objects in descriptive texts existed in space; those in narrative texts existed in time (Bal 1991a: 110).

3.   Bal recalls that Genette has shown that in *The Republic*, Plato tried to rewrite fragments of Homer so that they would be truly narrative. Even Homer himself attempted to avoid or at least disguise descriptions by making them narrative. Achilles' shield is described as it is in the process of being made; Agamemnon's armor as he puts it on' (Bal 1991a: 115).

4.   Bal's paper 'Description as Narration' presents a useful survey of the current theoretical discussions of description. Bal considers in particular the contribution of Hamon and develops it further. Nevertheless she acknowledges the theoretical impossibility of selecting descriptive text fragments in an unambiguous way although these fragments may be intuitively described as descriptive (Bal 1991a: 109-45).

5.   Thus a micro-narrative within a primary narrative may actually function as a description, despite its grammatical narrative form.

the information which is given ahead of its appearance within the story, as in Judas Iscariot, who became a traitor (Lk. 6.16).

The inside view which functions as narrative commentary is that which draws attention to the narrator rather than the character in the narrative world. In practice, this occurs when the narrator describes an inside view of the character's motives or thoughts which is unavailable within the story-world. This can be signalled to the narratee through either ignorance or dissonance. Ignorance is due to the character not revealing his motive in the story. Dissonance describes the occasion when the character seems to be doing one thing, while inwardly the character is involved in something quite different. These distinctions are able to distinguish the inner thoughts of the character which are expressed through their demeanour within the story-world. The implication is that not all inside views are examples of narrative commentary.

In literary studies of the New Testament Gospels, particularly in the Gospel of John, the presence of the narrator's commentary has long been recognized as important. In Lukan studies the study of narrative commentary is at an earlier stage, with the publication of the first monograph on the subject in Sheeley's *Narrative Asides in Luke–Acts* (1992).[6]

Sheeley addresses the concern 'to develop criteria to identify narrative asides in Luke–Acts...which include not only the insights of ancient handbooks on rhetoric but also the insight of modern narrative theory' (1992: 31). The present study treats what Sheeley calls narrative asides as one type of narrative commentary. Sheeley's criteria and his employment of them produce a small and at times surprising list of narrative asides, together with some surprising omissions.

Narrator's Commentary in the Lukan Narrative

The narrative material which is identified as commentary is listed below and is printed in italics. This extensive lists contrasts with the much shorter list compiled by Sheeley 1992. When an example of narrative commentary coincides with a suggestion of Sheeley, it is labelled with the numbered suffix S. This analysis does not accept all of Sheeley's proposals, which explains the omissions of S^{16} and S^{21}.

Prologue
1.1 S^1 *Since many have undertaken to set down an orderly account of the events...*

Act 1
1.6   *Both of them were righteous before God,* living blamelessly
1.8 S^2 he was chosen by lot, *according to the custom of the priesthood,* to enter
1.66   What will this child [John] become? *For the hand of the Lord was with him...*
2.02 S^3 *This was the first registration and was taken while Quirinius was governor of Syria.*

6.   Sheeley surveys the literature and concludes that no systematic study of this narrative technique has been attempted (1992: 27).

2.4	S⁴	to the city of David *called Bethlehem* because he was descended.
2.21		Jesus, *the name given by the angel before he was conceived in the womb*
2.23	S⁵	*(As it is written in the law of the Lord...designated holy to the Lord)...*
2.25		Simeon. *This man was righteous and devout...the Holy Spirit rested on him...*
2.40		The child grew...*and the favour of God was upon him.*
2.50		*But they [parents] did not understand what he said to them*
2.52		And Jesus increased in wisdom...and in *divine and* human favour...
2.04		*as it is written in the book of the words of the prophet Isaiah: The voice...*
3.15		*And all were questioning in their hearts whether he might be the Messiah*

Act 2

3.23	S⁶	He was the son (*as was thought*) of Joseph son of Heli...
4.13		When the devil had finished every test, he departed from him *until an opportune time*
4.16	S⁷	he went to the synagogue on the Sabbath day, *as was his custom*.
4.41		he would not allow them to speak, *because they knew that he was the Messiah...*

Act 3

5.17		*they had come from every village of Galilee and Judea and from Jerusalem...*
5.22		When Jesus *perceived their questionings* he answered them
5.24	S⁸	*he said to the one who was paralysed*
6.7		[they] watched him...*so that they might find an accusation against him*
6.8		*Even though he knew what they were thinking*, he said to the man...
6.16	S⁹	and Judas Iscariot, *who became a traitor*.
7.29	S¹⁰	*and all the people who heard this, including the tax collectors...*
8.29	S¹¹	*For many times it had seized him; he was kept under guard...*
9.14	S¹²	*For there were about five thousand men.* And he said to his disciples
9.31		speaking of his departure, *which he was about to accomplish at Jerusalem*
9.33	S¹³	Peter said, *not knowing what he said*
9.45	S¹⁴	they did not understand; *its meaning was concealed from them*
9.47		Jesus, *aware of their inner thoughts*, took a little child

Act 4

9.51		*When the days drew near for him to be taken up*, he set his face to Jerusalem
9.53		but they did not receive him, *because his face was set toward Jerusalem*
10.25		Just then a lawyer stood up *to test Jesus*. Teacher, he said....
10.29		But *wanting to justify himself* he asked Jesus
11.16		Others, *to test him*, kept demanding from him a sign...
11.17		But *he knew what they were thinking* and said to them...
11.54		lying in wait for him, *to catch him in something he might say.*
14.07	S¹⁵	*When he noticed how the guests chose the places of honour*, he told them...
16.14		The Pharisees, *who were lovers of money*, heard all this...
17.16	S¹⁷	He...thanked him. *And he was a Samaritan.* Then Jesus asked him...
18.1	S¹⁸	Then Jesus told them a parable *about their need to pray always and not to lose heart*
18.9		He told this parable *to some who trusted in themselves that they were righteous*

| 18.23 | But when he heard this he became sad, *for he was very rich.* |

18.23 | But when he heard this he became sad, *for he was very rich.*

18.34 | In fact *what he said was hidden from them*, and they did not grasp what was said

19.11 | he told a parable, *because he was near Jerusalem and they supposed the Kingdom...*

Act 5

19.48 | they did not find anything they could do, *for all the people were spellbound by what they heard...*

20.19 | they wanted to lay hands on him at that very hour, *but they feared the people*

20.20 | they sent spies who pretended to be honest, *in order to trap him by what he said...*

20.27 S[19] | Sadducees, *those who say there is no resurrection*, came to him...

20.40 | *for they no longer dared to ask him another question*

Act 6

22.01 S[20] | Festival of unleavened bread, *which is called the Passover*, was near...

22.02 | looking for a way of to put Jesus to death, *for they were afraid of the people.*

22.39 | He came out and went, *as was his custom*, to the Mount of Olives...

23.08 | When Herod saw Jesus he was very glad...*because he was hoping to see him perform some sign*

23.19 S[22] | Release Barabbas for us. *This was a man who had been put in prison for an insurrection that had taken place in the city and for murder.*

23.20 | Pilate, *wanting to release Jesus*, addressed them again

23.50 S[23] | Now there was a *good and righteous* man named Joseph...

Act 7

24.11 | But *these words seemed to them to be an idle tale* and they did not believe them.

24.12 | Peter went home, *amazed at what had happened*

24.16 | *but their eye were kept from recognizing him.*

24.27 | he interpreted to them things *about himself* in all the scriptures

24.31 | then *their eyes were opened,* and they recognized him...

24.37 | they were startled and terrified *and thought that they were seeing a ghost.*

24.41 | While in their joy *they were disbelieving and still wondering*, he said...

The Usefulness of Word Counts in Narrative Analysis

The narrative units of the Gospel of Luke have been analysed for the number of words employed in the Greek text of each unit, and also for the number of words in each discourse within the unit, both the primary discourse and the embedded discourses. The reading which is offered in Chapters 9, 10 and 11 attends to the discourses of the narrator, the character Jesus and the character of the demons. The narrator and Jesus are found all through the narrative, and so the table in Appendix C lists the word count for their respective discourses. The demons appear in just 14 narrative units, and so the word counts do not appear in these whole narrative statistics.

The value of these figures depends on the assumption that the word count gives the best approximation to the narrative time allocated to a particular discourse.[7] To appreciate the significance of this time the raw data of the number of words has to be integrated with the discussion of the function and content of the particular discourse, and all this with an eye to the wider narrative context.

Simple word counts can be misleading, and even provide the narratee (and thus the contemporary reader) with an illusory grasp of the narrative. The function of the particular discourse is very important when the reader interprets the word count. A discourse which rebukes is appropriately brief (as when Jesus rebukes the demons), whereas a discourse which teaches will inevitably tend to be longer (as in the parables or the Sermon on the Plain). Furthermore, the raw totals of word counts are in themselves meaningless. The significance of the word count is found primarily in the relation to the word counts of other discourses.[8]

The interest in word or line counts arose from the recognition that narrative presentations vary in the time taken to cover a particular event. In *Narrative Discourse*, Genette offers a scheme to organize this variety. Bal acknowledges the contribution of the German critic Günther Müller who wrote at length in the area of narrative time. Bal concludes that the narrative time which may be measured by such devices indicates something about how the *attention* is patterned. 'If we treat this division of attention as the main object of the investigation, we must not limit ourselves to counting lines only, but should aim at establishing comparisons (with) calculations as an aid' (Bal 1985: 69).

In this thesis word counts are used to identify which scenes have most narrative time allocated to them. This fact is established by comparison with other scenes, and is considered to be an indicator of the importance of the scene to the narrator.

The word count approach is developed further by using it at the level of individual discourses within a narrative unit. At this level, the word count offers another contribution to the critical reading of the text. The comparison between the primary discourse and the embedded discourse offers an insight into the strategy of the narrator. There are two important aspects.

The first aspect is the question of the importance of the embedded discourse, when it is found within a primary discourse. What does the narrator achieve through the device of allowing the character to speak their own discourse? In the Emmaus Road scene in Luke 24, Cleopas and his companion rehearse at great length (112 words, which is the longest discourse in the scene) the difficulties of the disciples, and Jesus begins his reply in his own words (26 words), and this is then completed in the narrator's report. The comparison with the total length of the scene

---

7.   Readers have used lines or pages as the unit of measurement for the narrative time taken to present an action. These are considered to be too crude an approach for a text which comprises many small narrative units, and within which there are several discourses embedded.

8.   The attention paid to each element can only be analysed *in relation* to the attention paid to all the other elements (Bal 1985: 69; Bal's italics).

and with the length of other discourses makes clear the unusual length of the disciples' discourse. Although Jesus teaches the disciples in a discourse, the narrator gives more attention to the disciples' questions.

The second aspect is the case of the report and embed pattern for the representation of dialogue. The narrator reports in the primary discourse one element in a dialogue, and then provides a response in the form of an embedded discourse of the other character.[9] I have been unable to trace work on this feature of Gospel narratives and its likely significance. As a preliminary comment, I suggest that the embedded discourse gives emphasis to the character who speaks and the substance of what they say. The comparison of the word count of the primary discourse report and the character discourse will then refine this emphasis. In the Gospel narratives there are rarely more than two characters who contribute their own discourse within a scene, and often just one. Consequently this report and embedded type of dialogue is all the more striking.

The suggested link between a discourse length and its narrative importance is a key which the reader uses in order to identify the focalization which is taking place within the narrative. Word counts are one element in the reader's repertoire for the recognition of the kind of ordering which is going on in the process of focalization. The results of this analysis are set out in the tables in Appendix C.

9.   Rimmon-Kenan correctly argues that all representation of speech is a form of narration or diegesis, even when the use of a separate embedded discourse creates the illusion of mimesis. She instances McHale's proposal of seven types of representation within this diegetic spectrum (Rimmon-Kenan 1983: 106-16). In the Gospel narrative there are three types of representation: (1) summary of the speech act (e.g. he began to teach in their synagogues [4.15]); (2) summary of the act and the content of the speech (e.g. the crowds wanted to prevent him from leaving them. But he said...[4.43]); and (3) the separate embedded character discourse.

Appendix C

TABLES OF ANALYSIS OF THE NARRATING SUBJECTS

Key to the Types of Narrative Unit

The Narrator's Report
The primary discourse is the product of the narrator's voice and may report an activity or a conversation or a state of affairs. There is no embedded discourse.

Report of an action	RpA
Report of a character's speech	RpSp

The Primary Discourse and the Character Discourses
If a story character has their own discourse embedded within the primary discourse the narrative unit is labelled a 'scene'. Scenes may also include action.

Scene with embedded speech of one or more characters	ScSp
Scene with embedded speech and description of action	ScA

The Character Discourses
Occasionally the narrator retires and hands over the narration to a character (or characters) so that the narrative unit comprises the character speech or discourse. Occasionally there is a minimal contribution from the narrator (e.g. 'he said to them'), which is noted by a lower case 'n'.

Character discourse of speech	Sp

Key to Abbreviations in Tables of Narrative Units

anon	anonymous individual
CP	Chief Priest
disc	disciple
Eld	Elders
J	Jesus
L	Lord
N (Nar)	Narrator
n	minor contribution for the narrator
NoL	Name of the Lord
P	Prophet
Ph	Pharisees
S	Son
s	Implied sonship from Jesus' use of Father
Sam	Samaritan
Scb	Scribe
Syn Ldr	Synagogue Leader
?	Signifies a possible but unconfirmed audience

Act 1 The Arrival of Jesus (1.5–3.20)

Ref.	Title of the Narrative Unit		Principal Voice	Other Voices	Unit Type	Unit Words	Narrative Discourse			Jesus' Discourse		
							Nar. Words	Jesus' Name	Jesus' Titles	Jesus' Words	Jesus' Titles	Jesus' Audience
1.01	The Promise of the Birth of John	1.5-23	N	2	ScA	347	195	—	—	—	—	—
1.02	The Conception of Elizabeth's Child	1.24-25	N	1	ScA	30	16	—	—	—	—	—
1.03	The Promise of the Birth of Jesus	1.26-38	N	2	ScSp	209	80	—	—	—	—	—
1.04	Mary's Visit to Elizabeth	1.39-56	Mary	2	ScA	232	72	—	—	—	—	—
1.05	The Birth of John the Baptist	1.57-58	N	—	RpA	31	31	—	—	—	—	—
1.06	The Circumcision/Naming of John	1.59-66	N	3	ScA	128	96	—	—	—	—	—
1.07	Zechariah Prophesies	1.67-79	Zech	n	Sp	148	11	—	—	—	—	—
1.08	The Childhood of John	1.80	N	—	RpA	19	19	—	—	—	—	—
1.09	The Birth of Jesus	2.1-7	N	—	RpA	104	104	—	—	—	—	—
1.10	The Shepherds Visit the Baby Jesus	2.8-20	N	2	ScA	207	143	—	—	—	—	—
1.11	The Circumcision of Jesus	2.21	N	—	RpA	26	26	1	—	—	—	—
1.12	The Presentation of Jesus	2.22-39	N	1	ScA	302	236	1	—	—	—	—
1.13	The Childhood of Jesus	2.40	N	—	Rp	14	14	—	—	—	—	—
1.14	The Boy Jesus in the Temple	2.41-51	N	2	ScA	180	152	1	—	15	s	parents
1.15	Jesus Grows Up	2.52	N	—	RpA	14	14	1	—	—	—	—
1.16	John Baptizes	3.1-14	N	2	ScA	240	113	—	—	—	—	—
1.17	Is John the Messiah?	3.15-18	John	N	ScSp	86	33	—	—	—	—	—
1.18	Herod Arrests John	3.19-20	N	—	RpA	34	34	—	—	—	—	—

Act 2 An Introduction to the Character Jesus (3.21–4.44)

Ref.	Title of the Narrative Unit	Principal Voice	Other Voices	Unit Type	Unit Words	Narrative Discourse			Jesus' Discourse		
						Nar. Words	Jesus' Name	Jesus' Titles	Jesus' Words	Jesus' Titles	Jesus' Audience
2.01	The Baptism of Jesus	3.21-22	N	1	ScA	43	33	1	—	—	—	—
2.02	The Genealogy of Jesus	3.23-38	N	—	Rp	165	165	1	—	—	—	—
2.03	The Temptations of Jesus	4.1-13	N	2	ScA	203	103	4	—	26	—	Devil
2.04	The Journey into Galilee	4.14-15	N	—	RpA	31	31	1	—	—	—	—
2.05	Jesus Preaches at Nazareth	4.16-30	J	2	ScA	271	129	—	—	137	P	crowd
2.06	Jesus Preaches at Capernaum	4.31-37	N	3	ScA	118	80	1	—	5	—	demon
2.07	The Healing of Simon's Mother-in-Law	4.38-39	N	—	RpA	38	38	—	—	—	—	—
2.08	The Sick Healed at Evening Time	4.40-41	N	1	ScA	52	46	—	—	—	—	—
2.09	Jesus Departs from Capernaum	4.42-44	N	J	ScA	54	39	—	—	15	—	crowd

Act 3 A Narrative Exposition of 'Who Jesus is?' (5.1–9.50)

Ref.	Title of the Narrative Unit		Principal Voice	Other Voices	Unit Type	Unit Words	Narrative Discourse			Jesus' Discourse		
							Nar. Words	Jesus' Name	Jesus' Titles	Jesus' Words	Jesus' Titles	Jesus' Audience
3.01	The Miraculous Draft of Fish	5.1-11	N	2	ScA	206	165	2	—	19	—	Simon
3.02	The Cleansing of the Leper	5.12-16	N	2	ScA	96	72	1	—	20	—	Leper
3.03	The Healing and Controversy (1)	5.17-26	N	2	ScA	214	143	2	—	53	SoM	man/Ph
3.04	The Call of Levi	5.27-28	N	J	ScA	24	22	—	—	2	—	Levi
3.05	Controversy (2): Mixing with Sinners	5.29-32	N	2	ScA	64	42	1	—	12	—	Ph & Scb
3.06	Controversy (3): Fasting & Prayer	5.33-39	J	n	ScSp	142	18	1	—	105	—	Ph & Scb
3.07	Controversy (4): Sabbath Grain	6.1-5	J	2	ScA	90	35	1	—	48	SoM	Pharisees
3.08	Controversy (5): Sabbath Healing	6.6-11	N	J	ScA	114	92	2	—	22	—	Scb & Ph
3.09	The Choosing of the Twelve	6.12-16	N	—	RpA	77	77	—	—	—	—	—
3.10	The Occasion of the Sermon	6.17-19	N	—	RpA	62	62	—	—	—	—	—
3.11	The Sermon: Blessing and Woes	6.20-26	J	n	Sp	127	11	—	—	116	SoM	disciples
3.12	But I Tell You: Love your Enemies	6.27-36	J	—	Sp	161	—	—	—	161	—	disciples?
3.13	Do not Judge, but Forgive	6.37-38	J	—	Sp	37	—	—	—	37	—	disciples?
3.14	The Need to See Clearly	6.39-42	J	n	Sp	98	5	—	—	93	—	disciples?
3.15	The Fruit of the Heart	6.43-45	J	—	Sp	63	—	—	—	63	—	disciples?
3.16	The Parable of the House Foundation	6.46-49	J	—	Sp	94	—	—	—	94	—	disciples?
3.17	The Centurion at Capernaum	7.1-10	N	2	ScA	186	102	4	—	9	—	crowd
3.18	The Widow's Son at Nain	7.11-17	N	2	ScA	126	109	—	—	6	—	widow/son
3.19	John's Questions and Jesus' Answer	7.18-23	J	2	ScSp	103	52	—	—	29	—	John's disc.
3.20	Jesus Speaks of John	7.24-35	J	N	ScSp	202	44	—	—	158	SoM	crowd
3.21	The Woman with the Ointment	7.36-50	J	2	ScA	273	118	1	—	125	—	Ph

Act 3 (continued)

						Narrative Discourse			Jesus' Discourse		
Ref.	Title of the Narrative Unit	Principal Voice	Other Voices	Unit Type	Unit Words	Nar. Words	Jesus' Name	Jesus' Titles	Jesus' Words	Jesus' Titles	Jesus' Audience
3.22	Jesus Proclaims the Kingdom	N	—	Rp	62	62	—	—	—	—	crowd
3.23	The Parable of the Sower	J	N	ScSp	90	17	—	—	73	—	disciples
3.24	The Parable Explained	J	2	ScSp	145	14	—	—	131	—	disciples
3.25	The Parable of the Lamp	J	—	Sp	61	—	—	—	61	—	crowd
3.26	Jesus' Mother and Brothers	N	2	ScA	54	27	—	—	15	—	disciples
3.27	The Stilling of the Storm	N	2	ScA	94	66	—	—	10	—	disciples
3.28	The Gerasene Demoniac	N	2	ScA	294	261	5	—	16	—	demon/man
3.29	Two Women in Need	N	3	ScA	287	233	5	—	39	—	woman/girl
3.30	The Commissioning of 'The Twelve'	J	N	ScA	94	43	—	—	51	—	twelve
3.31	Herod and John the Baptist	N	1	ScSp	52	41	—	—	—	—	—
3.32	The Return of the Apostles	N	—	Rp	40	40	—	—	—	—	—
3.33	The Feeding of the 5000	N	2	ScA	125	73	—	—	10	—	disciples
3.34	Jesus Asks 'Who do you say I am?'	J	3	ScSp	197	42	—	—	137	SoM2	disciples
3.35	The Transfiguration	N	3	ScA	173	142	2	—	—	—	—
3.36	The Disciples' Failed Exorcism	N	2	ScA	124	63	2	—	18	—	disciples?
3.37	The Second Passion Prediction	N	J	ScSp	54	35	1	—	19	SoM	disciples
3.38	Who Is the Greatest?	J	N	ScA	60	29	—	—	31	—	disciples
3.39	The Unknown Exorcist	J	2	ScSp	39	10	—	—	11	—	disciples

Act 4 Jesus in the Shadow of Jerusalem (9.51–19.44)

						Narrative Discourse			Jesus' Discourse		
Ref.	Title of the Narrative Unit	Principal Voice	Other Voices	Unit Type	Unit Words	Nar. Words	Jesus' Name	Jesus' Titles	Jesus' Words	Jesus' Titles	Jesus' Audience
4.01	The Decision to Go to Jerusalem	9.51									
		N	—	Rp	19	19	—	—	—	—	—
4.02	Jesus is Rejected by the Samaritans	9.52-56									
		N	1	ScA	55	36	—	—	—	—	James/John
4.03	On Following Jesus	9.57-62									
		J	4	ScSp	117	35	2	—	55	SoM	anon
4.04	The Commissioning of the 70	10.1-12									
		J	N	ScA	213	31	—	L	182	—	disciples
4.05	Woes Pronounced on Galilean Cities	10.13-16									
		J	—	Sp	68	—	—	—	68	—	cities
4.06	The Return of the 70	10.17-20									
		J	2	ScA	74	11	—	—	53	—	disciples
4.07	Jesus' Thanksgiving to his Father	10.21-22									
		J	N	ScSp	75	12	—	—	63	S	Father
4.08	Blessed Are the Disciples' Eyes	10.23-24									
		J	N	ScSp	38	8	—	—	30	—	disciples
4.09	The Lawyer's Question	10.25-37									
		J	2	ScSp	229	54	3	—	124	—	lawyer
4.10	Martha and Mary	10.38-41									
		N	2	ScSp	90	51	—	L	21	—	Martha
4.11	Prayer and the Lord's Prayer	11.1-4									
		J	2	ScSp	74	22	—	—	41	—	disciples
4.12	The Importunate Friend at Midnight	11.5-8									
		J	n	Sp	86	4	—	—	58	—	disciples
4.13	Encouragement to Pray	11.9-13									
		J	—	Sp	75	—	—	—	75	—	disciples
4.14	The Beelzebul Controversy	11.14-23									
		J	2	ScA	168	42	—	—	117	—	crowds
4.15	The Return of the Unclean Spirit	11.24-26									
		J	—	Sp	55	—	—	—	55	—	crowds
4.16	True Blessedness	11.27-28									
		N	2	ScSp	39	19	—	—	10	—	anon
4.17	The Sign of Jonah	11.29-32									
		J	N	ScSp	96	6	—	—	90	SoM	crowds?
4.18	Concerning Light	11.33-36									
		J	—	Sp	83	—	—	—	83	—	crowds?
4.19	Dining with Pharisees and Lawyers	11.37-54									
		J	2	ScSp	306	66	—	L	234	—	Ph & Law
4.20	The Leaven of the Pharisees	12.1-3									
		J	N	ScSp	63	17	—	—	46	—	disciples
4.21	Fear the One who Casts into Hell	12.4-7									
		J	—	Sp	70	—	—	—	70	—	disciples
4.22	The Importance of the Holy Spirit	12.8-12									
		J	—	Sp	94	—	—	—	94	SoM2	disciples

Act 4 (continued)

						Narrative Discourse			Jesus' Discourse		
Ref.	Title of the Narrative Unit	Principal Voice	Other Voices	Unit Type	Unit Words	Nar. Words	Jesus' Name	Jesus' Titles	Jesus' Words	Jesus' Titles	Jesus' Audience
4.23	Warning against Avarice	J	2	ScSp	54	15	—	—	29	—	anon
4.24	The Parable of the Rich Fool	J	n	Sp	94	6	—	—	88	—	crowd
4.25	Anxieties about Earthly Things	J	n	Sp	72	6	—	—	66	—	disciples
4.26	Strive for his Kingdom	J	—	Sp	37	—	—	—	37	—	disciples
4.27	Treasure in Heaven	J	—	Sp	50	—	—	—	50	—	disciples
4.28	Waiting for the Master's Return	J	—	Sp	67	—	—	—	67	—	disciples?
4.29	The Unexpected Thief	J	—	Sp	34	—	—	—	37	SoM	disciples?
4.30	Knowledge and Responsibility	J	1+n	ScSp	169	8	—	L	150	—	Peter
4.31	Jesus Brings Fire and Division	J	—	Sp	80	—	—	—	80	—	disciples?
4.32	Interpreting the Times	J	n	Sp	48	5	—	—	43	—	crowds
4.33	Agreement with One's Accuser	J	—	Sp	58	—	—	—	58	—	crowds
4.34	Unless You Repent You Will Perish	J	N	ScSp	86	25	—	—	61	—	anon
4.35	The Parable of the Barren Fig Tree	J	n	Sp	83	5	—	—	78	—	crowd?
4.36	The Healing of the Crippled Woman	N	2	ScA	160	93	2	L	49	—	Syn.Ldr
4.37	The Parable of the Mustard Seed	J	n	Sp	40	2	—	—	38	—	crowd
4.38	The Parable of the Leaven	J	n	Sp	25	3	—	—	22	—	crowd?
4.39	Jesus Continues toward Jerusalem	N	—	Rp	12	12	—	—	—	—	—
4.40	Exclusion from the Kingdom	J	2	ScSp	149	9	—	—	135	—	anon
4.41	The Pharisees' Warning of Herod	J	2	ScSp	56	12	—	—	35	P	Herod
4.42	The Lament over Jerusalem	J	—	Sp	53	—	—	—	53	NoL	Jerusalem
4.43	The Healing of a Man with Dropsy	N	J	ScA	82	59	1	—	23	—	Ph & Law
4.44	Teaching on Humility	J	N	ScSp	154	20	—	—	134	—	Ph's guests
4.45	The Parable of the Great Supper	J	2	ScSp	180	12	—	—	159	—	Ph's guest
4.46	Count the Cost of Discipleship	J	n	Sp	162	10	—	—	152	—	crowds

No.	Title	Ref										Audience
4.47	The Parable of Salt	14.34-35	J	—	Sp	29	—	—	—	29	—	crowds?
4.48	The Parable of the Lost Sheep	15.1-7	J	2	ScSp	117	30	—	—	81	—	Ph & Scrb
4.49	The Parable of the Lost Coin	15.8-10	J	—	Sp	53	—	—	—	53	—	Ph & Scrb?
4.50	The Parable of the Lost Son	15.11-32	J	n	Sp	391	2	—	—	389	—	Ph & Scrb?
4.51	The Parable of the Shrewd Steward	16.1-9	J	n	Sp	188	6	—	—	182	—	disciples
4.52	You Cannot Serve Two Masters	16.10-13	J	—	Sp	74	—	—	—	74	—	disciples?
4.53	The Pharisees Reproved	16.14-15	J	N	ScSp	38	14	—	—	24	—	Pharisees
4.54	The Law, the Kingdom and John	16.16-17	J	—	Sp	34	—	—	—	34	—	Pharisees?
4.55	Concerning Divorce	16.18	J	—	Sp	17	—	—	—	17	—	Pharisees?
4.56	The Parable of Rich Man and Lazarus	16.19-31	J	—	Sp	244	—	—	—	244	—	Pharisees?
4.57	Warnings: Causing to Stumble	17.1-4	J	n	Sp	71	6	—	—	65	—	disciples
4.58	On Faith	17.5-6	J	1+n	ScSp	34	10	—	L2	21	—	apostles
4.59	On Dutiful Service	17.7-10	J	—	Sp	68	—	—	—	68	—	apostles?
4.60	The Cleansing of the Ten Lepers	17.11-19	N	2	ScA	117	81	1	—	32	—	Sam Leper
4.61	The Coming of the Kingdom of God	17.20-21	J	N	ScSp	38	15	—	—	23	—	Pharisees
4.62	The Future Day of the Son of Man	17.22-37	J	2	ScSp	242	13	—	—	219	SoM4	disciples
4.63	The Parable of the Unjust Judge	18.1-8	J	N	ScSp	138	18	—	L	120	SoM	disciples?
4.64	The Pharisee and the Tax Collector	18.9-14	J	N	ScSp	117	19	—	—	98	—	crowd
4.65	Jesus Blesses the Children	18.15-17	J	N	ScA	57	21	1	—	36	—	disciples
4.66	The Rich Ruler	18.18-27	J	3	ScA	148	45	3	—	87	—	rich ruler
4.67	The Disciple's Reward	18.28-30	J	N	ScSp	54	8	—	—	39	—	Peter
4.68	Another Passion Prediction	18.31-34	J	N	ScSp	61	25	—	—	36	SoM	the twelve
4.69	The Blind Man near Jericho	18.35-43	N	3	ScA	108	86	2	—	10	—	blind man
4.70	Zacchaeus	19.1-10	N	3	ScA	147	90	3	L	90	SoM	Zacchaeus
4.71	The Parable of the Pounds	19.11-27	J	N	ScSp	279	26	—	—	253	—	crowd
4.72	Jesus goes up to Jerusalem	19.28	N	—	Rp	8	8	—	—	—	—	—
4.73	The Ride into Jerusalem	19.29-40	N	4	ScA	185	111	2	—	45	L	Pharisees
4.74	Jesus Weeps over Jerusalem	19.41-44	J	N	ScA	73	11	—	—	62	—	Jerusalem

Act 5 Jesus Reclaims the Temple (19.45–21.38)

						Narrative Discourse			Jesus' Discourse		
Ref.	Title of the Narrative Unit	Principal Voices	Other Voices	Unit Type	Unit Words	Nar. Words	Jesus' Name	Jesus' Titles	Jesus' Words	Jesus' Titles	Jesus' Audience
5.01	Jesus Cleanses the Temple	J	1	ScA	35	11	—	—	14	—	merchants
5.02	Chief Priests and Scribes Conspire	N	—	RpA	36	36	—	—	—	—	—
5.03	The Question about Authority	N	1	ScSp	98	31	1	—	25	—	CP/Scb/Eld
5.04	The Parable of Wicked Tenants	J	N	ScSp	200	47	—	—	151	—	crowd
5.05	On Paying Tribute to Caesar	N	1	ScSp	104	58	—	—	19	—	spies
5.06	The Question about the Resurrection	Sad	2	ScSp	185	30	1	—	75	—	Sadducees
5.07	The Question about David's Son	J	n	Sp	47	4	—	—	43	—	Sadducees?
5.08	Beware of the Scribes	J	n	Sp	48	9	—	—	39	—	disciples/ crowd
5.09	The Widow's Mite	J	N	ScSp	58	23	—	—	35	—	disciples/ crowd?
5.10	The Destruction of the Temple	J	2	ScSp	118	23	—	—	80	—	crowd?
5.11	Persecutions are Foretold	J	—	Sp	97	—	—	—	97	—	crowd?
5.12	The Fall of Jerusalem Foretold	J	—	Sp	93	—	—	—	93	—	crowd?
5.13	The Coming of the Son of Man	J	—	Sp	67	—	—	—	67	SoM	crowd?
5.14	The Parable of the Fig Tree	J	n	Sp	66	4	—	—	62	—	crowd?
5.15	Do Not Let that Day Catch you	J	—	Sp	57	—	—	—	57	SoM	crowd?
5.16	Jesus Continues to Teach	N	—	RpA	31	31	—	—	—	—	—

Act 6 The Suffering and Death of Jesus (22.1–23.56)

							Narrative Discourse			Jesus' Discourse		
Ref.	Title of the Narrative Unit		Principal Voice	Other Voices	Unit Type	Unit Words	Nar. Words	Jesus' Name	Jesus' Titles	Jesus' Words	Jesus' Titles	Jesus' Audience
6.01	Seeking a Way to put Jesus to Death	22.1-2	N	—	RpA	24	24	—	—	—	—	—
6.02	Satan enters Judas	22.3-6	N	—	RpA	44	44	—	—	—	—	—
6.03	Preparation for the Passover	22.7-13	J	3	ScSp	96	36	—	—	57	Teacher	disciples
6.04	The Last Passover	22.14-23	J	N	ScA	168	53	—	—	115	SoM	disciples
6.05	Which Disciple is the Greatest?	22.24-27	J	N	ScSp	67	16	—	—	51	—	disciples
6.06	A Place at the Table in the Future	22.28-30	J	—	Sp	43	—	—	—	43	s	disciples
6.07	Peter's Denial Foretold	22.31-34	J	2	ScSp	63	7	—	—	44	—	Simon
6.08	The Time to Buy a Sword	22.35-38	J	2	ScSp	80	16	—	—	58	—	disciples
6.09	Prayer on the Mount of Olives	22.39-46	N	1	ScA	114	82	—	—	32	s	disciples/Father
6.10	The Arrest of Jesus	22.47-53	N	2	ScA	124	75	4	—	44	SoM	Judas
6.11	The Denial of Jesus by Peter	22.54-62	N	4	ScA	142	101	—	L	—	—	—
6.12	The Captors Mistreat Jesus	22.63-65	N	1	ScA	27	21	—	—	—	—	—
6.13	Jesus before the Sanhedrin	22.66-71	N	2	ScSp	94	35	—	—	33	SoM	council
6.14	Jesus before Pilate	23.1-7	N	3	ScA	118	72	—	—	2	—	—
6.15	Jesus before Herod	23.8-12	N	—	RpA	91	91	1	—	—	—	—
6.16	Pilate Releases Barabbas	23.13-25	N	2	ScSp	163	92	2	—	—	—	—
6.17	The Daughters of Jerusalem	23.26-32	J	N	ScA	110	49	2	—	61	—	women
6.18	The Crucifixion	23.33-34	N	—	RpA	30	30	—	—	—	—	—
6.19	Jesus Derided on the Cross	23.35-38	N	3	ScSp	56	29	—	—	—	—	—
6.20	The Two Criminals	23.39-43	Crim	3	ScSp	73	20	—	—	10	—	criminal
6.21	The Death of Jesus	23.44-49	N	2	ScA	95	81	1	—	8	s	father
6.22	The Burial of Jesus	23.50-56	N	—	RpA	100	100	1	—	—	—	—

Act 7 The Triumph of Jesus (24.1–24.53)

Ref.	Title of the Narrative Unit		Principal Voice	Other Voices	Unit Type	Unit Words	Narrative Discourse			Jesus' Discourse		
							Nar. Words	Jesus' Name	Jesus' Titles	Jesus' Words	Jesus' Titles	Jesus' Audience
7.01	The Angels at the Tomb	24.1-12	N	1	ScA	176	136	1	L	—	—	—
7.02	The Road to Emmaus	24.13-35	N	3	ScA	391	190	1	—	36	M	disciples
7.03	Jesus Appears to the Disciples	24.36-43	N	1	ScA	101	56	—	—	45	—	disciples
7.04	Jesus Explains the Scriptures	24.44-49	J	n	Sp	101	17	—	—	84	s,M	disciples
7.05	Jesus Leaves the Disciples	24.50-53	N	—	RpA	49	49	—	—	—	—	—

Appendix D

THE PARABLES OF JESUS IN LUKE*

			Audiences		
No.	Ref.	Theme	Disciples	Crowd	Pharisees, etc.
Act 3					
01	6.47-49	The Two Houses	X	X	—
02	7.31-35	The Children in the Marketplace	—	X	—
03	7.41-43	The Two Debtors	—	—	X
04	8.5-8	The Sower	—	X	—
Act 4					
05	10.25-37	The Good Samaritan	—	—	Lawyer
06	11.5-8	The Friend who Asks for Help at Night	X	—	—
07	11.24-26	The Return of the Unclean Spirit	—	X	—
08	12.16-21	The Rich Fool	—	X	—
09	12.35-38	The Doorkeeper	X?	—	—
10	12.39-40	The Burglar	X?	—	—
11	12.42-48	The Servant with Responsibility	Peter	—	—
12	12.58	Going before the Judge	—	X	—
13	13.6-9	The Barren Fig Tree	—	X?	—
14	13.18-19	The Mustard Seed	—	X	—
15	13.20-21	The Leaven	—	X?	—
16	13.24-30	The Closed Door	—	anon	person
17	14.7-11	The Places at Table	—	—	X
18	14.16-24	The Great Supper	—	—	X
19	14.28-32	The Tower Builder and King on Campaign	—	—	X
20	15.4-7	The Lost Sheep	—	—	X
21	15.8-10	The Lost Coin	—	—	X
22	15.11-32	The Prodigal Son	—	—	X
23	16.1-8	The Unjust Steward	X	—	—
24	16.19-31	Rich Man and Lazarus	—	—	X?
25	17.7-10	The Servants Reward	X?	—	—

* Developed from Jeremias 1972: 247-48. 'X' signifies that the audience is present.

				Audiences	
No.	*Ref.*	*Theme*	*Disciples*	*Crowd*	*Pharisees, etc.*
Act 4 (cont.)					
26	18.1-8	The Unjust Judge	X?	—	—
27	18.9-14	The Pharisee and the Publican	—	Confident	
28	19.12-27	The Pounds and the Talents	—	X	—
Act 5					
29	20.9-18	The Wicked Tenants	—	X	—
30	21.29-31	The Budding Fig Tree	—	X?	—

Appendix E

ENGLISH TRANSLATIONS OF GREEK TEXTS INVOLVING THE DEMONS

Jesus and the Demons who Speak: Capernaum (4.31-41)

[31]He went down to Capernaum, a city in Galilee, and was teaching them, *Sabbath by Sabbath*.[1] [32]They were astounded at his teaching, because his *word*[2] had authority. [33]In the synagogue there was a man who had the spirit of an unclean demon, and he cried out with a loud voice, [34]'Let us alone![3] What have you to do with us, Jesus of Nazareth? *You have come to destroy us!*[4] I know who you are, the Holy One of God!'

[35]But Jesus rebuked him, saying: 'Be silent and come out of him!'

When the demon had thrown him down before them, he came out without having done him any harm. [36]They were all amazed and kept saying to one another, 'What kind of *word* is this? For with authority and power he commands the unclean spirits and out they come!'

1. The dative plural ἐν τοῖς σάββασιν literally translates as 'on the Sabbaths'. Thus v. 31b describes a general state of affairs, before a particular occurrence is introduced in the synagogue in v. 33. The typical situation is conveyed by the translation 'Sabbath by Sabbath', which is also supported by 'the periphrastic use of the imperfect plus present participle καὶ ἦν διδάσκων, which stresses the habitual character of Jesus' activity' (Fitzmyer 1981: 544).

2. This translation clearly represents the literary device of the *inclusio* in the Greek text between v. 32b: ὅτι **ἐν ἐξουσίᾳ** ἦν **ὁ λόγος αὐτοῦ** and 36b Τίς **ὁ λόγος οὗτος**, ὅτι **ἐν ἐξουσίᾳ**.

3. The three options are to translate this as: (1) an interjection of surprise or disbelief as in Attic poetry: 'Ah!' (RSV; or 'Na!' [Fitzmyer]); (2) as a translation of the Hebrew for 'Alas' (less likely, and adopted by no recent commentator); (3) as the imperative of the verb ἐάω 'Let us alone' (so NRSV; Nolland; Schürmann). There seems to be no persuasive reason for not following the NRSV, and the sense of this option fits well with the rest of the demon's discourse.

4. When translating ἦλθες ἀπολέσαι ἡμᾶς, the usual construction of this clause is in the interrogative mood (NRSV; Marshall; Fitzmyer). However, there is no grammatical reason for ruling out the indicative form, as the early MSS were not punctuated to make clear which mood (Funk 1961: 10). Though the indicative option is rarely adopted (cf. *UBSGNT*, 3rd edn, critical apparatus), the indicative form fits well with the knowledge which the demons clearly possess (so also Nolland 1989: 207, who traces a similar indicative form in LXX 1 Kgs 17.10).

Luke's Stories of Jesus

³⁷And a report about him began to reach every place in the region.

³⁸After leaving the synagogue he entered Simon's house. Now Simon's mother-in-law was suffering from a high fever, and they asked him about her. ³⁹Then he stood over her and rebuked the fever, and it left her. Immediately she got up and began to serve them.

⁴⁰As the sun was setting, all those who had any who were sick with various diseases brought them to him; and he laid his hands on each of them and cured them. ⁴¹*Out came*[5] demons from many, shouting, 'You are the Son of God!'

But he rebuked them and would not allow them to speak, because they knew he was *the Christ*.[6]

Jesus and the Demons who Speak: Gerasa (8.26-39)

²⁶They *sailed*[7] to the country of the Gerasenes,[8] which is opposite Galilee. ²⁷When *he*[9] stepped out on land, a man of the city who had demons met him. For a long time he had worn no clothes and he did not live in a house but in the tombs. ²⁸When he saw Jesus, *he shouted out*,[10] fell down before him and said at the top of his voice, 'What have you to do with me, Jesus? Son of the Most High God I beg you, do not *start tormenting* me!'[11]

---

5.   The translation brings out the emphatic position of the verb in the clause ἐξήρχετο δὲ καὶ δαιμόνια ἀπὸ πολλῶν, 'the bringing forward of the verb may accentuate Jesus' victory over the demons' (Marshall 1978: 196).

6.   In the clause ὅτι ᾔδεισαν τὸν Χριστὸν αὐτὸν εἶναι the definite article in the phrase τὸν Χριστὸν, which is the predicate of the verb 'to be', suggests that τὸν Χριστὸν is a title (cf. Nolland 1989: 214; Marshall 1978: 197 who agree that it is a title, and consider that the translation 'the Messiah' makes this sufficiently clear contra Fitzmyer 1981: 554).

7.   The literal translation of κατέπλευσαν is 'they sailed down' which more clearly links this scene and the preceding scene out on the lake.

8.   The difficulty of which reading to adopt is discussed in Marshall, Evans and other commentaries. Nolland (who eventually and curiously prefers Gadarenes) sums up the common view that 'if the original read Γερασηνῶν it would present difficulties because the territory cannot have reached the sea of Galilee', and these difficulties would explain the later alterations (1989: 406). The translation offered here follows *UBSGNT*, 3rd edn, NRSV and the majority of commentators since Plummer (Plummer 1901: 229).

9.   NRSV inserts the name Jesus to assist the reader. This masks the play within the Greek text between the name Jesus and the pronoun 'he'. In a narrative reading this distinction is significant.

10.   This syntax preserves the Greek text's unfolding of events ἰδὼν δὲ τὸν Ἰησοῦν ἀνακράξας προσέπεσεν αὐτῷ. which is reversed in the NRSV, presumably to allow the verb ἀνακράξας to be followed by what the demon shouts out.

11.   The clause μή με βασανίσῃς is translated in NRSV as 'do not torment me'. In English this clause implies that the torment has begun, although it is just possible that it may mean that it is imminent. The Greek construction of μή + aorist subjunctive βασα-

[29]For he was *about to*[12] command the unclean spirit to come out of the man. For many times it had seized him *violently*;[13] he was kept under guard and bound with chains and shackles, but he would break the bonds and be driven by the demon into the wilds.

[30]Jesus then asked him, 'What is your name?'

He said 'Legion', for many demons had entered him. [31]They begged him not to order them to go into the Abyss.

[32]Now, there on the hillside a large herd of swine was feeding there; and the demons begged Jesus *for permission*[14] for them to enter these. So he gave them permission. [33]Then the demons came out of the man and entered the swine, and the herd rushed down the steep bank into the lake and was drowned. [34]When the swineherds saw what had happened, they ran off and told it in the city and in the country.

[35]Then the people came out to see what had happened, and when they came to Jesus, they found *sitting there at the feet of Jesus*[15] the man from whom the demons had gone, clothed and in his right mind. And they were afraid. [36]Those who has seen it told them how the one who had been possessed by demons had been *saved.*[16]

ὑίσης usually means 'do not start tormenting me', which is made clear by the translation suggested here.

12. The MSS divide between an imperfect παρήγγελλεν or an aorist form παρήγγειλεν in the clause παρήγγειλεν γὰρ τῷ πνεύματι τῷ ἀκαθάρτῳ ἐξελθεῖν ἀπὸ τοῦ ἀνθρώπου. Though the *UBSGNT*, 3rd edn, and Nolland adopt the aorist, Marshall, Fitzmyer and Moule adopt the imperfect, even though 'an aorist might be expected' (Marshall 1978: 338). The translation offered here adopts the imperfect, which poses a further question. It could either be a periphrastic perfect or pluperfect: 'he had been commanding the spirit' (Moule 1959: 10), or the equivalent of an inceptive aorist: 'Jesus was about to charge the unclean spirit' (Fitzmyer 1981: 738). The narrative logic suggest the inceptive aorist, in the light of (1) there being no command given to the demon by Jesus in the narrative prior to this point; (2) the previous clause being most clearly translated: 'do not start tormenting me'. This then implies that all of v. 29 is narrator's commentary, to be marked in parenthesis.

As in the earlier note, the NRSV supplies 'Jesus' when the Greek text employs the pronoun.

13. The addition of 'violently' conveys the nuance of the verb συνηρπάκει, cf. Acts 6.12, 19.29 and 27.17; Bauer 1957: 792, 'seize by violence'; cf. Marshall, 1978: 338. The violence is confirmed in the next verse.

14. This translation better captures the interplay of request and response which is conveyed in the Greek by the use of the same verb: **ἐπιτρέψῃ** αὐτοῖς εἰς ἐκείνους εἰσελθεῖν· καὶ **ἐπέτρεψεν** αὐτοῖς.

15. The syntax followed in this translation retains the depiction in the Greek text of the first thing that the people notice: εὗρον καθήμενον τὸν ἄνθρωπον ἀφ᾽ οὗ τὰ δαιμόνια ἐξῆλθεν ἱματισμένον.

16. The NRSV choice of 'healed' well represents the new state of the man, but does not convey the associations of salvation which the Greek verb includes: πῶς ἐσώθη ὁ δαιμονισθείς. Other commentators suggest 'delivered'. In Luke, the verb σῴζω and the noun σωτηρία are used of Jesus (1.69, 71, 77, 2.30, *et al.*). Although not quite appropriate, the

[37]Then all the people of the surrounding country of the Gerasenes asked Jesus to leave them, for they were seized with great fear. So he got into the boat and returned.

[38]The man from whom the demons had gone begged that he might be with him; but Jesus sent him away, saying, [39]'Return to your home and declare how much *has been done for you by God.*'[17] So he went away, proclaiming throughout the city how much *had been done for him by Jesus.*

Jesus Exorcises where the Disciples Failed (9.37-43)

[37]On the next day, when they came down from the mountain, a great crowd met him.

[38]Just then, a man from the crowd shouted *and implored*[18] 'Teacher, I beg you to look at my son *with compassion*,[19] for he is my only child. [39]Suddenly a spirit seizes him and all at once he shrieks. It convulses him until he foams at the mouth; It mauls him and will scarcely leave him. [40]I begged your disciples to cast it out, but they could not.'

[41]Jesus answered, 'You faithless and perverse generation, how much longer must I be with you and bear with you? Bring your son here.'

[42]While he was coming, the demon dashed him to the ground in convulsions. But Jesus rebuked the unclean spirit, healed the boy and gave him back to his father.

[43]And all were astounded at the greatness of God.

The Crippled Woman with a Spirit (13.10-17)[20]

[10]Now he was teaching in one of the synagogues *Sabbath by Sabbath.*[21] [11]And just

word 'saved' allows the English reader to notice the association between these early references and Lk. 8.36.

17. The rearrangement of the NRSV syntax makes clear the emphasis in the Greek upon *who* has done these things, and underlines the narrator's deliberate parallelism between v. 39a and v. 39b.

18. 'and implored' captures the nuance of ἐβόησεν.

19. 'with compassion' conveys more of the verb ἐπιβλέψαι. The verb is also used of God in the Magnificat (1.48), and often in the LXX to represent 'appeals for divine succour' (Evans 1990: 423). The form is the active aorist infinitive (as NRSV, Plummer 1901: 254 and Marshall 1978: 390) and not an aorist middle.

20. Some raise the possibility that this story is not an exorcism but a healing (e.g. Easton 1926: 215; Evans 1990: 550; Nolland 1993: 724). Although this is the only example of πνεῦμα ἔχουσα ἀσθενείας, and the way in which Jesus deals with the person is more typical of a healing than an exorcism, on balance ot is treated here as an exorcism, because (1) there are literary parallels with the first exorcisms in Capernaum (the location, the source of the trouble—a spirit of uncleanness/infirmity; the laying on of hands); (2) the reference to the binding of Satan; (3) the phrase 'a spirit of infirmity' is an Aramaism which is used to describe demonic conditions (cf. Fitzmyer 1985: 1012).

21. Verse 10 reads ᾿Ην δὲ διδάσκων ἐν μιᾷ τῶν συναγωγῶν ἐν τοῖς σάββασιν. The combination of the periphrastic imperfect and the dative plural 'on the Sabbaths' suggests a

then there appeared a woman *who had had a spirit of infirmity*[22] for 18 years. She was bent over and was *completely*[23] unable to stand up straight. [12]When Jesus saw her, he called her over and said, 'Woman, *from now on you are released*[24] from your *infirmity*.'[25]

[13]*And*[26] he laid his hands on her and immediately she stood up straight and began praising God. [14]But the leader of the synagogue, indignant because Jesus had cured on the Sabbath, kept saying to the crowd, 'There are six days on which work ought to be done; come on those days and be cured, and not on the sabbath day.'

[15]But the Lord answered him and said, 'You hypocrites! Does not each of you on the sabbath untie his ox or his donkey from the manger, and lead it away to give it water? [16]And ought not this woman, a daughter of Abraham whom Satan bound for eighteen long years, be *untied*[27] from this bondage on the sabbath day?'

[17]When he said this, all his opponents were put to shame; and the entire crowd was rejoicing at all the wonderful things he was doing.

typical state of affairs (cf. Schürmann 1969: 227, and contra NRSV). The grammatical construction is similar to that of 4.31.

22. This translation 'smooths' the tense of the present participle in καὶ ἰδοὺ γυνὴ πνεῦμα ἔχουσα ἀσθενείας κ.τ.λ (13.11). The phrase is literally 'a spirit of infirmity' and evokes the first occasion that Jesus met a man in the synagogue at Capernaum ἔχων πνεῦμα δαιμονίου ἀκαθάρτου (4.33).

23. The translation 'completely' better represents the Hellenistic phrase εἰς τὸ παντε-λές (Evans 1990: 551). The absolute contrast is reinforced by the play on the Greek verbal stem κύπτω which is difficult to capture in English: συγκύπτουσα καὶ μὴ δυναμένη ἀνακύψαι εἰς τὸ παντελές. The 'reinforcement by opposites' is not unusual in Luke, even if the play on the verbal stem is not present (cf. 1.20) 'you will become mute, unable to speak' (cf. Goulder 1989: 565). This translation follows the NRSV in treating εἰς τὸ παντελές as qualifying the ability to straighten herself, rather than the extent of her straightening.

24. This translation seeks to capture the nuance of the perfect passive in Jesus' words: ἀπολέλυσαι τῆς ἀσθενείας σου.

25. The translation of τῆς ἀσθενείας σου in Jesus' response as 'your infirmity' makes clear the link with the narrator's description of the woman's need: πνεῦμα ἔχουσα ἀσθενείας (13.11).

26. NRSV chooses 'When' to represent the conjunction καὶ, which unfortunately loosens the relationship between Jesus' word and Jesus' act in her healing.

27. The translation of λυθῆναι as 'untied' makes clear the link to the untying of the ox or donkey in the previous verse: ἕκαστος ὑμῶν τῷ σαββάτῳ οὐ λύει τὸν βοῦν αὐτοῦ (9.15).

BIBLIOGRAPHY

The usual bibliographical convention is employed for all the entries except for those of the writings of Hans Frei. Many of his essays were written over decades and display the development of his thought but they were not published at the time. Eventually they were collected into anthologies whose single and later publication date masks this development. Accordingly, these essays are listed in chronological order of the date of their production, but with the pagination and the usual details of the later published form.

Aarde, A. van
    1991   'Narrative Criticism Applied to John 4:43-54', in Hartin and Petzer 1991: 101-28.

Abrams, M.H.
    1988   *A Glossary of Literary Terms* (New York: Holt, Rinehart & Winston).

Adam, A.K.M.
    1995   *What Is Postmodern Biblical Criticism?* (Minneapolis: Fortress Press).

Ahlstrom, G.W.
    1984   'Aspects of the Bible as Literature', *JR* 64: 520-29.

Alter, Robert
    1978   'Biblical Type-Scenes and the Uses of Convention', *CritInq* 5: 355-68.
    1981   *The Art of Biblical Narrative* (London: George Allen & Unwin).
    1992   *The World of Biblical Narrative* (London: SPCK).

Alter, Robert, and Frank Kermode (eds.)
    1987   *The Literary Guide to the Bible* (London: Collins).

Anderson, A.A.
    1972   *The Psalms*, I (London: Marshall, Morgan & Scott).

Anderson, Janice Capel, and Stephen Moore (eds.)
    1992   *Mark and Method* (Minneapolis: Fortress Press).

Atkins, Douglas, and Laura Morrow (eds.)
    1989   *Contemporary Literary Theory* (Massachusetts: Macmillan).

Auerbach, Eric
    1953   *Mimesis* (ET; Princeton, NJ: Princeton University Press [1946]) .

Aune, David E.
    1981   'The Problem of the Genre of the Gospels: A Critique of C.H. Talbert's *What Is a Gospel?*', in France and Wenham 1981: 9-60.
    1987   *The New Testament in its Literary Environment* (Philadelphia: Westminster Press).

Bailey, James, and Lyle Vander Broek
    1992   *Literary Forms in the New Testament* (London: SPCK).

Bailey, Kenneth
1976   *Poet and Peasant* and *Through Peasant Eyes* (Grand Rapids: Eerdmans).
Bal, Mieke
1977   *De theorie van vertellen en verhalen: inleiding in de narratologie* (Mulderberg: Coutinho).
1985   *Narratology: Introduction to the Theory of Narrative* (Toronto: University of Toronto Press).
1986   *Femmes imaginaires: L'Ancien Testament au risque d'une narratologie critique* (Utrect: A.G. Nizet).
1987   *Lethal Love: Feminist Literary Readings of Biblical Love Stories* (Bloomington: University of Indiana Press).
1988a   *Murder and Difference: Gender, Genre and Scholarship on Sisera's Death* (Bloomington: University of Indiana Press).
1988b   *Death and Dissymmetry: The Politics of Coherence in the Book of Judges* (Chicago: University of Chicago Press).
1989a   Review of *Story, Text and Scripture: Literary Interests in Biblical Narrative* (University Park: Pennsylvania State University Press, 1988), by W. Kurt, in *TTod* 45: 460-64.
1989b   Review of *The Literary Guide to the Bible* (London: Collins, 1987), by R. Alter and F. Kermode (eds.), in *JAAR* 57: 373-83.
1989c   *Anti-Covenant: Counter reading women's lives in the Hebrew Bible* (Sheffield: Almond Press).
1990   'Dealing/With/Women: Daughters in the Book of Judges', in Schwartz 1990: 16-39.
1991a   *On Story-Telling: Essays in Narratology* (Sonoma, CA: Polebridge Press).
1991b   'Murder and Difference: Uncanny Sites in an Uncanny World', *JLT* 5: 11-19.
1991c   *Reading "Rembrandt": Beyond the Word–Image Opposition* (Cambridge: Cambridge University Press).
Bal, Mieke (ed.)
1989   *Anti-Covenant: Counter-Reading Women's Lives in the Hebrew Bible* (Sheffield: Almond Press).
Barr, D., and J. Wentling
1984   'The Conventions of Classical Biography and the Genre of Luke–Acts', in Talbert 1984: 63-88.
Barr, James
1973   *The Bible in the Modern World* (London: SCM Press).
1977   *Fundamentalism* (London: SCM Press).
1981   'The Bible as a Document of Believing Communities', in Betz 1981: 25-47.
1986   'Review of Barton, *Reading the Old Testament*', *JTS* 37: 462-65.
1989   'The Literal, the Allegorical and Modern Biblical Scholarship', *JSOT* 44: 3-17.
Barrett, C. Kingsley
1961   *Luke the Historian in Recent Study* (London: Epworth Press).
Barthes, Roland
1974   *S/Z* (New York: Richard Miller).

1992 'To Write: An Intransitive Verb?', in Rice and Waugh 1992: 42-51.

Barton, John
1983 'Note upon Alter, *Art of Biblical Narrative*', in *N and Q* 1983: 452-53.
1984 *Reading the Old Testament: Method in Biblical Study* (London: Darton, Longman & Todd).
1987 'Reading the Bible as Literature: Two Questions for Biblical Critics', *JLT* 1: 135-53.

Barton, John (ed.)
1998 *Biblical Interpretation* (Cambridge: Cambridge University Press).

Bauer, David R.
1992 'The Major Characters of Matthew's Story', *Int 46*: 357-67.

Bauer, Walter, William Arndt and Wilbur Gingrich
1957 *A Greek–English Lexicon of the New Testament and Other Early Christian Literature* (Chicago: University of Chicago Press).

Beardslee, William A.
1970 *Literary Criticism of the New Testament* (Philadelphia: Fortress Press).
1989 'Recent Literary Criticism', in Epp, Eldon and MacRae 1989: 175-98.

Berendsen, Marjet
1984 'The Teller and the Observer: Narration and Focalization in Narrative Texts', *Style* 18.2: 140-58.

Berlin, Adele
1983 *Poetics and Interpretation of Biblical Narrative* (Sheffield: Almond Press).
1993 'The Role of the Text in the Reading Process', *Semeia* 62: 143-47.

Best, Ernest
1983 *Mark as Story* (Edinburgh: T. & T. Clark).

Betz, Hans D. (ed.)
1981 *The Bible as a Document of the University* (Chico, CA: Scholars Press).

Bloom, Harold (ed.)
1988 *The Gospels* (New York: Chelsea House Publishers).

Boobyer, G.H.
1975 'Review of *The Eclipse of Biblical Narrative*', *SJT* 28: 578-80.

Borsch, Frederick
1975 'Review of *The Eclipse of Biblical Narrative*', *RelE* 70: 571-72.

Brawley, Robert L.
1987 *Luke–Acts and the Jews: Conflict, Apology and Conciliation* (Atlanta: Scholars Press).

Brett, Mark
1990 'Four or Five Things to do with Texts', in Clines, Fowl and Porter, 1990: 357-77.
1993 'The Future of Reader Criticisms?', in Watson 1993a: 13-31.

Britt, Brian
1992 'Review of Schwartz, R. (ed.), *The Book and the Text*', *JR* 72: 93-104.

Brooks, Cleanth
1968 *The Well Wrought Urn* (London: Dobson, rev. edn).

Bronzwaer, W.
1981 'Mieke Bal's Concept of Focalization: A Critical Note', *PToday* 2.2: 193-201.

Brown, Raymond E.
    1977   *The Birth of the Messiah* (New York: Image).
    1986   'Gospel Infancy Narrative Research from 1976 to 1986: (Luke)', *CBQ*
              48: 660-80.
Brown, Schuyler
    1978   'The Role of the Prologues in Determining the Purposes of Luke–Acts',
              in Talbert 1978: 99-111.
    1988   'Reader Response: Demythologizing the Text', *NTS* 34: 232-37.
Brueggemann, Walter
    1989   'Review of Josipovici, *The Book of God: A Response to the Bible*', *TTod*
              46: 323-26.
    1993   *The Bible and the Postmodern Imagination* (London: SCM Press).
    1997   *Theology of the Old Testament* (Minneapolis: Fortress Press).
Buckley, James J.
    1990   'The Hermeneutical Deadlock between Revelationists, Textualists and
              Functionalists', *ModTh* 6: 325-39.
Burnett, Fred
    1990   'Postmodern Biblical Exegesis: The Eve of Historical Criticism', *Semeia*
              51: 51-80.
    1993   'Characterization and Reader Construction of Characters in the Gospels',
              Semeia 63: 3-28.
Cadbury, Henry J.
    1920   *The Style and Literary Method of Luke I and II* (London: Harvard Univer-
              sity Press).
    1922   'Commentary on the Preface of Luke', in Jackson and Lake 1922: 489-
              510.
    1927   *The Making of Luke–Acts* (London: Macmillan).
    1937   *The Peril of Modernizing Jesus* (London: SPCK).
Caird, G.B.
    1963   *The Gospel of Luke* (London: A. & C. Black).
    1980   *The Language and Imagery of the Bible* (London: Gerald Duckworth).
Callan, Terrance
    1985   'The Preface of Luke–Acts and Historiography', *NTS* 31: 576-81.
Carroll, John T.
    1988   'Luke's Portrayal of the Pharisees', *CBQ* 50: 604-21.
Cassidy, R.
    1993   'Review of Kingsbury: *Conflict in Luke: Jesus, Authorities, Disciples*',
              JBL 112: 150-52.
Castelli E., S. Moore and R. Schwarz (eds.)
    1995   *The Postmodern Bible* (New Haven: Yale University Press).
Chatman, Seymour B.
    1969   'New Ways of Analysing Narrative Structures', *Language and Style* 2: 3-
              36.
    1971   'The Structure of Fiction', *University Review* 37: 199-214.
    1973   *Approaches to Poetics* (New York: Columbia University Press).
    1978   *Story and Discourse* (Ithaca, NY: Cornell University Press).
    1981a   'What Novels Can Do That Films Can't (and Vice Versa)', in Mitchell
              1981: 117-36.

1981b   'Reply to Barbara Herrnstein Smith', in Mitchell 1981: 258-65.
1986   'Characters and Narrators', *PToday* 7: 189-204.
1988   'On Deconstructing Narratology', *Style* 22: 9-17.
1990a   *Coming to Terms: The Rhetoric of Narrative in Fiction and Film* (Ithaca, NY: Cornell University Press).
1990b   'What Can We Learn from Contextualist Narratology?', *PToday* 11: 309-28.

Chatman, Seymour B. (ed.)
1971   *Literary Style: A Symposium* (London: Oxford University Press).

Childs, Brevard
1977   'The *Sensus Literalis* of Scripture: An Ancient and Modern Problem', in Donner, Hanhart and Smend (eds.) 1977: 80-93.
1984   *The New Testament as Canon: An Introduction* (London: SCM Press).
1990   'Critical Reflections on James Barr's Understanding of the Literal and the Allegorical', *JSOT* 46: 3-9.
1992   *Biblical Theology of the Old and New Testament* (London: SCM Press).

Chilton, Bruce
1981   'Announcement in Nazara: An analysis of Luke 4.16-21', in France and Wenham 1981: 147-72.

Clines, David J.A.
1990   'Reading Esther from Left to Right: Contemporary Reading Strategies', in Clines, Fowl and Porter 1990: 31-52.

Clines, D.J.A., Stephen E. Fowl and Stanley F. Porter (eds.)
1990   *The Bible in Three Dimensions: Essays in Celebration of Forty Years of Biblical Studies in the University of Sheffield* (JSOTSup, 87; Sheffield: JSOT Press, 1990).

Coleridge, Mark
1993   *The Birth of the Lukan Narrative: Narrative as Christology in Luke 1–2* (JSNTSup, 88; Sheffield: JSOT Press).

Collins, Adela Y.
1988   'Narrative, History and Gospel', *Semeia* 43: 145-53.

Comstock, Gary
1986   'Truth or Meaning: Ricoeur versus Frei on Biblical Narrative', *JR* 66: 117-40.
1987a   'Two Types of Narrative Theology', *JAAR* 55: 687-717.
1987b   'Review of McConnell (ed.), *The Bible and the Narrative Tradition*', *JR* 67: 540-41.

Conzelmann, Hans
1960   *The Theology of St. Luke* (London: SCM Press).

Cook, Cornelia
1991   'The Sense of Audience in Luke: A Literary Examination', *NB* 72: 19-30.

Creed, John M.
1930   *The Gospel According to St. Luke* (London: Macmillan).

Crossan, John D.
1982   'Ruth amid the Alien Corn', in Polzin and Rothman (eds.), 1982: 199-210.

Culler, Jonathan
1975   *Structuralist Poetics* (London: Routledge & Kegan Paul).

1977	'Structuralism and Literature', in Schiff 1977: 59-76.
1980	'Fabula and Sjuzhet in the Analysis of Narrative', *PToday* 1.3: 27-37.

Culpepper, R. Alan

1983   *The Anatomy of the Fourth Gospel: A Study in Literary Design* (Philadelphia: Fortress Press).

Danker, Frederick W.

1983   'Review of Fitzmyer, *Luke I*', *Int* 37: 297-99.

1987   *Luke* (Philadelphia: Fortress Press).

1989   'Review of Tannehill, *Narrative Unity of Luke–Acts I*', *Int* 43: 78-82.

1992   'Review of Nolland, *Lk 1–9.20*', *CBQ* 54: 363-64.

Darr, John

1988   'Review of Alter and Kermode, *Literary Guide to the Bible*', *TTod* 45: 348-50.

1992   *On Character Building: The Reader and the Rhetoric of Characterization in Luke–Acts* (Louisville, KY: Westminster/John Knox Press).

1993   'Narrator as Character: Mapping a Reader-Oriented Approach to Narration in Luke–Acts', *Semeia* 63: 43-60.

1994   'Watch How You Listen (Lk 8.18)', in Malbon and McKnight 1994: 87-107.

Davies, Jon, Graham Harvey and Wilfred G.E. Watson (eds.)

1995   *Words Remembered, Texts Renewed: Essays in Honour of John F.A. Sawyer* (JSOTSup, 195; Sheffield: Sheffield Academic Press).

Dawsey, James M.

1986a   'What's in a Name? Characterization in Luke', *BTB* 16: 143-47.

1986b   *The Lukan Voice: Confusion and Irony in the Gospel of Luke* (Macon, GA: Mercer University Press).

Demson, David

1992   'Response to Walter Lowe', *ModTh* 8: 145-48.

1997   *Hans Frei and Karl Barth: Different Ways of Reading Scripture* (Grand Rapids: Eerdmans).

Detweiler, Robert

1980   'After the New Criticism: Contemporary Methods of Literary Interpretation', in Spencer 1980: 3-23.

Detweiler, R., and W. Doty

1990   *The Daemonic Imagination: Biblical Text and Secular Story* (Atlanta: Scholars Press).

Detweiler, R., and V. Robbins

1991   'From New Criticism to Poststructuralism: Twentieth Century Hermeneutics', in Prickett 1991: 225-80.

Dillistone, F.W.

1975   'Review of *The Eclipse of Biblical Narrative*', *JTS* 26: 223-24.

Donahue, John

1994   'Redaction Criticism: Has the *Haupstrasse* become a *Sackgasse*?', in Malbon and McKnight 1994: 27-57.

Doner, H., R. Hanhart and R. Smend (eds.)

1977   *Beiträge zur Alttestamentlichen Theologie* (Göttingen: Vandenhoeck & Ruprecht).

Doty, William G.
  1983   'Review of Rhoads and Michie, *Mark as Story*', *Int* 37: 302-304.
  1985   'Review of Culpepper, *Anatomy of the Fourth Gospel*', *Int* 39: 78-80.
Dunn, James
  1987   *The Living Word* (London: SCM Press).
Eagleton, Terry
  1983   *Literary Theory: An Introduction* (Oxford: Basil Blackwell).
  1996   *The Illusions of Postmodernism* (Oxford: Basil Blackwell).
Edwards, Michael
  1984   'Story: Towards a Christian Theory of Narrative', in Jasper 1984: 179-90.
Eliot, T.S.
  1935   'Religion and Literature', in *idem*, *Selected Essays* (London: Faber & Faber): 388-401.
Ellingsen, Mark
  1990   *The Integrity of Biblical Narrative* (Minneapolis: Fortress Press).
Elliott, J.K.
  1990   *Essays and Studies in New Testament Textual Criticism* (Cordoba, Spain: Ediciones el Almendro).
Ellis, Earle
  1974   *The Gospel of Luke* (London: Oliphants).
Epp, D., J. Eldon and G. MacRae (eds.)
  1989   *The New Testament and its Modern Interpreters* (Philadelphia: Fortress Press).
Evans, Craig A.
  1987   ' "He set his Face": Luke 9.51 Once Again', *Bib* 68: 80-84.
Evans, C.F.
  1990   *Luke* (London: SCM Press).
Evans, C.A., and J.A. Sanders
  1993   *Luke and Scripture* (Minneapolis: Fortress Press).
Fackre, Gabriel
  1983   'Narrative Theology: An Overview', *Int* 37: 340-52.
Fergusson, David
  1990   'Meaning, Truth, and Realism in Bultmann and Lindbeck', *RelS* 26: 183-98.
Fergusson, Duncan
  1986   *Biblical Hermeneutics: An Introduction* (London: SCM Press).
Fisch, Harold
  1990   'Character as Linguistic Sign', *NLH* 21: 593-606.
Fishelov, David
  1990   'Types of Character: Characterization of Types', *Style* 24: 422-39.
Fitzmyer, Joseph A.
  1978   'The Composition of Luke, Chapter 9', in Talbert 1978: 139-52.
  1981   *Luke 1–9* (New York: Doubleday).
  1985   *Luke 10–24* (New York: Doubleday).
  1989   *Luke: The Theologian* (London: Chapman).
Fodor, James
  1995   *Christian Hermeneutics* (Oxford: Clarendon Press).

Foerster, W.
1965   'δαιμόνιο̂', in *TDNT*, II: 1-20.

Ford, David F.
1989   'System, Story, Performance', in Hauerwas and Jones 1989: 191-215.
1992   'Hans Frei and the Future of Theology', *ModTh* 8: 203-14.

Forster, E.M.
1927   *Aspects of the Novel* (London: Edward Arnold).

Fowl, Stephen
1990   'The Ethics of Interpretation', in Clines, Fowl and Porter 1990: 379-98.

Fowler, Robert M.
1985   'Who Is the Reader in Reader Response Criticism?', *Semeia* 31: 5-23.
1992   'Reader-Response Criticism: Figuring Mark's Reader', in Anderson and Moore 1992: 50-83.
1993   'Characterizing Character in Biblical Narrative', *Semeia* 63: 97-104.

France, R.T., and D. Wenham (eds.)
1981   *Studies of History and Tradition in the Four Gospels*, II (Gospel Perspectives, 2; Sheffield: JSOT Press).

Frei, Hans W.
1966   'Theological Reflections on the Accounts of Jesus' Death and Resurrection', in Hunsinger and Placher 1993: 46-93.
1967a   'The Mystery of the Presence of Jesus Christ', *Crossroads*, January, February, March.
1967b   'Remarks in Connection with a Theological Proposal', in Hunsinger and Placher 1993: 27-44.
1974   *The Eclipse of Biblical Narrative* (New Haven: Yale University Press).
1975   *The Identity of Jesus Christ* (Philadelphia: Fortress Press).
1978   'Review of Busch, *Karl Barth: His Life and Letters and Autobiographical Texts*', in Hunsinger and Placher 1993: 147-63.
1982   'Theology and the Interpretation of Narrative: Some Hermeneutical Considerations', in Hunsinger and Placher 1993: 95-116.
1983   'The Literal Reading of Biblical Narrative in the Christian Tradition: Does It Stretch or Will It Break?', in McConnell 1986: 36-77.
1985a   'David Friederich Strauss' in N. Smart (ed.), *Nineteenth Century Religious Thought in the West*, I (Cambridge: Cambridge University Press, 1985): 215-57.
1985b   'Response to Narrative Theology: An Evangelical Appraisal', in Hunsinger and Placher 1993: 207-12.
1986   'Conflicts in Interpretation: Resolution, Armistice, or Co-Existence?', *TTod* 49 (1992): 344-56.
1988a   'Jesus and God' [a minor revision of chapter 11] of Frei 1975 in Bloom 1988: 25-33.
1988b   'Narrative in Christian and Modern Reading', in Marshall 1990: 149-63.
—   Commentary of the 39 Articles: Article IV Of the Resurrection of Christ', unpublished draft.
1988c   *Types of Christian Theology* (rev. G. Hunsinger and W. Placher; New Haven: Yale University Press, 1992).

Frein, Brigid C.
1992   'Fundamentalism and Narrative Approaches to the Gospels', *BTB* 20: 12-18.

Freyne, Sean
1988   *Galilee, Jesus and the Gospels: Literary Approaches and Historical Investigations* (Dublin: Gill & Macmillan).

Frow, John
1986   'Spectacle Binding', *PToday* 7: 227-50.

Frye, Roland M.
1979   'Literary Criticism and Gospel Criticism', *TTod* 36: 207-19.
1981   'Review of Caird, *Language and Imagery of the Bible*', *TTod* 38: 393-94.

Funk, Robert W.
1961   *A Greek Grammar of the New Testament and other Christian Literature* (Cambridge: Cambridge University Press).
1988   *The Poetics of Biblical Narrative* (Sonoma, CA: Polebridge Press).

Furst, L.R. (ed.)
1992   *Realism* (Harlow: Longman).

Geldenhuys, N.
1950   *A Commentary on the Gospel of Luke* (London: Marshall, Morgan & Scott).

Genette, Gérard
1977   'Boundaries of Narrative', *NLH* 8: 1-13.
1980   *Narrative Discourse* (Oxford: Basil Blackwell).
1982   'Structuralism and Literary Criticism', in D. Lodge (ed.), *Modern Criticism and Theory: A Reader* (London: Longman, 1988): 63-78.
1983   *Narrative Discourse Revisited* (ET; Ithaca, NY: Cornell University Press, 1988).

Gerhart, Mary
1979   *The Question of Belief in Literary Criticism* (Stuttgart: Akademischer Verlag Hans-Dieter Heinz).

Giblin, Charles J.
1985   *The Destruction of Jerusalem according to Luke's Gospel* (Rome: Biblical Institute Press).

Gill, Christopher
1986   'The Question of Character and Personality in Greek Tragedy', *PToday* 7: 251-73.

Goldberg, Michael
1988   'God, Action and Narrative: *Which* Narrative? *Which* Action? *Which* God?', *JR* 68: 39-56.
1991   *Theology and Narrative: A Critical Introduction* (Valley Forge, PA: Trinity Press International, 2nd edn).

Goldingay, J.
1990   *Approaches to Old Testament Interpretation* (Leicester: Apollos, rev. edn).

Gooding, David
1987   *According to Luke: A New Exposition of the Third Gospel* (Leicester: Inter-Varsity Press).

Goulder, Michael
    1964   'The Chiastic Structure of the Lucan Journey', *SE* 2: 195-202.
    1989   *Luke: A New Paradigm* (JSNTSup, 20; Sheffield: JSOT Press).
    1992   'Review of Evans, *Luke*', *SJT* 45: 116-17.
Gowler, David B.
    1989   'Characterization in Luke: A Socio-Narratological Approach', *BTB* 19: 54-62.
Graff, G.
    1970   *Poetic Statement and Critical Dogma* (Evanston, IL: Northwestern University Press).
Grant, Patrick
    1989   *Reading the New Testament* (Basingstoke: Macmillan).
Green, Garrett (ed.)
    1987   *Scriptural Authority and Narrative Interpretation* (Philadelphia: Fortress Press).
Green, Joel B. (ed.)
    1995   *Hearing the New Testament: Strategies for Interpretation* (Grand Rapids: Eerdmans).
Greenwood, David
    1985   *Structuralism and the Biblical Text* (Berlin: Mouton de Gruyter).
Griffin, D., W. Beardslee and J. Holland (eds.)
    1989   *Varieties of Postmodern Theology* (New York: State of New York Press).
Grundmann, W.
    1965   'δεῖ', *TDNT*, II: 21-25.
Gunn, David
    1990   'Reading Right', in Clines, Fowl and Porter 1990: 55-64.
    1993   'Narrative Criticism', in McKenzie and Haynes (eds.) 1993: 171-95.
Gunn, Giles (ed.)
    1971   *Literature and Religion* (London: SCM Press).
Gunton, Colin
    1993   *The One, the Three and the Many* (Cambridge: Cambridge University Press).
Hamm, Dennis
    1986   'Sight to the Blind: Vision as Metaphor in Luke', *Bib* 67: 457-77.
    1987   'The Freeing of the Bent Woman: Lk 13.10-17 as Narrative Theology', *JSNT* 31: 23-44.
Hartin P.J., and J.H. Petzer (eds.)
    1991   *Text and Interpretation: New Approaches in the Criticism of the New Testament* (Leiden: E.J. Brill).
Hauerwas, S., and L.C. Jones (eds.)
    1989   *Why Narrative?* (Grand Rapids: Eerdmans).
Harvey, A.E. (ed.)
    1985   *Alternative Approaches to New Testament Study* (London: SPCK).
Hernadi, Paul
    1980   'Afterthoughts on Narrative', in Mitchell 1981: 197-99.
Hill, David
    1984   'The Figure of Jesus in Matthew's Story: A Response to Prof. Kingsbury', *JSNT* 21: 37-52.

Hirsch, E.D.
    1967   *Validity in Interpretation* (New Haven: Yale University Press).
Hochman, Baruch, and Ilja Wachs
    1990   'Straw People, Hollow Men, and the Postmodernist Hall of Dissipating Mirrors: The Case of *David Copperfield*', *Style* 24: 392-407.
Houlden, Leslie
    1987   'Review of Kingsbury, *Matthew as Story*', *JSNT* 29: 125.
Hunsinger, George
    1992   'Hans Frei as Theologian: The Quest for a Generous Orthodoxy', *ModTh* 8: 103-28.
    1993   'Afterword', in Hunsinger and Placher 1993: 235-70.
Hunsinger, G., and W. Placher (eds.)
    1992   *Types of Christian Theology* (North Haven: Yale University Press).
    1993   *Theology and Narrative* (Oxford: Oxford University Press).
Hutcheon, Linda
    1988   *A Poetics of Postmodernism* (New York: Routledge).
Jackson, F.J.F. and K. Lake (eds.)
    1922   *The Beginnings of Christianity*. I. *The Acts of the Apostles* (London: Marshall, Morgan & Scott).
Jakobson, Roman
    1958   'Closing Statement: Linguistics and Poetics', in D. Lodge (ed.), *Modern Criticism and Theory* (London: Longman, 1988): 32-61.
Jasper, David
    1987   'The Limits of Formalism and the Theology of Hope: Ricoeur, Moltmann and Dostoevsky', *JLT* 1: 1-10.
    1989   *The Study of Literature and Religion: An Introduction* (Basingstoke: Macmillan).
    1992   'The Study of Literature and Theology: Five Years On', *JLT* 6: 1-10.
    1993   *Rhetoric, Power and Community* (Basingstoke: Macmillan).
    1995   'The Bible in Arts and Literature: Source of Inspiration for Poets and Painters', *Concilium* 1: 47-60.
Jasper, David (ed.)
    1984   *Images of Belief in Literature* (London: Macmillan, 1984).
Jeanrond, Werner G.
    1988   *Text and Interpretation* (Dublin: Gill & MacMillan).
    1991   *Theological Hermeneutics* (Basingstoke: Macmillan).
    1992   'Biblical Criticism and Theology: Towards a New Biblical Theology', *JLT* 6: 218-21.
    1993   'After Hermeneutics', in Watson 1993a: 85-102.
Jefferson, Ann
    1979   'Review of Bal, *Narratologie: Les instances du récit*', *PToday* 1: 402-404.
Jenson, Robert
    1976   'Review of Frei, *The Identity of Jesus Christ*', *Int* 30: 83-85.
Jeremias, J.
    1966   *The Eucharistic Words of Jesus* (London: SCM Press).
    1967   *The Prayers of Jesus* (London: SCM Press).
    1972   *The Parables of Jesus* (London: SCM Press, 3rd rev. edn).

Jobling, David
1992   'Review of *Literary Guide to the Bible*', *Int* 46: 181-82.
Johnson, Luke T.
1991   *The Gospel of Luke* (Collegeville, MN: Liturgical Press).
1992   'Review of Moessner, *Lord of the Banquet*', *NovT* 34: 101-102.
Josipovici, Gabriel
1988   *The Book of God: A Response to the Bible* (New Haven: Yale University Press).
1990   'The Bible in Focus', *JSOT* 48: 101-22.
Jüngel, Eberhard
1995   'The Dogmatic Significance of the Question of the Historical Jesus', in *idem*, *Theological Essays*, II (Edinburgh: T. & T. Clark): 83-119.
Kay, James F.
1991   'Theological Table Talk: Myth or Narrative?', *TTod* 48: 326-32.
Keck, Leander
1975   'Review of Frei, *The Eclipse of Biblical Narrative*', *TTod* 31: 367-70.
Keegan, Terence
1994   'The Parable of the Sower and the Markan Leaders', *CBQ* 56: 501-18.
1995   'Biblical Criticism and the Challenge of Postmodernism', *BibInt* 3.1: 1-14.
Kelber, Werner H.
1987   'Narrative as Interpretation and Interpretation of Narrative', *Semeia* 39: 107-33.
1988a   'Gospel Narrative and Critical Theory', *BTB* 18: 130-36.
1988b   'Narrative and Disclosure: Mechanisms of Concealing, Revealing and Reveiling', *Semeia* 43: 1-20.
Kelsey, David
1975   *The Uses of Scripture in Recent Theology* (London: SCM Press, 1975).
1987   'Biblical Narrative and Theological Anthropology', in Green 1987: 121-43.
Kermode, Frank
1967   *The Sense of an Ending* (New York: Oxford University Press).
1979   *The Genesis of Secrecy: On the Interpretation of Narrative* (Cambridge, MA: Harvard University Press).
1981   'Secrets and Narrative Sequence', in Mitchell 1981: 79-97.
1988   'Anteriority, Authority and Secrecy: A General Comment', *Semeia* 43: 155-67.
Kingsbury, Jack D.
1984   'The Figure of Jesus in Matthew's Story: A Literary-Critical Probe', *JSNT* 21: 3-36.
1985   'The Figure of Jesus in Matthew's Story: A Rejoinder to David Hill', *JSNT* 25: 61-81.
1986   *Matthew as Story* (Philadelphia: Fortress Press).
1987a   'Developing Conflict between Jesus and Jewish Leaders in Mt', *CBQ* 49: 57-73.
1987b   'The Place, Structure and Meaning of the Sermon on the Mount', *Int* 41:.131-43.

1988   'On Following Jesus: The Eager Scribe and Reluctant Disciple: Mt 8.18-22', *NTS* 34: 45-59.
1990   'The Religious Authorities of Mark', *NTS* 36: 42-65.
1991a   'Review of Howell, *Matthew's Inclusive Story*', *Bib* 72: 280-83.
1991b   *Conflict in Luke: Jesus, Authorities, Disciples* (Minneapolis: Fortress Press).
1992   'The Plot of Matthew's Story', *Int* 46: 347-56.
1993   'The Significance of the Cross within Mark's Story', *Int* 47: 370-79.
1994a   'Review of Moore, Mark and Luke in Poststructuralist Perspectives', *Int* 48: 92-93.
1994b   'The Plot of Luke's Story of Jesus', *Int* 48: 369-78.

Klemm, David E.
1986   *Hermeneutical Inquiry.* I. *The Interpretation of Texts* (Atlanta: Scholars Press).

Knapp, John V.
1990   'Introduction: Self-Preservation and Self-Transformation: Interdisciplinary Approaches to Literary Character', *Style* 24: 349-64.

Knight, Jonathan
1998   *Luke's Gospel* (London: Routledge).

Kodell, Jerome
1983   'Luke's Gospel in a Nutshell (Lk 4.16-20)', *BTB* 13: 16-18.

Kort, Wesley
1987   'Narrative and Theology', *JLT* 1: 27-38.
1988   *Story, Text and Scripture: Literary Interests in Biblical Narrative* (University Park: Pennsylvania State University Press).

Kümmel, Werner G.
1957   *Promise and Fulfilment* (London: SCM Press).
1975   *Introduction to the New Testament* (London: SCM Press, rev. edn).

Kurz, William S.
1984a   'Lk 3.23-38 and Greco-Roman and Biblical Genealogies', in Talbert (ed.) 1984: 169-87.
1984b   'Review of Talbert, *Reading Luke*', *Int* 38: 415-17.
1987   'Narrative Approaches to Luke–Acts', *Bib* 68: 195-220.

Landy, Francis
1986   'Review of Poland, *Literary Criticism and Biblical Hermeneutics*', *JR* 66: 466-68.

Leaney, A.R.C.
1958   *A Commentary on the Gospel According to St Luke* (London: A. & C. Black).

Lee, David
1993   'The Making and the Discovering of History: Contemporary Historiography and the Gospel Narratives', unpublished paper.

Lewis, C.S.
1958   *Reflection on the Psalms* (London: Collins).

Lentricchia, Frank
1980   *After the New Criticism* (London: Athlone Press).

Lindbeck, George
1984   *The Nature of Doctrine* (Philadelphia: Westminster Press).

1987   'The Story-Shaped Church: Critical Exegesis and Theological Interpreta-
           tion' in Green 1987: 161-77.

Loades, Ann, and Michael McLain (eds.)

1991   *Hermeneutics, the Bible and Literary Criticism* (Basingstoke: Macmillan).

Lodge, David

1980   'Analysis and Interpretation of the Realist Text', *PToday* 1 (in Rice and
           Waugh 1992: 24-40).

1981a   *Working with Structuralism* (London: Routledge & Kegan Paul).

1981b   'Ambiguously Ever After', in Lodge, 1981a: 143-55.

1984   'Mimesis and Diegesis in Modern Fiction', in A. Mortimer (ed.), *Con-
           temporary Approaches to Narrative* (Tübingen: Gunter Narr Verlag,
           1984): 89-108.

Louis, Kenneth (ed.)

1974   *Literary Interpretations of Biblical Narratives* (Nashville: Abingdon
           Press).

1982   *Literary Interpretations of Biblical Narratives*, II (Nashville: Abingdon
           Press).

Loughlin, G.

1995   'Using Scripture: Community and Letterality', in Davies, Harvey and
           Watson 1995: 321-39.

1996   *Telling God's Story: Bible, Church and Narrative Theology* (Cambridge:
           Cambridge University Press).

Lowe, Walter

1992   'Hans Frei and Phenomenological Hermeneutics', *ModTh* 8: 133-44.

Malbon, Elizabeth

1982   'Galilee and Jerusalem: History and Literature in Marcan Interpretation',
           CBQ 44: 242-55.

1983   'Fallible Followers: Women and Men in the Gospel of Mark', *Semeia* 28:
           29-48.

1986   'Disciples/Crowds/Whoever: Markan Characters and Readers', *NovT* 28:
           104-30.

1989   'The Jewish Leaders in the Gospel of Mark: A Literary Study of Marcan
           Characterization', *JBL* 108: 259-81.

1992a   'Narrative Criticism: How Does the Story Mean?', in Anderson and
           Moore 1992: 23-49.

1992b   'Review of Tolbert M., *Sowing the Gospel: Mark's World in Literary-
           Historical Perspective*', *JR* 72: 95-96.

1993a   'Echoes and Foreshadowings in Mark 4-8: Reading and Rereading', *JBL*
           112: 211-30.

1993b   'Text and Contexts: Interpreting the Disciples in Mark', *Semeia* 62: 81-
           102.

1994   'The Major Importance of the Minor Characters in Mark', in Malbon and
           McKnight 1994: 59-86.

Malbon, E., and E.V. McKnight (eds.)

1994   *The New Literary Criticism and the New Testament* (JSNTSup, 109;
           Sheffield: Sheffield Academic Press).

Malina, Bruce J.

1983   'Review of Rhoads and Michie, *Mark as Story*', *BTB* 13: 102.

Margolin, Uri
1983	'Characterization in Narrative: Some Theoretical Prolegomena', *NeoPh* 67: 1-14.
1986	'The Doer and the Deed', *PToday* 7: 205-25.
1987	'Introducing and Sustaining Characters in Literary Narrative: A Set of Conditions', *Style* 21: 107-24.
1988	'Review of Martin: *Recent Theories of Narrative*', *Style* 22: 137-39.
1990	'The What, the When and the How of Being a Character in Literary Narrative', *Style* 24: 453-68.
Marshall, Bruce D.
1990	'Absorbing the World: Christianity and the Universe of Truths', in Marshall (ed.) 1990: 69-102.
1992	'Meaning and Truth in Narrative Interpretation: A Reply to Schner', *ModTh* 8: 173-79.
1995	'We Shall Bear the Image of the Man of Heaven: Theology and Concept of Truth', *ModTh* 11: 93-117.
Marshall, Bruce D. (ed.)
1990	*Theology and Dialogue* (Notre Dame: University of Notre Dame Press).
Marshall, Christopher D.
1989	*Faith as a Theme in Mark's Narrative* (Cambridge: Cambridge University Press).
Marshall, I. Howard
1970	*Luke: Historian and Theologian* (Exeter: Paternoster Press).
1978	*Gospel of Luke: A Commentary on the Greek Text* (Exeter: Paternoster Press).
1987	'The Present State of Lucan Studies', *Themelios* 14: 52-57.
1991	'Review of Evans, *Luke*', *JTS* 42: 215-18.
Martin, James
1987	'Towards a Post-Critical Paradigm', *NTS* 33: 370-85.
Martin, Wallace,
1986	*Recent Theories of Narrative* (Ithaca, NY: Cornell University Press).
Matera, Frank J.
1987	'The Plot of Matthew's Gospel', *CBQ* 49: 233-53.
1993a	'He Saved Others; He Cannot Save Himself: A Literary Critical Perspective on the Markan Miracles', *Int* 47: 15-26.
1993b	'Jesus' Journey to Jerusalem: A Conflict with Israel', *JSNT* 51: 57-77.
McCabe, A., and C. Petersen (eds.)
1991	*Developing Narrative Structure* (New Jersey: Lawrence Erlbaum).
McClendon, James W.
1983	'More on Narrative', *TTod* 40: 49-53.
McConnell, Frank (ed.)
1986	*The Bible and the Narrative Tradition* (Oxford: Oxford University Press).
McKenzie, S., and S. Haynes (eds.)
1993	*To Each its Own Meaning* (Louisville, KY: Westminster/John Knox Press).
McKnight, Edgar V.
1978	*Meaning in Texts: The Historical Shaping of a Narrative Hermeneutics* (Philadelphia: Fortress Press).

1980a   'Review of Caird, *Language and Imagery of the Bible*', *Int* 34: 81-83.
1980b   'The Contours and Methods of Literary Criticism', in Spencer 1980: 53-69.
1985   *The Bible and the Reader* (Philadelphia: Fortress Press).
1989   'Review of Alter and Kermode, *Literary Guide to the Bible*', *JAAR* 57: 385-91.
1994   'A Sheep in Wolf's Clothing: An Option in Contemporary New Testament Hermeneutics', in Malbon and McKnight (eds.) 1994: 326-47.

Mead, Gerald
1990   'The Representation of Fictional Character', *Style* 24: 440-51.

Metzger, B.
1958   'Seventy or Seventy-Two Disciples?', *NTS* 5: 299-306.

Mitchell, W.J. (ed.)
1981   *On Narrative* (Chicago: Chicago University Press).

Moessner, David
1988   'The Leaven of the Pharisee and this Generation', *JSNT* 34: 21-46.
1989   *Lord of the Banquet* (Minneapolis: Fortress Press).

Monshouwer, D.
1991   'The Reading of the Prophet in the Synagogue at Nazareth', *Bib* 72: 90-99.

Moore, Stephen D.
1986   'Negative Hermeneutics, Insubstantial Texts', *JAAR* 54: 707-19.
1987   'Are the Gospels Unified Narratives?', in Kent H. Richards (ed.), *SBL 1987 Seminar Papers* (Atlanta: Scholars Press): 443-58.
1989a   *Literary Criticism and the Gospels* (New Haven: Yale University Press).
1989b   'Doing Gospel Criticism as/with a "Reader" ', *BTB* 19: 85-93.
1989c   'Post-Age Stamp: Does It Stick?', *JAAR* 57: 543-59.
1992a   'Illuminating the Gospels without the Benefit of Color', *JAAR* 60: 257-79.
1992b   *Mark and Luke in Poststructuralist Perspectives: Jesus Begins to Write* (New Haven: Yale University Press).
1993a   'God's (Pri)son', in Watson 1993a: 121-39.
1993b   'Mirror, Mirror: Lacanian Reflections on Malbon's Mark', *Semeia* 62: 165-71.
1994   *Poststructuralism and the New Testament* (Minneapolis: Fortress Press).

Morgan, R.
1995   'On the Unity of Scripture', in Davies, Harvey and Watson 1995: 395-413.

Morgan, Robert, with John Barton
1988   *Biblical Interpretation* (Oxford: Oxford University Press).

Mosher, Harold F.
1980   'Review of Chatman, *Story and Discourse*', *PToday* 1: 171-85.

Mosher, Harold F., and William Nelles
1990   'Guides to Narratology', *PToday* 11: 419-27.

Moule, C.F.D.
1959   *An Idiom-Book of New Testament Greek* (Cambridge: Cambridge University Press).
1989   'Review of Parsons, *The Departure of Jesus in Luke–Acts*', *JTS* 40: 187-89.

Moulton, J.H.
    1929   *Grammar of the Greek New Testament*, II (Edinburgh: T. & T. Clark).
Mowinckel, S.
    1962   'Literature', *IDB*, III: 139-43.
Noble, Paul R.
    1993a   'The Sensus Literalis: Jowett, Childs, and Barr', *JTS* 44: 1-23.
    1993b   'Synchronic and Diachronic Approaches to Biblical Interpretation', *JLT* 7: 130-48.
    1994   'Hermeneutics and Post-Modernism: Can We Have a Radical Reader Response Theory?', *RelS* 30: 419-36.
Nolland, John
    1989   *Luke 1–9.20* (Dallas: Word Books).
    1993a   *Luke 9.21–18.34* (Dallas: Word Books).
    1993b   *Luke 18.35–24.53* (Dallas: Word Books).
Nuttall, Anthony D.
    1983   *A New Mimesis* (London: Methuen).
Oakes, Edward T.
    1992   'Apologetics and the Pathos of Narrative Theology', *JR* 72: 37-58.
Ogden, Schubert
    1993   'Review of Frei, *Types of Christian Theology*', *ModTh* 9: 211-14.
Outler, Albert C.
    1985   'Toward a Postliberal Hermeneutics', *TTod* 42: 281-91.
Parsons, Mikeal C.
    1987a   *The Departure of Jesus in Luke–Acts: The Ascension Narratives in Context* (JSNTSup, 21; Sheffield: JSOT Press).
    1987b   'Reading Talbert: New Perspectives on Luke-Acts', in Kent H. Richards (ed.), *SBL 1987 Seminar Papers* (Atlanta: Scholars Press): 687-720.
Parsons, Mikeal C., and Richard Pervo
    1993   *Rethinking the Unity of Luke and Acts* (Minneapolis: Fortress Press).
Patte, Daniel
    1993   'Textual Constraints, Ordinary Readings, and Critical Exegeses', *Semeia* 62: 59-79.
Patte, Daniel, and Aline Patte
    1978   *Structural Exegesis: From Theory to Practice* (Philadelphia: Fortress Press).
Perrin, Norman
    1976   *Jesus and the Language of the Kingdom* (Philadelphia: Fortress Press).
    1986   'Historical Criticism, Literary Criticism and Hermeneutics', in Klemm 1986: 253-65.
Petersen, Norman
    1978a   *Literary Criticism for New Testament Critics* (Philadelphia: Fortress Press).
    1978b   'Point of View in Mark's Narrative', *Semeia* 12: 87-121.
    1980   'Literary Criticism in Biblical Studies', in Spencer 1980: 25-50.
Phillips, Gary A.
    1990   'Exegesis as Critical Praxis: Reclaiming History and Text', *Semeia* 51: 7-39.

1994 'The Ethics of Reading Deconstructively', in Malbon and McKnight (eds.) 1994: 283-325.

Placher, William C.
1989 'Postliberal Theology', in D. Ford (ed.), *The Modern Theologians*, II (Oxford: Basil Blackwell, 1989): 114-28.
1992 'A Modest Response to Paul Schwartzentruber', *ModTh* 8: 197-201.
1993 'Introduction', in Hunsinger and Placher 1993: 3-25.
1994a 'Gospel's Ends: Plurality and Ambiguity in Biblical Narratives', *ModTh* 10: 143-63.
1994b *Narratives of a Vulnerable God: Christ, Theology and Scripture* (Louisville, KY: Westminster/John Knox Press).

Plummer, Alfred
1901 *Critical and Exegetical Commentary on the Gospel According to Luke* (ICC; Edinburgh: T. & T. Clark).

Poland, Lynn
1985a *Literary Criticism and Biblical Hermeneutics: A Critique of Formalist Approaches* (Atlanta: Scholars Press).
1985b 'The New Criticism, Neoorthodoxy and the New Testament', *JR* 66: 459-77.
1988 'Defending Biblical Poetics', *JR* 68: 426-34.
1992 'Review of Schwartz, *The Book and the Text: The Bible and Literary Theory*', *JLT* 6: 90-92.

Polzin, Robert
1980 'Literary and Historical Criticism of the Bible: A Crisis in Scholarship', in Spencer 1980: 99-114.

Polzin, R., and E. Rothman (eds.)
1982 *The Biblical Mosaic* (Philadelphia: Fortress Press).

Porter, Stanley
1990 'The Parable of the Unjust Steward', in Clines, Fowl and Porter 1990: 127-53.
1995 'Literary Approaches to the New Testament', in Porter and Tombs 1995: 77-128.

Porter, S., and D. Tombs (eds.)
1995 *Approaches to New Testament Study* (JSNTSup, 120; Sheffield: Sheffield Academic Press).

Poster, Mark
1989 *Critical Theory and Poststructuralism* (Ithaca, NY: Cornell University Press).

Powell, Mark Allan
1990a *What Is Narrative Criticism?* (Minneapolis: Fortress Press).
1990b 'The Religious Leaders in Luke: A Literary-Critical Study', *JBL* 109: 103-20.
1991a *The Bible and Modern Criticism: A Critical Assessment and Annotated Bibliography* (Westport: Greenwood Press).
1991b *What Are They Saying about Luke?* (Mahwah, NJ: Paulist Press).
1992 'Towards a Narrative-Critical Understanding of Matthew', *Int* 46: 341-46.
1993 'Toward a Narrative-Critical Understanding of Mark', *Int* 47: 341-45.
1994 'Toward a Narrative-Critical Understanding of Luke', *Int* 48: 341-46.

Prickett, Stephen
    1986   *Words and 'The Word'* (Cambridge: Cambridge University Press).
    1989   'Poetics and Narrative', in D. Jasper and T. Wright (eds.), *The Critical Spirit and the Will to Believe* (London: Macmillan, 1989): 1-22.
Prickett, Stephen (ed.)
    1991   *Reading the Text* (Oxford: Basil Blackwell).
Prince, Gerald
    1987   *A Dictionary of Narratology* (Lincoln: University of Nebraska Press).
    1988   'The Disnarrated', *Style* 22: 1-8.
    1991   'Narratology, Narrative and Meaning', *PToday* 12: 543-52.
Resseguie, James L.
    1990   'Defamiliarization and the Gospels', *BTB* 20: 147-53.
Rhoads, David
    1982   'Narrative Criticism and the Gospel of Mark', *JAAR* 50: 411-34.
    1992   'Social Criticism: Crossing Boundaries', in Anderson and Moore 1992: 135-61.
    1994   'Jesus and the Syrophonecian Woman in Mark', *JAAR* 62: 343-75.
Rhoads, David M., and Donald M. Michie
    1982   *Mark as Story: An Introduction to the Narrative of a Gospel* (Philadelphia: Fortress Press).
Rice, Philip, and Patricia Waugh (eds.)
    1992   *Modern Literary Theory* (London: Edward Arnold).
Richard, Earl
    1983   'Luke—Writer, Theologian, Historian: Research/Orientation of the 1970s', *BTB* 13: 3-15.
Riches, John K.
    1976   'Review of Frei, *The Eclipse of Biblical Narrative*', *RelS* 12: 117-19.
Riches, John, and Alan Millar
    1985   'Conceptual Change in the Synoptic Tradition', in Harvey 1985: 37-60.
Ricoeur, Paul
    1970   'What Is a Text? Explanation and Interpretation', in Klemm 1986: 233-46.
    1976   *Interpretation Theory: Discourse and the Surplus of Meaning* (Fort Worth: Texas Christian University Press).
    1980   'Narrative Time', in Mitchell 1981: 165-86.
    1984a   'From Proclamation to Narrative', *JR* 64: 501-12.
    1984b   *Time and Narrative*, I (Chicago: University of Chicago Press).
    1985   *Time and Narrative*, II (Chicago: University of Chicago Press).
    1988a   *Time and Narrative*, III (Chicago: University of Chicago Press).
    1988b   'Narrative Identity', in Wood (ed.) 1991: 188-99.
    1991   'Life in Quest of Narrative Identity', in Wood (ed.) 1991: 20-33
    1992   'Interpretative Narrative', in Schwartz (ed.) 1990: 237-55.
Rigney, Ann
    1992   'The Point of Stories: On Narrative Communication and its Cognitive Function', *PToday* 13: 263-83.
Rimmon-Kenan, Shlomith
    1983   *Narrative Fiction: Contempory Poetics* (London: Routledge).

Robertson, D.
    1976   'The Bible as Literature', in *IDBSup*: 547-51.
Ryken, Leland (ed.)
    1984   *The New Testament in Literary Criticism* (New York: Frederick Ungar).
    1992   *Words of Delight* (Grand Rapids: Baker Book House, 2nd edn).
Ryle, Gilbert
    1949   *The Concept of Mind* (London: Hutchinson).
Sanders, E.P.
    1993   *The Historical Figure of Jesus* (Harmondsworth: Penguin Books).
Scalise, Charles J.
    1989   'The *sensus literalis*: A Hermeneutical Key to Biblical Exegesis', *SJT* 42:
                45-65.
Schiff, H. (ed.)
    1977   *Contemporary Approaches to English Literature* (London: Heinemann):
                59-76.
Schneidau, Herbert
    1987   'Let the Reader Understand', *Semeia* 39: 135-45.
Schner, George
    1992   'The Eclipse of Biblical Narrative: Analysis and Critique', *ModTh* 8: 149-
                72.
Scholes, Robert
    1974   *Structuralism in Literature: An Introduction* (New Haven: Yale University
                Press).
    1980   'Review of Chatman, *Story and Discourse*', *PToday* 1: 190-91.
Scholes, Robert, and Robert Kellogg
    1966   *The Nature of Narrative* (Oxford: Oxford University Press).
Schürmann, H.
    1969   *Das Lukasevangelium 1.1–9.50* (Freiburg: Herder).
Schwartz, Regina (ed.)
    1990   *The Book and the Text: The Bible and Literary Theory* (Cambridge, MA:
                Basil Blackwell).
Schwartzentruber, Paul
    1992   'The Modesty of Hermeneutics: The Theological Reserves of Frei',
                ModTh 8: 181-95.
Schweiker, William
    1988   'Beyond Imitation: Mimetic Praxis in Gadamer, Ricoeur and Derrida', *JR*
                6: 21-38.
Schweizer, Eduard
    1984   *The Good News According to Luke* (Atlanta: John Knox Press).
Scruton, Roger
    1994   *Modern Philosophy: A Survey* (London: Sinclair-Stevenson).
Seim, Turid Karlsen
    1995   'The Gospel of Luke', in E. Schüssler Fiorenza (ed.), *Searching the
                Scriptures. II. A Feminist Commentary* (London: SCM Press, 1995): 728-
                62.
Sell, Stephen L.
    1993   'Hermeneutics in Theology and the Theology of Hermeneutics', *JAAR*
                56: 679-703.

Sheeley, Steven M.
1988   'Narrative Asides and Narrative Authority in Luke–Acts', *BTB* 18: 102-107.
1992   *Narrative Asides in Luke–Acts* (JSNTSup, 72; Sheffield: Sheffield Academic Press).

Sheppard, Gerald
1982   'Beyond the Myth and Reality Debate: The Problem of History in a Realistic Reading of Biblical Narrative', unpublished MS.

Squires, John
1993   *The Plan of God in Luke–Acts* (Cambridge: Cambridge University Press).

Smith, Barbara Herrnstein
1977   'Surfacing from the Deep: A Review of Fowler (ed.), *Style and Structure in Literature*', *PTL* 2: 151-82.
1981   'Narrative Versions, Narrative Theories', in Mitchell 1981: 209-32.

Spencer, R.A. (ed.)
1980   *Orientation by Disorientation: Studies Presented in Honour of William Beardslee* (Pittsburgh: Pickwick Press).

Stanton, Graham N.
1984   'The Passing of an Era', *NTS* 30: 1-2.
1989   'Review of Patte, *The Gospel of Matthew: A Structuralist Commentary*', *Int* 43: 184-86.

Starobinski, Jean
1973   'The Struggle with Legion: A Literary Analysis of Mk 5:1-20', *NLH* 4.2: 331-56.

Steiner, George
1977   'Critical Discussion of *The Eclipse of Biblical Narrative*', *Phil & Lit* 1.2: 239-43.

Sternberg, Meir
1985   *The Poetics of Biblical Narrative* (Bloomington: University of Indiana Press).

Stibbe, Mark
1992   *John as Storyteller: Narrative Criticism and the Fourth Gospel* (Cambridge: Cambridge University Press).

Stroup, George
1981   *The Promise of Narrative Theology* (London: SCM Press).
1991   'Theology of Narrative or Narrative Theology', *TTod* 47: 424-32.

Talbert, Charles H.
1974   *Literary Patterns, Theological Themes, and the Genre of Luke–Acts* (Missoula, MT: Scholars Press).
1976   'Shifting Sands: The Recent Study of the Gospel of Luke', *Int* 30: 381-95.
1977   *What Is a Gospel?* (London: SPCK).
1982   *Reading Luke* (London: SPCK).
1988a   'Review of Fitzmyer, *Gospel of Luke (X-XXIV)*', *CBQ* 48: 336-38.
1988b   'Review of Tannehill, *Narrative-Unity of Luke–Acts*, I', *Bib* 69: 135-38.
1989   'Luke–Acts' in Epp, Eldon and MacRae 1989: 207-320.
1991   'Review of Tannehill, *Narrative-Unity of Luke–Acts*, II', *Bib* 72: 589-91.
1992   'The Place of Resurrection in the Theology of Luke', *Int* 46: 19-30.

Talbert, Charles H. (ed.)
    1978   *Perspectives on Luke–Acts* (Danville: Association of Baptist Professors).
    1984   *Luke–Acts: New Perspectives from the Society of Biblical Literature Seminar* (New York: Crossroad).

Tambling, Jeremy
    1991   *Narrative and Ideology* (Milton Keynes: Open University Press).

Tannehill, Robert C.
    1977   'The Disciples in Mark: The Functions of a Narrative Role', *JR* 57: 386-405.
    1979   'The Gospel of Mark as Narrative Christology', *Semeia* 16: 57-73.
    1980   'Tension in Synoptic Sayings and Stories', *Int* 34: 138-50.
    1985   'Israel in Luke–Acts: A Tragic Story', *JBL* 104: 69-85.
    1986a   *The Narrative Unity of Luke–Acts. I. A Literary Interpretation* (Philadelphia: Fortress Press).
    1986b   'Review of Fitzmyer, *Luke, 10–24*', *CBQ* 48: 336-38.
    1990a   *The Narrative Unity of Luke–Acts*, II (Minneapolis: Fortress Press).
    1990b   'Review of Moore, *Literary Criticism and the Gospels*', *TTod* 47: 337-40.
    1994   ' "Cornelius" and "Tabitha" Encounter Luke's Jesus', *Int* 48: 347-56.

Tanner, Kathryn E.
    1987   'Theology and the Plain Sense', in Green 1987: 59-78.

Tate, Allen
    1970   *Essays of Four Decades* (London: Oxford University Press).

Thiemann, Ronald F.
    1987   'Radiance and obscurity in Biblical narrative', in Green 1987: 21-41.

Thiselton, Anthony C.
    1992   *New Horizons in Hermeneutics* (London: HarperCollins).
    1994   'On Models and Methods: A Conversation with Robert Morgan', in Malbon and McKnight, 1994: 337-56.

Tiede, David L.
    1980   *Prophecy and history in Luke–Acts* (Philadelphia: Fortress Press).

Todorov, Tzvetan
    1977   'The Methodological Heritage of Formalism', in *idem*, *Poetics of Prose* (Oxford: Basil Blackwell).

Tolbert, Mary A.
    1989   *Sowing the Gospel: Mark's World in Literary-Historical Perspective* (Minneapolis: Fortress Press).
    1991   'A Response from a Literary Perspective', *Semeia* 53: 203-11.
    1993   'How the Gospel of Mark Builds Character', *Int* 47: 347-57.

Toolan, Michael
    1988   *Narrative: A Critical Introduction* (London: Routledge).

Tracy, David
    1978   'Metaphor and Religion: The Test Case of Christian Texts', *CritInq* 5: 90-106.
    1981   *The Analogical Imagination* (London: SCM Press).
    1987   *Plurality and Ambiguity* (London: SCM Press).
    1988   'A Response to the Symposium on Tracy, D., *Plurality and Ambiguity*', *TTod* 44: 513-19.
    1990   'On Reading the Scriptures Theologically', in Marshall (ed.) 1990: 35-68.

| 1991 | 'The Plurality of Readers and a Possibility of a Shared Vision', *Conc* 1991: 115-24. |

1994   'Theology and the Many Faces of Postmodernity', in Robert Gill (ed.), *Readings in Modern Theology* (London: SPCK, 1995): 225-35.

Trible, Phyllis
1978   *God and the Rhetoric of Sexuality* (Philadelphia: Fortress Press).

Tuckett, Christopher
1987   *Reading the New Testament* (London: SPCK).

Unnik, W.C. van
1968   'Luke–Acts, A Storm Centre in Contemporary Scholarship', in L. Keck and J. Martyn (eds.), *Studies in Luke–Acts* (London: SPCK): 15-32.

Valdés, Mario, and Owen Miller (eds.)
1978   *Interpretation of Narrative* (Toronto: University of Toronto Press).

Vanhoozer, Kevin J.
1990   *Biblical Narrative in the Philosophy of Paul Ricoeur* (Cambridge: Cambridge University Press).

1995   'The Reader in New Testament Interpretation', in Green 1995: 301-28.

Vermes, G.
1983   *Jesus and the World of Judaism* (London: SCM Press).

Ward, Graham
1991   'Biblical Narrative and the Theology of Metonymy', *ModTh* 7: 335-49.

1996   *Theology and Contemporary Critical Theory* (London: Macmillan).

Watson, Francis
1993   'Review of Loades A., and McLain, M., *Hermeneutics, the Bible and Literary Criticism*', *RelS* 29: 566-67.

1994   *Text, Church and World: Biblical Interpretation in Theological Perspective* (Edinburgh: T. & T. Clark).

1996   'Literary Approaches to the Gospels: A Theological Assessment', *Theology* 99: 125-33.

1997   *Text and Truth* (Edinburgh: T. & T. Clark).

Watson Francis (ed.),
1993   *The Open Text* (London: SCM Press).

Weeden, Theodore J.
1971   *Mark: Traditions in Conflict* (Philadelphia: Fortress Press).

Webster, John
1992   'Response to George Hunsinger', *ModTh* 8: 128-32.

Wellek, René
1960   'The Concept of Realism in Literary Scholarship', *NeoPh* 44: 00-00.

Wellek, René, and Austin Warren
1993   *Theory of Literature* (Harmonsworth: Penguin Books).

Wilder, Amos
1971   'The Uses of a Theological Criticism', in Gunn 1971: 37-52.

1980   'Review of Kermode, *Genesis of Secrecy*', *Int* 34: 296-99.

1983   'Story and Story World', *Int* 37: 353-64.

1991   *The Bible and the Literary Critic* (Minneapolis: Fortress Press).

Wiles, Maurice
1976   'Review of Frei, *Identity of Jesus Christ*', *JTS* 27: 261-62.

1987 'Scriptural Authority and Theological Construction: The Limitations of Narrative Interpretation', in Green 1987: 42-58.

Williams, Rowan

1991 'The Literal Sense of Scripture', *ModTh* 7: 121-34.

Wood, Charles

1976 'Review of Frei, *The Eclipse of Biblical Narrative*', *Int* 30: 80-82.

1981 *Formation of Christian Understanding* (New Haven: Yale University Press).

1987 'Hermeneutics and the Authority of Scripture', in Green 1987: 3-20.

1993 'Review of Frei, *Types of Christian Theology*', *Int* 47: 302-304.

Wood, David (ed.)

1991 *On Paul Ricoeur* (London: Routledge).

Wright, Terrance R.

1984 'Regenerating Narrative: The Gospels as Fiction', *RelS* 20: 389-400.

1988 *Theology and Literature* (Oxford: Basil Blackwell).

Yu, Anthony

1978 'Recovering the Sense of the Story: Review of Frei, *The Eclipse of Biblical Narrative*', *JR* 58: 198-203.

INDEXES

INDEX OF REFERENCES

OLD TESTAMENT

NEW TESTAMENT

INDEX OF AUTHORS

JOURNAL FOR THE STUDY OF THE NEW TESTAMENT
SUPPLEMENT SERIES